Children of
Incarcerated Parents

Children of Incarcerated Parents

Edited by

Katherine Gabel

Denise Johnston, M.D.

LEXINGTON BOOKS
An Imprint of The Free Press
New York London Toronto Sydney Tokyo Singapore

Library of Congress Cataloging-in-Publication Data

Gabel, Katherine.
Children of incarcerated parents / Katherine Gabel, Denise Johnston.
p. cm.
ISBN 0-02-911042-4
1. Children of prisoners—United States. 2. Prisoners—United States—Family relationships. 3. Prisoners' families—United States. I. Johnston, Denise II. Title.
HV8886.U5G33 1995
362.7—dc20
94-42219
CIP

Lexington Books
An Imprint of The Free Press
A Division of Simon & Schuster Inc.
866 Third Avenue, New York, N. Y. 10022

Printed in the United States of America

printing number
1 2 3 4 5 6 7 8 9 10

Contents

Part III CARE AND PLACEMENT

Part IV LEGAL ISSUES

Part V INTERVENTION

Part VI   POLICY ISSUES

Foreword

Jean Harris

> All men are caught up in an inescapable network of mutuality, tied in
> a single garment of destiny. Whatever affects one directly, affects all
> indirectly. I can never be what I ought to be until you are what you
> ought to be, and you can never be what you ought to be until I am
> what I ought to be.
>
> —Martin Luther King

As you read this book there are over 1,300,000 adults jailed or imprisoned in the United States, and over 3,000,000 on parole or probation. Seventy five to 80 percent of incarcerated women have children; 65 percent of incarcerated men have children.

In the course of the year 1993, 14 million people were jailed for periods anywhere from overnight to over a year. Approximately 70 percent had not been found guilty or finished plea-bargaining; they were in jail because they couldn't make bail. I know of a woman with eight children who spent three weeks on Rikers Island, the huge jail compound in New York City, because she couldn't raise $75 for bail. A local charitable group finally heard about her and bailed her out. It costs $56,000 per year to keep a prisoner on Riker's Island, so it cost the city of New York over $3,000 to hold this woman because she didn't have $75. In the meantime, she didn't know what had happened to her eight children, and they didn't know what had happened to her.

There are no precise statistics on how many children of incarcerated parents there are, for the simple reason that, with all the statistics we keep on prisoners, we haven't found it important enough to ask them about their children. A conservative estimate is that that one and a half million children in the United States have at least one incarcerated parent. We don't keep careful statistics on how many babies are born to incarcerated women, either. Our best guess is that somewhere between seven percent and 10 percent of all women prisoners enter jail or prison pregnant. That means that over 6,000 babies are born each year to incarcerated women. In all the billions of dollars that the US spends on jails, prisons, courts, police and a war on drugs, a very small percentage is used to help the children of prisoners.

The traumatic effect of having a parent in jail or prison is multiplied for children of incarcerated women, because their mothers were probably the main caregivers in their families. There are those who say, "Well, if she was a good mother she wouldn't be in prison, so her kids are probably better off without her." Not so. Twelve years of close, daily observation of children visiting their mothers at Bedford Hills Correctional Facility in New York convinced me that many women were working hard at motherhood before they came to prison. At least, they were doing the best they could with the knowledge of motherhood they had to work from. Their family histories are not unlike those of their children, histories of poverty, limited education, single parent households, incarcerated relatives, drugs, unemployment, a life of trauma and stress. Tragically, the cycle continues.

I remember that one day I stood in the lunch line at Bedford Hills prison asking a mother of three daughters, two of whom were then in college, how her children had reacted to her arrest. She looked directly at me and said, "My kids have known all their lives that I was out there hustling for them."

I remember a 12-year-old girl who had just spent a week of daily visiting with her mother at the prison, in a special summer program for inmates' children founded and run by Sister Elaine Roulet. At the end of the last day of the program, as she was about to leave, the girl turned and ran to Sister Elaine, hugged her around the waist and said, "Oh, Sister, this has been the happiest week of my life." If a week of prison visits with her mother can be the happiest week of a 12 year old's life, we are hard put to imagine what the rest of her life has been.

I often heard women at Bedford Hills say of their own mothers, "She done the best she could." That has been their motherhood goal as well. The goal of this book is to sound an alarm that such parents and their children need the public's concern and help if a large slice of our next generation is to have a fair chance at a decent, useful future. And, their future plays a more powerful role in our country's future than many Americans have yet to understand or acknowledge.

There are many ways other than parental incarceration that children suffer trauma, the loss of a parent, poverty and a limited education. As you read this book, you may recognize that children of prisoners in some ways represent these other, larger groups of children. The needs of such children are made clear as you read, and doable suggestions are made as to how to help them come to terms with their losses and find the solace and support they require in order to find a hopeful future.

This book takes children seriously, and in doing so it takes the fundamental causes of crime seriously, too, something our legislators and other policy-makers have been far too slow to do.

Foreword

Susan M. Hunter

In 1980, I conducted a study of women parolees and their children (Hunter, 1984). The study explored the various dimensions motherhood added to the experience of being in prison and being on parole. The study found that

> . . . the women seemed to be survivors in a complex world where power and opportunity were outside their grasp. The goals of these women were similar to the goals of many American women and mothers. The histories of these women were histories of people who had tried.

In spite of the fact that they had tried, and that they and correctional authorities agreed that parole processes should not interfere with family relationships, the women and their children struggled against multiple problems. The children were found to have experienced emotional problems, nightmares, fighting in school and a decline in academic performance as a result of being separated due to their mother's incarceration.

The study also provided new information about the relationship between women offenders and their children, and pointed to many areas of research which needed further study. Some of the questions which emerged from the study are explored by the authors of this book, such as:

- are children of incarcerated mothers more likely to have problems in school?
- are children of incarcerated mothers more likely to become involved in fighting behavior in school?
- is it more likely that the children of an incarcerated mother will be cared for by the woman's mother than by any other person?
- do frequent visits between incarcerated mothers and their children reduce feelings of abandonment among the children?
- are women with a history of drug use less likely to live with their children before or after incarceration?

- are women offenders less likely to lose custody of their children if they have knowledge of child custody laws and policies?

Other questions remain unanswered even in this book. One measure of how little has been done in pursuit of answers is the frequency with which the authors of all chapters cite the same authorities. There is a great deal we do not know.

Yet, in the past decade, there have been accomplishments. Sesame Street Goes to Prison has been duplicated in hundreds of other visiting area waiting rooms nationwide, creating child-adapted spaces for young visitors. The Prison MATCH model of extended parent-child contact visitation has been successfully implemented in dozens of US jails and prisons. Legal Services for Prisoners with Children, once the only legal advocacy agency of its kind, has been joined by Chicago Legal Aid to Incarcerated Mothers, the Child Custody Advocacy Services (CHICAS) Project and other groups working to help prisoners retain their parental rights. The number of mother-child, community-based correctional programs like North Carolina's Summit House have increased severalfold.

The founding of the Center for Children of Incarcerated Parents will move us farther in this direction. The Center was created specifically for the purpose of increasing documentation on and demonstrating model services for these special children. Its existence signals a move away from the early developmental stages of this field, in which knowledge about offenders and their families was derived largely from programs serving prisoners. Housed at Pacific Oaks College & Children's Programs and supported by that institution's nationally recognized leadership in work with children and families, the Center represents a new era in scholarship and services for incarcerated parents, their children and the professionals who serve them.

The authors of *Children of Incarcerated Parents* conclude that there is much that can be accomplished to assist children of offenders and their parents. Throughout the book, they echo the conclusion of my study:

> However, whatever programs/services are provided to . . . offenders, it is essential that the underlying attitude be that of respecting (their) human dignity and recognizing the many facets of their lives.

Reference

Hunter, SM. (1984). *The relationship between women offenders and their children*. Unpublished doctoral dissertation, University of Michigan.

PART I

Incarcerated Parents

1
Incarcerated Parents

Denise Johnston
Katherine Gabel

The majority of adults incarcerated in the United States are parents (Inter-University Consortium, 1991; U.S. Department of Justice [USDJ], 1993c). Incarcerated parents share the characteristics of other prisoners. They are low-income persons with limited education, job skills, and employment histories; their lives have typically included separations from their own parents as children, substance abuse, and exposure to a variety of traumatic experiences including battering, molestation, parental alcoholism/addiction, domestic violence, and community violence.

Prisoners also have unique characteristics as parents. As a group, incarcerated parents have appropriate parenting concerns and attitudes. Although it has been suggested that their parenting behaviors tend to be overcontrolling or even aversive, there is no evidence of a disproportionately high incidence of physical or sexual abuse of their children among jailed or imprisoned parents.

There are differences between incarcerated mothers and incarcerated fathers. Jailed and imprisoned mothers are half as likely to be married as incarcerated fathers, three times as likely to have lived with their children prior to arrest, and half as likely to be satisfied with their children's placement during their incarceration. They are visited less often than incarcerated fathers, and are usually incarcerated farther away from their children's homes. These and other differences are significant, and justify a separate examination of the status, characteristics, and needs of incarcerated parents by their sex.

Incarcerated Fathers

In 1992 the U.S. Department of Justice reported that there were approximately 690,000 fathers among more than 1.23 million incarcerated men in the United States (USDJ, 1993c). This number included about 466,000 imprisoned fathers and about 225,000 jailed fathers.

3

There is far less information available about incarcerated fathers than about incarcerated mothers. There has been no research that usefully compares large numbers of incarcerated fathers with other incarcerated males. Although extrapolation of general data to incarcerated fathers must be made with caution, basic information about jailed and imprisoned fathers can be obtained from large-scale studies of male prisoners by branches of the U.S. Department of Justice.

Characteristics of Male Offenders

In 1992 there were over 400,000 men in U.S. state or federal prisons and over 833,000 men in U.S. jails, representing an increase of about 6% over the number of men incarcerated in 1991. Ninety-three percent of all incarcerated persons in the United States are males (USDJ, 1993a).

Age. More than six out of 10 incarcerated adults are between 18 and 34 years of age. Incarcerated men have a slightly lower average age than incarcerated women, as the result of a greater proportion of male prisoners in the 18- to 24-year-old category. The mean age of all state and federal prisoners is increasing.

Personal and Family Characteristics. The typical male offender comes from a single-parent home and has a family member who has been incarcerated. About one in seven was raised by other relatives, and 17% spent some time in a foster care setting.

About 30% of male prisoners experienced parental substance abuse, either of alcohol (30%) or drugs (4%). Both forms of substance abuse are more common among the parents of white prisoners than those of black prisoners. Over one-third of all prisoners have an immediate family member who has also been incarcerated; black (42%) and Hispanic (35%) prisoners are slightly more likely than white prisoners to have had some family member incarcerated, but white prisoners are more likely to have had a parent who was jailed or imprisoned.

About 12% of males in jails and prisons report that they experienced physical or sexual abuse in childhood. This rate is approximately one-third of the rate among female prisoners and one-fourth of the rate among female jail inmates (USDJ, 1993c).

Education, Employment and Income. The level of education among persons admitted to prison has increased during the past 6 years. About 34% of all prisoners in 1991 had completed high school, compared to 29% in 1986.

Almost 90% of all prisoners in 1991 had an annual income of less than $25,000, and 69% had an income below the poverty level. Before incarceration, two-thirds of all prisoners had been employed; however, the level of prearrest employment has declined since 1986 and the number of prisoners who were employed full time or unemployed but looking for work also declined. About 13% of male prisoners in 1991 were receiving support from Social Security, a welfare agency, or charity before admission to prison (USDJ, 1993c).

Drug Use. Male offenders have lower rates of any drug use, use of a major drug, regular drug use, and drug addiction than female offenders. Males, however, are more likely to have been under the influence of a drug at the time they committed their offense. About three-quarters of all jailed males have used drugs, and over half have used a major drug such as heroin or cocaine (USDJ, 1991a, 1993b).

Among jail inmates studied in 1989, whites were most likely to have used any drug daily in the month before their arrest, but blacks and Hispanics were more likely to have used a major drug during that period. White jail inmates were also more likely to have ever used any drug than inmates in other racial or ethnic groups (USDJ, 1991a).

Drug use is not clearly reflected by criminal charges. In 1989 one in four convicted offenders with armed robbery charges, one in four with property offenses, and one in five with drug trafficking charges committed their crimes to obtain money to buy drugs (USDJ, 1991a).

Sentences. Most misdemeanants serve their sentences in jails, but offenders with multiple misdemeanor charges or a series of prior similar charges are increasingly likely to be sentenced to prison. This trend is due to mandatory sentencing formulas that frequently require an increase in sentence length for each prior conviction for the same offense. Other persons may serve jail time for serious—but usually nonviolent—felony crimes, especially if they are first offenders.

Male prisoners and jail inmates serve longer average sentences than their female counterparts. This difference is related to the nature of their crimes and previous arrest histories. However, only 11.6% of convicted and sentenced male offenders will serve their time in prison, compared to 15.4% of convicted and sentenced females.

The median jail sentence for both men and women is 6 months; the mean sentence for men is 18 months and for women 16 months. However, the majority of jail inmates serve 60 days or fewer. In 1989 male prisoners had a median sentence of 72 months, compared to 60 months or females, and a mean sentence of 103 months compared to 72 months for females (USDJ, 1992b).

Recidivism. Data on the frequency with which formerly incarcerated persons are rearrested are kept only for state and federal prisoners. Recidivism of jail inmates is not usually measured. Unlike state and federal correctional agencies, most jail systems do not assign inmates "main" or permanent identification numbers that carry over from incarceration to incarceration. However, the tremendous number of jail admissions per year, compared to

1-day or average population counts, suggests that many people go to jail again and again.

A 1989 report of a study of prisoners released in 1983 found an overall recidivism rate of 59%; more than two-thirds of all male prisoners were rearrested within 3 years (USDJ, 1989). More recent data shows that recidivism has increased, but less so among males than among female offenders (USDJ, 1992d).

Summary. Male offenders are most likely to be young adults from single-parent homes, with a limited education and poor employment skills. They serve longer sentences than females and are more likely to be rearrested and reincarcerated.

Studies of Incarcerated Fathers

There is a large body of documentation on male prisoners and their families, most of which has been conducted by interview or survey of the wives of incarcerated men and which examines the husband–wife relationship. There has been very little research on incarcerated men as fathers. The literature is so limited that it cannot even be divided into separate reviews of the jailed and the imprisoned populations, although they are likely to be somewhat different.

Bakker, Morris & Janus (1978) interviewed the wives of seven incarcerated men and wrote a very limited description of the lives of the families of male prisoners. The only information collected on the paternal role of the prisoners related to their children's understanding of the fathers' whereabouts.

Schneller (1978) closely examined the effects of incarceration on the families of black men in a Washington, D.C., prison. Ninety-three prisoners and their wives were interviewed and home visits were also conducted. The usefulness of this well-designed, scientifically conducted study is limited, however, because the study population was restricted to one racial group and excluded fathers who did not have legal or common-law marriages.

Fritsch and Burkhead (1982) surveyed a representative sample of prisoners in the federal minimum security prison in Lexington, Kentucky, and identified 91 parents of minor children from this group. These parents answered survey questions about their 194 children. The study focused on parents' perceptions of their children's behavioral reactions to parental incarceration.

Swan (1981) authored *Families of Black Prisoners*. He interviewed the wives of 192 men imprisoned in Alabama and Tennessee. His study focused on social and family effects of paternal incarceration; the role of the men as fathers prior to and during incarceration was not closely examined.

Koban (1983) studied 61 men in a Kentucky prison. She compared the effects of imprisonment on the parent–child relationship among incarcerated fathers and incarcerated mothers.

Lanier (1987) conducted a qualitative study of imprisoned fathers participating in the Eastern Fathers' Group, an educational and mutual support group.

Hairston (1989) studied 126 fathers incarcerated at one maximum security prison and one minimum security prison in a southeastern state. This research examined family ties among fathers in prison and their parenting issues and concerns.

Family and Social Characteristics of Incarcerated Fathers

The personal, family, and social characteristics of incarcerated fathers are similar to those of other incarcerated males with a few exceptions. Incarcerated fathers are more likely to be married or to have been divorced than other prisoners (Hairston, 1989; USDJ, 1993c). The average age of the fathers is higher than that of other prisoners.

Imprisoned fathers have complex family networks. Hairston (1989) found that a majority of men in all marital categories, including those who were single, were fathers. At least half of those with two or more children had had these children by different mothers. These circumstances are consistent with the finding that most incarcerated fathers do not share a marital bond or an ongoing relationship with the mothers of their children. Indeed, over half of the fathers in Hairston's study reported that their marriages had ended during their current incarceration.

At the Center for Children of Incarcerated Parents it has been our experience that jailed fathers are more likely than imprisoned fathers to maintain a current relationship with the mother of at least one of their children during their incarceration. The majority of jailed fathers who participate in the center's family life and parent education projects lived with the mother of at least one of their children prior to incarceration and plan to return to the same relationship following release.

Paternal Characteristics of Incarcerated Fathers

The concerns of imprisoned fathers, like those of incarcerated mothers, focus on the well-being of their children. However, unlike incarcerated mothers, fathers identify discipline, lack of guidance or supervision, and the possibility that their children might "get in trouble" as their greatest concerns. Significant numbers are also worried that their children might forget them, that they might be replaced in their children's lives, and that their children might lose respect for them (Fritsch & Burkhead, 1982; Hairston, 1989).

Incarcerated fathers often feel powerless in their role as parents. Only half of the fathers studied by Koban (1983) expected to be consulted about their childrens' problems or to participate in decision making related to their children. More than half of the fathers surveyed by Hairston (1989) did not respond when asked what they did to maintain their parent–child relationships. Most of the men who responded indicated that imprisonment limited paternal activities. There were almost no references to involvement or interest in children's daily activities, special celebrations, or education. These fathers described their paternal role in only the most general terms.

Such findings are consistent with the fact that many incarcerated fathers did not live with their children prior to arrest. Fritsch and Burkhead (1982) found that parents who lived with their children prior to incarceration were significantly more likely to be able to identify their children's problems than parents who had not lived with their children. This was also found to be true for incarcerated fathers who had regular contact with their children by phone, in visits, or during home furloughs.

Feelings of a lack of authority and control as parents undoubtedly contribute to the overcontrolling parental behaviors identified in incarcerated fathers by Adalist-Estrin (1986). However, the extent to which paternal behaviors prior to and during incarceration contribute to these feelings is unclear. Incarcerated fathers do appear to be less invested in their children's futures than incarcerated mothers and less often plan to reunite with their children after release (Hairston, 1989).

Parent–Child Contact among Incarcerated Fathers

Many incarcerated fathers have no contact with their children. Earlier studies (Fritsch & Burkhead, 1982) suggest that fathers who lived with their children and/or were married prior to arrest are more likely to visit or correspond with their children during their incarceration. More recently, Lanier (1987) reported limited contact between incarcerated fathers and their children. Hairston (1989) found that almost one-third of the incarcerated fathers she studied had not seen their children since they entered prison and over half had not seen their children in the 6 months preceding her survey. Telephone contact and correspondence was similarly limited. Fathers who do not receive visits identify transportation and escort problems as the main reasons their children are unable to visit them in prison. About one-fifth say their children do not visit because of opposition by the child's mother (Hairston, 1989). These figures are not surprising in light of the fact that most imprisoned fathers do not have an active relationship with the mothers of their children.

Jailed and imprisoned fathers who have little contact with their children often claim that this is intentional. Many jailed fathers participating in a family life education project conducted by the Center for Children of

Incarcerated Parents assert that they do not wish to have their children visit them in jail; in fact, the majority receive no visits from their children. Koban's (1983) study of federal prisoners found that 87% of unvisited fathers in her study claimed to have made the decision to forego father–child visits themselves. These findings may represent the need of relatively powerless incarcerated men to feel a sense of control over their activities as fathers.

Service Needs of Incarcerated Fathers

In addition to general services that would also benefit prisoners who are not parents, like education, drug treatment, job training, and job placement, incarcerated fathers have special service needs in three areas.

Parental Empowerment. The need for power and control in parenting by offenders is perhaps greatest among incarcerated fathers. These needs arise in part because of the disempowering nature of incarceration, but also out of prior and current parent–child separations. Incarcerated fathers need services that train, support, and empower them as parents.

Father–Child Separation. The outcomes of early father–child separations are primary or supplementary causes of succeeding separations. Inmate fathers need services that address the causes of preincarceration separations as well as those that support the amelioration of separation due to jail and prison sentences. Finally, they need prerelease and release-related services that will support father–child reunification.

Family Conflict. Although there is little evidence to support the theory that the children of prisoners are at increased risk for abuse *from their parents*, there is a compelling research that suggests that male offenders are likely to commit assaults on their wives and partners. Dutton and Hart (1992) found that the female partners of the male prisoners they studied are at high risk for physical abuse. Other authorities with a great deal of experience in working with prisoners also believe that the families of offenders experience serious conflict, particularly after an incarcerated father's release (Vachio, 1991). Incarcerated fathers therefore need services directed toward the root causes of domestic conflict and interpersonal violence, as well as services that assist prisoners and their families in achieving peaceful reunification.

Incarcerated Mothers

There were approximately 67,500 incarcerated mothers in the United States among the 90,000 U.S. women incarcerated in 1993. This number includes about 37,500 imprisoned mothers and about 30,000 jailed mothers (USDJ, 1993a). No large-scale studies of female offenders have identified significant differences in demographic or criminal justice descriptors between incarcerated mothers and other incarcerated women.

Characteristics of Jailed and Imprisoned Women

In 1992 about 50,000 (55.6%) of all incarcerated women were in state or federal prisons, while about 40,000 (44.4%) were in jails. There appear to be some differences between female jail inmates and female prisoners.

Age. Jailed women are younger on the average than imprisoned women, with a mean age of 29 years in 1989. The mean age of women in prison is approximately 32 years and increasing as the result of mandatory sentencing practices and longer sentences (USDJ, 1991b, 1992b).

Personal and Family Characteristics. According to the Task Force on the Female Offender (1990), created by the American Correctional Association, the typical female offender comes from a broken or single-parent home in which other family members have been incarcerated. About one in five women offenders has spent time in a foster home or institution as a child, and one in three has attempted suicide.

The proportions of jailed and imprisoned women who report prior physical or sexual abuse are similar, about four out of 10. For 31% of women in jail, and 22% of women in prison, the reported abuse occurred before age 18 (USDJ, 1992b).

Education, Employment, and Income. Female offenders are better educated now than in previous decades, and also better educated than male offenders. Nevertheless, the general level of education is low among women in jail and prison. The Task Force on the Female Offender (1990), in a study of a combined population from U.S. jails and prisons, found that 7.3% had not gone beyond elementary school and less than half had completed high school.

When examined separately, jailed women appear to be slightly better educated than imprisoned women. One in six women prisoners has completed the 8th grade or less, compared to one in eight jailed women. Over half (50.6%) of jailed women have completed high school, compared to 43% of imprisoned women (USDJ, 1991b, 1992b). In spite of these differences in educational attainment, jailed women were more likely to have been unemployed before their arrest than imprisoned women and had lower prearrest incomes (Task Force on the Female Offender, 1990; USDJ, 1991b, 1992b).

Drug Use. Drug-related arrests, convictions, and incarcerations of women have risen dramatically since 1960. Although most attention to increases in arrests among women during these decades was given to property offenses (Adler, 1975; Crites, 1976; Simon, 1975; Steffensmeier, 1980), it is clear from our current perspective that the most significant trend was the increase in drug-related crimes. One in four jail inmates with armed robbery charges, one in four with property offenses, and one in five with drug trafficking offenses, for example, committed their crimes to obtain money to buy drugs (USDJ, 1991a).

U.S. Department of Justice (1991b, 1992b) statistics suggest that jailed women more often have a history of drug use than imprisoned women. While about one-third of both groups were under the influence of a drug at the time they committed their offense, more jailed women (55.1%) than imprisoned women (49.6%) had used drugs in the month before their arrest, and of these women, jailed women were more likely to have used a major drug such as heroin or crack cocaine than imprisoned women (43.8% vs. 32.2%).

Sentences. Most misdemeanants serve their sentences in jails, but women with multiple misdemeanor charges or prior similar charges are increasingly likely to be sentenced to prison. This trend is due to mandatory sentencing formulas that frequently require an increase in sentence length for each prior conviction for the same offense. Other women may serve jail time for serious—but usually nonviolent—felony crimes, especially if they are first offenders.

In the past the vast majority of jail inmates were sentenced to a maximum of 1 year; women who spent over a year in jail were those whose cases were in prolonged ajudication. Currently, as a result of prison overcrowding, jails have been forced to hold convicted women awaiting transportation to state prison for prolonged periods. Also, courts in some areas are now imposing longer jail sentences. For example, the majority of jails in the Northeast and the South, and about one-third of all jails in the West, hold women serving jail sentences of over 1 year.

According to the U.S. Department of Justice (1993b), the median jail sentence for a woman is 6 months and the mean sentence is 16 months. Since jailed persons typically serve 50 to 75% of their sentences, the mean time served by jailed women is 8 months to 1 year. However, the great majority of jailed women serve 60 or fewer days. Imprisoned women have a mean sentence of 66 months (108 months for violent offenses), of which the average time served is 16 months (27 months for violent offenses).

Racidivism. Women are less likely to be rearrested than men following release from prison. In 1989, in a report on a study of prisoners who had been released in 1983, the U.S. Department of Justice found an overall recidivism rate of 59%; in this study, approximately four out of 10 women were rearrested, compared to more than two-thirds of the men. More recent data shows that women's recidivism has increased; among women prisoners released in 1989, 51.9% were rearrested, 38.7% were reconvicted, and 33% were returned to jail or prison (USDJ, 1992d).

There is no comparable data on the recidivism of jailed women; information on the recidivism of women in jail has been obtained only by self-report. Among jailed women, over 13% have been previously convicted but not incarcerated. Fifty-six percent have been previously incarcerated; 35% are multiple recidivists. One in six jailed women is a multiple recidivist who has been out of jail for less than 1 year (USDJ, 1992b).

Summary. Women offenders, including incarcerated mothers, are most likely to be young adults from single-parent homes, with limited education, poor employment skills, and histories of substance abuse. The majority have committed drug offenses or drug-related crimes. Following incarcerated and release, most women offenders will be rearrested and more than a third will be jailed or imprisoned again within 3 years.

Maternal Characteristics of Incarcerated Women

Much of the early research that has been done on women offenders in jails and prisons has examined their perceptions of the maternal role and their maternal concerns. This emphasis reflects the general impression of the public that offenders, but particularly women prisoners, are not good parents.

In fact, there is no objective evidence to support that impression. There has been almost no research on incarcerated offenders, for example, which compares them as parents to similar populations in studies controlled for the effects of race, income, education, employment, and adult or childhood victimization. LeFlore and Holston (1990) compared incarcerated mothers with demographically matched noncriminal mothers and found that parenting attitudes and self-ratings of parenting performance among the two groups were similar. Other studies that did not utilize matched controls have also found that incarcerated mothers have appropriate maternal behaviors and concerns.

Bonfanti, Felder, Loesde & Vincent (1974) examined maternal behaviors among incarcerated women and their perceptions of their dual roles as mothers and as prisoners. The majority of the mothers demonstrated a high degree of maternal behavior, such as attempts to maintain contact with their children through telephone calls and letters. Maternal behaviors were most often seen in women who had legal custody of their children, who had lived with their children prior to arrest, and who planned to reunite with their children after release. However, the way in which women prisoners perceived their role as mothers was unrelated to these or any variables. In other words, women who had a good chance of remaining with their children on the outside continued to act out the mother role while incarcerated, but women's perceptions of their role had nothing to do with the reality of their past and future lives with their children. Even women who had performed very poorly as parents and/or had little or no possibility of returning to active parenting were able to perceive themselves in the maternal role in a positive light.

Baunach (1979) reported that women in her study felt inadequate in the mother role, due to the limitations imposed by incarceration. Nevertheless, most of these mothers also exhibited a high degree of maternal behaviors, again directed toward maintaining their relationship with their children while incarcerated. Unlike Bonfanti et al., (1974) Baunach found the women she studied to have realistic expectations of their future as parents.

Henriques (1982) also examined her subjects' perception of the maternal role. The majority (59.8%) identified "providing emotional care and support" as the main component of a mother's role. Other significant maternal attributes identified included "teaching" (39.9%), "physical care and support" (33.3%), and personal attributes such as understanding, patience, and fairness (33.3%). Henriques's interviews with 21 outside agency personnel documented significantly different perceptions of the study subjects as mothers. Most (80.7%) of these correctional officers, social workers, police, and judges felt that the women in the study were "incapacitated" by poverty, lack of opportunities, lack of knowledge, lack of family support, and other problems. However, 28.6% described the women as "manipulative, exploitative or selfish," and 9.5% believed that they only fantasized about being good mothers. Less than 15% felt that the women were genuinely concerned about their children.

However, the concerns of incarcerated mothers appear to be generally appropriate (LeFlore & Holston, 1990). McGowan and Blumenthal (1978) found that these mothers were concerned about their child's placement; approximately half were either ambivalent or negative about their children's living situation while they were incarcerated. The mothers they studied contributed to the extensive list of program service suggestions collected by McGowan and Blumenthal (see below).

Henriques and Hairston also examined the concerns of jailed mothers in their respective studies. These are summarized in Table 1.1.

Table 1.1
Concerns of Incarcerated Mothers

Mothers' Concerns	Hairston, 1990 (N = 38)	Henriques, 1982 (N = 30)
Parent–child separation	70%	43.3%
Child placement and custody	Not measured	43.3%
Child health	"	30.0%
Protection and safety of child	"	30.0%
Contact with child	71%	26.7%
Loss of maternal influence	Not measured	13.3%
Financial support	"	13.3%

The Parental Rights of Incarcerated Mothers

Women offenders appear to be particularly at risk for loss of their parental rights. This risk is the result of two factors: maternal substance abuse and lack of family reunification services for women prisoners. Other significant issues include statutory timelines for reunification and limited child placement options for families with incarcerated mothers.

Although there have been dramatic increases in maternal substance abuse over the past 3 decades, the criminal and civil liability of pregnant and parenting addicts remains unresolved. In spite of existing legislation supporting treatment in lieu of prosecution for drug users, addicted women are increasingly sentenced to incarceration (Becker, 1991), and some jurisdictions are merging involuntary civil commitments with treatment with punitive sanctions (Garcia, 1992).

Intermediate sanctions that require participation in drug programs were created in recognition of the compulsive nature of addiction behaviors, yet many require the incarceration of mothers or the removal of their children when they fail in treatment. Since the vast majority of women's correctional facilities do not have drug treatment services, maternal incarceration merely adds the effects of mother–child separation to the earlier traumatic effects of maternal substance abuse. Addicted women offenders and their children are therefore subject to multiple jeopardy.

Statutory timelines for family reunification generally mandate that children in foster care be returned to their parents or placed with long-term guardians within 12 to 24 months after their removal from the parent's custody. However, imprisoned mothers will serve a mean sentence of 16 months in prison, a circumstance that results in their having little or no time to complete reunification requirements after release.

Women offenders are particularly at risk for termination of their parental rights to infants born while they are incarcerated. Inappropriate placements of very young infants in adoptive foster homes has been common in some jurisdictions (Barry, 1990). Family placements may also be difficult as a result of the reluctance of child welfare agencies to approve placement of children in homes whose family members have criminal histories. Given the reality that approximately half of all incarcerated females have an immediate family member who has been incarcerated, and that the goal of agency services is to reunite the child with a parent who is an offender, such guidelines are unduly restrictive and increase the number of children of women prisoners who enter foster care with strangers.

There are no studies that specifically examine the extent of loss and retention of parental rights among female offenders. However, there is some evidence that terminations occur disproportionately among women offenders. The Center for Children of Incarcerated Parents has found that parental rights to some or all of their children have been terminated among about 25% of women offenders whose children participate in the center's therapeutic programs (Johnston, 1992). Also, national samplings of court data on terminations of parental rights in black families have revealed that from 12 to 18% of all terminations occur among incarcerated parents (National Black Child Development Institute, 1989).

The Effects of Recidivism

Clearly, maternal incarceration has become more damaging to mother–child relationships over the past 3 decades. It is not clear exactly why this is so. There were far fewer women prisoners and fewer women's prisons 30 years ago, so that a greater proportion of women were imprisoned farther away from their children's homes. Sentences were longer in the past. For example, Zalba (1964) reported a mean time served of 22 months for all California women prisoners; this compares to a current mean of 17 months. In spite of these more detrimental conditions, mother–child contact was apparently better for previous generations of imprisoned women and their families. Similarly, involuntary termination of parental rights among women prisoners was less prevalent in the past than it is today.

The variable that has increased, as contact and visitation between incarcerated mothers and their children have decreased and terminations of parental rights have become more prevalent, is female recidivism. In 1964 Zalba reported that 80% of California's women prisoners were serving their first prison term, compared to only 28% of women currently imprisoned in the United States (USDJ, 1991b). Studies show that the likelihood of mother–child reunification after incarceration decreases with each prior incarceration (Gibbs, 1971; Hairston, 1990; McGowan & Blumenthal, 1978). As women are increasingly rearrested, reconvicted, and reincarcerated, the rates at which they are permanently separated from their children also rising. Although it is not apparent in their stated concerns, nor in the research literature, this relationship is perhaps the greatest problem facing incarcerated mothers.

Service Needs of Incarcerated Mothers

McGowan and Blumenthal (1978) asked incarcerated mothers about their concerns and the services that could meet their needs and the needs of their children. Their findings are summarized in Table 1.2. Three areas of need merit special attention.

Maternal Decision Making. Women prisoners surveyed by McGowan and Blumenthal (1978) identified eight areas of service needs for incarcerated mothers; a mother's ability to make decisions regarding her children was

Table 1.2
Service Needs Identified by Incarcerated Mothers

Area of Concern	Suggested Services
Adjustment to incarceration and release; mental health; reactions to trauma of maternal incarceration	Therapy/counseling
Protection of parental rights	Family legal services
Perinatal health	Improved medical services & sanitary condtions for pregnant prisoners
Financial assistance for families	Public assistance information; immediate post-release aid
Substance abuse/addiction	Drug treatment services
Maternal employment	Vocational & educational programs; expanded work release & furlough programs
Re-entry & family reunification	Reunification counseling; social services for assistance with housing/employment; childcare

Source: McGowan & Blumenthal, 1978

an important factor in each area. Children's placement at the time of arrest, selection of children's caregivers, participation in dependency hearings, and resolution of issues regarding children's schooling, health care, and religion have all been identified as decisions in which incarcerated mothers should participate (Johnston, 1994). Without such participation, maternal satisfaction with child placement decreases, parent/child/caregiver conflicts increase, and the mother's parental authority is weakened beyond what is common following parental arrest and incarceration.

Mother–Child Contact. Another critical need of incarcerated mothers is for contact with their children. Correctional agencies have generally recognized the need for visitation programs. Virtually all women's prisons allow mother–child contact visits. The prevalence of special, extended contact visitation programs varies by region, from a high of 62.5% in the Northeast to a low of 16.7% in the West. Nationally, on-site childcare for visitors is available in about one in eight women's prison (Task Force on the Female Offender, 1990).

However, when the National Council on Crime and Delinquency recently reprised McGowan and Blumenthal's (1978) study in 1992, it found that mother–child prison visitation had declined from 92% in 1978 to less than 50% in 1992. Continuing contact between parent and child is perhaps the most significant predictor of family reunification following parental incarceration. The worrisome decline in the ability of women prisoners to maintain contact with their children is due to:

restriction of prison telephone privileges to mutually exclusive systems of collect calls, which burden the children's caregivers, or to use of telephone credits, which severely limit calling by indigent prisoners;

construction of the majority of larger women's prison facilities in rural and outlying areas not easily accessible to the children of prisoners, most of whom reside in cities; and

lack of financial and worker support from the child welfare system for visitation between incarcerated women and their children in foster care.

Correctional and social service agencies have been extremely slow to address the needs of incarcerated mothers and their children in these areas.

Retention of Parental Rights. Women offenders with children in foster care do not receive adequate reunification services (Barry, 1985). In addition to the inability to maintain optimal mother–child contact, incarcerated mothers also do not have access to resources needed to meet other reunification requirements commonly imposed by dependency courts, including:

Parent education. Only 14% of women prisoners in the United States were enrolled in parenting programs in 1991 (USDJ, 1993a).

Drug treatment. Less than 10% of all U.S. prisoners were enrolled in residential drug treatment programs in 1991; the majority of these programs were located in male facilities (USDJ, 1993a).

Psychological counseling. Only about 10% of women prisoners were enrolled in psychological or psychiatric counseling in 1991 (USDJ, 1993a).

Employment training. Only 5.3% of all U.S. prisoners were enrolled in employment training programs in 1990 (USDJ, 1992c); the majority of these programs are located in male facilities, and, where they exist in coed facilities, women participants are relegated to sewing, clerical, and other types of training that lead to low-paid employment while male prisoners are more often trained for skilled occupations (U.S. General Accounting Office, 1980).

Conclusions

The justice process strips offenders of parental power and authority but not of their concerns about the well-being of their children and their desire for parent–child reunification. Incarcerated parents of both sexes are most powerless in the areas of parental decision-making and parent–child contact. Both need services that empower them as parents and increase their parental decision-making capabilities. However, incarcerated mothers and fathers differ significantly in other characteristics and concerns.

Incarcerated fathers less often resided or were involved with their children prior to their incarceration; yet, because the children of male prisoners almost always live with their natural mothers, incarcerated fathers have more contact with their children than do incarcerated mothers. Only one in five children of women prisoners live with their other natural parent and incarcerated mothers have a much greater proportion of their children in foster care. As a result, women prisoners not only have more difficulty receiving visits from their children, but they are also more likely to have their parental rights terminated during incarceration. Prisoners of both sexes need services supporting parent–child relationships and continued parent–child contact during incarceration, but incarcerated mothers need additional services specifically directed toward preventing the termination of their parental rights.

Gender-related differences in the parenting issues and behaviors of prisoners are based in part upon the sex roles and responsibilities traditionally assigned to parents in the larger society. They are also based upon gender-related differences in criminal activity, arrest, conviction, incarceration, and recidivism. Previously, female patterns of interaction with the criminal justice system—including lower arrest, incarceration, and recidivism rates—were complementary to their social role as the primary caregivers of children. Recent increases in female arrests, convictions, incarceration, and recidivism have resulted in greater conflicts with the traditional female role for women offenders. As female patterns of interaction with the criminal justice system become quantitatively more similar to male patterns, mother–child reunification among women offenders is decreasing, terminations of their parental rights are increasing, and we are seeing a greater number of women prisoners who, like men, did not live with their children prior to incarceration and will probably not live with them after release. This is not happening because women offenders are assuming what appear to be male patterns of parenting, but rather because dissolution of the family is the consequence of repeated parental incarcerations. Such circumstances require, perhaps as a first priority, services for incarcerated parents that address not only prearrest and postrelease reunification issues, but also the prevention of recidivism.

References

Adalist-Estrin, A. (1986). Parenting . . . from behind bars. *Family Resource Coalition Report*, 5(1):12–13.

Adler, F. (1975). *Sisters in crime*. New York: McGraw-Hill.

Bakker, L. J., Morris, B.A., & Janus, L.M. (1978). Hidden victims of crime. *Social Work*, 23:143–148.

Barry, E. (1985, July–August). Reunification difficult for incarcerated parents and their children. *Youth Law News*, pp. 14–16.

Barry, E. (1990). Women in prison. In C. Lefcourt (Ed.), *Women and the Law* (6:18.01–18.35). Deerfield, IL: Clark, Boardman & Callahan.

Baunach, P. J. (1979, November). *Mothering from behind prison walls*. Paper presented at the annual meeting of the American Society of Criminology, Philadelphia.

Becker, B. L. (1991). Order in the court: Challenging judges who incarcerate pregnant, substance-dependent defendants to protect fetal health. *Hastings Constitutional Law Quarterly*, 19:235–259.

Bloom, B., & Steinhart, D. (1993). *Why punish the children: A reappraisal of the children of incarcerated mothers in America*. San Francisco: National Council on Crime and Delinquency.

Bonfanti, M. A., Felder, S. S., Loesch, M. L., & Vincent, N. J. (1974). *Enactment and perception of maternal role of incarcerated mothers*. Master's thesis, Louisiana State University.

Crites, L. (1976). Women offenders: Myth versus reality. In L. Crites (Ed.), *The female offender* (pp. 33–44). Lexington, MA: Lexington Books.

Dutton, D. G., & Hart, S. D. (1992). Risk markers for family violence in a federally incarcerated population. *International Journal of Law and Psychiatry*, 15:101–112.

Fritsch, T. A., & Burkhead, J. D. (1982). Behavioral reactions of children to parental absence due to imprisonment. *Family Relations*, 30:83–88.

Garcia, S. (1992). Drug addiction and mother–child welfare: Rights, laws, and discretionary decision making. *Journal of Legal Medicine*, 13:129–203.

Gibbs, C. (1971). The effect of imprisonment of women upon their children. *British Journal of Criminology*, 11:113–130.

Hairston, C. F. (1989). Men in prison: Family characteristics and family views. *Journal of Offender Counseling, Services and Rehabilitation*, 14(1):23–30.

Hairston, C. F. (1990) Imprisoned mothers and their children. *Affilia*, 6(2).

Henriques, Z. W. (1982). *Imprisoned mothers and their children*. Washington, DC: University Press of America.

Inter-University Consortium for Political & Social Research. (1991). *Survey of Inmates of Local Jails, 1989*. Ann Arbor, Michigan: Authors.

Johnston, D. (1991). *Jailed mothers*. Pasadena, CA: Pacific Oaks Center for Children of Incarcerated Parents.

Johnston, D. (1992). *Children of offenders*. Pasadena, CA: Pacific Oaks Center for Children of Incarcerated Parents.

Johnston, D. (1994). *Caregivers of prisoners' children*. Pasadena, CA: Pacific Oaks Center for Children of Incarcerated Parents.

Koban, L. (1983). Parents in prison: A comparative analysis of the effects of incarceration on the families of men and women. *Research in Law, Deviance and Social Control*, 5:171–183.

Lanier, C. S. (1987, November 7). *Fathers in prison: A psychosocial exploration*. Paper presented at the annual meeting of the American Society of Criminology, Montreal, Quebec.

LeFlore, L., & Holston, M. A. (1990). Perceived importance of parenting behaviors as reported by inmate mothers: An exploratory study. *Journal of Offender Counseling, Services and Rehabilitation*, 14(1):5–21.

McGowan, B., & Blumenthal, K. (1978). *Why punish the children?* New York: Children's Defense Fund.

National Black Child Development Institute. (1989). *Who will care when parents can't? A study of black children in foster care*. Washington, DC: Author.

Schneller, D. P. (1978). *The prisoner's family*. San Francisco: R & E Research Associates.

Simon, R. (1975). *Women and crime*. Lexington, MA: Lexington Books.

Steffensmeier, R. J. (1980). Assessing the impact of the women's movement on sex-based differences in the handling of adult criminal defendants. *Crime and Delinquency*, 26:344–357.

Swan, A. (1981). *Families of black prisoners: Survival and progress*. Boston: G. K. Hall.

Task Force on the Female Offender. (1990). *The female offender: What does the future hold?* Arlington, VA: American Correctional Association.

U.S. Department of Justice. (1989). *Recidivism among prisoners released in 1983*. (Report No. NCJ-116261). Washington, DC: Bureau of Justice Statistics.

U.S. Department of Justice. (1991a). *Drugs and jail inmates, 1989* (Report No. NCJ-130836). Washington, DC: Bureau of Justice Statistics.

U.S. Department of Justice. (1991b). *Women in prison* (Report No. NCJ-127991). Washington, DC: Bureau of Justice Statistics.

U.S. Department of Justice. (1992a). *Correctional populations in the United States, 1990* (Report No. NCJ-134946). Washington, DC: Bureau of Justice Statistics.

U.S. Department of Justice. (1992b). *Women in jail, 1989* (Report No. NCJ-134732). Washington, DC: Bureau of Justice Statistics.

U.S. Department of Justice. (1992c). *Prisons and prisoners in the United States* (Report No. NCJ-137002). Washington, DC: Bureau of Justice Statistics.

U.S. Department of Justice. (1992d). Recidivism of felons on probation. (Publication No. NCJ-134177). Washington, DC: Bureau of Justice Statistics.

U.S. Department of Justice. (1993a). *Correctional populations in the United States, 1991* (Report No. NCJ-142729). Washington, DC: Bureau of Justice Statistics.

U.S. Department of Justice. (1993b). *Jail inmates 1992* (Report No. NCJ-143284). Washington, DC: Bureau of Justice Statistics.

U.S. Department of Justice. (1993c). *Prisoners in 1992* (Report No. NCJ-141874). Washington, DC: Bureau of Justice Statistics.

U.S. Department of Justice. (1993d). *Survey of state prison inmates* (Report No. NCJ-136949). Washington, DC: Bureau of Justice Statistics.

U.S. Department of Justice. (1992d). *Recidivism of prisoners released in 1989*. Report No. NCJ 134177. Washington, DC: Bureau of Justice Statistics.

U.S. General Accounting Office. (1980). *Women in prison: Inequitable treatment requires action* (Report No. GGD-81-6). Gaithersburg, MD: Author.

Vachio, A. (1991, November 16). *How we work with families*. Paper presented at the conference of the New Mexico Corrections Department, Santa Fe, NM.

Zalba, S. (1964). *Women prisoners and their families*. Sacramento, CA: Department of Social Welfare and Department of Corrections.

2
Imprisoned Mothers

Barbara Bloom

P arents who are in prison face many problems in maintaining meaningful relationships with their children, and this is especially true for
imprisoned mothers. When a father is imprisoned, responsibility for
his children is typically assumed by their mother. Families are more likely
to be disrupted by women's incarceration than by men's because, in most
cases, the mothers were the primary caregivers of their children prior to
imprisonment. Because many women provided the sole economic and
emotional support for their children prior to incarceration, maternal
incarceration is often far more unsettling to the family than paternal
incarceration.

It is estimated that between 75 and 80% of the women in U.S. prisons
are mothers. The U.S. Department of Justice (USDJ) reported that 76% of
incarcerated women in the United States were mothers in 1986. A study in
progress (Bloom & Owen, In progress) involving California women prisoners found that 80% of the respondents were mothers. The majority of
these mothers are single parents with an average of two children. Separation from and concern about the well-being of these children is often one
of the most damaging aspects of imprisonment for women (Baunach,
1979; Bloom & Steinhart, 1993; Henriques, 1982; McGowan & Blumenthal, 1978).

Women's Prisons

The Task Force on the Female Offender (1990), a study group created by
the American Correctional Association, reported that female prisoners in
the United States were housed in 71 state and federal correctional facilities
for women in 1989. Sixteen of these were maximum security prisons, 28
were medium security prisons, and 27 were minimum security prisons.
Although most women prisoners are classified as minimum security
inmates, the majority are held in medium or maximum security facilities
because their small numbers in each state do not justify the expense of
building more women's prisons. The conditions of maximum security

confinement may effect the development of parent–child programming and impact the experience of visiting children at these prisons.

About three-quarters of women in state prisons, and about one-third of those in federal prisons, are housed in female-only facilities with an average capacity of 390 women. One-third of women's prisons were originally designed and/or used as men's prisons. About two-thirds of women in state prisons and about half of the women in federal prisons are housed in multiple-occupancy living quarters; they are confined to their sleeping areas an average of 12 hours per day.

The range of educational offerings and other services is more limited in women's prisons than in men's prisons (U.S. General Accounting Office, 1980). Round-the-clock emergency care is unavailable in more than one-third of women's prisons and weekly prenatal/postpartum care is offered in less than three-quarters of women's prisons; about 80% of women's prisons report that they offer gynecological/obstetrical services (Task Force on the Female Offender, 1990).

Studies of Imprisoned Mothers

Studies of imprisoned mothers and their children have spanned more than 3 decades. The following summary reports some of the predominant research efforts in the United States.

Zietz (1963) examined child welfare services for 40 women imprisoned at the California Institution for Women. Although this was a small study, it was the first report based on well-designed research on incarcerated mothers to be published in the professional literature.

Zalba (1964) conducted one of the first large-scale studies of imprisoned mothers in the United States, surveying 460 prisoners at the California Institution for Women and interviewing 124 of these women. Zalba examined interagency cooperation in providing services for incarcerated mothers and their families.

Gibbs (1971) interviewed 223 incarcerated mothers with dependent children as part of a larger survey of over 600 women prisoners. This study was conducted in England and examined placement situations of the children of imprisoned women.

Bonfanti, Felter, Loesch and Vincent (1974) interviewed 71 mothers to study maternal role perception and behaviors among women incarcerated at the Louisiana Correctional Institution for Women.

DuBose (1975) interviewed women at the Federal Correctional Institution at Fort Worth, Texas, as part of a study of the effects of maternal incarceration.

Glick and Neto (1977) conducted a national study of 6,300 women incarcerated in 14 states. In their research on programming for women prisoners, the authors collected data on imprisoned mothers from correctional institutions.

McGowan and Blumenthal (1978) surveyed 9,379 women in U.S. prisons and jails; of those respondents, 3,121 were mothers. The results of this study were issued in the landmark Children's Defense Fund publication, *Why Punish the Children?*

Baunach (1979) interviewed 196 women prisoners, 138 of whom were mothers. The study was conducted in Washington and Kentucky state prisons for the purpose of examining the separation of incarcerated mothers and their children.

Koban (1983) studied 72 women in a Kentucky prison. She compared the effects of imprisonment on the parent–child relationship among incarcerated parents of both sexes.

LeFlore and Holston (1990) interviewed all 120 mothers imprisoned at Mississippi's only secure female facility and a matched-pair sample of non-incarcerated controls. All subjects rated parental behaviors by importance and their performance.

Bloom and Steinhart (1993) reprised the original "Why Punish the Children?" study. The authors surveyed 439 mothers incarcerated in eight states and the District of Columbia by mail; 80% of the respondents were state or federal prisoners.

Pregnant Women in Prison

Struggles with parent–child separation issues and retention of parental rights may be the greatest for the woman who is pregnant and delivers her baby while incarcerated. Approximately 8 to 10% of women offenders are pregnant when they enter prison. According to the Task Force on the Female Offender's (1990) national survey of female offenders, 6% of imprisoned women were pregnant at the time they were admitted. Bloom and Steinhart's (1993) found that 9% of the respondents gave birth while incarcerated.

Traditionally, the conditions of confinement, including nutrition and perinatal care, have been inadequate in women's institutions (Mann, 1984; McCall, Casteel, & Shaw, 1985). High miscarriage rates have been documented in correctional facilities throughout the nation. A significant study conducted by McCall, Casteel, and Shaw (1985) concluded that high miscarriage rates within three California correctional systems were related to severe problems in perinatal care including (1) difficulties in identification of women with high-risk pregnancies; (2) difficulties in transportation of pregnant women to outside medical facilities for routine treatment and; and (3) low levels of competence among correctional medical staff and community hospital staff. For example, the common practice of waiting until a pregnant prisoner is in labor before transporting her to the hospital can increase the risk of birth complications and infant mortality. Fortunately, medical care for pregnant prisoners has begun to improve in some states as a result of class action suits brought on behalf of pregnant prisoners (Barry, 1985b).

Other concerns regarding high-risk pregnant prisoners include the use of shackles and restraints in the delivery room, transportation methods, and the management of perinatal drug addiction. The problem of pregnant, substance-dependent prisoners is complex and has critical implications for both the mother and her unborn child, particularly relating to detoxification procedures and prenatal and postpartum care. Pregnant prisoners may also suffer emotional problems associated with denial of the right to choose between carrying the fetus to term or terminating the pregnancy.

In most instances, when a women gives birth during incarceration she is allowed to spend only several days with her newborn baby after delivery. Essential bonding of mother to infant cannot occur in such a short period of time, and this has serious implications for the future mother–child relationship. With the exception of some correctional facilities in the state of New York, U.S. prisons do not allow newborns and young infants to remain with their incarcerated mothers.

Some states, such as North Carolina, have enacted legislation that allows a judge to defer incarceration of a pregnant woman convicted of a nonviolent crime until 6 weeks after the birth of her child. This provision allows the mother to experience some bonding with her child and provides her an opportunity to establish adequate placement for the child.

Contact between Imprisoned Mothers and Their Children

Visitation is also more difficult for incarcerated mothers and their families. Koban (1983) concluded that female offenders have closer relationships with their children prior to incarceration than do men and that women's relationships with their children are more affected by incarceration. Koban also found that the women prisoners in her study experienced a significant disadvantage compared to male prisoners in attempting to maintain consistent contact with their children and the caregivers of these children—a factor that was associated with problems during reunification with their children. Koban reported that while more mothers than fathers received at least one visit from their children during incarceration, the frequency of parent–child visits decreased after 1 year for mothers, while it remained stable for fathers.

Only 8% of the women surveyed in the original, 1978 "Why Punish the Children?" (McGowan & Blumenthal, 1978) study had no visits from their children, while the 1993 reprise of that study (Bloom & Steinhart, 1993) found that 54% of the children had *never* visited their incarcerated mothers.

Some differences in the frequency of visits were noted between children who lived with their mothers prior to arrest and those who did not. Children who lived with their mothers prior to arrest were nearly twice as likely to visit their mothers in jail or prison (54%) as children who did not (28%). Even so, mother and children living together prior to arrest had an overall no-visit rate of 46%. Letters were the mothers' main form of contact with their families, followed by telephone calls.

The primary reason cited by Bloom and Steinhart (1993) for infrequent visitation or nonvisitation by children of mothers in their study was the distance between the child's residence and the correctional facility. Over 60% of the children lived more than 100 miles from the mother's place of incarceration. Women's prisons are often located in rural areas far from urban centers where the family members generally reside, and they are often inaccessible by public transportation. Incarcerated women are usually placed farther from their homes than their male counterparts because there are fewer prisons for women in most states.

Reluctance of the child's caregiver to allow visitation was cited by Bloom and Steinhart (1993) as another reason for lack of mother–child contact. Caregivers are sometimes angry with the mother for prolonged periods of substance abuse, criminal activity, or repeated incarcerations, and may believe that it is unhealthy for the child to have contact with her or his mother. Some foster parents are reluctant to assist children in maintaining contact with their imprisoned mothers due to concern about the mother's "fitness" as a parent or fear of losing their own relationship with the children.

Finally, some mothers do not want their children to visit them in prison. They may feel shame or embarrassment related to their children's awareness of their criminal involvement; indeed, some choose not to tell their children that they are in prison. The extent of powerlessness experienced by some mothers who are separated from their children is so severe that they sever their emotional ties to their children out of sheer self-preservation.

When children do visit their mothers in prison, contact may be quite limited. For example, some prisons offer minimal visiting opportunities or have stringent rules regarding legal guardianship, which make it difficult for the children's caregivers to bring them to see their mothers.

The Parental Rights of Imprisoned Mothers

Bloom and Steinhart (1993) found that 73% of incarcerated mothers reported that they had custody of their children at the time of arrest. In comparing data related to women in jails as opposed to prisons, there are substantial differences. Fifty-eight percent of jailed women had custody versus 76% of women in prison. This is supported by Hairston's 1990 study in which 60% of jailed mothers reported having one or more children living with them prior to arrest. The majority of incarcerated mothers plan to resume custody of all or some of their children upon release from prison.

Upon incarceration, many women prisoners face losing custody of their children. Some women have relatives or friends who will care for their children while they are incarcerated. Placement with relatives generally reduces the likelihood that children will be permanently separated from their mother and other family members. It also increases the chances that children will maintain some type of contact with their mothers. Maternal grandmothers most often care for the children of women prisoners (Baunach, 1984; Bloom & Steinhart, 1993; Hairston, 1990; McGowan & Blumenthal, 1978).

If a mother is unable to place her children with relatives or friends, the local child welfare agency will place them in foster care. It is estimated that between 7 and 13% of the children of incarcerated mothers are in foster care with nonrelatives (Bloom & Steinhart, 1993; McGowan & Blumenthal, 1978; USDJ, 1991). When children of imprisoned mothers are placed in foster care, caseworkers are expected to make concerted efforts to sustain family ties and encourage family reunification. This approach is mandated by the requirements of the Adoption Assistance and Child Welfare Act of 1980, which calls for caseworkers to make assiduous efforts to either achieve family reunification or provide children with alternatives that promise permanence. The law calls for the development of a case plan shortly after the child is placed in care and parental involvement in the development and implementation of that plan. One of the prerequisites of this permanency plan is regular contact between mothers and their children's caseworkers, including continual discussion of the intent and contents of the children's case plans and the purpose and outcome of each review proceeding (Beckerman, 1994). Failure to engage in such activities jeopardizes the parental status of the incarcerated mother.

Continuing contact between parent and child is a significant predictor of family reunification following parental incarceration. Child welfare laws provide for termination of parental rights (usually after 12 to 18 months) if the incarcerated mother, who lacks the freedom to maintain consistent contact, has failed to sustain an adequate relationship with her child who is in foster care. In addition to the inability to maintain sufficient mother–child contact, incarcerated mothers do not have access to the resources they need to meet other reunification requirements imposed by the court such as parent education, counseling, drug treatment, and job training.

Various authorities (Barry, 1985a, 1985b; Henriques, 1982; McGowan & Blumenthal, 1978) have suggested that contact between caseworkers and mothers is strained and infrequent and that mothers are uninformed about their legal status and responsibilities. Beckerman (1994) confirmed these perceptions in a recent study which found that the prerequisite conditions deemed necessary for a mother's involvement in permanency planning—including frequent interaction and collaboration between caseworker and parents of children in foster care—are not present among imprisoned women.

Although a mother's imprisonment alone should not precipitate termination of her parental rights, this does occur in some cases, particularly for an incarcerated mother who is confined for a significant period of time. At least 25 states have termination-of-parental-rights or adoption statutes that explicitly pertain to incarcerated parents. These states include: Alabama, Arizona, California, Colorado, Georgia, Idaho, Iowa, Kansas, Louisiana, Mississippi, Missouri, Montana, Nevada, New Hampshire, New Mexico, New York, Oklahoma, Oregon, Rhode Island, Wisconsin, and Wyoming (Genty, 1991).

The current foster care system is poorly equipped to deal with the growing population of incarcerated mothers who are serving lengthy sentences. This time-driven model of foster care placement simply cannot handle the situation of an imprisoned mother who has a relationship with her child but is unable to resume physical custody for many years.

Imprisoned mothers face enormous obstacles in maintaining contact with their children and in reunifying with their families once they are released. Prisoner-mothers are forced to navigate through a number of complex governmental and social service agencies in order to receive court-mandated reunification services.

Strengthening Family Relationships

The fact that a parent is incarcerated is disruptive to the entire family. Many experts believe that the state, instead of intervening to permanently sever the bonds between mother and child, should work toward preserving and strengthening the family relationship. Some states have enacted statutes that allow children to remain with their mothers in prison for designated time periods. For example, New York allows incarcerated mothers to keep their infants until they are 1-year-old or even longer if the mother's release is imminent. California allows women with children under the age of 6 to live with their mothers in a community-based facility in lieu of prison. However, most states have none of these provisions, and mothers and children are separated from the time of arrest through subsequent incarceration.

Nationwide, correctional policy and programs give minimal consideration to maintaining the mother–child relationship, and the fact remains
that no one in the criminal justice system has official responsibility for
assisting these families. In some states, there appears to be increasing recognition on the part of members of the judiciary, policymakers, and correctional agencies that existing criminal justice policies tend to adversely affect
imprisoned women and their families. State and local jurisdictions throughout the nation are beginning to examine the manner in which women
offenders are being treated. Task forces, commissions, conferences, and
publications are beginning to examine the special issues affecting imprisoned women.

Perhaps the most significant issue is the primary parenting role of the
women prisoner and the social, psychological, and economic impact of
incarceration on her entire family. There also appears to be a growing
recognition that experience with the criminal justice system is intergenerational and that the children of incarcerated parents may be at greater risk
than their peers for future involvement with the criminal justice system
(Johnston, 1991, 1992; Task Force on the Female Offender, 1990). Thus,
the impact of incarceration becomes a multigenerational problem that must
be addressed within this context.

Strengthening families should be the focus of a coordinated effort
between public and private agencies. Targeted resources and services must
be made available to the mothers, their children, and the children's caregivers in order to promote positive family relationships.

When mothers are imprisoned they do not automatically relinquish their
parental roles, obligations, or concerns. Although they may be separated
from their children, they continue to care about their children's well-being.
Consequently, it is of vital importance to maintain the integrity of the family whenever possible. Coordinated efforts should be taken by the criminal
justice and child welfare systems to ensure that mothers and their children
are able to sustain their relationships. If we continue to ignore the plight of
imprisoned women and their children, generations to come may suffer the
consequences.

References

Barry, E. (1985a). Reunification difficult for incarcerated parents and their children. *Youth Law News,* 5:14–16.

Barry, E. (1985b). Children of prisoners: Punishing the innocent. *Youth Law News,*
6:12–17.

Baunach, P. J. (1979). *Mothering from behind prison walls.* Paper presented at the
annual meeting of the American Society of Criminology, Philadelphia.

Baunach, P. J. (1984). *Mothers in prison.* NJ: Transaction Books Rutgers University
Press.

Beckerman, A. (1989). Incarcerated mothers and their children in foster care: The dilemma of visitation. *Children and Youth Services Review*, 11(2):175–183.

Beckerman, A. (1994). Mothers in prison: Meeting the prerequisite conditions for permanency planning. *Social Work*, 39(1):9–13.

Bloom, B., & Steinhart, D. (1993). *Why punish the children? A reappraisal of the children of incarcerated mothers in America*. San Francisco: National Council on Crime and Delinquency.

Bloom, B & Owen, B. (In progress). *Survey of Women in California State Prisons*. California Department of Corrections.

Bonfanti, M. A., Felter, S. S., Loesch, M. L., & Vincent, N. J. (1974). *Enactment and perception of maternal role of incarcerated mothers*. Unpublished master's thesis, Louisiana State Univeristy.

Datesman, S. K., & Cales, G. L. (1983). I'm still the same mommy: Maintaining the mother–child relationship in prison. *Prison Journal*, 63(2):142–154.

DuBose, D. G. (1977). *Incarcerated mothers and their Children in Texas*. Unpublished manuscript.

Genty, P. M. (1991). Procedural due process rights of incarcerated parents in termination of parental rights proceedings: A fifty state analysis. *Journal of Family Law*, 30(4).

Gibbs, C. (1971). The effect of imprisonment of women upon their children. *British Journal of Criminology*, 11:113–130. Glick, R. M., & Neto, V. V. (1977). *National study of women's correctional programs*. Washington, DC: National Institute of Law Enforcement and Criminal Justice.

Hadley, J. G. (1981). *Georgia women inmates and their families*. Atlanta: Georgia Department of Offender Rehabilitation Office of Research and Evaluation.

Hairston, C. F. (1990) Imprisoned mothers and their children. *Affilia*, 6(2).

Henriques, Z. W. (1982). *Imprisoned mothers and their children*. Washington, DC: University Press of America.

Hunter, S. M. (1984). *The relationship between women offenders and their children*. Unpublished doctoral dissertation, University of Michigan.

Johnston, D. (1991). *Jailed mothers*. Pasadena, CA: Pacific Oaks Center for Children of Incarcerated Parents.

Johnston, D. (1992). *Children of offenders*. Pasadena, CA: Pacific Oaks Center for Children of Incarcerated Parents.

Koban, L. A. (1983). Parents in prison: A comparative analysis of the effects of incarceration on the families of men and women. *Research in Law, Deviance and Social Control*, 5:171–183.

LeFlore, L., & Holston, M. A. (1990). Perceived importance of parenting behaviors as reported by inmate mothers: An exploratory study. *Journal of Offender Counseling, Services and Rehabilitation*, 14(1):5–21.

Mann, C. (1984). *Female crime and delinquency*. Birmingham: University of Alabama Press.

McCall, C., Casteel, J. & Shaw, N. (1985). *Pregnancy in prison: A needs assessment of perinatal outcome in three California penal institutions*. Sacramento: California Department of Health.

McCarthy, B. R. (1980). Inmate mothers: The problems of separation and reintegration. *Journal of Offender Counseling, Services and Rehabilitation*, 4(3):199–212.

McGowan, B. G., & Blumenthal, K. L. (1978). *Why punish the children?* Hackensack, NJ: National Council on Crime and Delinquency.

Neto, V. V., & Bainer, L. M. (1983). Mother and wife locked up: A day with the family. *Prison Journal*, 63(2):125–141.

Sametz, L. (1980). Children of incarcerated women. *Social Work*, 25(4):298–303.

Task Force on the Female Offender. (1990). *The female offender: What does the future hold?* Laurel, MD: American Correctional Association.

U.S. Department of Justice. (1991). *Women in prison* (Report No. NCJ-127991). Washington, DC: Bureau of Justice Statistics.

U.S. General Accounting Office. (1980). *Women in prison: Inequitable treatment requires action* (Report No. GGD-81-6). Gaithersburg, MD: Author.

Zalba, S. (1964). *Women prisoners and their families*. Sacramento, CA.: Department of Social Welfare and Department of Corrections.

Zietz, D. (1963). Child welfare services in a women's correctional facility. *Child Welfare*, 42:185–190.

3
Fathers in Prison

Creasie Finney Hairston

Fathers who are in prison are not just convicts: they are parents too. Although their family roles are seldom acknowledged in a prison setting, men, once incarcerated, do not give up their family identities or parental status. They have many of the same dreams and aspirations for their families and children as other men and share many of the same parenting joys and difficulties. Maintenance of responsible husband and father roles during imprisonment is related to prisoners' well-being during imprisonment, to the well-being of their families and children, and to their postrelease success (Curtis & Shulman, 1984; Flanagan, 1981; Glaser, 1969; Hairston, 1988; Holt, 1986; Holt & Miller, 1972; Richards, 1978; Swan, 1981; Walker, 1983).

The number of fathers who are in prison is large and, consistent with a rapidly growing prison population, increases considerably each year. At the end of 1992 there were more than 880,000 persons incarcerated in U.S. state and federal prisons. Based on survey data that show that more than 94% are men and at least 55% are fathers (U.S. Department of Justice [USDJ], 1993b), a conservative estimate of the number of fathers of dependent children who are in prison on any given day numbers close to half a million, and of the number of children with a father in prison, close to one million.

Although most prisoners are parents and maintaining relationships with their children during imprisonment is very important to these prisoner-parents, correctional policies and practices lack a family orientation (Hairston & Hess, 1989). Makers of social policy, providers of social services, and correctional administrators have limited knowledge and understanding of this area of prisoners' lives, and thus there is a critical need for basic research on the nature of family relationships during imprisonment. This is particularly the case with respect to fathers in prison, as they are generally not encouraged or expected to fulfill parental obligations or to carry out family commitments during their incarceration.

The research reported here was carried out as part of a larger project to test and evaluate a self-help, family support service model in several male prisons. The project was a collaborative effort between a community organization that provided social services to prisoners and a school of social work that conducted research and program evaluation in correctional settings. As an initial effort in program development, project staff conducted needs assessments in two of the prisons where the prison administration had expressed interest in adding social services.

The aim of the research was to define the nature of prisoners' family ties, to determine their family and parenting issues and concerns, and to assess their interest in organized family programs. The study findings were subsequently used to shape the development of administrative policy and a parent education curriculum and to set up program services. They are presented here not as a definitive statement of the status of all fathers in prison, but rather as a means of enhancing understanding of the social worlds of fathers in prison. Consequently, throughout this chapter, findings are discussed in the context of other research and general themes in the family and corrections literature.

Methods

The study population consisted of men incarcerated at two southeastern prisons: a maximum security facility and a minimum security facility. Both prisons are located in a major metropolitan area and limit visiting by families and friends to weekends and holidays. Neither prison allows overnight family or conjugal visits, though both provide limited opportunities for family-oriented social activities such as picnics and holiday parties. Both also offer parent education courses.

Study participants were recruited by a prisoner-led family support group organization at the maximum security prison and by the inmate council at the minimum security facility. The researcher conducted an orientation session covering the purpose of the survey and study procedures for the recruiters at each prison. Participants were recruited from all housing units in each prison. This approach provided representation of the different prison groups as defined by the prison administration. Different housing units (administrative segregation, death row, hospital, work assignments, honor units, etc.) are designated for different purposes, and these designations reflect service needs of prisoners, differences in sentences, and different security risks.

Data were collected using a self-administered questionnaire. Men who agreed to complete the questionnaire were given a written summary of the study's purpose, procedures, and sponsorship. They were also required to sign an informed consent form, a copy of which they maintained for their own records.

Questionnaires were hand-delivered and picked up within 2 to 3 days by the recruiters. Completed questionnaires were obtained from 92 men at the maximum security prison and from 34 men at the minimum security prison, thereby making a total of 126. This was only eight fewer than the target of 100 which the family support group had set for itself. The inmate council did not have a specific target but was given 35 questionnaires.

Records were not maintained at either facility on the number of persons who were approached but declined to participate. Two recruiters reported, however, that some men who initially agreed to participate later declined. They reported that the potential respondents felt the questions were too personal. One prisoner wrote the researcher a letter indicating that he did not believe anything in a prison was confidential, and therefore decided not to participate. A second advised the researcher that he would not participate because he did not believe participating would be helpful to him. He stated that the sponsoring organization had not helped him locate his children, despite several requests for assistance. A follow-up discussion with recruiters revealed that some prisoners were reluctant to participate in anything where they signed their names, despite promises of confidentiality.

Social Characteristics

The survey respondents were primarily unmarried fathers under age 40. They were serving long prison terms and were, by and large, in the early stages of their imprisonment. Forty-four percent of the respondents reported their current marital status as single, 25% as married, and 26% as divorced. Four men were widowed. About three-fourths (74%) of the men were parents. Of those who were parents, 88% had a child 12 years of age or younger; 42% had a teenager.

The average age of the men was 34. The youngest participant was 18; the oldest was 59. One-third of the men were under 30 years of age and four-fifths were under 40. Only four men were under the age of 21.

The men were not highly educated: 51% had not completed high school prior to entering prison and 14% had an 8th grade education or less. Thirteen percent had some college education and 8% had a college degree. Two-thirds of the maximum security respondents were African-American, and one-third were white. The racial percentages were the reverse for the minimum security respondents.

Most of the men were serving long prison terms with two-thirds of the men having sentences greater than 20 years. Twenty-six percent of the respondents were serving a life term and 10% were serving sentences of 99 years or more. One man was sentenced to death. Only 10% of the men had sentences of fewer than 10 years. One-third of the participants were in the early stages of their imprisonment and had served 3 years or less. A considerable number, however, had been in prison a long time. Fifty percent had served more than 5 years and 25% more than 10.

The social characteristics of these men are similar to those reported by other studies. National statistical reports, national surveys, and sociological studies (see, e.g., Hairston, 1989; Lanier, 1987; National Institute of Justice, 1988; U.S. Department of Justice, 1993a) have reported that male prisoners are mostly young and unmarried. A substantial number have not finished high school, and there is a disproportionate representation of African-Americans.

Researchers who have inquired about the parental status of men in prison (Hairston, 1989; Koban, 1983; Lanier, 1987; National Institute of Justice, 1988) also report that the majority are parents of dependent children. Percentages range from a low of 54 to a high of 84%. With respect to sentences, the participants differed from other prisoners in that they were serving and/or had served much longer sentences than the national norm. Since the focus of this chapter is on fathers in prison, the remainder of this analysis is based on responses of the men who had a child or children.

Parenting Roles and Responsibilities

Most fathers (69%) had more than one child. Thirty-three percent had two children; 21% had three, and 15% had four or more. The mean number of children per parent was 2.3. Almost all (88%) were fathers of children under the age of 13, though a few (9%) had children 3 years of age or younger. Forty-two percent had teenagers and 25% had adult children.

Used alone, these data on current ages of children provide a striking, though limited, picture of many children whose fathers are physically absent during significant stages in their growth and development. When placed in the context of the long prison terms these prisoners are serving, the data clearly show that many children will grow up while their fathers are in prison. Some men whose children were infants at the time of conviction are now the parents of elementary school children. Others have watched their children become adults during the incarceration period. Still others can expect their children to go through major developmental stages before their expected release dates. These periods in a child's life can never be recaptured and the parental nurturing so critical to growth during them cannot be placed on hold to be used "once I get out of prison."

Marital Ties and Relationships

Family networks are quite complex. The picture of a married man and wife with one set of biological children does not describe the family structure of these men. First, the majority of men in all marital status categories were fathers. Fifty-two percent of single men, 89% of divorced/separated men, and 97% of married men have children.

Second, most fathers do not share a marital bond or ongoing relationship with the mothers of their children. The majority of fathers were not currently, or had never been, married to the mother of one or more of their children. Among the men who had two or more children, about one-half indicated that their children had different mothers. This was the case for married, divorced, and single men.

When men did have a marital relationship that could be expected to strengthen, or at least sustain, their relationship with their children, the marital relationship was often ended during incarceration. Fewer than one-half of the men who were married at the time of their conviction were still married at the time of the study. In addition, the relationships of those who remained married were tenuous. For example, although all of the men who were currently married had received at least one visit from their wife during the 6 months preceding the study, only 23% identified their wife as their most frequent visitor. In addition, only 50% of married men indicated that their wife was their most important source of support during their imprisonment.

While many marital relationships disintegrated during incarceration, others developed. Ten men who were single or divorced at the time of their conviction married while in prison. One man divorced and remarried during his imprisonment. The study did not determine if these men married mothers of their children or if they became stepparents as a result of their new marital commitments. New marital commitments in families involving children might reasonably be expected, however, to generate related parenting obligations and issues.

Parenting Relationships

Fathers' relationships with children are tenuous at best. Only 50% were living in the same household as their youngest child prior to incarceration. Most children lived with their mothers or other relatives prior to their father's incarceration and maintained their same residences following their fathers' incarceration. Although fathers did not physically reside with their children, it cannot be assumed that their incarceration had no effect on their children. Two-thirds of the fathers indicated that they were contributing to the financial support of at least one child at the time of their conviction. For these children, there was, at a minimum, a change in financial well-being.

Most fathers seldom see their children. Thirty percent had not seen their children at all since they had entered prison and fewer than one-half had seen their children in the 6 months preceding the survey. Twenty-five percent had not been in touch by phone or letter with their children during the 6 months preceding the survey and one-fifth had been in touch only once or twice using these methods. Only 55% of the fathers had contact by phone, letter, or visit at least three times with any of their children in this 6-months period.

The major reason fathers gave for no or few visits by their children was that the child had no one to bring him or her (42%) or that the child's mother did not want the child to visit (22%). Only 5% of the fathers believed that his child did not want to visit. Since most minor children of incarcerated fathers currently live with their mothers (76%), women who have no enduring bond with these prisoners, it is not surprising that the mothers have little interest in facilitating children's visits with their incarcerated fathers.

These fathers' visiting patterns are similar to those found in previous research. Studies of fathers in prison conducted by Hairston (1989) and Lanier (1987) report limited contact between fathers and children. In addition, the previously cited studies show that fathers who are married to the mothers of their children or who lived with their children prior to imprisonment are more likely to see their children and/or to correspond with them during imprisonment than unmarried fathers and those who lived in separate households. These fathers' preprison life-styles and changing family structures during imprisonment place their father–child relationships at very high risk of disintegration during imprisonment and of eventual permanent severance.

The precarious nature of parent–child relationships is also reflected in responses to a question that asked what, if anything, fathers did to maintain their parent–child relationships. Fifty-seven percent of fathers did not answer the question. Of those who did answer, only three acknowledged that they were not doing what a father should do. Several others implied that there were limitations to what a father could do while in prison. Statements such as "I talk to her as much as possible" and "I try to do all that I can do for her within my power" or "My parenting is on hold" are examples. Most of those who answered the question said that they kept in touch with their children by writing to them or talking with them on the phone. Two men stated that their children visited often. Among the other things fathers did or tried to do were offer advice, tell the child he or she was loved, and encourage the children to do positive things such as "stay in school," "mind their mom," or "don't mess with drugs."

Providing financial support, a traditional father's responsibility, was mentioned by only one father. There was also almost no reference given to fathers' being interested in or knowledgeable about their children's day-to-day activities. Only one respondent reported involvement of this kind. He stated that he showed interest in the child's school, activities, and the like. No respondent mentioned celebrating holidays or birthdays, sending gifts to or receiving gifts from their children, participating with children in family functions at the prison, exchanging photos, and so on. It is possible that these kind of parenting activities were subsumed under such statements as "We share a father–son bond," "I keep a clear line of communication open for my son and me," and "I let them know that I love them and miss them." Nevertheless, they were not mentioned directly, thereby suggesting that they did not immediately come to mind as important ways of maintaining parent–child bonds.

These men had several concerns about their parent–child relationships and the well-being of their children. Only 11% of fathers indicated that they had no concerns as a parent. The major concerns focused on what was happening to the children. The largest number (42%) worried that their children lacked guidance and/or supervision and 29% were concerned that their children might get in trouble. Twelve percent believed that their children did not have a proper home. Some fathers were concerned about their own relationship with the child. Twenty-six percent worried that their children might forget them; 20% worried that their children might replace them with someone else such as a stepfather, and 18% worried that their children might not respect them anymore.

Parenting Needs and Organizational Supports

Several men stated that they needed to know much more about child development and how to be a good parent. They wanted service activities such as parenting courses and educational materials to help them better understand their children's needs and to help them better carry out their parenting roles and responsibilities.

Responses to the question "How can organizations help you and/or other fathers who are in prison be better parents?" indicated that family service organizations were viewed as needed and desirable. Several men indicated that organizations should work to improve opportunities for incarcerated fathers and children to spend time together. Generally, this view was specified simply in terms of better visiting hours and conditions. Others stressed the importance of family-oriented visiting activities.

One respondent noted that organizations could "teach prison fathers how to bring their children up in a way better than their way." Another remarked that family service programs could "help fathers not let their lives and their children's lives go by not knowing what and who their father is." A third felt that an important task would be to help fathers become aware of "the different types of stress and fears single-parent children face daily." With the exception of one participant who stated that parenting should be a joint mother–father effort, issues related to coparenting, often with a person who did not support children's visits, were not mentioned.

The idea of an organization that focused specifically on fathering concerns was viewed as a positive undertaking in and of itself. Creation of an atmosphere supportive of fathers, providing opportunities for incarcerated men to see and meet professional people, and letting folks know that there are people who care were all seen as important ways organizations could help fathers be better parents.

Although it is not common practice to think of men in prison as a viable service population for parenting courses and other forms of parenting supports, these men's views are not unusual or distinct. Eighty percent of the men in the Hairston (1989) survey in a maximum security prison, for example, indicated they were willing to strengthen and improve their parenting skills. Ninety-one percent of the fathers and 65% of the nonfathers in that survey expressed a desire to learn ways of becoming a better father.

Strengthening Family Ties

Participants were also asked how organizations could help prisoners maintain family ties. Providing more opportunities for visits was seen as the major means for doing so. The participants generally wanted help in getting better visiting hours and conditions, more frequent visiting, and informal, relaxed family outings and family-oriented activities such as "families attending worship services in the chapel together." One father asked for help in locating his children and in getting their caretaker to agree to children's visits.

Comments about the need for family contact extended to opportunities for families to problem-solve together. Family support groups, family therapy, and open information sessions involving family members and prisoners were all seen as desirable services. In general, any action that encouraged prisoners and families to keep in touch, to share their feelings, and to work through family problems were seen as ways to help strengthen family ties during imprisonment.

Summary and Conclusion

The participants in this study were primarily unmarried fathers under the age of 40 who were serving long prison terms. Their family networks are complex, their family relationships unstable, and their relationships with their children strained. Contrary to a widespread belief that fathers, unlike mothers in prison, are not cut off from their loved ones and have wives who willingly transport children over long distances to maintain family contact, (see Friends Outside, 1986), most fathers in prison do not have wives to bring children to visit. Fathers' contact with their children is very limited, and they too are cut off from their loved ones. Although most children of incarcerated fathers live with their mothers, the mothers either do not want children to visit, do not visit themselves, and/or do not bring children to visit.

Many fathers in prison are concerned about their children and want to be better parents. They need help, however, in finding responsible ways to be involved, concretely and emotionally, in their children's lives. A considerable number are interested in having parent education and family support services in prisons and believe that organizations can be helpful to them and their families. It must be recognized, however, that programs and services that are developed based on traditional models of a two-parent, white, middle-class family and using complex parent education reading materials will leave the majority of fathers in prison unaffected. Most fathers in prison are not currently, and have never been, married to the mothers of their children. Most are not white and most lack advanced education. They therefore can be expected to have limited interest in and use for complex reading materials that do not reflect understanding of their own culture, experiences, and life-styles.

From all of the available evidence, families and children are an important part of the identities of incarcerated men. Men who are in prison do not give up their family aspirations or their parental concerns. Not unlike many other men separated from their children, however, they need help in understanding and fulfilling their family commitments and parental responsibilities. With close to 900,000 men incarcerated in U.S. prisons and prison populations that are growing by leaps and bounds, it is irresponsible, given our national commitment to family preservation, to continue to ignore this population. Policies and programs can be implemented to help fathers in prison be parents too.

References

Curtis, R., & Schulman, S. (1984). Ex-offenders' family relations and economic supports: The significant women study of the TARP project. *Crime and Delinquency*, 30(4):507–528.

Flanagan, T. J. (1981). Dealing with long-term confinement: Adaptive strategies and perspectives among long-term prisoners. *Criminal Justice and Behavior*, 8(2):201–222.

Friends Outside. (1986). *Incarcerated mothers and their children* (Review draft). Salinas, CA: Author.

Glaser, D. (1969). *The effectiveness of a prison and parole system* (Abridged ed.). Indianapolis, IN: Bobbs-Merrill.

Hairston, C. F. (1988). Family ties during imprisonment: Do they influence future criminal activity? *Federal Probation*, 52(1):48–52.

Hairston, C. F. (1989). Men in prison: Family characteristics and family views. *Journal of Offender Counseling, Services and Rehabilitation*, 14(1):23–30.

Hairston, C. F. (1991). Family ties during imprisonment: Important to whom and for what? *Journal of Sociology and Social Welfare*, 18(1):85–102.

Holt, L. (1986). *Statistical tables describing the background characteristics and recidivism rates for releases from Massachusetts pre-release facilities during 1983*. Boston: Massachusetts Department of Corrections.

Holt, N., & Miller, D. (1972). *Explorations in inmate–family relationships*. Sacramento: California Department of Corrections.

Koban, L. A. (1983). Parents in prison: A comparative analysis of the effects of incarceration on the families of men and women. *Research in Law, Deviance and Social Control*, 5:171–183.

Lanier, C. S. (1987, November). *Fathers in prison: A psychosocial exploration*. Paper presented at the annual meeting of the American Society of Criminology, Montreal, Canada.

National Institute of Justice. (1988). *Report to the nation on crime and justice* (2nd ed.). Washington, DC: Author.

Richards, B. (1978). The experience of long-term imprisonment. *British Journal of Criminology*, 10(2):162–169.

Swan, A. (1981). *Families of black prisoners: Survival and progress*. Boston: G. K. Hall.

U.S. Department of Justice. (1993a). *Report of the National Corrections Reporting Program, 1990*. Washington, DC: Author.

U. S. Department of Justice. (1993b). *Survey of state prison inmates, 1991*. Report No. 136949 Washington, DC: Bureau of Justice Statistics.

Walker, N. (1983). Side-effects of incarceration. *British Journal of Criminology*, 23(1):61–71.

4
Jailed Mothers

Denise Johnston

J ailed mothers, like other jailed women, are somewhat different from women incarcerated in state or federal prisons. Most research on incarcerated women has focused on combined populations of jailed and imprisoned women, and has not examined differences between these groups. Recent small-scale studies of jailed mothers have identified some unique characteristics and service needs of this population.

Women's Jails

Jails have traditionally housed persons awaiting trial and those sentenced for misdemeanor crimes to less than 1 year of incarceration. About one-third of all arrested women are unable to obtain pretrial release on bond and must remain in jail during ajudication of their charges. Ultimately, about half of all arrested women are convicted and sentenced to jail. In 1993 the average daily female population of U.S. jails was about 40,000 women, but there were over 1.2 million female jail admissions (U.S. Department of Justice [USDJ], 1993b).

In a recent survey of women's correctional facilities, the Task Force on the Female Offender (1990) found that 80% of U.S. jails that house women were built specifically for female inmates or have separate temporary holding areas for women. Four out of 10 of these jails were less than 10-years-old, but one in six was over 40-years-old. The majority of these jails were small facilities (nine-bed average) located in cities or towns with populations of less than 100,000 persons. Like jails for men, women's jails were occupied at 99% capacity in 1992 (USDJ, 1993b).

The Task Force study found that only 17.6% of women's jails had a female administrator. About half of all women's jails required inmates to perform insitutional work assignments, the majority of which were janitorial or in the jail laundry. Some jurisdictions required jailed women to use income earned in jail to pay room and board (21.4% of U.S. jails), restitution to victims (11.6%), and/or child support (12.3%). Vocational training was reportedly available to jailed women in 27.1% of jails. On-site

41

emergency health care was reported to be available in about half of all women's jails, OB/GYN services in 52.9%, prenatal/postpartum care in 58.8%, and mental health/psychiatric care in over three-quarters of U.S. jails for women. The average annual cost per female jail inmate varied from about $13,000 in the Midwest to $16,000 in the West.

Studies of Jailed Mothers

Approximately 80% of all jailed women are mothers (Inter-University Consortium, 1991). There have been very few attempts to systematically study this population. Most research on mothers in local correctional facilities has resulted from large-scale studies that combined data on jailed and imprisoned women with and without children (Bloom & Steinhart, 1993; McGowan & Blumenthal, 1978; Task Force on the Female Offender, 1990) or on small self-selected groups of mothers (Henriques, 1982).

Brenda McGowan and Karen Blumenthal (1978) conducted what remains the largest study of incarcerated mothers in the United States. The purpose of the study was to document the events and effects of maternal incarceration. The main portion of the study surveyed over 3,000 mothers in 46 prisons and jails by mail, but data was not broken down by type of facility, so that information on jailed and imprisoned mothers was combined.

However, in a supplement to their national survey, McGowan and Blumenthal conducted a local study at the New York City Correctional Institution for Women on Riker's Island. Detained women were selected for screening on the basis of their availability during adjudication procedures; sentenced women were selected by length of sentence (at least 2 months) and length of incarceration at the time of the interview (at least 60 days). Only women who agreed to come to the social service interview area were screened. The final sample included 64 sentenced and 80 detained women out of a count of 402 female inmates; of this group, 65 mothers with dependent children were interviewed.

The mothers in this study were young, unmarried, and poorly educated, with an average of 1.8 children each. Almost all were women of color. A third had not held a job for at least 5 years. They were charged primarily with property offenses and "victimless" crimes like prostitution and drug possession. Two-thirds had a history of prior incarcerations; one in four had been previously incarcerated more than five times. Demographic and criminal justice data from this study is summarized in Tables 4.1 and 4.2.

These jailed mothers were concerned about their children's placement; approximately half were either ambivalent or negative about the children's living situation while they were incarcerated. The mothers in the local study contributed to the extensive list of program and service suggestions

Table 4.1
Demographic Characteristics of Jailed Mothers

Characteristic	McGowan & Blumenthal (1978) N = 63		Stanton (1980) N = 54		Henriques (1982) N = 30		Hairston (1990) N = 38	Johnston (1991) N = 100	
Age in years									
	≤ 20	22.2%	18–25	37%	16–20	23.3%	Range = 18–57	≤ 20	4%
	21–24	30.2%	26–30	33%	21–24	40.0%	Mean = 28	21–24	25%
	25–34	36.5%	31–35	17%	25–30	26.7%	Median = 28	25–30	30%
	≥ 35	11.1%	36–50	13%	≥ 31	10.0%		31–34	17%
								≥ 35	24%
Race/ethnicity									
Black	84.1%		48%		73.3%		45%	18%	
Hispanic	7.9%		15%		23.3%		7%	31%	
Native American	0%		5%		0		0	7%	
White	7.9%		32%		3.3%		47%	42%	
Marital status									
never married	50.8%		20%		50.0%		54%		
married	14.3%		30%		6.7%		18%	Not measured	
previously married	41.3%		33%		29.9%		28%		
common-law	4.8%		17%		13.3%				
Dependent children	Mean = 1.8		Not measured		Mean = 2.5		Mean = 1.4	Mean = 2.3	
Education									
≤ 8th grade	11.1%		18%		13.3%			8%	
9th–11th grade	49.2%		39%		63.3%			45%	
≥ 12th grade	39.7%		43%		23.4%		2/5	47%	

Table 4.2
Criminal Justice Histories of Jailed Mothers

Criminal Justice History	McGowan & Blumenthal (1978) N = 63	Stanton (1980) N = 54	Henriques (1982) N = 30	Hairston (1990) N = 38	Johnston (1991) N = 100
Age at first arrest in years	Not measured	32% ≤ 20 26% 21–25 22% 26–30 15% 31–35 06% ≥ 36	Not measured	Not measured	09% ≤ 12 18% 13–15 22% 16–18 23% 19–25 28% ≥ 26
Prior arrests	Not measured	Adult arrests: 59% Yes 41% No	33.3% None 16.7% 1 16.7% 2–5 20.0% 6–10 13.3% ≥ 11	Not measured	15% None 11% 1 11% 2 06% 3 06% 4 46% ≥ 5
Prior incarcerations	33.3% None 29.6% 1–2 11.1% 3–5 25.9% ≥ 6	Adult incarcerations: 52% None 30% 1–2 19% ≥ 3	40.0% None 13.3% 1 23.3% 2 10.0% 3 13.3% ≥ 4	1/3 None 2/3 ≥ 1	Incarcerations > 30 days: 23% None 31% 1 23% 2 08% 3 15% ≥ 4
Current offense category	12.9% "against persons" 40.3% "against property" 38.7% "victimless" 08.1% multiple categories	22% violent 50% property 26% drug 02% other	23.3% violent 43.3% property 20.0% drug 13.3% other	2/3 "economic"	Not measured

made by all women surveyed by McGowan and Blumenthal and reproduced in Table 1.2.

Anne Stanton (1980) studied women jailed in four northern California counties. The purpose of the study was to distinguish the effects of parent–child separation due to incarceration from the general effects of the mother's criminal involvement. To accomplish this purpose, Stanton compared children of jailed mothers with children of women probationers.

Criteria for participation of jailed women included sentenced status and a release date within the temporal limits of the study. From this group, 54 mothers who had been living with a child over 4 years of age at the time of arrest were selected. Twenty-two women probationers with similar living arrangements prior to arrest were also selected. Jailed mothers, their children, their children's caregivers, and school personnel were interviewed during the mother's incarceration and 1 month after her release.

The mothers in Stanton's study were mostly young women convicted of property crimes. While about two-thirds had been married at some time, only one-third were married at the time of the study and the one in four who had been living with a man prior to arrest had been living with him for less than a year. These mothers were poorly educated and the majority had been unemployed and on welfare at the time of arrest. They came from families with extensive histories of criminal involvement. Two out of five had juvenile arrest records and one out of five had been incarcerated as juveniles. The majority had been previously arrested as adults, and half had a history of adult incarceration. Demographic and criminal justice data from this study are summarized in Tables 4.1 and 4.2.

The majority of women Stanton studied had substance abuse problems. Fifty percent reported problems with drug use or addiction, 15% problems with alcoholism, and 6% problems with both drug and alcohol addiction. (See Table 4.4.)

Fifty percent of the mothers studied by Stanton could not be located for follow-up after release. Of the 27 women that could be located, 33% had returned to the living arrangement they had had prior to arrest and 4% had been returned to jail in the month after their release. Of the follow-up mothers, 70% were living with their children, 22% had not been reunited after release, and the remainder had been separated from their children again. Only 11% had found employment at the time of follow-up; 41% identified financial and employment problems as their greatest obstacles to reentry.

Zelma Henriques (1982) also conducted a survey of jailed mothers in New York City, attempting to identify and examine the perceptions of these mothers regarding their children's situations. Henriques interviewed 30 of 325 women inmates at the Riker's Island Jail. No selection criteria or methodology of selection are described in the published report of the study.

Henriques's population was very young; one in four women was under 20 years of age. All but but one woman were black or Hispanic. They were also less educated than most women offenders; more than three-quarters had not completed high school. This group was similar to Stanton's in the distribution of offenses, prior arrests, and prior incarcerations; the majority were multiple recidivists. Demographic and criminal justice data from this study is summarized in Tables 4.1 and 4.2.

Unlike Stanton, who was interested in the effects of maternal incarceration on children, Henriques examined the concerns of jailed mothers. These are presented in Table 1.1.

Henriques found that her subjects' perceptions of the maternal role were appropriate and included "providing emotional care & support", as well as "teaching" and providing "physical care & support". These results contrasted with Henriques' findings among personnel of correctional and criminal justice agencies; most believed that the vast majority of incarcerated mothers were not genuinely concerned about their children.

Creasie Finney Hairston (1990) studied mothers jailed in a large metropolitan area of the Midwest. The purpose of the study was to examine parenting roles and responsibilities, plans for family reunification, and visiting concerns among jailed mothers.

All 80 women incarcerated at the selected facility were invited to participate in the study. Fifty-six women (70%) accepted and completed structured interviews over a 3-week period in 1990. Of the women interviewed, 68% had dependent children; this group of 38 mothers formed the study population.

The mothers in this study were young and unmarried. They were disproportionately women of color. However, this group included a larger number of white women than the other studies just summarized, in a proportion more similar to their representation in national correctional population counts. The mothers in Hairston's study were slightly older than the previously described populations. Approximately four in 10 had completed high school. Three-quarters had been unemployed, on welfare, or engaged in illegal occupations prior to arrest. Over two-thirds were charged with nonviolent and property offenses; two-thirds had a history of prior incarceration. Demographic and criminal justice data from this study is summarized in Tables 4.1 and 4.2.

These women had small families, with an average of 1.4 children. Sixty percent had lived with one or more of their children prior to incarceration; of these, three-quarters (45% of the total) had been solely responsible for their children's care. Most mothers in this study (70%) identified parent–child separation as the most negative consequence of incarceration. Other concerns related to the effects of maternal incarceration, including financial problems, changes of school, and emotional disruptions in their children's lives.

The Jailed Mothers Study

The Center for Children of Incarcerated Parents conducted a study of jailed mothers at the Robert Presley Detention Center [RPDC] in downtown Riverside, a city of 240,000 population in an increasingly suburban southern California county 50 miles outside of Los Angeles. The RPDC jail is a new cocorrectional facility, and housed 120–140 detained and sentenced women at the time of the study.

All mothers incarcerated during the last 2 weeks of December 1990 were asked to participate in the study. There were no other selection criteria. One hundred and fourteen women, or about 80% of all female prisoners, were identified as possible subjects. All women who elected not to participate in the study cited concerns about confidentiality as the reason they declined. One hundred women consented to the study and were interviewed by former prisoners; the study instrument contained 138 items with multiple response categories.

The mothers in this study were somewhat older than the subjects of earlier research; one in four were 35 years of age or older. They were 18% black, 42% white, 31% Hispanic, and 7% Native American. Fifty-three percent had not completed high school, and most were on welfare or unemployed at the time of arrest. Two-thirds had previously served a sentence to incarceration; however, only one in four of these recidivists had served time in prison. Demographic and criminal justice data on women participating in this study is summarized in Tables 4.1 and 4.2.

The criminal careers and substance abuse history of these mothers intertwined. Two subgroups were identified, characterized by age at first drug use and arrest. One group (23.5% of the total) began using drugs at an early age and were first arrested before the age of 16. Women in this group typically went on to juvenile incarceration and/or adult arrests, adult incarceration, and multiple episodes of recidivism, usually with 1 to 3 years between incarcerations. Another group began using drugs as adults and were first arrested after age 25. Women in this group (24.7% of the total) typically had three or fewer total arrests and two or fewer total incarcerations.

The family histories of these mothers included parental or sibling alcoholism, drug addiction, sexual molestation, and physical abuse. One-third of the women had a parent who had been jailed or imprisoned. Approximately eight out of 10 had other immediate relatives who had been incarcerated and 59% had multiple family members in this category. Ten percent of the women had children who had served time in juvenile or adult correctional facilities. Family histories and characteristics of study participants are summarized in Table 4.3.

The women's personal histories (see Table 4.4) were litanies of victimization. One-third reported having been sexually abused as children; one-third had been physically abused. About six in 10 had been physically

Table 4.3
Parent and Family Characteristics of Jailed Mothers

Characteristic	Frequency (N = 100)
Mother's parent was physically abused as a child	39%
Mother's parent was sexually abused as a child	4%
Mother's parent was battered as an adult	23%
Mother's parent was sexually abused as an adult	4%
Mother's parent is/was alcoholic	39%
Mother's parent is/was addicted to drugs	18%
Mother's parent is/was incarcerated	34%
Mother's child is/was incarcerated	10%
Mother's other family member is/was incarcerated	77%
Mother has multiple family members who have been incarcerated	59%

Source: Johnston, 1991.

abused as adults; the majority of these were victims of domestic violence. Many were sexually active as preadolescents; 28% had their first pregnancy by the age of 16. The great majority of these mothers (76%) reported that they had problems with drug abuse or addiction, and 23% reported alcoholism or alcohol abuse.

These mothers had an average of 2.3 children each. Prior to arrest, most of those with minor children lived with at least one of these children in a variety of settings, and most had full legal custody of their children.

The majority of the mothers studied reported that they had faced multiple reentry problems. (See Table 4.5 and 4.6). About six in 10 women experienced immediate reentry problems; this number increased during the first month after release. Problems with drug and alcohol use began immediately for approximately a third of the women; at 1 month after release, over half had substance abuse or dependency problems. Significantly, about one in five reported difficulty in finding drug or alcohol treatment services.

While major problems in their first week after release were related to subsistence needs for shelter, transportation, and other material resources, women reported that family relationship problems became more important when they had been out of jail for a longer period of time. The increasing level of stress after release is reflected in reports of "emotional problems" among about one-third of the women in the later reentry period; "emotional problems" were not reported by any women as a concern in the first week after release from jail.

The Jailed Mothers Study asked participating women about the likelihood that they would return to jail in the future (see Table 4.7). Only 56% percent believed that they would never return to jail again. Answers to this question varied by criminal justice history; more than nine out of 10

Table 4.4
Personal Characteristics of Jailed Mothers

Characteristic	Stanton (1980) N = 54	Henriques (1982) N = 30	Hairston (1990) N = 38	Johnston (1991) N = 100
Age at birth of first child, in years	Not measured	$\leq$ 14 10.0% 15–16 30.0% 17–18 40.0% 19–21 20.0%	Not measured	12–14 04% 15–16 24% 17–18 27% 19–21 20% $\geq$ 22 24%
Physically abused as a child	"	Not measured	"	31%
Sexually abused as a child	"	"	"	31%
Battered as an adult	"	"	"	58%
Sexually abused as an adult	"	"	"	34%
Alcoholic/alcohol abuse problem	15%	"	25%	23%
Addiction/drug abuse problem	50%	"	50%	76%
Drug and alcohol abuse problem	6%	"	Not measured	Not measured

Table 4.5
Early Reentry Problems of Jailed Mothers

First-Week Reentry Problems, Last Release from Jail	% (N = 100)
Drug or alcohol use	37
No transportation	28
Unable to get into substance-abuse-treatment program	21
Unable to visit children	20
Homeless, needed shelter	18
Needed food	16
Needed clothes	11
Multiple problems	58
No problems during first weeks after release	41

Source: Johnston, 1991.

Table 4.6
Late Reentry Problems of Jailed Mothers

Reentry Problems after First Month, Last Release from Jail	% (N = 100)
Drug or alcohol use	52
Difficulty in family relationships	39
Unable to find employment; need job training	30
Emotional problems	28
Child custody problems	18
Problem obtaining public assistance	14
Needed regular assistance in obtaining food	13
Multiple problems	66
No problems during first months after release	34

Source: Johnston, 1991.

mothers who were incarcerated for the first time believed that they would not return to jail, while almost two-thirds of mothers who were multiple recidivists felt that it was probable they would be jailed again.

Discussion

Although about two-thirds of jailed women have been previously convicted, more than half have been previously incarcerated, and about one in six are recidivists who have been out of jail less than 1 year, only 5.5% were on parole when arrested (USDJ, 1992b). This suggests that many jailed women recidivists have repeatedly served jail sentences without ever going

Table 4.7
Predicted Probability of Future Incarceration, Jailed Mothers

Probability of Future Incarceration	All Mothers (N = 100	Mothers Serving First Jail Sentence (N = 16)	Mothers Who Have Served Multiple Jail Sentences (N = 66)
Certain ("I am sure I will be coming back to jail")	7%	None	12.1%
Very good ("There is a very good chance that I will be coming back to jail")	12%	None	16.6%
Some ("There is some chance that I will be coming back to jail")	25%	6.3%	33.3%
None ("I am sure I will never come back to jail")	56%	93.7%	38.0%

Source: Johnston, 1991.

to prison. This impression is confirmed by the Jailed Mothers Study, which found that only one-fourth of the recidivists studied had ever served a prison sentence.

The research reported here found that women recidivists who serve multiple sentences to incarceration in jails are usually convicted of a series of nonviolent, misdemeanor crimes. They are arrested more than twice as often as they are detained or sentenced to time in jails. Their interactions with the criminal justice system appear to occur in a typical cycle.

This cycle begins with accelerated drug use followed by drug-related crime. Increasingly disorganized behavior, compulsive crime habits, and/or the lack of resources to modify the pattern and site of their criminal activity lead these women to arrest. If they are not detained or jailed, they return to the street until arrest results in incarceration. If they are sentenced to more than a few days, incarceration interrupts their increasing drug use. Upon release from jail, the women attempt reentry in sobriety or with reduced drug needs. Drug use increases again as reentry efforts fail.

Most of the women who go to jail in this fashion have long histories of untreated abuse and/or exploitation, addiction, minimal education, and poor job skills. Regardless of whether these problems lead to repeated incarceration or are compounded by it, none can be seriously addressed or resolved within the short periods of stable street life women experience between release and rearrest. Indeed, for some, the temporal distinctions of this cycle do not exist, and their lives are disorganized and even chaotic from the moment of release until they are once again jailed.

The implications of such a pattern for the children and families of jailed women are grave. While the problems of families where the parent is addicted to drugs or a survivor of childhood abuse can be great, there is also evidence that they can be managed with intervention and produce successful outcomes for children (Kaplan-Sanoff & Fitzgerald, 1992). The lives of the families of jailed mothers, however, are complicated not only by these two issues, but also by the traumas and disorganization produced by parental crime, arrest, and incarceration. Successful intervention for these families requires multiple services for multiple circumstances, is extremely costly, and often overwhelms and defeats individual providers.

Systemic interventions for jailed mothers clearly must address root causes of and contributors to their criminal behavior patterns, and specifically include services for substance-dependent women with children, for survivors of abuse in childhood, and for victims of domestic violence. Services should also prepare these women for alternatives to survival by crime, with general education, job skills training, and actual job placement. Of equal importance for jailed mothers, who have no reporting requirements and face release-related problems more frequently and with less resources than women on parole, are reentry support services that will reduce the likelihood of their immediate return to addiction.

Summary and Conclusions

Jailed mothers come from troubled families with histories of substance abuse, physical and sexual victimization, criminal activity, and other compulsive behaviors. A significant number of these mothers are second- or third-generation offenders. Most jailed mothers began using drugs in their teens. They experienced teenage pregnancies. Most did not finish high school and were unemployed or on welfare at the time of arrest. Jailed mothers were usually arrested for the first time as teenagers or young adults. The majority have had multiple arrests prior to their current incarceration; over half have been previously incarcerated. Their criminal histories are most commonly related to substance abuse and the public order or property crimes that support drug addiction.

The majority of jailed mothers lived with their children before their arrest and retained legal custody of their children during incarceration. Their primary concerns relate to the effects of their incarceration on their children's lives. Even when these mothers (and the risks related to their criminal activity and arrest) are no longer in the home, they perceive their children as vulnerable to placement problems, custody disputes, ill health, physical injury, and abuse. They relate these risks to parent–child separation and their inability to protect, control access to, and retain parental authority over their children while incarcerated.

In spite of having served short sentences, jailed mothers experience major problems at reentry. Most are unable to find employment after release; postrelease homelessness and immediate return to substance abuse are increasing among this population. The lack of personal and public resources to meet their reentry needs contributes to a high rate of recidivism and hopelessness among these mothers. The majority of those who have been previously incarcerated believe that they might be jailed again, and this is an accurate assumption.

References

Adler, F. (1975). *Sisters in crime*. New York: McGraw-Hill.

Barry, E. (1985, July–August). Reunification difficult for incarcerated parents and their children. *Youth Law News*, pp. 14–16.

Barry, E. (1990). Women in prison. In C. Lefcourt (Ed.), *Women and the law* (6:18.01–18.35). Deerfield, IL: Clark, Boardman, and Callahan.

Baunach, P. J. (1979, November). *Mothering from behind prison walls*. Paper presented at the annual meeting of the American Society of Criminology, Philadelphia.

Becker, B. L. (1991). Order in the court: Challenging judges who incarcerate pregnant, substance-dependent defendants to protect fetal health. *Hastings Constitutional Law Quarterly*, 19:235–259.

Bloom, B., & Steinhart, D. (1993). *Why punish the children? A reappraisal of the children of incarcerated mothers in America*. San Francisco: National Council on Crime and Delinquency.

Bonfanti, M. A., Felter, S. S., Loesch, M. L. & Vincent, N. J. (1974). *Enactment and perception of maternal role of incarcerated mothers*. Unpublished master's thesis, Louisiana State University.

Crites, L. (1976). Women offenders: Myth versus reality. In L. Crites (Ed.), *The female offender* (pp. 33–44). Lexington, MA: Lexington Books.

DuBose, D. G. (1977). *Incarcerated mothers and their children in Texas*. Unpublished manuscript,

Garcia, S. (1992). Drug addiction and mother–child welfare: Rights, laws, and discretionary decision making. *Journal of Legal Medicine*, 13:129–203.

Gibbs, C. (1971). The effect of the imprisonment of women upon their children. *British Journal of Criminology*, 11:113–130.

Glick, R. M., & Neto, V. V. (1977). *National study of women's correctional programs*. Washington, DC: National Institute of Law Enforcement and Criminal Justice.

Hairston, C. F. (1990). Mothers in jail: Parent–child separation and jail visitation. *Affilia*, 6(2).

Henriques, Z. W. (1982). *Imprisoned mothers and their children*. Washington, DC: University Press of America.

Inter-University Consortium for Political & Social Research. (1991). *Survey of Inmates of Local Jails, 1989.* Ann Arbor, Michigan: Authors.

Johnston, D. (1991). *Jailed mothers.* Pasadena, CA: Pacific Oaks Center for Children of Incarcerated Parents.

Johnston, D. (1992). *Children of offenders.* Pasadena, CA: Pacific Oaks Center for Children of Incarcerated Parents.

Kaplan-Sanoff, M., & Fitzgerald, K. (1992). Working with addicted women in recovery and their children. 0–3, 13(1):17–22.

Koban, L. (1983). Parents in prison: A comparative analysis of the effects of incarceration on the families of men and women. *Research in Law, Deviance and Social Control,* 5:171–183.

LeFlore, L., & Holston, M. A. (1990). Perceived importance of parenting behaviors as reported by inmate mothers: An exploratory study. *Journal of Offender Counseling, Services and Rehabilitation,* 14(1):5–21.

McGowan, B., & Blumenthal, K. (1978). *Why punish the children?* New York: Children's Defense Fund.

National Black Child Development Institute. (1989). *Who will care when parents can't? A study of black children in foster care.* Washington, DC: Author.

Phase ReEntry Programs. (1991). *StreetReady: A release-planning handbook for jailed women.* Pasadena, CA: Pacific Oaks Center for Children of Incarcerated Parents.

Simon, R. (1975). *Women and crime.* Lexington, MA: Lexington Books.

Stanton, A. (1980). *When mothers go to jail.* Lexington, MA: Lexington Books.

Steffensmeier, D. J. (1980). Assessing the impact of the women's movement on sex-based differences in the handling of adult criminal defendants. *Crime and Delinquency,* 26:344–357.

Task Force on the Female Offender. (1990). *The female offender: What does the future hold?* Arlington, VA: American Correctional Association.

U.S. Department of Justice. (1991a). *Drugs and jail inmates, 1989* (Report No. NCJ-130836). Washington, DC: Bureau of Justice Statistics.

U.S. Department of Justice. (1991b). *Women in prison* (Report No. NCJ-127991). Washington, DC: Bureau of Justice Statistics.

U.S. Department of Justice. (1992a). *Correctional populations in the United States, 1990* (Report No. NCJ-134946). Washington, DC: Bureau of Justice Statistics.

U.S. Department of Justice. (1992b). *Women in jail, 1989* (Report No. NCJ-134732). Washington, DC: Bureau of Justice Statistics.

U.S. Department of Justice. (1992c). *Prisons and prisoners in the United States* (Report No. NCJ-137002). Washington, DC: Bureau of Justice Statistics.

U.S. Department of Justice. (1993a). *Correctional populations in the United States, 1991* (Report No. NCJ-142729). Washington, DC: Bureau of Justice Statistics.

U.S. Department of Justice. (1993b). *Jail inmates 1992* (Report No. NCJ-143284). Washington, DC: Bureau of Justice Statistics.

U.S. Department of Justice. (1993c). *Prisoners in 1992* (Report No. NCJ-141874). Washington, DC: Bureau of Justice Statistics.

U.S. Department of Justice. (1993d). *Survey of state prison inmates* (Report No. NCJ-136949). Washington, DC: Bureau of Justice Statistics.

U.S. Department of Justice. (Forthcoming). *Recidivism of prisoners released in 1989.* Washington, DC: Bureau of Justice Statistics.

U.S. General Accounting Office. (1980). *Women in prison: Inequitable treatment requires action* (Report No. GGD-81-6). Gaithersburg, MD: Author.

Zalba, S. (1964). *Women prisoners and their families.* Sacramento, CA: Department of Social Welfare and Department of Corrections.

Zietz, D. (1963). Child welfare services in a women's correctional institution. *Child Welfare,* 42:185–190.

PART II

Effects of Parental Incarceration

5
Effects of Parental Incarceration

Denise Johnston

P arental crime, arrest, and incarceration have profound effects on children. Professionals in all fields, including the social services, medicine, education, legal services, childcare, and mental health, will encounter children of offenders regularly and should be familiar with their demographics, life experience, and special characteristics.

Population Size

Most children who have experienced parental incarceration do not have a currently incarcerated parent. The great majority of persons under correctional supervision in the United States, for example, are on probation or parole and are not being held in locked facilities. Since unduplicated data on the number of adults who have been jailed or imprisoned in the past 2 decades has not been collected, we cannot make reliable estimates of the number of children who have had the experience of parental incarceration at least once in their lives.

Estimation of the number of children of current prisoners poses fewer challenges. Estimates are based on data obtained from studies of large numbers of incarcerated parents. Direct measurement of the size of the population of prisoners' children has not been attempted.

Problems in Counting the Children of Prisoners

We possess no reliable way to directly measure the number of prisoners' children. Official mechanisms to collect information about offenders' children during arrest and ajudication do not exist. All such information is necessarily derived from the self-reports of offenders, which may be inaccurate and which would be costly to verify. Moreover, it is not clear that offenders can legally or ethically be required to provide researchers with information about their families.

Lack of Official Data Collection Methods. Most jurisdictions do not request or collect family information from arrested persons. A few jurisdictions require law enforcement officers to inquire about the dependent children of arrested persons, but mechanisms for this information to follow the offender through ajudication do not exist. Similarly, although some jurisdictions require that information about convicted persons' family responsibilities be included in presentencing reports, the majority of sentences are imposed without such reports.

Even when such information is available to the courts, little or none of it is contained in the official documentation that accompanies persons sentenced to incarceration. Jails and prisons have no mandate to collect or verify data on the families of prisoners.

Limitations of Self-Reported Data. At all stages of the justice process, for the great majority of those with criminal charges, information about their families must be obtained by self-report. The reluctance of this population to provide family-related information in response to official or independent inquiries has been well documented (Baunach, 1979; Hairston, 1990; Hunter, 1984; McGowan & Blumenthal, 1978); this reluctance stems from legitimate concerns about confidentiality, criminal liabilities, child custody matters, and public assistance.

Family information provided by offenders may also be inaccurate. There have been no structured attempts to examine the reliability of family data reported by prisoners; however, Zalba (1964) found several areas, including the identity of childrens' caregivers, in which information provided by incarcerated mothers proved to be incorrect upon investigation. Hunter (1984) also found discrepancies between the reports of paroled women about their family circumstances and the official information provided by supervisory agencies.

Confidentiality Issues. While basic information on the identity, offense, ajudication, conviction, and incarceration of offenders is available to the public, unrelated information is not. Offenders have no legal obligation to provide the police or the courts with information about their families. Except where it is related to the direct security concerns of correctional institutions, as in contact visitation activities, information about their families cannot be ethically or legally demanded from prisoners.

Estimating the Number of Children of Incarcerated Parents

As a result of these difficulties in direct measurement, the number of children of prisoners in any given jurisdiction has only been estimated by extrapolation of data collected in large-scale studies of their parents. Estimated counts of prisoners' children can be made by determining an approximate number of incarcerated parents and multiplying by the average number of children per prisoner for each sex.

Average Proportions of Parents among Prisoners. Over the last 3 decades, virtually all studies of incarcerated women have found that about three-quarters of them are mothers (Baunauch, 1979; Glick & Neto, 1977; Johnston, 1991; McGowan & Blumenthal, 1978; Stanton, 1980; Task Force on the Female Offender, 1990). Less consistently, these studies and others (U.S. Department of Justice [USDJ], 1993) have found that up to 80% of incarcerated mothers, or two-thirds of all incarcerated females, have minor children. Data on the percentage of incarcerated men who have children is much more limited. Only one large-scale study, the Survey of State Prison Inmates conducted by the U.S. Department of Justice (1993), has reported data on this topic; the survey found that 56% of men in state prisons have minor children.

Average Number of Children per Incarcerated Parent. This number has been extremely consistent among incarcerated mothers studied in a variety of settings and circumstances over the past 30 years (Baunauch, 1979; Bloom & Steinhart, 1993; Gibbs, 1971; Johnston, 1991; Koban, 1983; Stanton, 1980; Task Force on the Female Offender, 1990; Zalba, 1964). These and other studies found a mean of 2.3–2.4 children per incarcerated mother. Small studies of incarcerated fathers found a significantly lower mean number of children per prisoner (Koban, 1983; Sack, Seidler, & Thomas, 1977). However, the national Survey of State Prison Inmates (USDJ, 1993) found that imprisoned men have an average of 2.0 children each.

Consideration of Living Arrangements Prior to Arrest. In calculating the number of prisoners' children, some jurisdictions have excluded those who were living apart from their parents at the time of parental arrest (Virginia Commission on Youth, 1992). This approach decreases the accuracy of numerical data on these children. In addition, there is some evidence that offenders who do not officially "live with" their children do, in fact, have regular and even daily contact with them (Miller, 1986). Finally, since one outcome of parental recidivism is permanent parent–child separation, eliminating children who have not been living with their parents from study also eliminates from consideration those who are likely to have been most negatively affected by previous experiences with parental incarceration. This creates a distorted perception of the characteristics of the population. All categories of minor children of prisoners should be counted when estimating their numbers.

Formula for Estimating the Number of Prisoners' Children. For any given population of incarcerated adults, estimation of the number of prisoners' children can be made by using the following formula, where .67 an average percentage of incarcerated women with minor children, 2.4 is the mean number of minor children per incarcerated mother, .56 is an average percentage of incarcerated men with minor children and 2.0 is the mean number of minor children per incarcerated father:

(# incarcerated females x .67 x 2.4) + (# incarcerated males x .56 x 2.0)

By this formula, 90,000 incarcerated U.S. women have an estimated 145,000 minor children and 1.23 million incarcerated U.S. men have an estimated 1.38 million minor children. There are therefore approximately 1.53 million minor children of incarcerated parents in the United States.

Research on Children of Prisoners

Most information on prisoners' children is actually derived from surveys of their parents. Very few studies have directly examined the children themselves. The difficulties that prevent accurate counts of children of incarcerated parents also prevent the collection of representative descriptive data on these children. Since the entire population has not been measured or identified, it is impossible to know if smaller groups are typical of the whole group. The consistency of data in some categories over several decades suggests that existing studies have produced some reliable information about prisoners' children; however, without research on large, well-selected populations, this assumption cannot be confirmed.

Zalba (1964) collected data on the 460 incarcerated mothers among all of California's women prisoners, and on their 1,085 children. The study was conducted by survey and review of correctional and other agency records. Children and their caregivers from two selected counties were also interviewed. The other children in this study were not interviewed or directly examined. Zalba's data focused on the children's placement. This study is one of the few that have actually examined a representative sample (in this case, all) of a specific correctional population.

Friedman and Esselstyn (1965) studied teacher ratings of academic performance and classroom behavior of 117 children of men incarcerated in Santa Clara County, California. Children were accessed through their fathers; the sampling method used is not described. Children were matched by grade with controls; the offender status of the parents of controls was not determined. The experimental group was 60% Mexican-American; no other socioeconomic or personal descriptors of the children were obtained. Findings were reported in subjective terms; actual data was not presented in the published report of the research, limiting the usefulness of this study.

Morris (1965) interviewed 932 prisoners from 17 of 45 prisons in Great Britain, and 676 of their wives. The study is remarkable for its breadth and the intensive interviews conducted with a small subgroup of 35 wives who were followed for 18 months. The children of these families were not directly examined.

Sack, Seidler & Thomas (1976) studied a nonrandom sample of 73 children of 20 imprisoned fathers and 11 imprisoned mothers. Information was obtained by interview of the incarcerated parents and the wives of the male prisoners. No children, and none of the partners of the female prisoners, were directly examined. The study focused on the effects of parental imprisonment on the family and children's reactions to parental incarceration.

Sack (1977) reported on a small, clinical sample of the sons of imprisoned fathers. The eight boys studied had been referred for psychiatric care as a result of aggressive behaviors following parental imprisonment. Sack's report provides detailed family and behavioral characteristics of these children.

McGowan and Blumenthal (1978) surveyed a national sample of 3,121 incarcerated mothers and interviewed a local sample of 63 jailed mothers. Their study examined living arrangements prior to incarceration, placement, visitation, and reunification plans. Information on the children was obtained from the mothers only. The national study population included approximately half of the mothers incarcerated in the United States at the time the research was conducted.

Stanton (1980) attempted to distinguish the effects of maternal criminal involvement from the effects of mother–child separation among a nonrandom sample of 54 jailed women and 118 of their children. This is one of the few studies of incarcerated parents to directly access the children; demographic data, pre- and postarrest placement, school performance, the child's knowledge of the mother's legal situation, welfare status, and the child's legal socialization were all documented through interviews with the children, the mothers, the caregivers, and school personnel. This work was the first thorough and direct examination of the effects of maternal incarceration, and remains one of the most important studies in this area to date.

Swan (1981) interviewed the wives of 192 men imprisoned in Alabama and Tennessee. His study focused on the economic, social, and family effects of paternal incarceration. Effects on the children of male prisoners was not a primary subject of this work, and the children were not directly examined.

Fritsch and Burkhead (1982) surveyed a representative sample of prisoners in the federal minimum security prison in Lexington, Kentucky, and identified 91 parents of minor children from this group. These parents answered survey questions about their 194 children. The study focused on children's behavioral reactions to parental incarceration. The children were not directly examined.

Shelton, Armstrong & Cochran (1983) conducted an early study of the outcomes of pregnancy among incarcerated mothers. The small sample of 12 women and 13 children was followed clinically through the perinatal period and the mothers were interviewed.

Hunter (1984) studied women on parole in Michigan, examining a random sample of 55 mothers and their 165 children. Hunter's data was derived from interviews with the mothers and their parole agents, and from the records of the state parole agency. There was no direct examination of the children. The report included information on mother–child separation during maternal imprisonment, child custody, child care, and placement.

McCall and Shaw (1985) studied perinatal outcomes among a sample of 110 prisoners in both of California's women's prisons and one large women's jail. Mothers were interviewed; prison and community medical records were reviewed for 66 of the women.

Johnston (1991) interviewed 100 of 114 jailed mothers in Riverside County, California. The study examined children's pre- and postincarceration living arrangements, risk factors, and behavior problems.

Bloom and Steinhart (1993) reprised McGowan and Blumenthal's "Why Punish the Children?" study. A nonrandom, national sample of 439 jailed and imprisoned women with 866 minor children were surveyed by mail; also, 35 caregivers were interviewed for information about the 66 children in their care. There was no direct examination of the children; the report focused on mother–child contact and the role of the caregiver.

Gabel and Shindledecker (1991) examined a small, clinical sample of children of incarcerated parents. The subjects were in day treatment for emotional disturbances. Like other studies of clinical samples, this report did not produce data that can be applied to larger populations of prisoners' children.

The Virginia Commission on Youth (1992) issued a report on the needs of children whose parents are incarcerated. The report, based on a review of existing literature, estimated the number of children of prisoners in the Commonwealth of Virginia. No other demographic or descriptive data was collected.

Johnston (1992, 1993a) directly examined 56 children in 1992 and 202 children in 1993. Nine out of 10 of the children studied had experienced parental crime, arrest, and incarceration; one in four had a parent who was incarcerated at the time of the study. Assessments included child interviews by a clinical psychologist, parent/caregiver interviews, school records reviews, classroom observations, and standardized measurements of the childrens' home and classroom behaviors. The study focused on children of offenders whose school behavioral and disciplinary problems appeared to be leading them toward delinquency and second-generation incarceration.

Table 5.1
Perinatal Problems among Incarcerated Mothers

Perinatal Problem	Shelton et. al. (1983) (N = 11)	McCall & Shaw (1985) (N = 110)	Cordero et al (1991) (N = 106)	Egley et al. (1992) (N = 69)
Complications of pregnancy	65.1%	20–50%	Not measured	10%
Miscarriages	None	33.7%	short-term incarceration = 7%	None
			long-term incarceration = None	
Total live births	91.7%	44.5%*	short-term incarceration = 93%	100%
			long-term incarceration = 100%	

*Includes data on electively terminated pregnancies.

The Prison Visitation Project (1993) surveyed a nonrepresentative sample of 184 parents incarcerated in Virginia jails and prisons, and interviewed the caregivers of 234 of their minor children. The children were not directly examined. This study collected demographic data and information on caregiver characteristics, living conditions, behaviors, and services available for children of parents incarcerated in the Commonwealth of Virginia.

The design and implementation of research on children of prisoners and other offenders has clearly been difficult. Only four of the studies described here were based on direct assessments of the children, and only two of those four examined nonclinical samples. A study involving direct examination of a large numbers of prisoners' children has yet to be conducted.

In addition, most of the research on prisoners' children just described has focused on their problems (see Tables 5.1, 5.2, 5.3, 5.4, and 5.5) and has not attempted to create a rounded picture of their lives. It is important to remember that even among groups of prisoners' children selected for study because of their emotional, behavioral, or disciplinary problems, few of the children had problems in every area and all of the children were performing adequately in one or more areas (Johnston, 1993a).

Life Experience

The studies just described paint a compelling picture of the experience of children of offenders. Parental incarceration, and the crime and arrests that preceed it, produce a typical series of events in the lives of these children. The Children of Offenders Study (Johnston, 1992) identified three factors

Table 5.2
Neonatal Problems of Children Born to Incarcerated Mothers

Neonatal Problem	Shelton (1983) (N = 11)	Cordero et al. (1991) (N = 106)	Egley et al. (1992) (N = 69)
Complications, including illness, birth injuries, and neonatal intensive care unit (NICU) admissions	37.2%	short-term incarceration = 33% long-term incarceration = 9%	9%
Neonatal deaths	27.9%	None	None

Table 5.3
Behavioral Problems of Prisoners' Children

Study	Problem	Incidence
Sack et al. (1976)	aggressive reactions	19.2%
Baunach (1979)	aggression, tension, withdrawal	69.9%
Hunter (1980)	fighting, hostility	"frequent"
Fritsch & Burkhead (1982) troubled children of female prisoners	acting out withdrawal	31.8% 68.3%
Fritsch & Burkhead (1982) troubled children of male prisoners	acting out withdrawal	58.8% 41.2%

Table 5.4
School Problems of Prisoners' Children

Study	Problem	Incidence
Sack et al. (1977)	academic, aggressive behavior	over 50%
Baunach (1979)	academic	15%
Stanton (1980)	classroom behavior problem poor performance	50% 70%
Henriques (1982)	truancy, attendance academic or classroom behavior	12.5% 62.5%

Table 5.5
Delinquency among Children of Prisoners and Other Offenders

Study	Delinquency	Gang Involvement	Incarceration
Breckenridge & Abbot (1912)	17.4%	Not measured	Not measured
Glueck & Glueck (1950)	45.6%	Not measured	Not measured
McCord & McCord (1958)	60.0%	Not measured	Not measured
Sack et al. (1976)	12.2%	Not measured	Not measured
Stanton (1980)	24.0%	Not measured	Not measured
Johnston (1991)	Not measured	Not measured	10.0%
Johnston (1992)	29.6%	22.2%	Not measured

that were consistently present in the majority of children studied. These factors—parent–child separation, enduring traumatic stress, and an inadequate quality of care—can affect each stage of child development (see Table 5.6).

Prenatal Life

Pregnant prisoners and their unborn infants are at extremely high risk for morbidity and mortality. Some of this risk accompanies their socioeconomic status, since the great majority of prisoners are low-income persons. Some risk has also been associated with poor-quality obstetrical and medical care for women prisoners (McCall & Shaw, 1985). However, more recent research suggests that obstetrical care for prisoners has improved dramatically over the past decade, perhaps as the result of litigation (Barry, 1989).

Cordero, Hines, Shibley & Lauton (1991), for example, have found that drug use, hepatitis, poor nutrition, and poor prenatal care are more common among women serving short terms of incarceration. Thirty-three percent of such women had stillbirths or infants with neonatal morbidity compared to 9% of women serving longer prison terms. These authors suggest that women serving longer sentences had better perinatal outcomes as a result of extended periods of better nutrition and prenatal care than they would have had on the street.

Prenatal Substance Abuse. Most risk among pregnant offenders, however, has been attributed to maternal behaviors, including use of tobacco and illicit drugs (King & Whitman, 1981; Miller, 1984). The incidence of prenatal exposure to drugs or alcohol among children of offenders appears to be high. The Children of Offenders Study (Johnston, 1992) found that

Table 5.6
Possible Developmental Effects of Parental Crime, Arrest, and Incarceration in Children

Developmental Stage	Developmental Characteristics	Developmental Tasks	Influencing Factors	Effects
Infancy (0–2 years)	Limited perception, mobility, and experience. Total dependency.	Development of attachment and trust.	Parent–child separation.	Impaired parent-to-child bonding.
Early childhood (2–6 years)	Increased perception and mobility. Improved memory. Greater exposure to environment. Ability to imagine.	Sense of autonomy and independence. Sense of initiative	Parent–child separation.	Inappropriate separation anxiety; other developmental regression. Impaired development of initiative
	Incomplete individuation from parent at younger ages.		Trauma.	Acute traumatic stress reactions; survivor guilt.
Middle childhood (7–10 years)	Increased independence from caregivers. Increased ability to reason. Peers become important.	Sense of industry. Ability to work productively.	Parent–child separation.	Developmental regressions. Poor self-concept.
			Enduring trauma.	Acute traumatic stress reactions. Trauma-reactive behaviors. Impaired ability to overcome future trauma.
Early adolescence (11–14 years)	Organization of behavior in pursuit of distant goals.	Ability to work productively with others.	Parent–child separation.	Rejection of limits on behavior.
	Increased aggression. Puberty. Increasing abstract thinking.	Control of expression of emotions.	Enduring trauma.	Patterning of trauma-reactive behaviors.
Late adolescence (15–18 years)	Emotional crisis and confusion. Adult sexual development and sexuality. Formal abstract thinking.	Achievement of cohesive identity. Resolution of conflicts with family and society.	Parent–child separation.	Premature termination of the dependency relationship between parent and child.
	Increased independence.	Ability to engage in adult work and relationships.	Enduring trauma.	Characteristic legal socialization Intergenerational crime and incarceration.

over half of the children of women who had been arrested, and 77% of the children of currently or previously incarcerated women, had been prenatally exposed to drugs or alcohol.

However, more recent studies suggest that the direct, chemical effects of illicit drugs on the fetus are overshadowed by the effects of the living conditions of women offenders. Egley, Miller, Granatos & Fogel (1992) found that perinatal outcome was better among women prisoners than matched controls, even though the use of major drugs and tobacco continued among the incarcerated subjects. The authors concluded that the adequate diet, reduced stress, and regular prenatal care received by women prisoners resulted in fewer medical complications from pregnancy and childbirth in spite of drug use. Similarly, comprehensive behavioral, developmental, and academic assessments could not distinguish between 11- to 14-year-old children who had been prenatally exposed to drugs and other children of offenders (Johnston, 1992).

Prenatal Stress. Whether it is their mothers or their fathers who are involved in activities leading to arrest and incarceration, it is likely that the stress and trauma that will characterize the lives of children of offenders begins before birth. Shelton (1983) found that the majority of the incarcerated mothers in her small study experienced emotional problems, including one suicide attempt. McCall and Shaw (1985) found that most pregnant prisoners have guilt and anxiety related to their circumstances, and suffer stress related to the manner in which obstetrical care is provided in jails and prisons.

Summary. The children of offenders experience prenatal stress related to their parent's criminal activity, arrest, and/or incarceration. The children of pregnant, substance-abusing women are subject to prenatal exposure to drugs. Women serving short terms of incarceration appear to continue to be at extremely high risk for poor perinatal outcomes. The children of women serving longer sentences recently have begun to have better perinatal outcomes, as a result of long periods of adequate nutrition, a stable lifestyle, and regular, improved prenatal care in prison. Maternal drug use appears to have less direct effects on the outcomes of pregnancy among prisoners than the conditions of life that accompany addiction on the street.

The First Two Years of Life

The basic tasks of social-emotional development in infancy are the development of attachment and subsequent learning of trust. *Attachment* is an emotional closeness between people that lasts over an extended period of time. While parents and caregivers bond to highly dependent infants by meeting their needs, attachment is learned by infants while their needs are being met. The need for infants to have at least one nurturing caregiver to whom they are attached is well established (Bowlby, 1983). However, although child welfare experts and juvenile courts often follow the "psychological parent" theory (Goldstein et al., 1973), which asserts that a child can have only one primary attachment figure for normal emotional development, there is in fact no evidence in the behavioral science, child development, or child welfare literature that this is so (Kadushin, 1974). Indeed, there is evidence to the contrary (Bush & Goldman, 1982; Lamb, 1977). Infants have been found to be capable of developing multiple attachments. It is nevertheless important to note that infants do not become attached to persons who are not regularly involved in meeting their needs. Infants cannot express their attachments verbally; therefore, attachment behaviors are used as a measurement of development in this area. Attachment behaviors include differentiation between known and unknown persons and smiling and other movements that express pleasure at interaction with significant others.

Babies develop a sense of *trust* in others when their needs are met in a caring and consistent way. Infants whose needs go unmet may become difficult to manage as they express feelings of stress; they may experience a narrower range of emotions when they do not receive emotionally nurturing care.

Effects of Trauma in Infancy. Infants have very little awareness of the events of their parents' lives that do not directly involve them. Only profound deprivation or abuse will significantly affect the great physical and intellectual development that takes place in infants. However, social-emotional development is more likely to reflect stress or trauma in children of any age, including infants. The sequence of developmental reactions to stress/trauma at all ages is transient developmental regression   deceleration of development   arrest of development   developmental delay. It is important to understand that general developmental delay does not occur before a slowing of the normal process of development, or before regression. Developmental delay only occurs in response to profound insults or to stress/trauma that is continuous over a long period of time.

Most offenders have low incomes, and their infants suffer the moderate deprivations that accompany poverty in Western nations (Duncan, Brooks-Gunn, & Kelbanov, 1994). However, there is no evidence that the infants of incarcerated parents, as a group, experience significant delays in physical or intellectual development (Catan, 1992). Parental crime, arrest, and incarceration mainly affects social-emotional infant development through parent–child separation.

Effects of Parent–Child Separation. The separation of infants from their parents produces great risks. Adults with emotional and behavioral problems have often been found to have histories of separations from their parents in early childhood (Rutter, 1966).

No studies have documented serious or lasting primary attachment disorders among young infants of prisoners. This may be because many infants of incarcerated parents are placed with nurturing primary caregivers soon after birth, a factor that Rutter (1981) and others (Bowlby, 1983) have found to greatly ameliorate the effects of maternal–child separation in early infancy. However, Catan's (1992) examination of infants born in British prisons found that nearly half experienced two to four caregiver changes in the first year of life, suggesting that at least some infants born to incarcerated mothers are at risk for attachment problems.

Some authorities (Adalist-Estrin, 1986, 1993) have speculated that offenders have had early separation experiences that impaired development of their sense of trust and that this basic mistrust makes it likely that they will be unable to instill trust in others, including their own children. According to this model, the early experience of offenders may impair their ability to become attached to others. Thus, since moral development is based upon empathy and the development of empathy is based upon attachment, crime must be related to disorders of primary attachment. Because persons with primary attachment disorders and empathic dysfunction are unable to form normal emotional attachments to others, the implications of this theory for the infants of offenders are grave. However, there has been no research that supports such speculations. There is no evidence that most prisoners or other offenders have identifiable empathic dysfunction (Halleck, 1967). Similarly, while the children of parents with primary attachment disorders would presumably have a very high incidence of major attachment problems themselves, this does not appear to be the case, even among delinquent children of offenders (Johnston, 1992, 1993a).

Of greater concern than attachment disorders in infants is the impaired bonding that can result from the incarceration of a parent and the parent's physical separation from the infant. This is a profound loss that can interfere with the full flowering of parental feelings and the sense of parental responsibility that grows out of the bond between a parent and a totally dependent infant. Ultimately, such a diminished relationship may produce more negative outcomes than any direct effects of parent–child separation on the infant.

Summary. Infants of prisoners experience few direct effects of parental incarceration on their physical and intellectual development. Multiple caregiver changes for infants born to women prisoners seem likely to produce attachment difficulties, but there has been no research on this topic. The most significant effect of parental incarceration in the first year of life may be that it prevents the development of bonding of incarcerated parents with their infants.

Early Childhood (2 to 6 Years)

Young children are very dependent upon and strongly identify with their parents or primary caregivers. The social and emotional developmental tasks for this age group result in the emergence of independence, called autonomy, and a sense of initiative. A child's success at these tasks is challenged by parental crime, arrest, and incarceration in several ways.

The first experience of parental crime, arrest, or incarceration that many children can recall usually occurs in early childhood. There are several reasons for this, including improved memory, increased awareness, and greater exposure. Central nervous system development normally provides an increasing capacity for memory at this age. Earlier experiences of all types are unlikely to be recalled. Moreover, early childhood is the age at which children become aware of violence, crime, law enforcement, and incarceration. Even when these are not topics of family discussion, children observe these events in the media and discuss them with peers.

Stanton (1980) found that 53% of the 4- to 8-year-olds she studied had witnessed the arrest of a family member. Johnston (1991) found that only one-fifth of all children studied had witnessed their mother's arrest, but over half of these were 3- to 6-years-old. These findings might be due to the increased mobility of children at this stage, combined with the fact that they do not yet attend school. In other words, young children are most likely to be in the home at the time of a domestic crime, and the most likely of children of all ages to accompany their parent on a excursion for criminal activity.

The nature and timing of parental crime, and the extent to which it removes the parent from the home, determine its effects on young children. The activities of parents who leave their children at home and take their criminal behavior to the streets affect young children primarily through parent–child separation. Crime that occurs in their presence at home or in their neighborhoods may be traumatic for young children. This is also true of parental arrest. Finally, several studies and authorities have found that some groups of prisoners have overcontrolling parental behaviors (Adalist-Estrin, 1986; Kolman, 1983).

Effects of Parent–Child Separation on Young Children. The identity and sense of security of young children are still dependent on the presence of the parent or primary caregiver. As older infants and toddlers begin to recognize the separate identity of parents, and the potential for parental absence and loss of security, separation anxiety occurs. Children learn to overcome this stressful experience as part of their normal development of autonomy and initiative.

When separation from their parent is sudden, traumatic, or prolonged, children who have mastered separation anxiety may regress and experience it again. When such separations recur, separation anxiety may persist indefinitely. In addition, parent–child separation may slow or alter the normal development of autonomy, causing children to become excessively dependent and fail to develop appropriate self-confidence. Parent–child separation has also been found to produce a variety of emotional reactions in young children, who may act out their emotions in behaviors that include other anxiety states, aggression, and withdrawal.

Effects of Early Childhood Trauma. Young children have several capabilities that make them more susceptible to negative outcomes of trauma than infants. Their perception has improved and they see, hear, and otherwise sense more than infants. They have a greater range of knowledge than infants and are able to imagine, which infants appear not to do. As a result, they are afraid of more things. However, just like infants, young children do not have the developmental skills to process frightening experiences. Unlike older children and adults, they cannot mentally create alternative scenarios or verbally express their emotional reactions to trauma.

Young children are also particularly vulnerable to the traumatic effects of parental arrest and incarceration for several other reasons, including identification with the parent, survivor guilt, and forced silence.

Identification with the Parent. Children at this age do not recognize their parent as a completely separate individual; they tend to experience injuries or threats to the parent as injuries or threats to themselves. Events that result in parent–child separation, like parental arrest, are especially traumatic because they eliminate the opportunity for children to observe their parents following trauma and be reassured of their well-being; this type of reassurance is often critical to children's adjustment. Also, a major role of parents is to assist children in mastering the effects of trauma; when a bad experience traumatizes a child *and* removes the parent (as in parental arrest), the child's helper is also gone and the child's ability to overcome future traumatic experiences may be severely or permanently impaired (Furman, 1983).

Survivor Guilt. Young children normally believe that all events center around themselves. Like other children, they have ambivalent feelings toward their parents, but unlike older children, they cannot be sure that these feelings do not cause their parents injury. Parental arrest and incarceration typically follows a period of family stress related to parental crime; children and other family members may be angry with and resentful of a criminal parent. When the parent is arrested and goes away, their angry feelings may cause young children to feel guilty and responsible.

Forced Silence. Children need to express their feelings in order to overcome the effects of trauma. This is particularly difficult following parental arrest and incarceration because family members may order children not to speak about what happened or may conduct themselves as if the events never occurred, avoiding the topic and ignoring children's questions. There may be very good reasons for such a forced silence; family jobs, welfare payments, child custody, and even housing may be jeopardized when others become aware of the parent's whereabouts. However, children of prisoners are more likely to have negative reactions to their experience when they cannot talk about it (Hannon, Martin, & Martin, 1984; Schwartz & Weintraub, 1974).

The long-term effects of traumatic stress are greatest in this age group. This is especially true when there is no intervention following trauma.

The Effects of Overcontrolling Parent Behaviors. Kolman (1983) and Adalist-Estrin (1986) have studied the parental control behaviors of inmate parents and found both mothers and fathers to be overcontrolling. The parents they observed exhibited coercive and authoritarian patterns in managing their children's behavior. Other studies have similarly found aversive interactions to be common among substance-dependent parents and their children (Bauman & Dougherty, 1983).

Authoritarian behaviors among persons subject to overcontrolling, authoritarian environments may be expected. However, young children who are in the process of developing a sense of initiative may be susceptible to the negative effects of this parenting style. Overcontrolling parents may stifle young children's growing ability to think and act without being urged, and may make them feel they are "wrong all the time." This is particularly important in young children of prisoners and other offenders, because of the tendency of these children to experience survivor guilt. Although the extent to which these behaviors occur among all incarcerated parents is unknown, where they exist they are likely to have long-term effects on the development of initiative in young children.

Summary. The development of autonomy and initiative in very young children of prisoners may be damaged by traumatic experiences of parental criminal activity and/or parental arrest, the overcontrolling parent behaviors of some offenders, and parent–child separation due to parental incarceration. The long-term effects of these experiences may be worse at this stage of childhood than at any other stage because young children have the ability to perceive and remember traumatic events, but they cannot process or adjust to trauma without assistance.

Middle Childhood (7 to 10 Years)

The developmental tasks of middle childhood prepare children to work with others. Although the significant adults in their lives continue to provide models and guidance, children at this age are increasingly independent of their caregivers and becoming more socially aware. Children's own self-concept and the interrelated esteem of their peers become more important in middle childhood.

Children of offenders at this age are most likely to have had previous experiences, which they can recall, with parental crime, arrest, and/or incarceration. Because they are in school or able to engage in out-of-the-home play and recreation, these children are less likely to be present at the time of a parent's crime and arrest. Nevertheless, such events may have profound emotional and developmental effects in middle childhood.

Effects of Parent–Child Separation. This is a source of emotional injury to children of prisoners. Parent–child separation due to parental incarceration produces its effects through several mechanisms, including a sense of loss, multiple placements, and lack of a parental role model. First, the children of prisoners, like other children separated from their parents, miss their mothers and fathers. Even in households that were disrupted by parental crime, children who have an incarcerated father miss his affection (92%) and feel lonely (59%) as a result of his absence (Schneller, 1978).

Second, in themselves, multiple placements of children living out of the home are a source of traumatic stress (Doyle & Bauer, 1989). Several studies have found that a significant proportion of the children of women prisoners experience multiple placements while their parents are incarcerated (Baunach, 1979; Johnston, 1991; Zalba, 1964). The life experience of school-age children of offenders is characterized by this problem, and it is associated with some of the worst outcomes of parental incarceration. Examining older children of offenders, the majority of whom were delinquent or gang-involved by early adolescence, Johnston (1992) found that only one in 11 children studied had lived continuously with one primary caregiver since birth.

Third, in middle childhood parents continue to serve as their children's models, demonstrating gender roles and productive behavior. Children whose parents are incarcerated lose a significant role model at a critical period in their lives. A small number of prisoners' children do not have a traditional parent–child relationship with their incarcerated parent (LaPointe, Picker & Harris, 1985) and manage to find adult models elsewhere. For the majority, parental role modeling can be assumed by a responsible caregiver when a parent is incarcerated. However, children's acceptance of these other adults in the parental role may not be complete. This is particularly true for older children who are placed with a caregiver who is significantly different in attributes from the parent (e.g., in sex, race, age, etc.) or who is a stranger to the child.

Effects of Enduring Trauma in Middle Childhood. Typical emotional responses to childhood trauma include anger, sadness or grief, and anxiety. In most cases, children's natural resiliency allows them to recover from these immediate reactions to trauma. However, children with poor coping skills, and children whose families are so stressed that they cannot offer support, are more likely to be unable to overcome the emotional effects of trauma (Brett, Spitzer & Williams, 1988; Krupnick, 1984; Payton & Krocker-Tuskan, 1988). This is particularly true of children who have enduring (multiple or recurrent) exposure to traumatic events.

When children are unable to recover from their emotional responses to trauma, they may begin to express these persistent emotions in reactive behaviors. The most typical trauma-reactive behavior seen in children of offenders is aggression (Johnston, 1993a); others include hypervigilance and other anxiety states, attention and concentration problems, and withdrawal. Aggressive behaviors and attention/concentration difficulties lead to academic and disciplinary problems at school; the Children of Offenders Study (Johnston, 1992, 1993a) found that these problems typically appear when children are in grades 4 and 5. Since a sense of industry and productivity in middle childhood is largely achieved through success in school, the experience of trauma at this age can impair or prevent achievement of this critical developmental task.

Trauma also interferes with the process of learning to control emotions, another developmental task of middle childhood. All children at this stage need to be encouraged to express their feelings while controlling the behaviors that arise from them. This is especially difficult for older children of prisoners who are increasingly concerned about the opinions of others and so are reluctant to share feelings about their situation.

The relationship between childhood trauma and all its effects is cyclical. For example, children with a weak self-concept respond poorly to trauma, but repeated trauma weakens self-concept. One of the most important long-term effects of childhood trauma is that it impairs children's ability to recover from future traumatic events.

Summary. The development of children's abilities to work and to get along with others—including achievement in school and the control of emotions—may be significantly impaired by parental crime, arrest, and incarceration. In middle childhood, the development of trauma-reactive behaviors, particularly aggression, is characteristic of many children of offenders.

Early Adolescence (11 to 14 Years)

A major developmental task of children in this age group is the organization or patterning of behavior in pursuit of distant goals. This task not only involves abstract thinking and and a willingness to accept delayed gratification, it also requires the ability to work productively with others. Many of the activities traditionally offered to adolescents assist them in learning how to pattern their behavior, reason abstractly, and delay gratification.

These activities often allow children to utilize the normal increase in physical aggression that occurs at adolescence and to act within peer groups that foster increasing independence from adults in the areas of self-control, emotional support, and information sharing.

Adolescent children of prisoners have typically had multiple experiences with parental crime, arrest, and incarceration; Stanton (1980) found that seven out of 10 children in this age group had witnessed a family member's arrest. As with younger children, these experiences affect older children through parent–child separation and enduring stress/trauma. However, at adolescence, normal developmental tasks and the outcomes of the life experiences of prisoners' children are more compatible than at any previous age.

Effects of Parent–Child Separation in Early Adolescence. Older children of prisoners have usually had at least one prior experience with a parent–child separation of over 3 months (Johnston, 1991). Fanshel and Shinn (1978) and others have clearly established the damaging effects of multiple, long-term separations of children from their parents.

Assumption of the Parental Role. It has been suggested that children of offenders, like other children of absent parents, frequently attempt to assume the roles of those parents (Osborne Association, 1993). This has not been directly observed or measured in objective studies of prisoners' children; studies that have examined children's behavioral reactions to incarceration have actually documented increased dependency and/or regression (Fritsch & Burkhead, 1982; Johnston, 1992, 1993a). However, parentification was identified in 10% of the mother–child dyads examined in a study of black incarcerated mothers (LaPointe, Picker & Harris, 1985). This type of role reversal is more commonly seen in the children of impaired parents, including the children of severely substance-dependent parents; these children assume a parental role in the family even when the parent is present. They are essentially neglected, and their assumption of adult responsibilities is an indication that the parent is not fulfilling the parental role.

Rejection of Limits. An important role for parents is to guide children's behavior and development through encouragement and limit setting. When children are young, parents fulfill this role in the home through intimate interactions. Young children learn that parents set limits out of love and concern, and this understanding foster their acceptance of the limits parents and other adults set in the larger, more public arena of social conduct. Parental incarceration may undermine this process. Older children recognize that their parents voluntarily engaged in the activities that resulted in parent–child separation. This leads them to reasonably question their parents' love and concern, the basis upon which they agreed to accept limits on their behavior. In addition, the testing of limits on social conduct is a normal activity of adolescents. Children in this age group are therefore very likely to reject parental limit setting and, by extension, the limits set by other adults in parental roles. It is important to understand that rejection of limit setting by parents and other adults does not represent a confusion about values among older children of prisoners. There is no moral component to this behavior, which is a reaction to feelings of grief and loss.

Effects of Enduring Trauma in Early Adolescence. Trauma-reactive behaviors like aggression and anxiety states appear in middle childhood (Johnston, 1992). They are difficult to manage for both the adults who work with traumatized children and the children themselves. When intervention does not occur as these children get older, they may attempt to pattern or organize their behaviors to make them more manageable. Activities like team sports, marching bands, orchestras, youth choirs, and boys/girls clubs are often unavailable to older children from highly stressed families, who attend failing schools, and who live in poor communities. For some highly traumatized children, aggression, disorganized behavior, and poor social skills interfere with the ability to participate in these activities even when they are available. As a result, these children may adopt other patterns of behavior that fulfill their needs for an increased sense of control, achievement, and peer acceptance.

Patterns of asocial behaviors (lying and stealing), gang activity, and interpersonal violence may meet all or some of these needs. Some examples:

> The daughter of a drug-addicted parent has been lying about her family circumstances since early childhood. She has learned to express her anger and grief with this form of verbal aggression. This behavior helped her to feel more successful and more in control of her life as a young child. In adolescence, she has begun to use more organized expressions of verbal aggression, such as forging her mother's name on notes to her school, to achieve a sense of control.

> An angry child from a home torn by domestic violence has been aggressive since he was in elementary school. Physical intimidation and fighting with his peers has allowed him to feel a greater sense of control during middle childhood; as an adolescent, he has become increasingly aggressive and abusive in his relationships with females.

> An anxious child of a highly stressed, immigrant family has been "hyperactive" and aggressive throughout his school years. As an adolescent, gang activity allows him to pattern his physical aggression and anxiety in ways that make his behavior less disorganized and help him to feel more in control.

These stories are tragedies because the children's development of patterned behaviors like interpersonal violence and theft represents an adaptive response to the threatening environments in which they have been raised. These responses allow them to be more effective than they would be with emotional illness or other forms of withdrawal. However, although these patterned behaviors may help children to cope with stress and address developmental tasks, they typically become compulsive and ultimately maladaptive. Maladaptive coping mechanisms are common among children of prisoners and other offenders (Johnston, 1992, 1993a, 1993b).

Summary. Some adolescents are able to overcome the absence of a parent, caregiver stress, lack of finances, stigma, and/or changes of placement with their own internal and external resources. Others may supplement the developmental imperatives of adolescence with the effects of these experiences to organize their behavior into stable, productive patterns. However, many children of prisoners and other offenders will organize their behavior into patterns that are ultimately maladaptive. Some children will also reject limitations on their behavior, in reaction to parental activities that lead them to question their parents' love and concern.

Late Adolescence (15 to 18 Years)

The developmental tasks of older teenagers are to achieve a cohesive identity and to develop the related ability to successfully engage in adult work and relationships. Teenagers must learn to think formally and abstractly, to acquire work skills, to function in sexual relationships, and to become independent and self-sufficient. However, the later teenage years are also a time of crisis and confusion, in which children must resolve conflicts within themselves, within their relationships, and between themselves and society.

Teenage children of prisoners typically have experienced a lifetime of disruptions related to their parent's criminal activities, arrests, and incarcerations. The cumulative effects of repeated parent–child separations, enduring trauma, and/or inadequate care may be expressed in their school performance, legal socialization, or other conduct. Intergenerational crime and incarceration begins to appear as a significant pattern in families when children reach this age.

Effects of Parent–Child Separation: Decreased Likelihood of Reunification. While some researchers (Prison Visitation Project, 1993) have suggested that teenagers visit their incarcerated parents less frequently than younger children, this is not borne out in the literature (McGowan & Blumenthal, 1978; Stanton, 1980). In spite of the fact that they visit and appear interested in reunifying with their parents, the cumulative effects of multiple parent–child separations due to parental incarceration reduce the likelihood of reunification for these older children (Morris, 1965). McGowan and Blumenthal (1978) found that incarcerated mothers' plans for immediate reunification with their children declined from 73.3% for infants to 41.7% for teenagers.

Effects of Enduring Trauma: Intergenerational Crime and Incarceration. Traumatized children who have organized their reactive behaviors into maladaptive coping patterns are at extremely high risk for delinquency. Many maladaptive coping patterns, like theft and sexual aggression, are illegal in themselves. Others, like substance abuse and gang involvement, have a strong association with crime. Two separate studies found that children of offenders are far more likely than other children to enter the criminal justice system. Twenty-nine percent of the 11- to 14-year-olds in the Children of Offenders Study (Johnston, 1992, 1993a) had been arrested and/or incarcerated. The Jailed Mothers Study (Johnston, 1991) found that 11.4% of children of participating women had been arrested and 10% had been incarcerated.

The Center for Children of Incarcerated Parents has developed a model for intergenerational crime and incarceration, illustrated in Table 5.7. According to this model, children exposed to enduring trauma develop trauma-reactive behaviors. These behaviors are disorganized and difficult to manage, particularly in a context marked by parent–child separation and lack of an adequate quality of care. Traumatized children attempt to cope with challenges and increase their sense of control by organizing these behaviors into patterns. When options for utilizing adaptive patterns of coping behaviors do not exist, trauma-reactive children will chose accessible but maladaptive coping mechanisms, such as gang activity, that meet the same needs. The long-term outcome of most maladaptive coping mechanisms is delinquency or adult crime.

This sequence of events typically begins in early childhood and results in arrest in adolescence or young adulthood (Johnston, 1993b). Earlier research on the effects of parental crime support this theory (Breckinridge & Abbott, 1912; Gluek & Glueck, 1950; Otterstrom, 1946; McCord & McCord, 1958; Robins, West, & Herjanic, 1975). However, the sequence is not unique to the children of offenders. When it occurs in other children, it produces first-generation offenders. When it occurs among children of prisoners, it produces intergenerational crime and incarceration.

Other Effects. Experience with parental crime, arrest, and incarceration may also produce effects on patterns of legal socialization, sexual behavior, and substance abuse among older children of offenders.

Legal Socialization. Stanton (1980) studied the legal socialization of the children of jailed mothers. She found that children who had not witnessed their mothers' arrests had generally positive impressions of the police, but that most children who had been present at such arrests had mixed (20%) or negative (47%) impressions. Stanton identified an important difference in these children's attitudes toward police by age: only 33% of the older teenagers of women offenders would call upon the police for assistance, even in situations of danger, compared to 83% of children under the age of 14.

Table 5.7
Intergenerational Behaviors, Crime and Incarceration

Childhood Trauma	Emotional Response	Reactive Behavior	Coping Pattern	Criminal Activity
Example: Physical Abuse	Anger	Physical aggression	Fighting with peers	Assault
Example: Parent–child separation	Sadness, grief	Withdrawal	Substance Abuse	Drug possession
Example: Witness to violence	Anxiety	Hypervigilence	Gang activity	Accessory to homicide
Example: Parental substance abuse	Anger	Verbal aggression	Asocial behaviors (lying and stealing)	Fraud
Example: Sexual molestation	Fear, anxiety	Sexualized behavior	Promiscuity	Prostitution
Children are vulnerable to trauma when exposed to dangers or when their families cannot protect them. There is no direct relationship between specific traumas and specific posttraumatic emotional and behavioral reactions.	Childhood traumas normally produce emotional responses. There is no direct relationship between specific emotional responses to trauma and subsequent reactive behaviors.	Without intervention, posttraumatic emotional responses lead to *reactive* behaviors. Specific reactive behaviors appear to be related to development of specific patterns of coping behaviors.	Without intervention, reactive behaviors become fixed in patterns that help children to cope. Fixed patterns of coping behaviors may become compulsive when children have no other resources for support. Although they may initially be adaptive for highly stressed children, the compulsive coping behaviors that occur after trauma are ultimately maladaptive because they often lead to crime and incarceration.	

Sexual Behavior. Problems related to sexual behavior appear to be minimal among older children of offenders. Jose-Kampfner of the Children's Visitation Project in Michigan has reported (1991) that she has seen a small number of teenage girls become pregnant after their mothers were sentenced to long terms of imprisonment. Kampfner speculates that these pregnancies represent "emotional replacements" for the mothers, rather than the results of sexual acting out. This interpretation is supported by other sources. Bloom and Steinhart (1993) found that teenage pregnancy among their female children was a concern of only 1.1% of the incarcerated mothers and 1.5% of the caregivers surveyed. Johnston (1993a) also noted that neither caregivers nor school officials identified sexual acting out as a problem among the teenagers in the Children of Offenders Study; there have been no pregnancies among girls who entered the study at 11 to 14 years of age and have been followed for 3 years. Similarly, 50% of the 12- to 18-year-old children studied by Virginia's Prison Visitation Project (1993) were reported to be sexually inactive. These findings suggest that the children of offenders may be less likely than their peers to engage in sexual activity as a form of acting out behavior.

Early Substance Abuse. The substance abuse literature suggests that children of alcoholics and drug addicts are more likely than other children to have their own substance abuse problems (Bauman & Doherty, 1983; Bohman, Sigrardsson & Cloninger, 1981; Goodwin, Schulsinger, Hermausen, Guze & Winokur, 1973). Because the majority of offenders are substance abusers, it is reasonable to assume that substance abuse would be a significant problem among their children. But this does not appear to be the case.

Bloom and Steinhart (1993) found that drug and alcohol problems among the children of women prisoners were a concern of only 1.3% of incarcerated mothers and 3.0% of the caregivers of their children. None of the children followed by the Children of Offenders Study (Johnston, 1993a) have been referred for a substance abuse problem during the first 3 years of that project. Finally, the Prison Visitation Project (1993) found that 84% of the teenage children of incarcerated parents they studied were not involved in drug or alcohol use. Indeed, none of the studies cited in this chapter have identified substance abuse as significant problem among the minor children of prisoners.

Summary. The cumulative effects of parental crime, arrest, and incarceration are seen in teenagers. Their experiences have left many with negative attitudes toward law enforcement and the criminal justice system. The parents of many have served multiple jail and/or prison sentences and will not reunify with them. A large but unknown proportion will engage in criminal activity; about one in 10 will have been incarcerated themselves as juveniles and/or adults.

Special Issues

Numerous issues deserving special consideration arise in a discussion of the children of incarcerated parents. Two related issues merit general discussion, the effects of shame and stigma on children of offenders, and the children of first-time prisoners.

Shame and Stigma

Much of the literature on parental incarceration has identified social stigma and/or shame as an important issue for children of prisoners (Bakker, Morris & Janus, 1978; Blackwell, 1959; Gabel, 1992; Hannon et al., 1984; Henriques, 1982; Sack et al., 1976; Swan, 1981). However, none of these reports is based on direct examination of the children in question. Studies that more closely or directly examined incarcerated parents and their children have found shame or social stigma to be major themes among the concerns of the children's caregivers, but not among the concerns of incarcerated parents or the children themselves.

In his study of imprisoned women and their children, Zalba (1964) found significant differences between what children were told by their caregivers, what they believed, and what they told others about their mothers' absence. While four out of 10 children knew that their mother was incarcerated, only 6% gave this explanation to others. Zalba reported that many caregivers admitted that the children did not believe the various explanations given for maternal absence, and also tried to avoid the issue. The report found that "it was evident that families considered it inappropriate [for children] to discuss the mother's whereabouts" (p. 86).

Schneller (1978) surveyed 93 black men imprisoned in the District of Columbia, and their wives. He asked about the extent to which the children of these couples had lost or gained friends, had been insulted, felt the need to avoid people or places, or found themselves embarrassed as a result of their father's incarceration. In every category, 15% or less of the children reported that they suffered these forms of stigma or shame. Most concerns about shame and stigma were found among a small group of wives.

Baunach (1979) devoted a significant part of her report on imprisoned mothers to what and how children knew about their mother's incarceration. The 196 women studied did not identify shame or social stigma as problems for their children, over two-thirds of whom were aware of their mother's whereabouts.

Recent studies and those that have directly examined the children of prisoners have not found shame or social stigma to be a significant concern of incarcerated parents or a significant factor in producing the effects of parental incarceration (Bloom & Steinhart, 1992; Johnston, 1991, 1992, 1993a). This may be because parental arrest and incarceration is increasingly common in the communities in which many offenders live, and because the families of many offenders have several members who have been arrested and/or incarcerated too.

The Children of First-Time Prisoners

Most sentences to incarceration are not the result of first offenses. About nine out of 10 state and federal prisoners, for example, have prior convictions (USDJ, 1993). Therefore, while about 28% of female and 19% of male prisoners are incarcerated for the first time, their children are likely to have had prior experiences with parental crime, arrest, and detention.

Nevertheless, there are some differences between these and other families of offenders. Morris (1965) found that social stigma and shame related to paternal incarceration were mainly felt by the families of first offenders, and that these reactions occurred immediately after the father's imprisonment. Similar findings were reported by Lowenstein (1986), who concluded that stigma was a special problem for children of prisoners convicted of atypical offenses (e.g., sex crimes, tax fraud, and embezzlement) because these children were unfamiliar with crime and the criminal justice system. The concerns of parents and children in these categories may be closer to those of some of the children's caregivers and mainstream society.

Conclusions

Parental crime, arrest, and incarceration interfere with the ability of children to successfully master developmental tasks and to overcome the effects of enduring trauma, parent–child separation, and an inadequate quality of care. The combination of these effects produce serious long-term outcomes, including intergenerational incarceration. Children of prisoners and other offenders have multiple service needs that human services professionals and the criminal justice system must begin to meet in order to reduce the profound risk the experience of parental incarceration presents for these children and for society.

References

Adalist-Estrin, A. (1986). Parenting . . . from behind bars. *Family Resource Coalition Report*, 5(1):12–13.

Adalist-Estrin, A. (1993, October). *Moral development and attachment: Disruptions that create cycles of criminal behavior.* Paper presented at the annual conference of the Family and Corrections Network, Quebec City, Quebec.

Bakker, L. J., Morris, B. A., & Janus, L. M. (1978). Hidden victims of crime. *Social Work*, 23:143–148.

Barry, E. (1989). Recent developments: Pregnant prisoners. *Harvard Women's Law Journal*, 12:189–205.

Bauman, P. S., & Dougherty, F. E. (1983). Drug-addicted mothers' parenting and child development. *International Journal of the Addictions*, 18(3):291–302.

Baunach, P. J. (1979, November). *Mothering from behind prison walls*. Paper presented at the annual meeting of the American Society of Criminology, Philadelphia.

Blackwell, J. E. (1959). *The effects of involuntary separation on selected families of men committed to prison from Spokane, Washington*. Unpublished doctoral dissertation, State College of Washington.

Bloom, B., & Steinhart, D. (1993). *Why punish the children? A reappraisal of the children of incarcerated mothers in America*. San Francisco: National Council on Crime and Delinquency.

Bohman, M, Sigrardsson, S. & Cloninger, C. R. (1981). Maternal inheritance of alcohol abuse. *Archives of General Psychiatry*, 38:965–969.

Bowlby, J. (1983). *Attachment and loss*. New York: Basic Books.

Breckinridge, S. P., & Abbott, E. (1912). Chicago housing problems. *American Journal of Sociology*, 16:289–308.

Brett, E., Spitzer, R.C. & Williams, J. B. W. (1988). DSM-III-R criteria for post-traumatic stress disorder. *American Journal of Psychiatry*, 145(10):1232–1236.

Bush, M., & Goldman, H. (1982). The psychological parenting and permanency principles in child welfare: A reappraisal and critique. *American Journal of Orthopsychiatry*, 52(2):223–235.

Catan, L. (1992). Infants with mothers in prison. In R. Shaw (Ed.), *Prisoners' children*. London: Routledge. Pages 13–28.

Children's Defense Fund. (1978). *Children without homes*. Washington, DC: Author.

Cordero, L., Hines, S., Shibley, A., & Lauton, M. B. (1991). Duration of incarceration and perinatal outcome. *Obstetrics and Gynecology*, 78:641–645.

Doyle, J. S., & Bauer, S. K. (1989). Post-traumatic stress disorder in children. *Journal of Traumatic Stress*, 2(3):275–288.

Duncan, G. Brooks-Gunn, J., & Klebanov, P. K. (1994). Economics deprivation and early childhood development. *Child Development*, 65:296–318.

Egley, C. C., Miller, D. E., Granatos, J. L. & Fogel, C. I. (1992). Outcome of pregnancy during imprisonment. *Journal of Reproductive Medicine*, 37(2):131–134.

Fanshel, D., & Shinn, E.B. (1982). *Children in foster care*. New York: Columbia University Press.

Friedman, S., & Esselstyn, T.C. (1965). The adjustment of children to parental absence due to imprisonment. *Family Relations*, 30:83–88.

Fritsch, T. A., & Burkhead, J. D. (1982). Behavioral reactions of children to parental absence due to imprisonment. *Family Relations*, 30:83–88.

Furman, E. (1983). Studies in childhood bereavement. *Canadian Journal of Psychiatry*, 28(4):241–247.

Gabel, S. (1992), Behavioral problems in sons of incarcerated or otherwise absent fathers: The issue of separation. *Family Process*, 31:303–314.

Gabel, S., & Shindledecker, R. (1992). Incarceration in parents of day hospital youth: relationship to parental substance abuse and suspected child abuse/maltreatment. *International Journal of Partial Hospitalization* 8(1):77–87.

Gibbs, C. (1971). The effect of the imprisonment of women upon their children. *British Journal of Criminology*, 11:113–130.

Glueck, S., & Glueck, E. (1950). *Unraveling Juvenile Delinquency*. Cambridge, Massachusettes: Harvard University Press.

Glick, R. M., & Neto, V. V. (1977). *National study of women's correctional programs*. Washington, DC: National Institute of Law Enforcement and Criminal Justice.

Goldstein, A., Freud, A. & Solnit, A. (1973). *Beyond the best interests of the child*. New York: Free Press.

Goodwin, D. W., Schulsinger, F., Hermausen, L., Guze, S., & Winokur, G. (1973). Alcoholic problems in adoptees raised apart from alcoholic parents. *Archives of General Psychiatry*, 28:238–243.

Halleck, S. (1967). *Psychiatry and the dilemmas of crime*. New York: Harper and Row.

Hannon, G., Martin, D., & Martin, M. (1984). Incarceration in the family: Adjustment to change. *Family Therapy*, 11:253–260.

Henriques, Z. W. (1982). *Imprisoned mothers and their children*. Washington, DC: University Press of America.

Hunter, S. M. (1984). The relationship between women offenders and their children. *Dissertation Abstracts International*, (University Microfilms No. 8424436).

Johnston, D. (1991). *Jailed mothers*. Pasadena, CA: Pacific Oaks Center for Children of Incarcerated Parents.

Johnston, D. (1992). *Children of offenders*. Pasadena, CA: Pacific Oaks Center for Children of Incarcerated Parents.

Johnston, D. (1993a). *Children of the Therapeutic Intervention Project*. Pasadena, CA: Pacific Oaks Center for Children of Incarcerated Parents.

Johnston, D. (1993b). *Intergenerational incarceration*. Pasadena, CA: Pacific Oaks Center for Children of Incarcerated Parents.

Jose-Kampfner, C. (1991, May). *Children of Women Prisoners*. Presentation at the 6th National Roundtable for Women in Prison, Chicago, Illinois.

Kadushin, A. (1974). Beyond the best interests of the child: An essay review. *Social Services Review*, 48(4):508–516.

Kelmer, M. L., & Clifford, L. (1962). Conditions associated with emotional maladjustment among children in care. *Education Review*, 14(2):112–123.

King, L. N., & Whitman, S. (1981). Morbidity and mortality among prisoners: An epidemiological review. *Journal of Prison Health*, 1:7.

Koban, L. A. (1983). Parents in prison: A comparative analysis of the effects of incarceration on the families of men and women. *Research in Law, Deviance and Social Control*, 5:171–183.

Kolman, A. S. (1983). Support and control patterns of inmate mothers: A pilot study. *Prison Journal*, 63(2):155–166.

Krupnick, J. (1984). Bereavement during childhood and adolescence. In M. Osterweiss (Eds.), *Bereavement: Reactions, consequences and care*. Washington, DC: National Academy Press.

Lamb, F. (1977). Father–infant and mother–infant interaction in the first year of life. *Child Development*, 48:167–181.

LaPointe, V, Picker, O. & Harris, B. F. (1985). Enforced family separation: A descriptive analysis of some experiences of children of black imprisoned mothers. In Spencer, A. (ed.) *Beginnings: The social and affective development of black children.* Hillsdale, NJ: Erlbaum. 239–255.

Littner, N. (1981). The importance of the natural parents to the child in placement. In P.A. Sinanoglu & A.N. Maluccio (Eds.), *Parents of children in placement.* New York: Child Welfare League. Pages 269–276.

Lowenstein, A. (1986). Temporary single parenthood: The case of prisoners' families. *Family Relations,* 36:79–85.

McCall, C., & Shaw, N. (1985). *Pregnancy in prison: A needs assessment of prenatal outcome in three California penal institutions* (Contract No. 84-84085). Sacramento, CA: Department of Health Services, Maternal and Child Health Branch.

McCord, J., & McCord, N. (1958). The effects of parental role model of criminality. *Journal of Social Issues,* 14:66–75.

McGowan, B. G., & Blumenthal, K. L. (1978). *Why punish the children?* Hackensack, NJ: National Council on Crime and Delinquency.

Miller, E. (1986). *Street woman.* Philadelphia: Temple University Press.

Miller, R. E. (1984). Nationwide profile of female inmate substance involvement. *Journal of Psychoactive Drugs,* 16:319.

Morris, P. (1965). *Prisoners and their Families.* New York: Hart.

Osborne Association. (1993). *How can I help?* New York: Author.

Otterstrom, S. (1946). Juvenile delinquency and parental criminality. *ACTA Pediatrica Scandinavica,* 33(Suppl. 5):1–326.

Payton, J. B., & Krocker-Tuskan, M. (1988). Children's reactions to loss of a parent by violence. *Journal of the American Academy of Child and Adolescent Psychiatry,* 27(5):563–566.

Prison Visitation Project. (1993). *Needs assessment of children whose parents are incarcerated.* Richmond, Virginia: Department of Mental Health, Mental Retardation & Substance Abuse Services.

Robins, L. N., (1975). Arrests and delinquency in two generations: A study of black urban families and their children. *Journal Child Psychology and Psychiatry,* 16:125–140.

Rutter, M. (1981). *Maternal deprivation reconsidered.* Oxford: Oxford University Press.

Rutter, M. (1983). *Children of sick parents.* Oxford: Oxford University Press.

Sack, W. H. (1977). Children of imprisoned fathers. *Psychiatry,* 40:163–174.

Sack, W. H., Seidler, T. & Harris, S. (1976). Children of imprisoned parents: A psychosocial exploration. *American Journal of Orthopsychiatry,* 46(4):618–628.

Schneller, D. P. (1978). *The prisoner's family.* San Francisco: R&E Research Associates.

Schwartz, M. C., & Weintraub, J. (1974). The prisoner's wife: A study in crisis. *Federal Probation,* 38:20–26.

Shelton, B., Armstrong, F. & Cochran, S. E. (1983). Childbearing while incarcerated. *American Journal of Maternal Child Nursing,* 8:23.

Stanton, A. (1980). *When mothers go to jail.* Lexington, MA: Lexington Books.

Swan, A. (1981). *Families of black prisoners: Survival and progress*. Boston: G. K. Hall.

U.S. Department of Justice. (1992). *Prisons and prisoners in the United States* (Report No. NCJ-137002). Washington, DC: Bureau of Justice Statistics.

U.S. Department of Justice. (1993). *Survey of state prison inmates* (Report No. NCJ-136949). Washington, DC: Bureau of Justice Statistics.

Virginia Commission on Youth. (1992). *The study of the needs of children whose parents are incarcerated*. Richmond, VA: Author.

Zalba, S. (1964). *Women prisoners and their families*. Sacramento, CA: Department of Social Welfare and Department of Corrections.

6

Post-Traumatic Stress Reactions in Children of Imprisoned Mothers

Christina Jose Kampfner

I began to work with women in prison 14 years ago, and the first thing that struck me was that the women were always talking about the children they had left on the "outside." These mothers were very concerned about their children and often felt powerless in the face of prison restrictions and the minimal contact that they were allowed with the outside world. After I completed my dissertation, a study of incarcerated women, I asked my informants what I could do for them to repay their generosity. All of them wanted to see their children, wanted to know if there was anything I could do to arrange a visit. No one asked for food or candy, jewelry or money. Each wanted only to see her child, to have a visit without the unnaturalness of normal visiting hours, without the usual restrictions of movement that they were subject to in the noisy and distracting visiting rooms. These women loved their children so much!

Issues Raised by the Separation of Incarcerated Mothers and Their Children

Bonds between Women Prisoners and Their Children

Children suffer deeply when their mother is taken from them and imprisoned. The vast majority of these women were the primary caregivers for their children. These children spent most of their time with their mothers, and looked first to their mothers for support, even when the women were still dependent on their own mothers. When this was not the case, when the mother was often absent from the children's home or "neglectful" by the standards of the middle class, she was still of integral importance to the lives of her children. For example, Louis, a young man whose mother had been incarcerated years before and who was himself in prison at the time of our interview, explained:

89

> My mother was a drug addict when she was on the street and she would buy us anything we wanted but did not have time to spend with us. She would drop us here and there, and I used to wonder if she loved us. The day the cops came to take my mother for questioning sticks in my mind as a very sad, frightening day. We went to my grandmother's house. We did not see our mother for another year. My grandmother is an alcoholic and has been one since I can remember. She did not have time to look after us. She was very busy drinking. I missed my mother very much. I used to think of her all the time. I felt left behind. My mother used to write to me and stuff but I did not want to answer her letters. I was angry and missed her. She would tell me all this stuff about what I should do but she was not there to help me sort out how to do it. I wanted her to go to my basketball games. I used to be very good at basketball, you know, but I did not have anybody to cheer for me that could help me continue.

This young man felt very much alone when his mother was taken away. Although she was by no means a good mother by most standards, he had very strong feelings for her and her absence from his life was traumatic. After the loss of his mother, Louis began to run away from his grandmother's house and eventually dropped out of school. At the time of our interview, he was serving a life sentence.

As providers, we need to understand the deep emotional bonds that exist between children and their mothers. Often the pain that children experience because of forced separation from their mothers is ignored because it is assumed that the women involved could not be good mothers if they ended up in prison. The necessary role these mothers play in the lives of their children is discounted.

Traumatic Experiences

The long road that children travel between maternal arrest and maternal imprisonment is filled with traumatic experiences. Children are perpetually concerned about the possible outcomes of their mothers' cases, unsure if they will return, worried that they will be swept off to prison for the rest of their lives. Furthermore, they are forced to live without their mothers. Just as they are unsure of the outcome of their mothers' cases, they are unsure about how they should adjust, and about what they should expect in the future. These feelings add to the instability of situations in which they move from home to home, from caregiver to caregiver.

During this process children's emotional needs are essentially ignored. These children witness their mothers' powerlessness and violation. Such experiences often leave children feeling extremely vulnerable; this is especially true for young children who have trusted in the omnipotence of their mother and her capacity to provide emotional sustenance even under duress. Furthermore, police officers are frequently insensitive to the terror that young children experience during maternal arrests, and will subject children to the same kind of searches and arrest tactics that they use on adults.

The criminal justice system fails to keep accurate records of the existence of offenders' dependent children, let alone who they are and who is caring for them. Arrested mothers lose almost all control over the lives and well-being of their children. Because they fear the unknown, most women will not choose foster care arrangements at the time of arrest. One prisoner explained, "I had no choice. The choices were my mother's, where at least I knew what kind of home it was, or someone else that I would not know." Another agreed: "When I was arrested, the only person that offered to take care of my daughter was my aunt. I had mixed feelings, because I was so unhappy growing up with her, but I had no choice. It was either her or foster care."

It is often suggested that children of prisoners should become wards of the state. But for most women, turning to the social services represents a huge failure. The women feel that the services are inadequate, and that the agencies do not recognize the special needs of children. The women were concerned that the social services would not be careful to put black children with black families, or Latinos with Latinos. They feared they would never see their children again, and that the children would feel that their family had failed them.

In addition, foster care does not necessarily offer stability. Children are often moved from home to home, or live in less than ideal situations. One mother reported: "While I had been in the county jail, they made my son a ward of the court. They put him in a foster home and a daycare center. Then he went back to a foster care home. The foster mother there got sick and he was changed to another placement. . . ." Another woman was concerned that her child would share her childhood experiences: "I grew up in a foster care home. I know what they are like. A kid goes through a lot of changes. They used to beat me because I did not function the way they wanted me to. It hurts me to think that my child is probably going through the same pain I had."

When children are placed in foster care, it can take 6 months for mothers to discover where they are and even more time before a judge can grant visiting privileges for the children. These privileges can be removed at any time. If children appear to be upset before or during the course of a visit, this is seen as evidence that the visits are bad for them. Consequently, social workers or foster parents can ask that visitation be suspended.

Women serving long prison terms are often especially leery of state intervention on behalf of their children. They are well aware that most state facilities for children are grossly overcrowded and underfunded. Incarcerated women with long sentences frequently lose custody of their children after a 2-year period. If women have family members who are willing to take responsibility for childcare, the courts will often grant temporary custody to these relatives. However, many of these relatives, like the women in prison, are poor and lack resources to support the children. Very often the maternal grandmothers will struggle to support their daughters' children by means of small welfare or Social Security allowances. The children are relegated to an existence at poverty level; most welfare payments do not provide an income that is adequate to sustain family unity in situations of parental incarceration. Many families are permanently dissolved.

A mother who lost custody of her child recalled, "I begged the social worker for months to take my child to a psychologist. He never saw me again after the arrest. He has to talk about it with someone. The worker said that the foster parents did not think [the child] needed it. They thought he should forget. The worker said he was doing fine. He may be doing fine now, but who knows in 10 years? Maybe it will all come out at once." The children of women prisoners are often figuratively homeless. They go where there is someone who will take them in, and their situation changes with the availability of care. One child wrote to her mother, "Dear Mama, come home, I love you, and anyway don't nobody else wants Harry and me" (Harry is her little brother). Many children of prisoners report having similar feelings.

The Conspiracy of Silence

Frequently, children whose mothers are in prison are not allowed to talk about their traumatic experiences. Their caregivers attempt to downplay their pain, or even mandate silence about their mother's crime, arrest, and incarceration. Often the families of women prisoners feel that the incarceration of their relative gives the family a bad image. Or new caregivers may believe that they can write the experience out of the lives of the children by ignoring it. Children in these circumstances suffer the consequences of maternal imprisonment every day, for they themselves are sentenced to a "forced silence" that compounds the isolating effects of their treatment by the criminal justice and social service systems. This conspiracy of silence exists in spite of the fact that children need to talk about their feelings in order to overcome the effects of traumatic experiences. Forced silences limit the support that children can find following trauma because they fear repercussions if they speak about forbidden topics. Forced silences therefore shape children's subsequent reactions to trauma and may have a lifelong effect.

Some children are not informed about their mothers' whereabouts. They may be told that their mothers are "away at college" or "in the hospital." These kind of lies underestimate the acuity of children. After visiting her mother, a child said that she had a secret that could not be told to her grandmother. "This," she explained, "is a not a hospital, it is a prison. My grandmother thinks my mother is sick, but she's really in prison." One 11-year-old said, "My grandmother tells me to forget about it, and just not think about my mother, but the more I try not to think about my mother, the harder it is. . . ."

Mother–child visits may improve the situation, but they often do not take place. Traveling expenses are often more than families can afford and, because most states have only one women's correctional facility, mothers' prisons can be up to 600 miles away from the homes of their children. Contact is further diminished when caregivers cannot afford to pay for collect telephone calls from imprisoned mothers to their children. The children cannot call the prison, and many incarcerated women can only make collect calls. It is common for phone lines in the homes of caregivers to be disconnected because they cannot pay the bills that accrued for collect phone calls between imprisoned women and their children.

Ashamed, instructed not to talk about their experiences, and unable to communicate with their mothers, children of incarcerated women are forced to work through their reactions to the traumatic events of their lives in silence.

A Study of Traumatic Stress Reactions

The combination of the severance of the mother–child bond, other traumatic events, and a "conspiracy of silence" that prevents children of prisoners from being able to talk about these experiences suggests that they may be subject to acute traumatic stress reactions. In order to examine this possibility, and to examine other effects of maternal incarceration, I conducted a study of children who have lost their mothers to imprisonment.

Methods

The first part of the study compared children of incarcerated mothers with children from the same high-risk background whose mothers were not in prison. Children were matched for age, race, sex, and social class. The goals of this study were (1) to identify the range of psychological and educational difficulties that are experienced by children of incarcerated mothers; (2) to identify factors that increase the risk of these difficulties; and (3) to identify sources of resiliency in these children. The experimental group included 36 children and their caregivers who were participants in a Children's Visitation Program at a women's prison. The control group was created with the help of a multicultural research team. Interviews were conducted in the children's homes; consent for participation of the experimental group of children was obtained from both the incarcerated mothers and the children's caregivers, while consent for participation of the control group was obtained from their parents or caregivers in the home. A standardized instrument for assessing child behavior was used to measure the parent/caregiver's perception of each child's competence in a variety of domains.

The second part of the study was conducted among children of imprisoned mothers and focused on their behavior while visiting their mothers in prison. Observations of mother–child prison visits were conducted during a monthly program of special visits. During special visits mothers were free to move around the visiting room, to hug and hold their children, to take their children to the bathroom, and to do their hair. Children were free to move around the visiting room and to interact or play with other visiting children. These activities are not allowed during regular visits. Uniformed guards were not present in the visiting area, although there was a nonuniformed correctional staff member in the room. Special visits lasted 3 hours. Systematic, naturalistic observations, self-reports from participants, and in-depth interviews with seven children were the principle methods of data collection. Observations of 50 children who participated in a weekend children's visitation program on Saturdays were collected over a period of 6 months. Mothers of participating children were interviewed about the childrens' experiences during their arrests. The children's caregivers were interviewed and asked about child behavior in the home.

Results

There are significant differences between children of women prisoners and children of similar backgrounds whose mothers remain in the home. Children of incarcerated mothers have sustained recall of traumatic events. Even though many of the children in the experimental group had been separated from their mothers for 2 to 3 years at the time of their interviews, each child could still vividly remember his or her mother's arrest and his or her experiences in the courtroom. There was also a striking difference in perceived resources between the two groups. Many children of incarcerated mothers reported having no emotional supports; they could not identify people who might be sources of support, and they felt that they had no one with whom they could talk about their mothers. This was not true of children in the control group.

The majority (85%) of the mothers of children interviewed for the second part of the study were women of color and single heads of households. Eight out of 10 were between 13 and 18 years of age when they gave birth to their children. Half were the primary caregivers of their children prior to incarceration. About 45% shared their childcare responsibilities with their own mothers prior to incarceration.

The children observed for this study ranged in age from 5 to 16 years.

Seventy percent of this group had been present at their mothers' arrests. Eighty percent of the children lived in the inner city. Almost all came from low-income families; the mothers of 85% had been unemployed prior to arrest and 85% were living in poverty at the time of their interview. Five children had changed homes two or more times while their mother was incarcerated.

About 75% of the children studied reported symptoms including depression, difficulty in sleeping, concentration problems, and flashbacks about their mothers' crimes or arrests. Four of the seven children interviewed in depth reported hearing their mother's voice calling to them after she had gone to prison. A common problem for most of the children in the study was poor school performance. Children reported difficulty in concentrating, daydreaming about their mothers, and lack of motivation as their main problems. One child said, "The teacher asked me if I don't understand her. I told her that I hear her, but then I start thinking about what happened to my mommy and I can't concentrate."

Seventy-five percent of the caregivers interviewed reported similar symptoms among the children in their care. Only a minority of the caregivers, however, attributed these symptoms to the loss of the children's mothers. The majority identified the problem as the children's misbehavior. The case histories of four of the seven children interviewed in depth were characteristic of the larger group of children of incarcerated mothers:

Case 1: Tom, a 5-year-old boy, was present when his mother and other adults he knew were arrested for possession of drugs. The police burst into the apartment with their guns drawn and made everyone, including Tom, stand against the wall to search them for drugs and weapons. Tom was frightened and started to cry. When he attempted to go to his mother, the police officers prevented him from approaching her. Before she was taken away, Tom's mother was allowed to console him. Tom did not see his mother again for 11 months while she was in the county jail awaiting trial. During this time Tom developed behavior problems and an eating disorder.

Case 2: Leonard, an only child, had lived with his mother just down the street from the house where he now lived with his grandmother at the time of the interview. In his interview, Leonard said, "My mother and I were always together." The night of the crime, Leonard's mother and her friends were having a party. Leonard was playing when he heard loud screaming and yelling coming from the kitchen. His mother was fighting with her boyfriend, and they had both picked up knives. Leonard does not remember what happened from that moment until the police arrived, but his mother had stabbed her boyfriend to death. Leonard recalled, "It was blood all over the place. I had his blood on my hands. They asked me what happened and I told them what I knew." The police took his mother away; he remembers begging the officers to let him go with her. Leonard was taken in by his maternal grandmother; his mother remained in jail because the family did not have enough money to bail her out.

She was eventually sentenced to 10 years in prison. After the night of the crime, Leonard did not see his mother for 8 months. He says that when he finally saw his mother, "I kept looking at her hands, thinking that those are the hands that killed him." Leonard had nightmares, heard his mother's voice talking to him, and had the "shakes" every time he saw the house where he used to live with his mother. He has done poorly in school, reporting constant preoccupation with thoughts of his mother and trouble concentrating. His grandmother told me that he "cannot sit still." Leonard also reported that he was worried he was losing his mind because he saw blood on his hands, but when he tried to tell his grandmother, she told him not to think about it and it would go away. Additionally, his grandmother has instructed him not to tell anybody about what has happened or where his mother is. Leonard reported feeling burdened by this secret, especially when other children at school talked freely about their mothers.

Case 3: At the time of her mother's arrest, 12-year-old Kristin was returning home from school. She was met by her 7-year-old brother, who told her that the police were searching their apartment and were going to take their mother away. She remembers thinking, "I will not let them take my mother away." She entered the apartment, ran to her mother's side, and hugged her. The police demanded to know who she was. Kristin says, "I was terrified. I thought, 'They will not take her unless they take me, too.' I held on for as long as I could. My mother's girlfriend came and took us away after the police took my mother. The information about her mother's crime remained a secret. She thought her mother must have done something very bad, and that the police who took her away would kill her. She felt powerless in this situation. Kristin's mother was sentenced to 3 to 5 years in prison for possession of drugs. Kristin did not see her mother for the next 12 months because the jail where her mother was first detained did not allow visitors under 16 years of age. The prison to which her mother was sent was too far away for frequent visits, and Kristin's new caregivers felt that prison visiting was not a good idea because it "upset her more." These caregivers also told Kristin to say her mother was in the hospital if anyone asked. Kristin became withdrawn and refused to go to school. When asked why, she said she was afraid her brothers would not be there when she came home. She remembered feeling scared about what would happen to her, and often dreamed about her mother calling to her for help. She also reported feeling guilty about the role she played in her mother's arrest, and worried about having said the wrong thing to the police. She has done poorly in school, and developed behavior problems. Her caregiver reported that Kristin exhibits poor impulse control, irritability, and angry outbursts.

Case 4: Although his mother had been in prison for 5 years at the time of the interview, Marcus remembered her arrest in intricate detail. He remembered what his mother was wearing, what he was wearing, and the "ugly" faces of the police officers. He remembered how angry he was when the police handcuffed his mother. As his mother was being taken away, she told him that she would be back soon, that it was all just a big mistake. But, he said, "She has not come back to this day." Once his mother was in prison, Marcus's life became more difficult. "After she left," he said, "things went very bad for me in all ways." He recalled fantasizing about freeing her, and would often daydream about "the good times my mother and me had together" before the police took her away. He was very resentful toward the police and felt they were responsible for his mother's absence. Marcus had trouble sleeping and difficulty concentrating in school. He lived with his grandmother and they did not get along; he felt unwanted and kept running away, although he had no place to go. When he was 14, Marcus dropped out of school, became involved in selling drugs, and was soon arrested. He had been in and out of detention centers for over a year at the time of his interview.

Discussion

Up to 50% of juveniles who are incarcerated have a parent who has been incarcerated (Task Force on the Female Offender 1990). Baunach (1985), found that 70% of the children of imprisoned mothers she studied were reported as having psychological or emotional problems. These problems were mainly restlessness or "hypertension," as the mothers called it, aggressive behavior or withdrawal. Clearly, the traumas that these children experience due to an early separation from their primary caregiver and the difficult life that follows impact their mental health.

Following exposure to a disaster, many children may experience persistent distress (Lyons, 1987). The incarceration of a parent is a disaster in any child's life, and it is compounded by related situational stresses, like worrying about their own and their mother's safety. The problem is intensified when children experience this loss after witnessing their mother's arrest.

The psychological impact of parent–child separation among children of prisoners also resembles others forms of loss in childhood, such as those related to parental divorce. Some children of incarcerated women seem to experience this loss as a "temporary death" of the mother. Studies of childhood bereavement (Krueger, 1983) have found that the impact of temporary losses may be as traumatic as that of permanent loss. Because the missing parent is not emotionally available, children experience his or her loss like they experience death.

Children with incarcerated mothers cannot negotiate day-to-day interactions with them. Most forms of communication between mothers and children are cut off. Children often are limited to writing to their mothers, and for younger children even this form of communication is not an option.

It is not surprising that children of women prisoners often report depression, feelings of anger and fear, guilt, flashbacks, and the experience of hearing their mothers' voices. These symptoms have been associated with post-traumatic stress disorder (PTSD). As defined by Lyons (1987), the diagnostic criteria for PTSD are (1) exposure to an event that could be traumatic, (2) intrusive reexperiencing of this trauma, (3) numbness of responsiveness to or reduced involvement with the external world, and (4) at least two of a variety of other symptoms, including hyperalertness/startle, sleep disturbance, survivor guilt, impaired memory/concentration, avoidance of trauma-related cues, and intensification of symptoms when exposed to trauma-related stimulus. Some research has suggested a link between bereavement in young children and hallucinations, particularly hallucinations related to the lost person (Balk, 1983; Garfalda, 1982; Simonds, 1975). Children of imprisoned mothers are constantly preoccupied with their mothers' safety, making it difficult to acknowledge concerns about their own safety; the long-term implications of this phenomenon, especially among children who witness crimes against persons, are not known, but may be related to the change in future orientation that is one of the hallmarks of traumatic stress reactions in childhood (Terr, 1983). In addition, children with mothers in prison will often have to change caregivers at least once. Some—for example, those placed in the foster care system—may have to move from home to home throughout their mother's incarceration. Multiple placements have been recently suggested as a source of PTSD symptoms in children (Doyle & Bauer, 1989). Finally, the importance of the children's loss of their mothers is often downplayed by caregivers. Previous studies of children who have been traumatized report that caregiver attitudes toward lost parents are an important variable in the ability of children to grieve and overcome the effects of their loss (Yates & Bannard, 1988).

Quality of care, stability in the home, and family support in the face of loss are important factors in determining whether children will suffer from the long-term emotional and psychological consequences of trauma. The great majority of children in this study were traumatized when their mothers went to prison. Their subsequent experiences have contributed to the development of PTSD symptoms.

Conclusions

Children with mothers in prison are a high-risk population, especially when they were present at their mothers' arrests. Children in this study were traumatized by their experiences of maternal crime, arrest, and incarceration; they showed several symptoms associated with acute post-traumatic stress disorder. However, their circumstances—including the social stigma attached to maternal incarceration, caregivers' well-intentioned efforts to protect them from trauma-related cues, and their lack of emotional supports—combine in ways that make it difficult for them to overcome the effects of trauma.

These symptoms and circumstances need recognition. The relationships that children have with their mothers are important and necessary, do not disappear with maternal incarceration, and must be fostered. Children need opportunities to work out their emotional trauma, including access to social services, traditional psychological resources, and new forms of therapy and counseling that recognize the special cultural, class, and family circumstances of the families of prisoners. They also need social support networks, based on resources that already exist within their communities.

Children are traumatized when they lose their mothers to incarceration. They have the right to have the enormity of that loss acknowledged and should be be given appropriate forms of help to enable them to recover.

References

Balk, D. L. (1983). Adolescent grief reactions and self-concept perceptions following sibling death: A study of 33 teenagers. *Journal of Youth and Adolescence,* 12(3):159.

Baunach, P. J. (1985). *Mothers in prison.* New Brunswick, NJ: Transaction Books Rutgers University Press.

Bifulco, A. T., et al. (1987). Childhood loss of parent: Lack of adequate parental care and adult depression. *Journal of Affective Disorders,* 12:115–128.

Birtchnell, J. (1970). Depression in relationship to early and recent parental death. *British Journal of Psychiatry,* 116:229–306.

Bowlby, J. (1946). *Forty-four juvenile thieves: Their characters and home-life.* London: Tindall & Cox.

Bowlby, J. (1951). Adverse effects of maternal deprivation. In *Maternal Care and Mental Health.* Geneva: World Health Organization.

Bowlby, J. (1973). *Separation: Anxiety and anger.* New York: Basic Books.

Bowlby, J. (1980). *Attachment and loss.* New York: Basic Books.

Brown, F. (1961). Depression and childhood bereavement. *Journal of Mental Science,* 107:754–777.

Cain, A. C., & Fast, J. D. (1966). Children's disturbed reactions to parent suicide. *American Journal of Orthopsychiatry,* 36:873–880.

Doyle, J. S., & Bauer, S. K. (1989). Posttraumatic stress disorder in children. Journal of Traumatic Stress, 2(3):275–288.

Garfalda, M. E. (1982). Hallucinations in psychiatrically disordered children: Preliminary communication. *Journal of Sociological Medicine,* 75:181–184.

Glick, R., & Neto, V. (1977). *National study of women's correctional programs.* Washington, DC: National Institute of Law Enforcement and Criminal Justice.

Jose, C. (1985). *Women doing life sentences: A phenomenological study.* Unpublished doctoral dissertation, University of Michigan.

Kruger, D. (1983). Psychotherapy of adult patients with problems of parental loss in childhood. *Current Concepts in Psychiatry.*

LaPoint, V., Picker, M. O. & Harris, S. (1985). Enforced family separation: A descriptive analysis of some experiences of children of black imprisoned mothers. In Spencer, A. (ed.), *Beginnings: The social and affective development of black children.* Hillsdale, NJ: Erlbaum. Pages 239–255.

Lyons, J. (1987). Post-traumatic stress disorder in children and adolescents: A review of the literature. *Developmental and Behavioral Pediatrics*, 8(6):349–356.

McGowan, B. G., & Blumenthal, K. L. (1978). *Why punish the children? A study of the children of women in prison*. Hackensack, NJ: National Council on Crime and Delinquency.

Payton, J. B., & Krocker-Tuskan, M. (1988). Children's reactions to loss of a parent through violence. *Journal of American Academy of Child and Adolescent Psychiatry*, 27(5):563–566.

Schwartz, I. M., (1989). *The incarcerations of girls: Paternalism or juvenile crime control?* Unpublished manuscript.

Simonds, J. F. (1975). Hallucinations in non-psychotic children. *British Journal of Psychiatry*, 129:267–276.

Stanton, A. M. (1980). *When mothers go to jail*. Lexington, MA: Lexington Books.

Task Force on the Female Offender. (1990). *The Female Offender: What Does the Future Hold?* Laurel, Maryland: American Correctional Association.

Terr, L. (1983). Forbidden games: Posttraumatic child's play. *Journal of American Academy of Child and Adolescent Psychiatry*, 20:741–760.

Yates, T., & Bannard, J. (1988). The "haunted" child: Grief, hallucinations, and family dynamics. *Journal of American Academy of Child and Adolescent Psychiatry*, 27(5):573–581.

PART III

Care and Placement

7

The Care and Placement
of Prisoners' Children

Denise Johnston

A great deal of the research on children of prisoners has focused on their placements and caregivers prior to and during parental incarceration. This is an important topic, not just because the quality of care during these critical separations may have lifelong effects, but also because the circumstances of placement often determine the success of parent–child reunification.

Living Arrangements Prior to Parental Incarceration

Approximately three-quarters of imprisoned mothers and about one-half of imprisoned fathers lived with at least one minor child prior to incarceration (U.S. Department of Justice [USDJ], 1993). Fewer than half of prisoners' minor children lived with their parents before parental incarceration. (See Tables 7.1 and 7.2.)

Children of male prisoners who did not live with their fathers before paternal arrest most often lived with their natural mothers. The prior living arrangements of children of incarcerated mothers were more varied, but the greatest numbers of those who did not live with their mothers lived with their grandparents or natural fathers. In Great Britain, Gibbs (1971) found a significant number of children in foster care prior to their mother's incarceration. However, U.S. studies show that only a small number of children of prisoners of either sex are in foster care before parental arrest.

Previous incarcerations appear to have an impact on the living arrangements of women offenders and their children prior to the mother's arrest (see Table 7.3). As McGowan and Blumenthal (1978) concluded, "An increased number of previous incarcerations decreases the likelihood of a child's living with his mother before [her] arrest."

Table 7.1a
Living Arrangements of the Children of Incarcerated Mothers Prior to Incarceration, by Mother

Arrangement	McCarthy, 1980 (N = 31)	Koban, 1983 (N = 95♀)	Hunter, 1984 (N = 55)	USDJ, 1993 (N = 2,783)
At least one child lived with mother	58.1%	74.3%	82.1%	~70%
Children lived with other natural parent	0	7.1%	Not measured	Not measured
Children lived with grandparent	12.9%	Not measured	Not measured	Not measured
Children lived in foster care	16.1%	Not measured	Not measured	Not measured
"Other" arrangement	Not measured	18.6%	17.9%	Not measured

Table 7.1b
Living Arrangements of the Children of Incarcerated Fathers Prior to Incarceration, by Father

Arrangement	Koban, 1983 (N = 111 ♂)	Hairston, 1989 (N = 126)	USDJ, 1993 (N = 11,203)
At least one child lived with father	24.5%	50%	~50%
Children lived with other natural parent	60.7%	Not measured	Not measured
Children lived with grandparent	Not measured	Not measured	Not measured
Children lived in foster care	Not measured	Not measured	Not measured
"Other" arrangement	14.8%	Not measured	Not measured

Table 7.2
Living Arrangements of Children Prior to Maternal Incarceration, By Child

Living Arrangement	Zalba, 1964 (N = 299)	McGowan & Blumenthal, 1978(N = 112)	Baunach, 1979 (N = 285)	Bloom & Steinhart, 1993 (N = 866)
With mother, total[1]	56.0%	40.2%	73.7%	67%
With mother alone	38.0%	33.9%	Not measured	Not measured
With mother and father or mother's partner	18.0%	6.3%	Not measured	Not measured
With natural father	9.0%	1.8%	9.2%	Not measured
With grandparent(s)	20.0%	23.2%	5.7%	Not measured
With other relative(s)	4.0%	29.5%[2]	Not measured	Not measured
With friends	2.0%	Not measured[2]	1.1%	Not measured
In foster care	7.0%	5.4%	3.2%	Not measured
Other	2.0%	Not measured	5.7%	Not measured

1. Includes children who lived with their mothers alone and children who lived with their mothers and other adults.

2. McGowan and Blumenthal included living arrangements with other relatives and with friends in the same category.

Emergency Placement at Parental Arrest

Almost no one knows exactly when they will be arrested. This fact makes emergency placements a necessity for arrested parents who are the primary caregivers of dependent children.

When Children Are Present at Arrest

About one in five children are present at their mothers' arrest; half of these children are between 3 and 7 years of age, and in their mothers' sole care (Johnston, 1991). There is no similar information available about the children of arrested men.

Some arrested parents may have no opportunity to participate in emergency placements, even when their children are present. In some cases, the arresting officers decide where the children should go without consulting the parent. In other cases, parents who are intoxicated, violent, or otherwise difficult prisoners are not allowed to participate in emergency placement decisions.

There are a variety of ways in which emergency placements are made. The American Bar Association's study, *Children on Hold* (1993), found that law enforcement officers often make these decisions in the field when children are present at arrests, usually after consulting arrested parents about possible substitute caregivers. Arresting officers may also call in special police units (e.g., juvenile divisions) to handle placement, or they may request that the child protective services (CPS) take custody of the children at the site of parental arrest. Finally, some officers will transport children to their stations before contacting caregivers or the CPS.

Children of arrested parents may thus be placed informally with their immediate or extended family members, with friends or neighbors, or in emergency private placements like crisis nurseries. Each of these placements is legal and proper if made by or with the consent of the custodial parent.

Table 7.3
Living Arrangements of Children Prior to Maternal Incarceration,
By Mother's Previous Incarcerations (N = 39)

Living Arrangement Prior to Mother's Arrest	*Number of Previous Incarcerations*		
	None	*1–2*	*3 or More*
Lived with mother	80.0%	55.6%	33.3%
Did not live with mother	20.0%	44.4%	66.7%

Placements made by the CPS are always documented, even when the agency involved elects not to file a dependency petition for the children put in its care. Children placed by the CPS at the time of arrest may end up in any of the above placements; the agency then has the option of making a quick approval of the caregiver and withdrawing, or of initiating dependency proceedings. Children may be placed in emergency shelters with the possibility of being released to family members without extensive investigation if claimed within 48 to 72 hours. CPS workers may also place children with foster families or in other public placements; dependency petitions are usually initiated for all children in these circumstances.

When Children Are Not Present at Arrest

In most cases, children are not present at their parent's arrest. Parents usually are not asked and/or do not volunteer information about dependent children in their care (McGowan & Blumenthal, 1978; American Bar Association, 1993). Although there has been no research on this subject, data on children's living arrangements during parental incarceration suggests that most placements after parental arrests are made informally and do not result in children entering the foster care system.

Based on studies of incarcerated parents, it can be assumed that the placements of a significant number of children will not be affected by parental arrest. Up to one-half of prisoners' children were not living with them prior to incarceration (Baunach, 1979; Hairston, 1989, 1990; McGowan & Blumenthal, 1978; Zalba, 1964). For example, 5 to 7% of the children of incarcerated mothers were living in foster care at the time of their mother's arrest (Baunach, 1979; McGowan & Blumenthal, 1978; Zalba, 1964). Emergency placement decisions are unnecessary in these circumstances.

Living Arrangements During Parental Incarceration

Most studies that have followed child placements prior to and during parental incarceration have been conducted on the families of women prisoners (Baunach, 1979; Gibbs, 1971; McGowan & Blumenthal, 1978; Zalba, 1964;).

Placements and Caregivers of the Children of Women Prisoners

Children who lived with their mothers before her incarceration are typically divided up among their natural fathers, their grandparents, and other caregivers after maternal arrest. Most, but not all, children who lived with both parents prior to maternal incarceration remain with their fathers. Following maternal arrest, the number of children who are in the sole care of their fathers doubles, as fathers take in children who had previously lived apart from them. The number of children of women offenders in the care of their grandparents more than doubles following maternal incarceration. Ultimately, over half the children of women prisoners remain with or are placed in the care of their grandparents (most often the maternal grandmother), and up to one-fourth remain with or are placed in the care of their fathers during maternal incarceration. Five to ten percent of all children of women prisoners enter or remain in foster care (USDJ, 1993).

There are placement and caregiver differences among subgroups of the children of incarcerated mothers. For example, Zalba (1964) found:

> Placements with the father were more common among the children of (1) older women, (2) married and divorced—but not separated—women, and (3) white and Mexican-American women. They were less common among (1) younger women, (2) single, separated, and widowed women, and (3) black women.
>
> Placements with relatives other than fathers and grandparents were more common among the children of black women.
>
> Foster care placements were more common among the children of young women, white women, Mexican-American women, and women with larger numbers of children. They were less common among the children of black women and women with smaller families. Foster care placements were significantly less common among children of women offenders from large metropolitan areas than among children of women offenders from smaller, rural communities.

Placements and Caregivers of the Children of Incarcerated Men

Unlike the above data, statistics on the placements and caregivers of the children of male prisoners have been reported by parent rather than by child (Koban, 1983; USDJ, 1993). These studies have found that the vast majority of children do not change placements or caregivers after paternal incarceration, and about nine out of 10 live with their natural mothers. One to two percent of the children of male prisoners are placed in foster care following their father's arrest. Most of these are children whose mothers are also incarcerated. The remaining 8 to 10% live with their grandparents during their father's time in jail or prison.

Caregiver Counts for All Children of Incarcerated Parents

The relationships of children of prisoners to their caregivers during parental incarceration is illustrated in Tables 7.4 and 7.5. Based on an estimated 1.53

Table 7.4
Relationships of Prisoners' Children to Their Caregivers

Relationship to Child	Total Children	Number of Children
Other natural parent	80.4%	1,230,000
Grandparent(s)	14.7%	225,000
Foster care	2.7%	42,000
Other relative; friends	2.3%	35,000
Totals*	100.1%	1,532,000

*total is greater than 100% due to rounding.

million children of prisoners in the United States in 1993 (Center for Children of Incarcerated Parents, 1993), the greatest number, or about 1.23 million prisoners' children, are in the care of their other natural parents. Eighty-seven percent, or 1.20 million, children of male prisoners are in the care of their natural mothers (Koban, 1983; USDJ, 1993). About one in five, or 29,000 children, of female prisoners are in the care of their natural fathers (McGowan & Blumenthal, 1978; Stanton, 1980; Task Force on the Female Offender, 1990; USDJ, 1993; Zalba, 1964).

The next largest group, or about 225,000, children of prisoners live with their grandparents; at least half of this group live with their mother's mother, their maternal grandmother (Hunter, 1984; Henriques, 1982; Bloom & Steinhart, 1993; USDJ, 1993).

Approximately 42,000 of the remaining children are in foster care. This includes about 2%, or about 27,500, of the children of incarcerated fathers and about 10%, or about 14,500, of the children of incarcerated mothers (Johnston, 1991; Stanton, 1980; USDJ, 1993).

The remaining 35,000 children are placed with other relatives or friends. This number includes less than 3% of the children of male prisoners, and about 10% of the children of female prisoners (USDJ, 1993).

At least some mothers of the children of male prisoners will have another partner living in the home. However, it is important to note that significant numbers and perhaps a majority of children of all prisoners live in single-parent households and/or households with an older caregiver.

Separation from Siblings

Children of prisoners of both sexes are often separated from their siblings. Hairston (1989) found that about half of the incarcerated fathers she studied had children by different mothers. Zalba (1964) found that over half of the children of California's women prisoners lived apart from at least one brother or sister. However, only 19% of the 1,085 children he studied were separated from their siblings as the result of maternal incarceration;

Table 7.5
Relationships of Prisoners' Children to Their Caregivers, by Sex of the Incarcerated Parent

Relationship to Child	Children of Incarcerated Mothers (N = 145,000)	Children Incarcerated Fathers (N = 1,380,000)
Other natural parent	20%	87%
Grandparents	60%	9%
Foster care	10%	2%
Other relative, friends	10%	2%
Total	100%	100%

the majority who lived apart from their brothers and sisters had been separated prior to the mother's arrest. Stanton (1980), who studied only children who had lived with their mother prior to her arrest, found that 25% of these children were separated from their siblings during the time of their mother's jail sentence. Koban (1983) compared separation of siblings among the children of imprisoned parents of both sexes; she found that placements separating siblings occurred among one-third of the children of incarcerated mothers and were about twice as common among the children of women prisoners as among the children of imprisoned men.

Changes of Placement

Most children of women prisoners will experience at least one change in placement or caregiver during maternal incarceration. Changes in placement may occur without changes in caregiver, and vice versa. Zalba (1964) found that two-thirds of the children he studied had at least one change in their caregiver during maternal imprisonment; only about 60% of this group also had changes in placement, suggesting that some children remained in the same household while different adults assumed responsibility for their care.

A small number of children experience multiple changes in placement and/or caregiver (Baunach, 1979; Johnston, 1991, 1992; Zalba, 1964). Up to 14% change households two or more times during their mother's incarceration, while up to 11% experience two or more changes of caregiver.

The child welfare literature has established the detrimental effects of multiple out-of-home placements for children separated from their parents (Children's Defense Fund, 1978; Fanshel & Shinn, 1978; Littner, 1956). While it has been assumed that this is true for children of incarcerated parents, there have been no formal comparisons of prisoners' children who experience multiple changes in placements or caregivers with those who do not.

Table 7.6
Effects of Multiple Placements/Caregivers on Children of Jailed Mothers

Number of Caregiver or Placement Changes	0–1 (N = 116)	2 (N = 10)	3+ (N = 6)
School problems[1]	19.1%	30.0%	50.0%
Reactions to maternal incarceration[2]	36.4%	30.0%	100%

1. Includes academic/performance, behavior/discipline, attention, and attendance problems.
2. Includes emotional reactions, aggression, other problem behaviors, delinquency, sexual acting out, and other behaviors that occurred only following maternal incarceration.
Source: Johnston, 1991.

The Jailed Mothers Study (Johnston, 1991) compared children who had experienced different numbers of placement and caregiver changes. Only two outcomes, maternal perceptions of the children's "school problems" and "reactions to maternal incarceration," were examined (see Table 7.6). Although the size of the study group was too small for results to be generalized, the findings suggest that there may be an association of school problems and negative reactions to maternal incarceration with increased number of placements.

The Caregiver Experience

The caregivers and caregiving arrangements for prisoners' children fall roughly into five groups: (1) related caregivers who lived with the parent and shared caregiving responsibilities prior to parental incarceration; (2) related caregivers who lived with the children and separately from the parent prior to parental incarceration; (3) related caregivers who did not care for or live with the children prior to parental incarceration; (4) unrelated caregivers who lived with the children and separate from the parent prior to parental incarceration; and (5) unrelated caregivers who did not care for or live with the children prior to parental incarceration. The experience of each of these categories of caregiver is different.

Experiences Prior to Parental Incarceration

The experiences of the caregivers of prisoners' children prior to parental incarceration have significant effects on their abilities to meet the challenges that follow. The caregiver experiences of this period tend to be more varied than the experiences that occur during and after parents' jail and prison sentences.

Related Caregivers Who Lived with the Parent and Child(ren) Prior to Parental Incarceration. This group is mostly made up of the spouses/partners and mothers of prisoners. Their commonalities include shared responsibilities for childcare and homemaking with the parent prior to arrest, and the experience of the parent's crime-related behavior.

Fifty percent of all incarcerated fathers lived with their children prior to arrest (Hairston, 1989; USDJ, 1993). The roles and responsibilities of these men have not been thoroughly investigated. The Children of Offenders Study (Johnston, 1992) found that about half of the currently incarcerated fathers who had been living with their children prior to arrest had been employed and had carried out household responsibilities; the other half had been present in the home irregularly and had not assumed household responsibilities. Men who had been living with their wives or partners and their children were more likely to be working and involved in family life than men who were living with their own mothers and their children.

Prior to arrest, incarcerated mothers often lived in the same households as their mothers or other relatives with whom they shared childcare and other homemaking responsibilities (Hunter, 1984; LaPointe, Picker & Harris, 1985; Miller, 1986). Shared caregiving and domestic networks have been found to be a norm in the African-American community (Hogan & Kitagawa, 1990; Stack, 1974), and extended households with shared household responsibilities are common among Hispanics (Angel & Tienda, 1982). However, although they were less common among the families of white women, multigenerational households with shared childcare were prevalent in all racial/ethnic groups among the jailed women studied by Johnston (1991).

Caregivers who have lived with offenders and their children typically have had a series of experiences related to the parents' crimes. These include parental absences, parental substance abuse, domestic violence, other offenders in the home and around the children, repeated police contacts, and/or parental arrests. In many instances where parental criminal activity did not disrupt the family, this was because the parent was frequently out of the home (Miller, 1986).

Parental arrest may be both a trauma and a relief for these caregivers. Following parental incarceration, household life frequently stabilizes (Miller, 1986; Schneller, 1978), although resources may become more limited (Bakker, Morris & Janus, 1978; Lowenstein, 1986; Swan, 1981). Because there was a preexisting caregiver–child relationship, children who lived with both caregiver and parent prior to parental arrest have fewer problems adjusting to the changes in their care that followed their parents' incarceration.

All caregivers face similar challenges in working with incarcerated parents and their children, as well as from dealing with the social service, criminal justice, and corrections systems. However, caregivers in this group may have to face these challenges with fewer resources and greater levels of stress than others as a result of their recent experiences living with an active offender.

Related Caregivers Who Lived with the Child(ren) and Apart from the Parent Prior to Parental Incarceration. This group of caregivers is made up of former spouses/partners, parents, and other relatives of incarcerated parents. They either have always or have sometime previously assumed responsibility for the care of the children of these parents. They did not share their household and childcare responsibilities with the arrested parent prior to the parent's arrest and usually had only indirect experiences with the parent's most recent criminal activities.

Parental crime, arrest, detention, and incarceration causes the least amount of disruption in the lives of this group of caregivers. There are no crises in child placement, no emergency needs to be met, and no direct traumatic events from which to recover. There is no need for these caregivers to establish a new parenting relationship with the children in their care, and the children do not need to adjust to living apart from their arrested parent. Although they face the same challenges as other caregivers of prisoners' children following parental incarceration, these caregivers are, relatively, in the best possible position to meet them.

Related Caregivers Who Lived Apart from the Parent and Child(ren) Prior to Parental Incarceration. This group consists mostly of the former spouses/partners of female prisoners, and of the parent(s) and other relatives of prisoners of both sexes. These caregivers did not share household and childcare responsibilities for prisoners' children prior to the parents' arrests. They usually have had only indirect experiences with the parents' criminal activities. However, many caregivers in this category have previously assumed the care of the children.

Parental arrest and detention is not experienced as a stabilizing event that produces a sense of relief by this group of caregivers. They are much more likely to experience such events as an unexpected crisis that produces sudden demands on their time and resources. Unlike caregivers who have been living with the children of prisoners, these caregivers must move children into a new household, provide for their immediate material and emotional needs, seek long-term resources for their support, and work to establish a parenting relationship with them. In many cases, these caregivers must also provide assistance and liaison for the parent with criminal justice and social service agencies.

Caregivers in this category face the same challenges as others following parental incarceration. But they may come to these challenges in crisis, under conditions of stress on their emotional and material resources.

Unrelated Caregivers Who Lived with the Child(ren) and Apart from the Parent Prior to Parental Incarceration. This small group is comprised mostly of the foster parents of prisoners' children. Parental crime, arrest, and incarceration usually cause minimal physical disruption in the households of these caregivers. However, the children in their care are likely to have had multiple previous traumas related to similar events. Awareness of what has most recently happened in the lives of their parents may stimulate memories of previous traumas, emotional upheavals, and/or behavioral reactions in the children.

Caregivers in this group face less challenging experiences with social service and corrections agencies following parental incarceration than do others. However, they have in their care the most damaged children of offenders and must assist these children in adjusting to a new and painful but familiar trauma.

Unrelated Caregivers Who Did Not Live with the Child(ren) Prior to Parental Incarceration. This smallest group includes primarily foster caregivers of children who enter the child welfare system as a result of their parents' incarceration. These caregivers usually have no knowledge of or contact with the incarcerated parents of the children placed in their care, and parental criminal activity and arrest have had no effects on them.

Unlike caregivers who had previously lived with the children of prisoners, these caregivers must move children into a new household, provide for their immediate material and emotional needs, and establish a foster parent relationship with them. However, unlike related caregivers, these persons are strangers to the children and have no preexisting relationship upon which to build. They are not members of the family and do not have the benefit of that shared identity while attempting to forge a bond with the children.

These caregivers face the same challenges as others following parental incarceration. As trained foster parents who automatically receive income for the children of prisoners from the state, they come to these challenges better prepared and with greater supports than other caregivers. However, the children in their care face more new problems and their futures are much more at risk than most other children of prisoners.

Experiences during Parental Incarceration

All caregivers of prisoners' children face a series of challenging tasks during parental incarceration. They must not only provide for the children's material needs, but often must also explain parental absence, develop and maintain a caregiver–child relationship, develop and maintain a caregiver–parent relationship, foster parent–child communication, support parent–child jail or prison visits, and/or work toward family reunification.

Providing for Children's Material Needs. This may be the most challenging task faced by the caregivers of prisoners' children. Like most offenders and their families, most caregivers and their families are poor. Zalba (1964) found that 43% of the caregiver households he studied were supported by public assistance alone. Over half of the households of caregivers interviewed by Bloom and Steinhart (1993) were supported by Aid to Families with Dependent Children (AFDC) or foster care payments, while three-quarters of the caregivers surveyed by the Prison Visitation Project (1993) and 90% of the grandmother caregivers in the Aid to Imprisoned Mothers program received some form of public assistance (Dressel & Barnhill, 1990).

How the effects of low income are expressed in the lives of the children of incarcerated parents and their caregivers has not been closely examined. The Prison Visitation Project (1993) surveyed 184 caregivers who reported that their households had problems with maintaining heat and air conditioning (22.8%), access to medical/dental care (21.7%/35.9%), and lack of dependable transportation (35.3%). The nature and frequency of these problems suggests a degree of material need seen only in the poorest families in our society. This kind of poverty enhances the difficulty of every task faced by caregivers by decreasing their ability to access resources and increasing their level of stress. It also limits their ability to support parent–child communication, visitation, and reunification.

Explaining Parental Absence. The majority of children of prisoners are not present at their parent's arrest and must be informed of what happened by others. This difficult task often becomes the responsibility of caregivers by default, and they bear the brunt of the children's reactions, which normally include grief, anxiety, and/or anger. It is also normal for children to "blame the messenger" and to act out their emotions immediately or in the months following this event.

Developing and Maintaining a Caregiver–Child Relationship. During parental incarceration, caregivers must develop or expand a parenting relationship with the children in their care. For caregivers who have lived with the children and apart from the parent, this new role may require only minor adjustments to an existing relationship, as children react to and recover from this latest experience. For caregivers in other circumstances, this new role may require major and persistent efforts. For caregivers who have lived with the children and the incarcerated parent, arrest of the parent produces shifts in the household balance of power. The remaining parent or the caregiver must suddenly assume much or all of the control and authority of the arrested parent, as well as continue to carry out his or her regular household responsibilities. These shifts in role and responsibilities and related time demands may drastically alter the relationship of the remaining parent or caregiver with the children. Depending on the age of the children involved, caregivers in their new roles may face child confusion, child resistance, and even child rebellion.

Caregivers who were not living with the children at the time of parental arrest may need to construct an entire parenting relationship. Related caregivers have the benefit of a shared background and preexisting, if distant, relationships upon which to build. Unrelated caregivers who are strangers to the children must start from scratch. The emotional basis for the relationship, the nature and distribution of power/authority, the expected behaviors of participants, the penalties for failure to meet the terms of the relationship, the role of the parent, and a timeline are terms of caregiver–child relationships that are usually defined explicitly or implicitly at the outset.

The development of a healthy parent–child relationship normally takes a child's lifetime. In the case of children of incarcerated parents and their caregivers, the rushed nature of this activity creates a great amount of stress for both parties.

In establishing their temporary parenting relationships, caregivers of prisoners' children must give special attention to several issues that are specific to this population:

> *False information.* Caregivers of the children of incarcerated parents, and particularly the wives of prisoners, are most concerned about the shame and stigma of parental incarceration (Schneller, 1978; Zalba, 1964). This may lead them to misinform children about their parents' whereabouts. The damaging effects of lying to children about their incarcerated parent have been well documented (Gabel, 1992; Hannon, Martin & Martin, 1984; Schwartz & Weintraub, 1974).

> *Forced silences.* Out of similar concerns, or their own discomfort with the topic, caregivers may directly order or indirectly cue children of prisoners to avoid discussing their incarcerated parents. These forced silences are detrimental because children are unable to process the effects of trauma, including the trauma of parent–child separation, without expressing their feelings verbally. Caregivers must balance their own needs in this area with the equally important need for children of prisoners to avoid further emotional damage.

> *Hostile messages.* It is common for a caregiver to have experienced stress and anger as the result of the parent's criminal behavior and/or incarceration. These feelings may spill over into the emotional content of the discussions caregivers have with children of prisoners about their parents. Such hostile but hidden messages can be harmful to children. Since children identify with their parents, these messages may damage self-esteem; and, since children also identify with their caregivers, these messages may cause the children to experience conflicts about loyalty and authority. Anger and hostility toward incarcerated parents are real and reasonable feelings, and success in caring for their

special children requires that caregivers learn how to frankly express their mixed emotions about the parent in ways children can recognize and understand.

Identification of the child with the parent. Some caregivers who have had a negative or hostile relationship with an absent parent may extend the effects of that conflict into their relationship with the parent's child(ren). Caregivers in these cases invoke the parents when they are angry with the children, making disparaging ("You're going to turn out as bad as your dad") or warning ("This is how your mother started out") remarks. Specialists in childhood trauma have found that children who are raised in these circumstance often have negative, long-term outcomes following loss or separation from their parents (Brier, Kelsoe, Kirwin, Beller & Wolkowitz, 1988; Elizur & Kauffman, 1983). Offenders are the most likely among parents to have engendered negative feelings in their relationships with others, including the caregiver; good quality care of offenders' children avoids the incorporation of such feelings about the parent into the developing caregiver–child relationship.

Developing and Maintaining a Caregiver–Parent Relationship. The relationships between the caregivers of prisoners' children and incarcerated parents are built on the preincarceration caregiver–parent relationship and the acceptability of the placement to both parties. When the preexisting relationship was positive and the placement is acceptable to both the caregiver and the parent, the relationship between the two during the parent's jail or prison term will also be positive. When the preexisting relationship was stressful and one or both parties are not happy with the placement, the relationship between incarcerated parents and the caregivers of their children is less likely to be satisfactory.

The goal of the caregiver–parent relationship is the improvement of the well-being and adjustment to parental incarceration of all three parties: parent, child(ren), and caregiver. In this work, caregivers and parents have the following tasks:

Setting ultimate goals for the care of the children. Most caregivers and incarcerated parents informally set goals for the material and emotional well-being of the children. An often unstated but implicit goal is the ultimate reunification of parent and children, or the permanent placement of the children away from the parent. There is less conflict within caregiver–parent relationships when the ultimate goals of care are agreed upon and articulated.

Allocation of decision-making rights and responsibilities. Prisoners are often dissatisfied with child placements as the result of their inability to participate in decision making about their children (Baunach, 1979; Henriques, 1982; McGowan & Blumenthal, 1978). Lack of participation in decision making also contributes to a sense of powerlessness among incarcerated parents. The caregiver–parent relationship is more satisfactory when decision-making rights and responsibilities are agreed upon, articulated, or even documented (Hunter, 1984).

Completion of these two tasks will reduce the amount of conflict in caregiver–parent relationships, and allow caregivers and parents to pursue the expression of their agreements in the daily care of the children, parent–child contact and visitation, management of children's problem behaviors, and planning for family reunification or permanent placement of the children. It requires ongoing caregiver–parent communication, which now occurs in the case of less than half of all the childen of incarcerated parents (Bloom & Steinhart, 1993; Hairston, 1989).

However, it is common for prisoners and the caregivers of their children to have experienced conflicts in their relationships prior to the parent's current incarceration and/or to disagree on the placement. In fact, parent satisfaction with placement is probably a function of the degree to which parents and caregivers have gotten along in the past. Where preincarceration caregiver–parent conflicts exist, parents are unlikely to be completely satisfied with their child(ren)'s placement. Mediation or counseling between caregivers and incarcerated parents has been recommended as the best means to ameliorate such conflict (Vachio, 1991).

Finally, some authorities have suggested that caregivers serve as role models for parents whose children are in placement (Davies & Bland, 1981). In this view of the caregiver–parent relationship, caregivers model positive parenting behaviors and provide support for parents who are attempting to modify their parenting attitudes and expectations.

Working toward Family Reunification. This activity includes fostering parent–child communication and supporting parent–child visitation. Almost all caregivers of women prisoners' children who have been studied believe that contact between incarcerated parents and their children is helpful for the children. Over two-thirds of caregivers generally support the maintenance of the parent–child relationship by accompanying children to visits, by encouraging parent–child correspondence, and/or by allowing parent–child long distance telephone calls (Bloom & Steinhart, 1992).

The Role of Foster Parents. Incarcerated parents and their children often face long-term separations that extend beyond the mandated time frame for regular foster care in many jurisdictions. In these cases, the caregivers of prisoners' children may become the childrens' legal guardians or accept the responsibilities of long-term foster care. Especially in cases where prisoners' children have not been abused or neglected, and where parents participate in all required family reunification activities, it is important for caregivers to have a clear understanding of the role of foster parents.

Incarceration of the natural parent does not remove the responsibility of foster parents to work toward family reunification. The length of the parent's sentence or the distance of the parent's correctional facility from the foster home should not be used as a criteria to determine the appropriateness of visitation, telephone calls, and other forms of parent–child communication when these have not been forbidden by the court. Confusion over the role of the foster parent frequently leads to lack of support for reunification and custody conflicts, especially in the case of infants and young children. It is the responsibility of the supervising child welfare agency to ensure that foster parents have a clear understanding of their roles and responsibilities while caring for prisoners' children.

Experiences Following Parental Incarceration

Caregivers in all categories face a series of challenges as parents complete their jail or prison sentences and begin reentry into society. The difficulty of each task varies with the relationship of the caregiver to the parent and child. The challenges facing caregivers following parental incarceration include reintegration of the parent, shifting childcare and household responsibilities, continuing the caregiver–child relationship, and dealing with special issues.

Related Caregivers Who Will Live with the Parent and Child(ren) Following Parental Incarceration. The wives, mothers, and other relatives of prisoners who form this group often lived with the parent and children prior to parental arrest. Reintegration of the formerly incarcerated parent into the family may involve redistribution of power and authority among the adults. Particularly in the area of management of financial resources, these changes may lead to conflict between caregivers and formerly incarcerated parents.

Conflicts may also occur around issues of responsibility for childcare and household maintenance, including employment. Caregivers and reentering parents may differ in their assessments of the parent's ability to resume responsibilities and the time frame within which they should be resumed. While caregivers in this situation will maintain their existing relationship with the children, changes in the distribution of work and authority will effect the caregiver–child relationship to some extent.

Caregiver–parent conflicts during reentry can be minimized by prerelease planning, including the articulation or documentation of caregiver–parent agreements at the beginning of the parent's sentence, caregiver–parent visitation (with mediation, if necessary) during the parent's incarceration, and prerelease planning for family reentry. The focus of such planning should be to decrease or eliminate conflicts in the highly stressful reentry period.

Related Caregivers Who Will Live Apart from the Parent and Child(ren) Following Parental Incarceration. This group of caregivers is comprised of other natural parents, grandparents, friends, and other relatives of the children of prisoners. Most caregivers in this category did not have the care of the child prior to the parent's incarceration and will return the child to the parent's care after the parent's release. They face few issues related to the parent's reentry into the family and shifting childcare/household responsibilities.

However, these caregivers may have ambivalent feelings about returning children to the care of their formerly incarcerated parent. These feelings may arise because the caregiver has bonded to the children and wishes to continue to parent them. But caregivers are also often concerned about the ability of the reentering parent to responsibly care for his or her children. Just as care agreements made early in the incarceration period can facilitate a parent's reentry into the family, caregiver–parent agreements made after the parent's release can help to reassure caregivers who must relinquish the children's care.

Caregivers in this group also face diminished relationships with the children who have been in their care. Separation of caregivers and children can be experienced as a loss by both, especially where the caregiver and children have lived together for a long period, and where the relationship has been of mutual emotional benefit. Therefore, parents and caregivers need to plan for a gradual change in the caregiver–child relationship, from full-time care, to frequent visits and other contacts, to a regular pattern of limited contact.

Unrelated Caregivers. This group is comprised of foster parents who will not need to address issues of parent reentry into the family or shifting childcare/household responsibilities.

These caregivers may also have ambivalent feelings about returning children to the care of their formerly incarcerated parent. These feelings may arise because the caregiver has bonded to the children and wishes to continue to parent them. Like related caregivers, foster parents are also often concerned about the ability of the reentering parent to responsibly care for his or her children. However, unlike most related caregivers, foster parents have the formal responsibility to foster family reunification until the juvenile court orders that reunification services shall no longer be given, and to channel their reservations about reunification through the child welfare system.

Like some related caregivers, foster parents also face diminished relationships with the children who have been in their care. Separation of caregivers and children can be experienced as a loss by both, especially where the caregiver and children have lived together for a long period, and where the relationship has been of emotional benefit to the child. Therefore, natural and foster parents need to plan for a gradual change in the foster parent–child relationship, from full-time care, to frequent visits and other contacts, to the level of long-term contact agreed upon by all parties.

Quality of Care of Prisoners' Children

The inability of researchers to identify a representative sample of children of prisoners in the community has made investigation of the quality of their care almost impossible. Zalba's (1964) study of 95% of California's imprisoned mothers and their families selected all the subjects from Los Angeles and Alameda counties as subgroups for in-depth examination. Although this research design offered the opportunity for collection of data on a representative sample, Zalba did not investigate the material circumstances of the children's care. Two other large-scale studies of representative samples of correctional populations (McGowan & Blumenthal, 1978; Hunter, 1984) also failed to examine this topic.

Schneller (1978), in his study of the families of black prisoners in Washington, D.C., examined the living conditions of these families through survey of the prisoners and their wives, and home visits. One-quarter of the families lived in "poor" housing; the living conditions of the families were the same or worse than when the father went to prison in the areas of housing (75%), food (85%), clothing (82%), and transportation (99%).

The Children of Offenders Study (Johnston, 1992) also looked at quality of care. However, this study examined small, nonrepresentative groups in a high-crime, low-income community of African-American and Hispanic families. The mean per capita income for the children studied was $2900, or very nearly what is provided by AFDC. The children lived in medium- or high-density, older housing in poor repair; the childrens' households had an average of 5.5 persons living in 4.4 rooms. About one-third of the families had no car.

Although this study does not accurately reflect the status of the whole population of children of incarcerated parents, it helps to confirm the general impression that children of prisoners are poor and have multiple material needs. The study did not identify homelessness or the medical problems indicative of the most serious type of poverty. However, it also found no differences in availability of material resources between households of children whose parents were currently incarcerated and those whose parents had been incarcerated in the past. This finding suggests that the presence of formerly incarcerated parents in the home results in a balance of new income and expenses, or a deficit, and does not significantly improve the material quality of life for their children.

Conclusions

Although most incarcerated parents have at some time lived with at least one of their children, most children of prisoners did not live with their parent before the parent's incarceration. The families of most prisoners have been broken up prior to the prisoner's current incarceration, either because of separation/divorce between the parents (as in the case of male prisoners) or as the result of previous parental incarcerations (as is the case among women prisoners).

The great majority of prisoners' children live with female caregivers in single-parent households, either with their natural mothers or their maternal grandmothers. Significant numbers are separated from their siblings. Only a small minority are in the foster care system.

The prearrest and postrelease experiences of the caregivers of prisoners' children vary with the living arrangements of the caregiver, parent, and children prior to the parent's arrest. However, the caregiver experience during incarceration has similarities for all caregivers, who must deal with explaining parental absence, providing for the children's material and emotional needs, developing or maintaining a caregiver–child and/or caregiver–parent relationship, and working towards parent–child reunification. In all of these areas, caregivers must give special attention to the quality of their interaction with the children. Caregivers, parents, and children may be assisted by agreements and written contracts that set the terms of the caregiving arrangement.

The living conditions of prisoners' children are poor. A limited number of studies have documented high-density, low-quality housing and lack of transportation as common problems. These children live in poverty before, during, and after their parents' incarceration. In order to be truly effective, interventions for children of offenders must recognize and address this primary source of their needs.

References

American Bar Association. (1993). *Children on hold: What happens when their primary caregiver is arrested?* Washington, DC: Author.

Angel, R., & Tienda, M. (1982). Determinants of extended household structure: Cultural pattern or economic need? *American Journal of Sociology,* 87:1360–1383.

Bakker, L. J., Morris, B. A. & Janus, L. M. (1978). Hidden victims of crime. *Social Work,* 23:143–148.

Baunach, P. J. (1979, November). *Mothering from behind prison walls.* Paper presented at the annual meeting of the American Society of Criminology, Philadelphia.

Bloom, B., & Steinhart, D. (1993). Why punish the children? A reappraisal of the children of incarcerated mothers in America. San Francisco: National Council on Crime and Delinquency.

Breier, A., Kelsoe, J. R., Kirwin, P. D., Beller, S. A., Wolkowitz, D. M. & Pickar, D. (1988). Early parental loss and development of adult psychology. *Archives of General Psychiatry,* 45:987–493.

Center for Children of Incarcerated Parents. (1993). *Data sheets on children of prisoners.* Pasadena, CA: Pacific Oaks College.

Children's Defense Fund. (1978). *Children without homes: an examination of public responsibility.* Washington, D.C.: Authors.

Davies, L. J., & D. C. Bland. (1981). The use of foster parents are role models for parents. In P. A. Sinanoglu & A. N. Maluccio (eds.), *Parents of children in placement.* New York: Child Welfare League of America.

DeToledo, S. (1991, September). *Grandparents as parents, grandchildren as children.* Paper presented at the Colloquium of the Center for Children of Incarcerated Parents, Pasadena, California.

Dressel, P., & Barnhill, S. (1990). *Three generations at risk.* Atlanta, GA: Aid to Imprisoned Mothers.

Elizur, E., & Kauffman, M. (1983). Factors influencing the severity of childhood bereavement reactions. *American Journal of Orthopsychiatry,* 53(4):668–676.

Fanshel, D., & Shinn, E. B. (1978). *Children in foster care.* New York: Columbia University Press.

Gabel, S. (1992). Behavioral problems in sons of incarcerated or otherwise absent fathers: The issue of separation. *Family Process,* 31:303–314.

Gibbs, C. (1971). Effects of imprisonment of women on their children. *British Journal of Criminology,* 11:113–130.

Hairston, C. F. (1989). Men in prison: Family characteristics and family views. *Journal of Offender Counseling, Services and Rehabilitation,* 14(1):23–30.

Hairston, C. F. (1990). Mothers in jail: Parent–child separation and jail visitation. *Affilia,* 6(2).

Hannon, G., Martin, D. & Martin, M. (1984). Incarceration in the family: Adjustment to change. *Family Therapy,* 11:253–260.

Henriques, Z. W. (1982). *Imprisoned mothers and their children.* Washington, DC: University Press of America.

Hogan, D. P., & Kitagawa, M. (1985). The impact of social status, family structure, and neighborhoods on the fertility of black adolescents. *American Journal of Sociology,* 90:825–855.

Hunter, S. M. (1984). *The relationship between women offenders and their children.* Dissertation Abstracts International. (University Microfilms No. 8424436)

Johnston, D. (1991). *Jailed mothers.* Pasadena, CA: Pacific Oaks Center for Children of Incarcerated Parents.

Johnston, D. (1992). *Children of offenders.* Pasadena, CA: Pacific Oaks Center for Children of Incarcerated Parents.

Koban, L. A. (1983). Parents in prison: A comparative analysis of the effects of incarceration on the families of men and women. *Research in Law, Deviance and Social Control,* 5:171–183.

LaPointe, V., Picker, M. O. & Harris, B. F. (1985). Enforced family separation: A descriptive analysis of some experiences of children of black imprisoned mothers. In A. Spencer (Ed.), *Beginnings: The social and affective development of black children.* Washington, DC: Pgs 239–255.

Littner, N. (1956). *Some traumatic effects of separation & placement.* New York: Child Welfare League of America.

Littner, N. (1981). The importance of natural parents to the child in placement. In P. A. Sinanoglu & A. N. Maluccio (Eds.), *Parents of children in placement.* New York: Child Welfare League of America. Pgs 269–276.

Lowenstein, A. (1986). Temporary single parenthood: The case of prisoners' families. *Family Relations*, 36:79–85.

McCarthy, B. R. (1980). Inmate mothers: Problems of separation and integration. *Journal of Offender Counseling, Services and Rehabilitation*, 4(3):199–212.

McCord, J., & McCord, N. (1958). The effects of parental role model of criminality. *Journal of Social Issues*, 14:66–75.

McGowan, B. G., & Blumenthal, K. L. (1978). *Why punish the children?* Hackensack, NJ: National Council on Crime and Delinquency.

Miller, E. (1986). *Street woman.* Philadelphia: Temple University Press.

Poe, L. (1992). *Black grandparents as parents.* Unpublished manuscript, University of CA, Berkeley.

Prison Visitation Project. (1993). *Needs assessment of children whose parents are incarcerated* (Grant No. 720-93616D). Richmond, VA: Department of Mental Health, Mental Retardation, and Substance Abuse Services.

Schneller, D. P. (1978). *The prisoner's family.* San Francisco: R&E Research Associates.

Schwartz, M. C., & Weintraub, J. (1974). The prisoner's wife: A study in crisis. *Federal Probation*, 38:20–26.

Stack, C. (1974). *All our kin: Strategies for survival in the black community.* New York: Harper Colophon Books.

Stanton, A. (1980). *When mothers go to jail.* Lexington, MA: Lexington Books.

Swan, A. (1981). *Families of black prisoners: Survival and progress.* Boston: G. K. Hall.

Task Force on the Female Offender. (1990). *The female offender: What does the future hold?* Arlington, VA: American Correctional Association.

U.S. Department of Justice. (1993). *Survey of state prisoners.* Report No. NCJ 136949. Washington, DC: U.S. Bureau of Justice Statistics.

Vachio, A. (1991, November 16). *How we work with families.* Paper presented at the Conference of the New Mexico Corrections Department, Santa Fe, NM.

Zalba, S. (1964). *Women prisoners and their families.* Sacramento, CA: Department of Social Welfare/Department of Corrections.

8
Children of Prisoners in Foster Care

Julie A. Norman

While most children enter the state foster care system as the result of parental neglect and/or abuse, the majority of children of incarcerated parents who come to the attention of child welfare authorities do so because there are no relatives or close friends available provide care for them following parental arrest. Nevertheless, the experience of children of incarcerated parents in foster placement is in many ways similar to that of other children. They undergo the trauma of removal from familiar surroundings, the loss of significant relatives and friends, the entry of powerful strangers into their homes and lives, the feeling of being helpless and lost, and the sense that placement is somehow their fault. Even though the reasons for placement may seem quite clear to adults, to most children these reason are vague. Children entering foster care feel that their parent is being taken from them, *not* that they are being removed from their parent for their protection or support. Children ask themselves why they are in placement, and answer "There must be something wrong with me, I must be so bad nobody could love me" (Young, 1950).

All children are subjected to separation, for example, when they are left at the baby-sitters and on the first day of kindergarten. First experiences of separation are known to be somewhat traumatic for children. However, when children have experienced parental crime, have witnessed domestic violence, or have been present at a parent's violent arrest, separation trauma is magnified. The aftereffects of separation have been well documented, they include: increased sensitivity to later separation experiences, fear of emotional closeness, the expectation of rejection, and the tendency to reproduce in one's own children the separation trauma (Littner, 1981). Although it is also believed that a child who has had a warm, secure relationship with parents before separation occurs will suffer less trauma, all children who are placed and re-placed—like 55% of children in foster care (Tatara, 1990)—will experience increasing emotional damage from each separation.

When a child is placed in the custody of the state following a parent's arrest, the juvenile court petition may simply request the court to recognize the child as a dependent minor because the parent is unable to provide or care for him or her. The dependency allegation exists when a parent cannot continue to care for a child due to mental or physical illness or other disability. While neglect is often considered to exist as a result of omission of care by a parent, abuse is defined as commission of an act. Parental arrest alone should not constitute child abuse or neglect. Often, however, the fact of the parent's arrest is presented as evidence of neglect, especially in drug-related arrests.

When children are placed in substitute care, the best and most often considered placements are with relatives. Maternal or parental grandparents, aunts, uncles, first cousins, and older siblings are all acceptable to child welfare authorities. If none of these relatives are known or acceptable to child welfare authorities, children may be placed in the state or private foster care systems.

Some common instances that require placement decisions when the parent is a criminal offender include:

1. *Children present at the time of arrest.* Children may be informally placed by police with neighbors or relatives, or returned to the other custodial parent. When no acceptable substitute caregiver can be found, the child welfare authorities will be called. They may conduct a more thorough search for a possible caregiver within the family, they may place the children in an emergency shelter, or they may put the children in a foster placement.

2. *Children left at home alone.* The children may be removed at once by police or if the child protection system in that jurisdiction has homemakers/caretakers available to remain with the children until the parents return to the home. The parents may be charged later for neglect.

3. *Parent arrested for a drug-related crime.* The child may be placed temporarily in foster care or an emergency shelter until the parent is released and enters treatment. However, if other risks exist (such as substandard housing, imminent eviction, or homelessness), or if the drug abuse is chronic, the child may be placed for a longer period of time.

4. *Parent on probation, or under other supervision, is rearrested.* Children most often do not end up in placement after their parents' first arrests. However, once child placement does occur, dual supervision of the family by child welfare and criminal justice or correctional authorities may result in children being immediately placed after the parents' subsequent arrests, as a result of agency information sharing.

When parents are arrested for offenses unrelated to child abuse/neglect, and their children are placed in state custody (whether with relatives or foster care), other issues arise. The most immediate of these issues is the length of time of incarceration. When parents are able to post bond, the initial disruption in children's lives may be short term. However, even a short placement can be traumatic (Littner, 1981). In instances where the child welfare or juvenile court authorities become involved, even a brief jail stay for the parent can result in months (or even years) of social services intervention on behalf of the child.

Because of the overwhelming number of children in state child welfare care, it is reasonable to be concerned that children and relative caretakers may become "lost" in the system and not receive the kinds of services they could or should (National Commission on Children, 1990). When parents maintain contact with the child welfare authorities through their assigned caseworkers or through their attorney, they can be assured that their children are safe and receiving proper care and services. Concerns about placement, or replacement, can be discussed. When siblings are separated by placement, parents can ensure that siblings do not become lost to each other.

When children are placed in foster care, their best interests generally require that early and regular parent and sibling visits should occur, communication by letters and telephone calls should be facilitated, and cultural issues should be taken into account by the child welfare agency. Whenever possible, natural parents should meet the foster parents or at least have telephone contact with them to discuss their concerns. Contact with a sensitive foster parent can offer support to both parent and children, and foster parents may often serve as models for troubled parents. Parental contact with children, relatives or foster parent caretakers, and an assigned caseworker is often the key to successful family reunification.

Visitation

So important is the contact between parents and children that without adequate human touch an infant will die. Removal from a parent is experienced by a child as a kind of death. Traumatic separations from a parent can cause symptoms of traumatic stress (described by Kampfner in Chapter 6). The loss of a parent can affect a child's learning in school and her or his ability to trust, to sleep, and to eat. The interruption of natural development of attachment behaviors in infants can lead to severe personality disorders in adulthood.

Children need stability in their care, and consistency in their relationships with their caregivers. Bowlby (1983) asserts that considerable damage is done to a child separated from his mother, with the amount of damage depending on the age of the child, the length of separation, and the quality of substitute care. Fanshel and Shinn (1982) observed that children experiencing sustained, long-term separation from their parents are most vulnerable to serious cognitive and personality disorders.

Historically, the lack of nurturance for children reared in orphanages was recognized as a form of deprivation. Placing children in foster homes was promoted as a better alternative for children by their advocates and has since become the standard procedure in child welfare cases. In the present child welfare system parents are assured visitation with their children on a weekly basis, and if these contacts do not occur regularly, the juvenile court will order them. Federal legislation (Public Law 96-272, the Child Welfare and Adoption Assistance Act) addresses these issues of parent–child contact because it is well known that long-term separation interrupts bonding, and that in the prolonged absence of their natural parents young children will bond instead with foster parents and other caregivers who continuously meet their needs for an extended period. P.L. 96-272 attempted to address children's needs for continuity of care and reduce the number of traumatic separations by mandating short stays in the foster care system. If parents and their children in placement are to reunify quickly, visitation must occur.

Visits between parents and children in foster care are therefore the rule. Most parents and children visit at or near the child's foster home and this visitation takes place with a minimum of supervision. Even though visits are sometimes withheld because of a parent's behavior (e.g., threatening caseworkers or caregivers, or coming to visits intoxicated), they will usually be attempted again. Even in cases where child abuse has occurred, visits will be allowed, although the courts will order supervised contact between children and their parents.

Visit "supervisors" are sometimes caseworkers or therapists, but often they are the relatives who are caring for the children. Supervised visits take place in the child welfare offices, or the offices of private social service agencies working with the family. The child protective agency will also sometimes allow supervised visits to occur at the children's or parent's home. Supervised visits are usually tense for both parent and child. With a caseworker or relative present to document the parent–child interaction and to observe any inappropriate behavior, the parent feels an unnatural quality, and the child often feels guarded as well. Sometimes certain topics, such as an upcoming court date, or where a child will be placed, are "off limits." Often parents and children are not allowed to talk about what brought the child into placement, when the child can go home, or if the parent still loves and wants the child to return. Sometimes parents are not allowed to tell children about their efforts toward rehabilitation or toward changing other circumstances of their home lives. If caseworkers are unfamiliar with placement trauma, they may try to "protect" the child from these topics because they are upsetting rather than using them to reassure the child that his feelings are okay and that his parent cares for him. Recalling that children experience placement as their own fault, and that their parent was taken from them, it is crucial that caseworkers allow children and parents time to talk about these circumstances.

Supervised visits continue until parents have made positive progress toward correcting the behaviors that brought their child into placement. At this point, unsupervised contact will begin, at first usually for an hour or two, and then extending to all day, overnight visits, and weekend visits.

Jail and Prison Visitation for Children in Foster Care

While visits between parents and children in the context of juvenile court cases or divorce custody battles are difficult, visits between incarcerated parents and their children are doubly difficult. This increased difficulty is related to two factors, the quality of parent–child visits in jail or prison, and the frequency of visitation.

The Quality of Jail and Prison Visitation

Contact visits between a parent and child are more natural and are preferred. However, many jails and prisons do not allow them and visitation rooms are not set up for use by young children. Sometimes visiting rooms are loud, with several visits taking place at once; communication through thick glass barriers between prisoners and their visitors may require shouting. Where glass visiting windows are not used, the partitions separating visitors and inmates often are high, and children need to be held up to see their parent. Except for extended-contact visitation programs, most correctional facilities do not allow prisoners and visitors to touch during their visits; not being able to touch their parents is very upsetting to children. Contact visits can be difficult, too, depending on the setting. Some prisons have very rigid criteria for visits, for example, demanding that a prisoner and his visitors sit on benches side by side rather than across from each other. Other prisons have no space for toys that would allow a parent to play more naturally with a child. However, some states do have prisons with playgrounds, play rooms with toys, or supervised play rooms (Boudouris, 1990; Cannings, 1991). These are the most satisfying settings for children.

The Frequency of Visitation

Frequency of visits is affected by the distance of the prison from the child's home and by the feelings of caretakers. Most prisons are located far from major cities. Because the majority of incarcerated parents and their families come from low socioeconomic groups, the cost of transportation to distant prisons makes frequent visitation impossible (Bloom & Steinhart, 1993). The feelings of caregivers toward incarcerated parents may also effect parent–child visitation. Caregivers may feel anger at the incarcerated parent for committing a crime. Caregivers also sometimes feel that visits at a prison are not "good for children" and that visits "upset the children." The fact that children will cry and misbehave after visits is part of the separation process. Children's behavioral reactions to prison visits were examined by the Center for Children of Incarcerated Parents; "acting out" and excitability were found to be common and transient behaviors (see Chapter 7).

The feelings and attitudes of the incarcerated parents themselves also influence the frequency of visitation. Some parents report that they do not want their children to see them in jail or prison (Hairston, 1989, 1990; Stanton, 1980); a number of these parents instruct caregivers to tell their children that they are sick or away at school (Kiser, 1991).

Children who are wards of the state see their parents least frequently, or not at all (Hairston, 1990). This is in part due to child welfare agency policies, which often set geographical limits beyond which parent–child visitation is not required as part of the reunification plan, and in part due to limited resources to help caregivers pay for visitation costs. It is also the result of rulings in family court cases, where judges who have limited experience with parents who are offenders may bar visits at jails or prisons as not appropriate for children.

Family Reunification

According to the National Commission on Children (1990), the number of children in foster care decreased in the late 1970s. There were 502,000 children in care in 1977, but the number had dropped to 302,000 in 1980, and to 275,000 in 1983. But by 1989 the number of children in substitute care had risen to 340,000. It is projected that the number could continue to rise, reaching over a half a million by 1995.

The majority of these children come from abusive or neglectful families. With all other factors taken into account, only family income is consistently related to all categories of abuse and neglect (National Commission on Children, 1990). Children from minority and single-parent families are overrepresented in the child welfare population, and many of these families are impoverished. While poverty alone is not the cause of abuse, it places many stresses on poor parents, and contributes to frustration and inappropriate discipline.

The child welfare system was designed to protect vulnerable children and, if the need arose for their placement away from home, to provide treatment and concrete services to reunify them with their families. However, it has been established that 14% of children remain in the system for more than 5 years (National Commission on Children, 1990; Tatara, 1990) The system has been overloaded in the past 10 years mainly due to the increase in substance dependency among parents. Caseworkers have far too many cases, and states are inadequately funding their child welfare departments.

Parent–child reunification is the goal mandated by P.L. 96-272 for every child coming into the child welfare system. However, Title IV-E of this act provides open-ended funds to states for out-of-home placement. With $1.8 billion budgeted for foster care in 1991, Title IV-E funds unfortunately provide a strong incentive for states to remove children from parents rather than to offer services to prevent placement or to reunite families. Title IV-B of the same act provides for funding to the states for family preservation and reunification services; however, the resources so mandated are not open-ended and must be appropriated by Congress. These funds consistently fall short of the actual need. The amount appropriated by Congress each year between 1979 and 1989 was $325 million. In 1991 funding was decreased to $273 million (National Commission on Children, 1991).

In addition, state child welfare agencies are overwhelmed, and staffed with workers who are overloaded, underpaid, and undertrained. Often, caseworkers are poorly supervised and have no specialized training. Private social service agencies, which are funded by the state and provide foster homes or residential facilities, are often focused only on maintaining placements. These agencies receive state funds only for children in state custody. Once a child is returned home, their funding for that child ceases. Although such mercenary concerns are not openly voiced, the focus is established by the top administration of these agencies, and filters down to direct-service staff. In some cases, government agencies overlook deficiencies or outright child abuse in these private agency foster homes (Henriques, 1982).

Family Reunification for Prisoners and Their Children in Foster Care

Problems with the child welfare system most strongly affect prisoners with children in foster care. These families have multiple needs and require the most services, but because incarcerated parents have little or no access to the system, these needs are likely to go unmet. Unlike other parents with children in foster care, prisoners cannot advocate for themselves, seek services in the community to meet their needs, or communicate with their caseworkers. Incarcerated parents with children in foster care may even have trouble meeting the simplest procedural requirements for reunification (Beckerman, 1994).

Unable to communicate with child welfare system representatives and uninformed about child welfare system policies, incarcerated parents are at great risk of losing their children. The most critical situations involve long-term placements resulting from a parent's incarceration while awaiting trial or serving a long prison sentence. Although recidivist offenders may consider 6 months to be a short period of time, child welfare authorities view a long-term placement as one extending for this length of time or longer. Parents in these situations are often unaware of the expectations of child welfare departments, which view parents' failure to keep in contact with their children through visits, letters, or telephone calls as lack of parental interest. Even when children are placed with relatives while in state custody, the same set of expectations exist. Parents who view themselves as serving relatively short sentences, and who feel that their child's custody is secure because the child is living with relatives, often fail to meet state agency expectations.

Outcomes of Placement

Administrative case reviews at the state child welfare department take place once every 6 months while a child remains in foster care. Permanency goals will be discussed at these meetings, which can be attended by parents, relatives, advocates, therapists, foster parents, and older children. The state child welfare agency then will review progress in meeting the goals.

State child welfare agencies will begin thinking of a permanent plan within 6 to 12 months of a child's entry into foster care. By 18 months, the law requires a formal review of permanency goals. Because of the backlog of cases in juvenile courts, very often no review takes place or no adequate review takes place for months or years. These situations persist in spite of attempts at legal remedies. In 1988, for example, the American Civil Liberties Union sued the Illinois Department of Children and Family Services for failure to provide judicial permanency reviews (B. H. et al. *v* Sliter) and, although there was an agreed consent decree in this case, the state department continues to fall behind and the overload in juvenile court also continues.

When 18-month-reviews of foster care cases do take place, they consider permanent placements for the children. The ideal "permanent home" is the household from which the children were taken, headed by their natural parent(s). This is the mandated goal of reunification efforts, but when it is not attainable, a "permanent home" may also be a foster home licensed by the state, in which the foster parents agree to care for children for a long period of time or indefinitely. Similarly, it can be the home of a relative, approved by the state, who receives foster care payments. In either of these circumstances, the foster caregivers may be urged to assume legal guardianship of the children, thereby relieving the state of the burden of foster care payments and the child welfare system of the burden of supervising the child's care.

Permanent placements also include adoptions. In order for a child to be freed for adoption, the rights of the parents to that child must be terminated by the court, with or without the parents' consent. Adoptions may be traditional or "open." In traditional adoptions, the parent loses all rights to and will be given no further information about the child. In "open" adoptions, the adoptive parents agree to allow some contact between the child and the natural parents. Sometimes this contact is as minimal as a letter and photo once a year; in other cases, parents are allowed visits or calls. Open adoptions allow children to keep in contact with siblings and other relatives. Few states allow open adoption; in most jurisdictions, parents formally loses all legal rights to their adopted children and the open adoption is an individualized, negotiated agreement between the birth and the adoptive parents.

These are sensitive issues, and must be decided on a case-by-case basis. Each child, and each family situation, is different. There are many well-meaning people working within the child welfare system, but there is often a lack of training or consultants available to assist these professionals in their decision making. Decisions about a child's life are emotionally loaded. Many court dramas are played out with all players, including the professionals, acting on their *personal feelings*. Many of these professionals have had unhappy childhoods, or have themselves been victims of abuse and neglect, and the urge to save themselves is transformed into the urge to save all the children with whom they work.

Outcomes of Placement for Children of Prisoners

No one knows how the outcomes of placement differ for children of prisoners in foster care, compared to other children. However, the average amount of time served in U.S. prisons is 16 months for females and 66 months for males (USDJ, 1993), so that most prisoners with children in foster care face the federally mandated deadline for permanent placement of their children before or immediately after their release.

Studies (McGowan & Blumenthal, 1978; Hairston, 1990) have found that prior incarcerations reduce the likelihood that a mother and child will be reunited after the mother's current jail or prison term. These studies also suggest that incarcerated mothers and their children in foster care will be less likely to achieve reunification than other mothers with children supervised by the child welfare system.

The National Black Child Development Institute's (1989) survey of black children in foster care found that 12 to 18% of all terminations of parental rights within this population occurred among families with an incarcerated parent, where the child had entered the child welfare system because of the parent's incarceration. This group accounted for the largest proportion of terminations. The study did not determine what percentage of children who entered the system in other categories (e.g., allegations of abuse, neglect, or abandonment) had incarcerated parents, nor what percentage of those parents had their rights terminated. The findings of this study suggest that terminations of parental rights may occur disproportionately among incarcerated parents, and especially among those whose children entered foster care only because their parents could not materially provide for them while in jail or prison.

Conclusions

While there are fundamental similarities in the experience of foster care for all children, children of prisoners and their parents have significantly different experiences in the areas of visitation, family reunification services, and the outcomes of placement. These differences may lead to a different rate of termination of parental rights among incarcerated parents, and should be explored with further research.

References

Beckerman, A. (1994). Mothers in prison: Meeting the prerequisite conditions for permanency planning. *Social Work*, 39(1):9–14.

Bloom, B., & Steinhart, D. (1993). *Why punish the children? A reappraisal of the children of incarcerated mothers in America.* San Francisco: National Council on Crime and Delinquency.

Boudouris, J. (1990). *Prisons and kids.* Laurel, MD: American Correctional Association.

Bowlby, J. (1983). *Attachment and loss.* New York: Basic Books.

Cannings, K. (1991). *Bridging the gap: Programs and services to facilitate contact between inmate parents and their children.* Ottawa: Ministry of the Solicitor General of Canada.

Fanshell, D., & Shinn, E. B. (1982). *Children in foster care.* New York: Columbia University Press.

Hairston, C. F. (1989). Men in prison: Family characteristics and family views. *Journal of Offender Counseling, Services and Rehabilitation*, 14(1):23–30.

Hairston, C. F. (1990). Mothers in jail: Parent–child separation and jail visitation. *Affilia*, 6(2).

Henriques, Z. W. (1982). *Imprisoned mothers and their children.* Washington, DC: University Press of America.

Kiser, G. (1991, September). Female inmates. *Federal probation*, 54: 56–63.

Littner, N. (1981). The importance of the natural parents to the child in placement. In P.A. Sinanoglu & A. N. Maluccio (Eds.), *Parents of children in placement*. New York: Child Welfare League of America.

National Black Child Development Institute. (1989). *Who will care when parents can't? A study of black children in foster care*. Washington, DC: Author.

National Commission on Children. (1990). *Beyond rhetoric*. Washington, DC: Author.

Stanton, A. (1980). *When mothers go to jail*. Lexington, MA: Lexington Books.

Tatara, T. (1990). *Characteristics of children in substitute and adoptive care: A statistical child welfare data base*. Washington, DC: American Public Welfare Association.

U.S. Department of Justice. (1993). *Survey of state prison inmates, 1991* (Report No. NCJ-136949). Washington, DC: Bureau of Justice Statistics.

Young, L. (1950). Placement from the child's perspective. *Social Casework*, 17:133–47.

9

Parent–Child Visitation in the Jail or Prison

Denise Johnston

Adults who work with or care for children of incarcerated parents often express concerns about parent–child visitation in jails and prisons. Some feel that it is inappropriate for children to visit in these settings. Others are concerned about the emotional reactions of the children prior to, during, and following visitation, and about the difficult behaviors that arise from these emotions.

There is little or no research literature on children who visit parents removed from the home by arrest and incarceration. However, the issue of visitation for children and parents who have been separated by the child's removal from the home has been carefully examined in the child welfare literature.

Parent–Child Separation

Parent–child separation is traumatic. Even during short-term separations, parents and children experience grief and a sense of loss.

The Child Welfare League of America (Littner, 1956) has identified common reactions of children separated from their parents, including painful feelings of rejection, loss of identity, anger, and guilt. Children develop increased fear of emotional closeness and increased sensitivity and reactions to later separations. Separation was found to make the child highly vulnerable to both emotional and cognitive problems.

Forced parent–child separations are even more traumatic. This is also true of separations that are perceived by the child as forced or violent. A major role of parents is to assist children in adjusting to and overcoming the effects of trauma. When a traumatic experience also includes parent–child separation, children lose their helpers and their ability to master future trauma may be significantly and even permanently impaired (Furman, 1983).

It is important to understand that children commonly experience threats to their parents as threats to themselves. This is particularly true for children who have not completed the process of separation-individuation from the parent, which normally occurs by age 3. The traumatic effects on children of threats to or separation from their parents cannot be compared to the effects of any similar event on adults.

Children of Offenders and Parent–Child Separation

Children of offenders are particularly vulnerable to the trauma of parent–child separation. They are more likely than other children to have suffered previous traumatic experiences. As a result, they are more likely to have weakened family support systems and a less adequate quality of care than their peers.

These children have commonly been exposed to a series of preceding traumas. Like other recent investigations (Bloom & Steinhart, 1993; Task Force on the Female Offender, 1990) studies of children of jailed mothers and of children of offenders in the community by the Center for Children of Incarcerated Parents have found that a majority had experienced substance abuse in the home and/or domestic violence. One in three of the children we studied in south-central Los Angeles had lost a parent, sibling, or other adult household member to community violence. While the incidence of child abuse and neglect among these children was not significantly higher than that among their neighborhood peers, they were significantly poorer and more highly mobile.

These children have endured multiple separations from their parents, siblings, and caregivers. Since 78% of jail inmates (U.S. Department of Justice [USDJ], 1991) and 81% of prisoners (USDJ, 1993) are recidivists, most children of offenders experience parental arrest and detention at least twice. One in five have been present at the time of their parents' arrest, and approximately half of this smaller group are at the developmentally vulnerable stage of 3- to 7-years-old (Johnston, 1991). Many children of women offenders experience more than one change of caregiver during their mother's incarceration; this is significant because multiple placements of children separated from their parents have been identified as a source of traumatic stress (Doyle & Bauer, 1989). For all these reasons, children of offenders are increasingly susceptible to traumatic reactions from each additional parent–child separation.

In work with over 3,000 individual clients in a variety of therapeutic, educational, and family reunification projects since 1990, we have observed patterns in immediate trauma-reactive behaviors among children of arrested and detained parents. Acutely, children are frightened, distressed, and anxious. We have observed or verified reports of rare but extreme reactions, including mutism, conversion reactions, and dissociative states. Children are typically concerned with the physical well-being and safety of their arrested parents, and may interpret parental arrest and subsequent separation as a parental loss. Indeed, some children believe their parent is dead following arrest; we are aware of children up to 7 years of age who refuse to accept hearing their mother's voice over the telephone as evidence that she is alive.

In the period immediately following separation, children often grieve. They may be withdrawn and may experience changes in appetite, sleep, and activity level. For children who normally react to stress by acting out, this period may be characterized by agitation, hyperactivity, and other disruptive behaviors. It is common, acutely and in the immediate postseparation period, for children to identify the arrest and incarceration of their parent as the source of their distress.

Over time, most children of incarcerated parents become angry. More than 90% of the adolescent children we studied were found to be oppositional/defiant; a smaller number become depressed. Very young children may have very disorganized emotions and reactive behaviors. They may be emotionally labile and may have difficulty in their relationships with peers; they may also have concentration, sleep, and attention problems. Older children more often display consistent patterns of behavior. Both oppositional/defiant and depressed children can act out aggressively; the large majority of older children referred to our therapeutic programs have been fighting in school. As a result of these and other behavioral problems, children of offenders often have both academic and classroom disciplinary problems.

In addition, children of offenders may experience parental arrest and detention as rejection. Young children, who are developmentally unable to understand concepts of accountability, are frequently also unable to understand the concept of forced detention. For these children, the parent's absence is perceived as voluntary. While children at these ages are particularly susceptible to "survivor guilt" following the arrest and removal of a parent, most children of offenders report some feelings of inferiority or unworthiness and a sense of responsibility for the separation.

As they are separated from the experience by time, children are less likely to identify parental arrest and incarceration as the source of their reactive behaviors and more likely to attribute their behavioral problems to their own character deficits. "We're the bad kids" is how many children in our public school therapeutic programs collectively identify themselves. This opinion is reflected in their performance on the standardized measurements of self-esteem; their ratings on most categories of these scales fall into the normal range, but self-ratings of their behavior fall at the lowest levels.

We have concluded from our research that parent–child separation within families of offenders is one of three major contributors to increasing intergenerational incarceration.

Parent–Child Visitation Following Separation

Parent-child visitation is a critical intervention following forced separations, such as those that occur when a child is removed from the home by child welfare authorities or when a parent is arrested. Extensive reviews of the current and historical child welfare literature support the importance of frequent, regular parent–child visitation following separation (Hess, 1987).

Parent–child visitation following separation has beneficial effects on the emotional adjustment of children (Kelmer & Clifford, 1962; Weinstein, 1960; White, 1981). Weinstein found that the average well-being of children who visited with parents after separation was higher than the well-being of those who did not visit. It has also been found that parent–child visitation contributes to greater gains in IQ scores and emotional adjustment measurements in children separated from their parents, as well as to improvements in child behavior (Fanshell & Shinn, 1982).

Why does parent–child visitation produce beneficial effects?

1. Visits allow children to express their emotional reactions to the separation, which they may not be allowed to do elsewhere. According to Ner Littner (1981) of the Child Welfare League of America, the more disturbed children are by parent–child separation and the poorer their adjustment, the more important it is that visitation occur.

2. Visitation allows parents to work out their feelings about separation and loss, and therefore helps them become better able to help their children with the same issues.

3. Visitation allows children to see their parents realistically. Parent–child separation normally produces irrational feelings and fears within children about their parents; children also entertain unrealistic fantasies when contact with their parent does not occur. Visits allow children to release these feelings, fears, and fantasies and to replace them with a more realistic understanding of their parents' characteristics and circumstances.

4. Visits allow parents to model appropriate interactions for children who react inappropriately, but understandably, to the circumstances of separation. This is particularly important for children who do not accept their new caregivers and/or whose reactive behaviors are difficult to manage.

5. Visitation allows parents and children to maintain their existing relationship, and therefore allows the family to reunite more successfully following separation.

The timing of visitation is also important. Anna Freud (1965) has noted that the traditional delay in parent–child visitation after separation is wrong. She and other authorities (Jolowicz, 1981) believe that it is better for the parent and child to visit as soon as possible after placement. Victor Pike (1976) director of the landmark Oregon study on permanent placement for foster children, has written that visits between parents and children "should begin instantly" following separation.

Parent–Child Prison Visitation

In spite of the literature on parent–child visitation, there is persistent concern among child protective services workers (Johnston, 1994), caregivers (Bloom & Steinhart, 1993; Hairston, 1989), and prisoners themselves (Bloom & Steinhart, 1993; Hairston, 1990) about the possible negative effects of jail or prison visitation on children. Some caseworkers and caregivers report that children have undesirable reactions to visitation, and justify the suspension of visitation on this basis (Johnston, 1994).

A Study of Children's Reactions to Prison Visits

The Center for Children of Incarcerated Parents and Centerforce Visitors' Hospitality Network documented caregiver reports of children's behavioral reactions to parent–child prison visitation. The study examined children visiting six California prisons during October 1992. During 2 consecutive weekends, adults accompanying children to visit at five prisons for men and one prison for women were surveyed as they waited for visits to take place.

Results. The adults surveyed were supervising 240 visiting children between 3 months and 17 years of age. One hundred and thirty-nine children (57.9%) were visiting male prisoners, and 101 (42.1%) children were visiting females (see Table 9.1). The majority of children in each group were visiting their natural parents or stepparents. Seven out of 10 children had lived with the prisoners they were visiting for at least 6 months. Almost all the children visited the prison frequently; 80% visited at least once a month.

About half of the children had behavioral reactions to prison visits (see Table 9.2). The most common reaction was excitability or hyperactivity before visits. Most reactions (74.2%) lasted less than 1 week and more than half (53.9%) occurred only on the day of the visit. None of the children had ever had a serious or sustained reaction to prison visitation.

Table 9.1
Child Prison Visitors, by Relationship to Prisoner

Relationship of Prisoner to Visiting Child		No. (%)
Male prisoners (N = 139)	Natural father	68/139 (48.9)
	Stepfather	25/139 (18.0)
	Brother	9/139 (6.5)
	Grandfather	3/139 (2.1)
	Other relative	15/139 (10.8)
	Friend	13/139 (9.4)
Female prisoners (N = 101)	Natural mother	71/101 (70.3)
	Sister	6/101 (5.9)
	Grandmother	8/101 (7.9)
	Other relative	16/101 (15.8)

There was no relationship between reactions to visits and the age or sex of the child, the sex of the parent visited, or the frequency of visits. However, there was a relationship between the incidence of reactions to parent–child visits and the length of time the parent and child had lived together (see Table 9.3). More than four out of 10 children who had lived with the parent they visited for more than 6 months reacted to visits, compared to less than one in six children visiting a parent with whom they had never resided.

Discussion of the Findings. Up to half of all incarcerated parents do not receive visits from their children, and most of those that do receive visits do not receive them regularly or frequently (Bloom & Steinhart, 1993; Hairston, 1989). This study examined a subgroup of prisoners' children who visit prisons at short, regular intervals. Children who rarely visit their parents in prison may have different patterns of reaction to visitation.

The findings of the reported survey suggest that behavioral reactions to prison visitation are common and most often limited to the period immediately preceding and following the visits. They never involve serious emotional disturbances. They appear to occur more frequently among children who have lived with the parents they are visiting, suggesting that the behaviors are effects of parent–child separation.

Like other children who suffer parent–child separation, children of prisoners benefit from visits with their parents. Immediate visitation following parent–child separation due to arrest and detention also reassures these children that their parents are alive, are relatively well, and have not been injured by arrest. Visitation dispels common feelings of rejection and guilt. In addition, as with children in placement, visitation is the first and perhaps

Table 9.2
Children's Behavioral Reactions to Prison Visits

Group of Children	Timing of Reaction	No. (%)
All children	Before, during or after visits	128/240 (53.3)
Reactive children	Before visits	110/128 (85.9)
	After visits	75/128 (58.5)
	Both before and after visits	71/128 (55.5)

Table 9.3
Child Reactions to Prison Visits by Previous Living Arrangement

Visit Participants	Previous Living Arrangement	Frequency of Child Reactions
Father/child	lived together > 6 months	44.2%
	never lived together	13.5%
Mother/child	lived together > 6 months	48.6%
	never lived together	6.9%

most important step toward family reunification. There is no evidence in the literature, either from empirical studies or statements of expert opinion, that parent–child visitation in the jail or prison setting has any significant or long-term negative consequences for participating children.

Conclusions

Child welfare experts assert that there is cumulative evidence that the frequency, nature and duration of parent–child contacts following separation play a critical role in determining a child's future development (Klein, 1960). Speaking of children separated from their parents, Laird (1981, p. 110) says, "In situations where the physical and emotional cutoffs are intense, [children separated from their parents] may be even more prone to duplicate destructive family patterns in their own adult interpersonal and family relationships." This is particularly important for children of incarcerated parents, where physical and emotional separation of parent and child is abrupt and forced (or perceived as forced), and where there is commonly a history of destructive family patterns such as crime, substance abuse, or domestic violence.

As evidence of intergenerational crime and incarceration continues to mount, every criminal justice and corrections policy affecting children of offenders should be scrutinized for its long-term implications. In the case of parent–child visitation in jails or prisons, it is clear that this beneficial, low-cost intervention reduces the negative effects of parent–child separation and may therefore also contribute to a reduction of future crime and incarceration among prisoners' children.

References

Bloom, B., & Steinhart, D. (1993). *Why punish the children? A reappraisal of the children of incarcerated mothers in America.* San Francisco: National Council on Crime and Delinquency.

Doyle, J. S., & Bauer, S. K. (1989). Post-traumatic stress disorder in children. *Journal of Traumatic Stress,* 2(3):275–288.

Fanshell, D., & Shinn, E. B. (1982). *Children in foster care.* New York: Columbia University Press.

Freud, A. (1965). Cindy. In J. Goldstein & J. Katz (Eds.), *The family and the law* (pp. 1051–1053). New York: Free Press.

Furman, E. (1983). Studies in childhood bereavement. *Canadian Journal of Psychiatry,* 28(4):241–247.

Hairston, C. F. (1989). Men in prison: family characteristics & family views. *Journal of Offender Counseling, Services & Rehabilitation,* 14(1):23–30.

Hess, P. M. (1987). Parental visiting of children in foster care: Current knowledge and research agenda. *Children and Youth Services Review,* 9:29–50.

Johnston, D. (1991). *Children of jailed mothers.* Pasadena, CA: Center for Children of Incarcerated Parents.

Johnston, D. (1993). Helping children of offenders through intervention programs. In *The state of corrections.* Laurel, MA: American Correctional Association. Pgs. 238–244.

Johnston, D. (1994). *Child custody issues of offenders: A preliminary report on the CHICAS Project.* Pasadena, CA: Center for Children of Incarcerated Parents.

Jolowicz, A.R. (1981). A foster child needs his own parents. *Child,* 12(2):18–21.

Kelmer, M. L., & Clifford, L. (1962). Conditions associated with emotional maladjustment among children in care. *Education Review,* 14(2):112–123.

Kline, D. (1960). Service to parents of placed children. In *Changing needs and practices in child welfare.* New York: Child Welfare League of America, pp. 37–40.

Laird, J. (1981). An ecological approach to child welfare. In P. A. Sinanoglu & A. N. Maluccio, (eds.), *Parents of children in placement.* New York: Child Welfare League of America, pp. 97–132.

Hairston, C. F. (1990) Imprisoned mothers and their children. *Affilia,* 6(2).

Littner, N. (1956). *Some Traumatic Effects of Separation and Placement.* New York: Child Welfare League of America.

Pike, V. (1976). Permanent planning for foster children. *Children Today,* 5(6):22–25.

Task Force on the Female Offender. (1990): *The female offender: What does the future hold?* Laurel, MD: American Correctional Association.

Weinstein, E. A. (1960). *The self image of the foster child.* New York; Russell Sage Foundation.

White, M. S. (1981). Promoting parent–child visiting in foster care. In P. A. Sinanoglu & A. N. Maluccio, (Eds.), *Parents of children in placement*. New York: Child Welfare League of America. Pages 461–475.

U.S. Department of Justice. (1991). *Profile of jail inmates, 1989*. (Report No. NCJ-129097). Washington, DC: Bureau of Justice Statistics.

U.S. Department of Justice. (1993). *Survey of state prison inmates, 1991*. (Report No. NCJ-136949). Washington, DC: Bureau of Justice Statistics.

PART IV

Legal Issues

10

Legal Issues for Prisoners with Children

Ellen Barry

with River Ginchild and Doreen Lee

Incarcerated parents and their children are faced with enormous obstacles, emotionally, psychologically, socially, and legally. Legal obstacles pervade every aspect of the relationship between these parents and their children. While the social services system is designed to assist and support families in crisis, the practical reality for incarcerated parents and their children is that this system more often works to separate families than to reunify and heal them. There are several major legal issues confronting incarcerated parents and their children and some significant policy considerations that must be addressed in order to assist these families in crisis.

All 50 states have a system established for providing foster care and assistance to children in need, either because their parents have abused or neglected them or because their parents are unable to care for them for wide variety of reasons. In some instances, parents are institutionalized or hospitalized, in other instances they are alcohol- or drug-addicted, and in still other cases they are incarcerated. In the vast majority of cases, incarcerated parents have not had their children removed from their care because of abuse or neglect, but simply because they are unable to care for their children due to the fact of their incarceration. For example, a 1986 study of women prisoners in the largest U.S. prison for women indicated that less than 0.5% of the mothers surveyed were incarcerated for abusing their children (Barry & Reid-Green, 1990).

When parents are incarcerated, the lives of their children can be seriously disrupted because the systems that exist to address the legal arrangements for custody and care of children are not as responsive to the special needs of these children as they should be. When fathers are incarcerated, the family unit often experiences severe trauma, but families are much more likely to remain legally intact because the children's mother is usually present to maintain the structure of the family and to provide ongoing parenting. Indeed, some wives or partners of male prisoners relocate to the

147

area where the children's father is incarcerated to enable frequent visits with the prisoner and thus to keep the family unit intact. Of course, this is not always the case; a significant number of families fall apart under the strain of the arrest and incarceration of the father, and in these circumstances many wives of prisoners separate from their partners or initiate divorce actions (Hairston, 1989). While the anger and recrimination felt by some wives or partners is often clearly justified, it is important for these families to be able to go through the divorce process with the least amount of trauma and damage to the children involved. Just as all parents need to be sensitive to the impact of divorce on their children, a prisoner and his or her spouse need to pay special attention to the needs of their children— who may have already been traumatized by their father's arrest and incarceration—in approaching the process of divorce.

As difficult at it may be for incarcerated fathers to deal with the separation from their families and children, such separation is substantially more complex and difficult for incarcerated mothers. When women are incarcerated, it is very rarely the case that the father of their children remains with the children or moves with the children to enable them to be closer to their mother during her incarceration (Task Force on the Female Offender, 1990; U.S. Department of Justice [USDJ], 1993). Many women, in fact, never see their children once during their incarceration because of the problems posed by geographic distance, financial burdens for the family, and the lack of family members available to bring the children to visit (Bloom & Steinhart, 1992).

As a result, incarcerated mothers are far more likely to have to deal with a social services system that is not always responsive, one that in some cases is extremely hostile to the mother in prison. If a mother is arrested and there is no relative available to take the child immediately, the child is often taken into custody by the child welfare department. Unless a relative is able to claim the child within a short time after he or she is detained, the child is likely to become a dependent of the local juvenile court. Although a child may have been detained by the child welfare department strictly because of the arrest of the mother, the department may well include many other allegations about the mother in the petition that it is required to file with the juvenile court. For example, the mother's previous drug or alcohol history, history of homelessness, history of unemployment, or history of mental illness may be raised even though it is not technically relevant to the grounds for removing the child and even though such allegations may be based on hearsay.

Once her child is made a dependent of the juvenile court, a mother will find it very difficult to play an active part in her child's life or to take effective action to reunite with her child. Unfortunately, this situation may eventually lead to the termination of the incarcerated parent's parental rights. This is one of the most severe and devastating events that can occur to a parent and child, particularly if the only factor separating the parent and the child is the parent's incarceration and there has been no abuse by the parent.

While parent–child separation is difficult for all incarcerated parents and their children, the trauma experienced by pregnant women in prisons and jails, and new mothers and their infants, is particularly wrenching. Characteristically, most incarcerated mothers are separated from their newborns within 24 to 48 hours after birth. While there are some exceptions to this rule, and while some model programs have been designed to minimize the separation between mothers and newborns, few correctional systems allow even the most minimal time for mothers and their newborns to be together immediately after birth.

Approximately 10% of incarcerated women nationwide are pregnant while incarcerated (USDJ, 1993), and an additional 15% have been estimated to be in the postpartum period—that is, within the 12-month period after giving birth (McCall, Casteel & Shaw, 1985). The vast majority of jails and many prison systems provide poor to inadequate reproductive health care for women prisoners (Standing Committee on Legal Services for Prisoners, 1993). Some prison and jail systems do provide adequate to good care for pregnant women prisoners, often because they have been required to do so by court order, as the result of litigation (*Harris v. McCarthy*, 1985; *Jones v. Dyer*, 1986; *Yeager v Smith*, 1987). For pregnant, substance-dependent women, the issues of adequate pregnancy care, treatment, and recovery are even more complex. Adequate medical care, access to viable treatment and recovery services, and the need for effective alternatives to incarceration are the most critical issues facing these women, their infants, and society.

One of the most effective options for minimizing the risks and trauma of separation for the children of prisoners during their parents' incarceration is placement of the children with grandparents and other relative caregivers. When families have the ability to plan for the separation, many incarcerated parents turn to their mothers, sisters, and other relatives for assistance in caring for their children during the period of their incarceration. However, in some instances, families do not have the luxury of planning for this period of separation. All too often grandparents, aunts, and other relatives get a frantic call in the middle of the night from parents who have been arrested and need to make plans for the care of their children. In still other cases, parents are not allowed to call relatives, and children are taken at the same time their parents are arrested and placed in an emergency shelter. Relatives must then move quickly to pick up these children. If no relative is able to retrieve the children within a brief period of time, the children may become dependents of the juvenile court.

In each of these areas, alternatives to parental incarceration, and to the current procedures by which public agencies supervise and "protect" the children of prisoners, clearly represent a potential solution to these problems. Yet the limited number of existing alternatives have not been easily established. Legislation and/or litigation have often been necessary for the creation and implementation of such alternatives, suggesting that legal issues will remain central to the topic of incarcerated parents and their children for some time to come.

Challenges to Separation of the Family

Parental incarceration can have a lasting, disruptive effect on the family unit. The current growth in prison and jail populations has resulted in a significant increase in the number of incarcerated parents, and hence an increase in the number of families in crisis due to parental incarceration. The difficulty in overcoming this basic separation is exacerbated by often inadequate visitation policies and complications within the juvenile dependency court system.

When parents are incarcerated, visitation with their children becomes one of the few means of maintaining the family unit. Experts have concluded that visitation helps children adjust to parental incarceration (Editors of Yale Law Review, 1978), and that this consistent parent–child contact is critical for long-term healthy child development (Call, 1976; LaPoint, Picker & Harris, 1985). Although visitation rights are not directly guaranteed by the Constitution, they can be established by state law and protected by due process (Schoenbauer, 1986). Most states have acknowledged to some degree the importance of visitation rights for incarcerated parents and their children. According to the First Circuit Court of Appeals, "Visitation rights, besides having to meet the . . . due process standard, reflect First Amendment values, most clearly the rights of association" (*Feeley v Sampson*, 1978).

While many courts have upheld statutes granting visitation rights to incarcerated parents, many legal and practical barriers still exist. When a parent who has physical custody of the children is arrested, he or she must give temporary custody to another adult. In order to obtain visitation, the original custody order must be altered to reflect the circumstances of incarceration. This process is very difficult because prisoners have extremely limited access to legal services for family law issues. Indeed, incarcerated parents only have a right to a court-appointed attorney if their parental rights are in danger of being terminated. For all other situations, such as visitation and custody, they must represent themselves or secure an attorney who will work pro bono (without charge) to represent them.

Another difficulty in obtaining visitation is acquiring transportation to court hearings. Although incarcerated parents are usually entitled to be transported to court for hearings related to termination of parental rights, judges are not required to allow incarcerated parents to attend hearings for issues such as visitation rights.

Even if an incarcerated parent is able to obtain a visitation order, there is no guarantee that it will be enforced. Circumstances are often such that there is no one willing or able to bear the responsibility and expense of bringing the children to visit the parent.

As such, legal barriers have made the process of obtaining visitation rights extremely frustrating for incarcerated parents. About half of all imprisoned men do not receive visits from their children (Hairston, 1989), and over half of the women in prison and jail have never been visited by their children (Bloom & Steinhart, 1992). However, the significant number of incarcerated parents not visited by their children may be due to practical considerations as well as legal obstacles. Prisons are generally located in rural communities far from the cities where most prisoners' families live, and transportation to and from these institutions is severely limited by time and cost factors (Schoenbauer, 1986).

Many incarcerated parents also raise concerns about inappropriate and oppressive visiting conditions. County jail facilities often require children to speak by phone with their incarcerated parents who sit behind glass partitions. In addition, there have been several instances where children have been strip-searched or pat-searched by correctional staff who claimed they had to do so because of "security concerns" (*Blackburn v Snow*, 1985).

Ultimately, if incarcerated parents are unable to overcome such barriers, they may lose their parental rights altogether. The "termination" or "severance" of parental rights permanently curtails a parent's right to communicate with, and care for, his or her children. The probability of termination increases as a result of the limited contact incarcerated parents have with their children.

If a parent is able to place his or her children with relatives or other responsible adults upon arrest, the family will most likely be reunified when the parent is released. However, in many instances, parents are unable to make such arrangements at the time of arrest. They often do not have the time nor the access to resources to arrange a long-term care plan for their children. If a parent is unable to find a suitable place for the children, the children will be made dependents of the court, usually within 48 to 72 hours after arrest. As dependents of the court, the children are placed in foster care and either reunified with their parents upon release, or placed through adoption if parental rights are ultimately terminated.

Incarcerated parents can lose their parental rights if the court decides that the circumstances fall roughly within three basic areas: (1) abandonment, (2) the nature of the felony conviction, and (3) the length of time in foster care (Barry, E., Kojimoto, C., Issacs, R., Lujan, G., Kandel, M., et. al., 1993).

In some states, incarceration has been construed as a form of abandonment and used to justify termination of parental rights (Arizona Rev. Stat.

Ann., 1974; *In re Neal*, 1987; Michigan Comp. Laws Ann., 1986). Many courts, however, have decided otherwise. Indeed, a growing number of states allow incarcerated parents who maintain contact with their children and follow reunification plans to avoid termination on the grounds of abandonment (see *In re Adoption of Herman*, 1980; *In re Dolores B.*, 1988; *In re H.G.B., M.A.B., & D.J.B.*, 1981; *Jordan v Hancock*, 1974).

The nature of the felony conviction is generally another reason for termination. Several states terminate parental rights if the felony committed is determined as proof of "parental unfitness" (California Civil Code, 1994; California Welfare and Institutions Code, 1994; *Matter of Vernia*, 1989; Michigan Comp. Laws Ann., 1986). Although the statutory language describing what can be construed as "unfit" is vague, incarceration in and of itself does not automatically indicate a parent's inability to care for a child after release. For example, in order for termination to occur, California courts require clear evidence that incarcerated parents cannot be rehabilitated to support their children after release (*In re Terry E.*, 1986).

The third major reason that termination occurs for incarcerated parents is the length of time that a child is in foster care. After a child has been in foster care for 12 to 18 months, parental rights can be terminated by the state. The 1980 Adoption Assistance and Child Welfare Reform Act (P.L. 96-272) places this limit on the time children may remain in foster care in an attempt to avoid "foster care drift." Legislators are legitimately concerned about the negative effects that movement from one foster home to another over a lengthy period of time has upon children of incarcerated parents (Barry, Kojimoto, Issacs, Lujan, Kandel et. al., 1993).

The 1-year time limit, however, places an additional burden upon incarcerated parents, who are physically unable to assume care of their children until after release. Because prisoners incarcerated on even minor felony charges face sentences of at least 1 year, many incarcerated parents are unable to establish permanent homes or meet other reunification requirements within the allotted time. These circumstances increase the probability that they will lose their parental rights.

In order to address this issue, many states have held that if incarcerated parents maintain contact with their children and follow reunification plans, such positive actions deserve due consideration and often should forestall termination of parental rights. For example, the Arkansas Supreme Court held that while incarceration is an "impediment to a normal parent–child relationship," it is not conclusive evidence that parental rights should be terminated (*Bush v Dietz*, 1984).

It is therefore essential that incarcerated parents and their children remain in contact throughout the period of incarceration. This is particularly important when parents have more than a year to serve. Indeed, the necessity for active involvement with their children on the part of incarcerated parents is reflected by P.L. 96-272. In order to receive federal foster care funding, state agencies are required to provide reasonable assistance to all parents in the dependency court process. Incarcerated parents are clearly entitled to these services. Such assistance includes notification about juvenile court dates, development—with parents—of case plans that parents must follow if they are ultimately to be reunified with their children, and specific services to assist parents in reunifying with their children.

Unfortunately, although P.L. 96-272 seeks to support eventual reunification, the services available to assist incarcerated parents are with children in foster care often inadequate. The presence of incarcerated parents at dependency court proceedings is important not only as a means of their participation in permanency planning, but also as evidence of their interest in the child's life. Notification of court proceedings, however, is often insufficient. In many cases, notification is not timely and the parent is unable to arrange for transportation to court, or has missed the date altogether (Barry & Reid-Green, 1990; Beckerman, 1994). In other cases, vital information such as dates, addresses, and procedures for attending court hearings are not clearly stated by social services and judicial agencies in materials provided to incarcerated parents.

P.L. 96-272 also requires state agencies to work with incarcerated parents to develop individual case plans that must be followed to avoid termination. However, much like notification services, this requirement often goes unmet (Beckerman, 1994). A case plan must be developed for each individual case, and should reflect the special circumstances of an incarcerated parent. Unfortunately, due to their heavy caseloads and lack of adequate funding, caseworkers have very limited access to incarcerated parents; as a result, they often submit court reports that do not even include the parents' statements (Schoenbauer, 1986). The lack of communication between caseworkers and incarcerated parents can lead to distorted court reports and inappropriate reunification plans.

Upon release, for a variety of reasons, many parents will face tremendous obstacles in reunifying with their children. Some of these reasons are within their control, but many others are completely beyond their control. In many cases, parents will have been incarcerated for over a year and during that period of incarceration will have had limited contact with their children. Many of these parents will not have been able to attend relevant court hearings and will have been unable to fulfill all the requirements in their case plans. Most parents who have been ordered by the court to attend parenting classes, to get counseling, to attend drug or alcohol rehabilitation, or to obtain employment will not have been able to comply with these requirements because such programs were not available in the prison or jail. Without adequate reunification services, most of these parents will have their parental rights terminated. It is clear that improvements must be made in the dependency court system as well as in prison and jail visitation policies if states are to more effectively support the reunification of incarcerated parents and their children.

Modifications designed to make prison and jail facilities more conducive to visitation between incarcerated parents and their children should include both economic and structural enhancements. Because prisons are often located far from urban centers, transportation to and from facilities is difficult and expensive. Children who must be placed in foster care outside of their families should be placed in homes as near to their parents as possible in order to decrease traveling time and distance, or, alternatively, should be placed with foster parents or group homes willing and able to assist in facilitating visitation between parents and children. To make visitation more financially feasible for all caretakers of children whose parents are incarcerated, the state should fund transportation to and from prison facilities as part of its reunification services plan.

Structurally, prisons and jails are not designed to promote visitation. However, if eventual reunification is indeed a goal of the state, visitation facilities that foster supportive, family environments should to be established. Unreasonably intrusive practices such as strip-searching children without clear justification must be prohibited.

Other changes to better facilitate reunification can be made within the dependency court system itself. The reunification services required by P.L. 96-272 should be clearly defined so that social service agencies are able to provide adequate and uniform support to these families in crisis. Available services should also reflect the special needs of incarcerated parents and their children, and state laws governing dependency should have specific language addressing the provision of these services (California Welfare and Institutions Code, sect. 361.5). In order to ensure the availability of appropriate services, communication between state agencies and incarcerated parents must be improved. Because lack of communication is often due to parents' limited access to social service caseworkers, funding should be provided in all jurisdictions for parents to make collect phone calls to their caseworkers.

While notification of dependency court hearings is one of the most fundamental requirements of P.L. 96-272, it is also one of the most inadequate and functionally ineffective elements of the statute. Notification of dependency hearings should be made well in advance of the date the incarcerated parent is expected to appear in court. Enough time must be allowed to enable the parent to make arrangements for transportation to court. In addition, all relevant information, such as dates, addresses, and instructions for attending, should be clearly indicated on notification papers.

In the end, modifications to the dependency court system and to prison and jail visitation policies will more adequately respond to the needs of incarcerated parents and their families. Ultimately, the availability of effective services to facilitate reunification will not only benefit these families, but enhance the community at large.

Legal Issues for Grandparent and Other Relative Caregivers

The majority of the children of incarcerated parents are spared the risks of foster care because they remain with their other natural parent or because they are placed with related caregivers. Over a quarter of a million children of prisoners are in the care of their grandparents or other relatives (Johnston, 1994), and this number is increasing yearly. Among the factors contributing to this rise are growing rates of incarceration, substance dependency, and HIV/AIDS. Grandparents and other relatives have stepped in to stabilize the situation for these children, to share resources, and to prevent another generation from cycling into the criminal justice system.

Extended family caregiving is not a new phenomenon and has been extensively documented, particularly in African-American (Stack, 1974) and Latino families (Angel & Tienda, 1982). Miller (1986) has examined extended households among families and kinship networks of offenders. However, new attention has been called to this phenomenon in two recent and helpful studies: *Black Grandparents as Parents* (Poe, 1992) and *Grandmothers as Caregivers: Raising Children of the Crack Cocaine Epidemic* (Minkler, 1993).

The recent attention is warranted because of the dramatic increase— 40% in the last decade—of grandparents as primary caregivers (Minkler, 1993). Statistically, the burden falls most heavily on the African-American community. According to the U.S. Bureau of the Census (1991), nearly four times as many African-American grandparents have primary responsibility for their grandchildren as do their white counterparts and there are twice as many African-American grandparent caregivers as there are Latino grandparent caregivers.

However, regardless of the community, white, black, and Latino families share many of the same problems. The children suffer the trauma of separation from their parents. Families headed by grandparent and relative caregivers often struggle as a result of low, fixed incomes and inadequate resources (Dressel & Barnhill, 1990; LaPoint, Picker & Harris 1985). One of the major issues confronting grandparent caregivers is the necessity for obtaining adequate benefits and services for their grandchildren.

The majority of grandparent caregivers assume responsibility for their grandchildren through informal arrangements with the children's parents or by default when a parent is absent due to incarceration and/or substance abuse. In many of these cases, grandparents who meet AFDC eligibility guidelines may qualify for aid for the care of their grandchildren, but there are few, if any, sources for other essential support services for these families, such as children's counseling, family counseling, and respite care.

In some instances, grandparents are able to obtain legal assistance to file for guardianship of their grandchildren, although few legal services offices are able to provide such assistance on a regular basis. A guardianship action is often the most appropriate and effective legal avenue for a grandparent to use if she or he is caring for an infant or child who is drug-exposed. The guardianship creates a legal structure that offers the grandparent a certain measure of control over the custodial situation. If necessary, a grandparent can obtain a temporary restraining order in connection with the order of guardianship. Yet, if the parent successfully enters recovery from drug or alcohol addiction, the guardianship is easily modifiable in order to permit more parental involvement with the child, including eventual reunification with the child, where appropriate.

The second major custodial option for grandparent caregivers is to ask to have the child placed with them through the foster care system. However, specific conditions must be present in order for a grandparent to qualify for more than basic AFDC payments. Title IV-E (Foster Care) benefits are only available to grandparent caregivers in cases in which children are receiving AFDC or are AFDC-eligible when they are removed from the parental home by an order of the juvenile court and subsequently placed in foster care with the grandparent. If a child is already living with his or her grandparent at the time that dependency is declared by the juvenile court, the child would *not* be eligible for Title IV-E benefits, regardless of whether the child and grandparent are eligible to receive AFDC payments. Thus, the grandparent and grandchild will receive the minimal AFDC payment, but will not be eligible to receive critically necessary supplemental services in cases where children are suffering serious physical and emotional needs. If the child is removed from another relative's home and placed with a grandparent by order of the juvenile court, Title IV-E funds *may* be available to the child and grandparent. However, very few grandparent caregivers fit the precise circumstances required by federal and state foster care regulations to entitle them to additional services or payment beyond the AFDC level.

In *King v. McMahon* (1986), the California Court of Appeals held that children who were placed with relatives in foster care were not entitled to foster care payments and benefits. In *Lipscomb v. Simmons* (1990), the Ninth Circuit Court in Oregon originally held that the state's denial of foster care benefits to children in relative foster care was unconstitutional. But the State of Oregon requested a rehearing en banc, and the decision was reversed without comment.

In response to the need of grandparent caregivers and the children in their care, there has been an impressive and creative outpouring of involvement and action by community activists, professionals, and families, particularly in the African-American community. By and large, this grassroots response has emphasized the need for additional services and support for grandparents and their grandchildren and, at the same time, the need for treatment for drug- and alcohol-dependent family members.

Conditions of Confinement for Pregnant Prisoners

While U.S. prison and jail populations have climbed significantly over the past decade, the number of incarcerated women has grown at a markedly higher rate than the number of men. Daily local jail populations of women rose at almost twice the rate of that of men during the period between 1984 and 1989 (USDJ, 1992). A similar rate of increase has also occurred in state and federal institutions. The U.S. Department of Justice (1991) reports that between 1980 and 1989, the female prisoner population had grown by over 200%.

Studies have indicated that up to 25% of women in prisons and jails are pregnant or have been pregnant within the previous year (McCall, Casteel & Shaw, 1985; USDJ, 1993). In addition, there is an increasing trend toward sentencing pregnant, substance-abusing women to prison or jail in an attempt to protect the health of the fetus (Becker, 1991). This objective, however well intentioned, is misguided in effect, as the following Case Examples indicate:

Annette H. was incarcerated for a 1-year term for violation of probation on two counts of possession for the sale of marijuana. When she was approximately 5 1/2 months pregnant, she began to experience cramping and vaginal bleeding. As the symptoms worsened throughout the following weeks, she repeatedly requested medical attention but was never seen by an obstetrician. After almost 3 weeks, she was finally seen by the head physician at the prison. The doctor, who was an orthopedist by training, did not physically examine her, and in fact prescribed Flagyl, a drug usually contraindicated during pregnancy. The following day, Annette went into premature labor and delivered in the ambulance on the way to the hospital. The baby died 2 hours later. (*Harris v McCarthy*, 1985)

Louwanna Y. was incarcerated for a 1-year term at the Kern County Jail in Bakersfield, California, on a charge of welfare fraud when she was approximately 5 months pregnant. She was forced to sleep on a thin mattress on the floor of the jail for almost 2 weeks after she arrived at the jail. Although she was a low-security prisoner, she was confined 24 hours a day for several months in grossly overcrowded cells. She was exposed to several contagious diseases, including tuberculosis, measles, head lice, and crabs. She was never seen by an obstetrician during the course of her pregnancy. When she went into labor on a Friday evening, she reported her condition to the guards on duty, but was told that she would have to wait until the next morning for medical assistance because there was no medical staff available at the time. Early the next morning, she gave birth on a thin mat outside the door of the jail clinic with only the assistance of an untrained guard. (*Yeager v Smith*, 1987)

Many pregnant, incarcerated women have little or no access to medical care that adequately meets their specialized needs. Often these women are not provided with proper diets, decent living conditions, or adequate treatment by medical staff. Indeed, the American Correctional Association (Task Force on the Female Offender, 1990) found that only about half of all jails and seven out of 10 prisons report having the equipment and staff necessary to adequately attend to the needs of pregnant women at least once a week. The paucity of such necessities as pre- and postnatal services and regular visits with obstetricians has resulted in the use of inappropriate and often dangerous methods of treatment for pregnant prisoners.

A 1985 survey of women incarcerated in three California correctional facilities (McCall, Casteel & Shaw, 1985) serves to further illustrate the lack of adequate and effective care received by pregnant prisoners. Less than half (44.5%) of the 464 women respondents in the state prison system had pregnancies resulting in live births. Thirty-three percent had suffered miscarriages, with many of these occurring late in gestation.

Pregnancy outcome statistics in the county jail system were even more disturbing. In a limited sample, only 21% of the respondents had live births, with miscarriages after the 20th week of pregnancy occurring 73% of the time. According to the study, miscarriages in the county jail system were occurring at 50 times the California state average for miscarriages among pregnant women.

Despite the alarming statistical evidence that incarcerated, pregnant women are not receiving adequate medical care, few changes have been made to rectify the serious problems that exist in many correctional systems. Policymakers have failed to effect the widespread change necessary to remedy such a burgeoning problem. This failure is due in part to the lack of national protocols and minimum standards that would define the scope of care recommended for pregnant women prisoners (Barry, 1989). The current standard of pregnancy-related care for incarcerated women is based upon the constitutional standard for prisoners in general (Barry, Kojimoto, Issacs, Lujan, Kandel et. al., 1993). This standard, established in *Estelle v Gamble* (1976), outlines the responsibility of the government to provide adequate medical care to prisoners. The Supreme Court stated that "deliberate indifference to serious medical needs of prisoners constitutes the unnecessary and wanton infliction of pain proscribed by the Eighth Amendment" (*Estelle v Gamble*, 1976, citing *Gregg v Georgia*, 1976).

As a result of the creation of this standard, courts have since found that medical care in prisons has fallen below minimum guidelines whenever prisoners have been denied reasonable access to medical care (*Newman v*

Alabama, 1980; *Ramos v Lamm*, 1981), where correctional staff has inter-fered with treatment prescribed by medical personnel (*Martinez v Mancusi*, 1970, 1971), and where there has been a consistent pattern of neglect on the part of prison medical staff (*Ramos v Lamm*, 1981).

Todaro v Ward (1977) was the first major lawsuit brought specifically on behalf of women prisoners regarding inadequate medical care. Using the *Estelle* standard, the court held that the correctional officials' repeated fail-ure to provide adequate medical treatment violated women prisoners' consti-tutional rights. While the holding set a precedent for overall improvement of conditions for incarcerated women, *Todaro* did not directly address the specific concerns of pregnant prisoners (Barry, 1989).

One of the first lawsuits to raise the issue of inadequate pregnancy care in a correctional facility was *West v Manson* (1983). Plaintiffs alleged that pregnant prisoners were not receiving adequate diets and prenatal educa-tion, were being deprived of reasonable access to toilets and showers, and were being shackled in leg irons late in pregnancy. Addressing these claims, the settlement agreement provided for dietary improvements, prenatal classes, placement of pregnant women in cells with toilets, and limits on the use of shackles.

In the past decade a growing number of advocates and community-based organizations have focused attention on the issue of adequate med-ical care for pregnant prisoners. Between 1985 and 1989, five class action lawsuits were filed to improve the conditions for pregnant women in Cali-fornia prisons and jails.

Harris v McCarthy (1985) was the first of the five suits to be filed. It was brought on behalf of pregnant and postpartum prisoners at the California Institution for Women (CIW), which at the time was the largest women's prison in the world. Plaintiffs alleged that the California Department of Corrections had been failing to provide adequate pre- and postnatal care, proper diets, and sufficient exercise. There was no obstetrician on the prison medical staff at the time, and no existing standards to guide the small, ill-equipped staff with regards to the specialized needs of pregnant, incarcerated women. A comprehensive settlement agreement required the prison to hire an obstetrician/gynecologist who would provide appropriate treatment and supervision of pregnant prisoners; to adopt extensive proto-cols to address high-risk pregnancies and pregnancy emergencies; to increase medical staffing, record keeping, and equipment; to create a "pregnancy-related health care time" to assess all pregnant women; and to set up a specialized obstetrical-unit for pregnant women.

The second lawsuit, *Jones v Dyer* (1986), was filed on behalf of the incarcerated women at Santa Rita County Jail, a large, urban, northern California jail facility in Alameda County, California. The plaintiffs alleged that pregnant prisoners were not provided with adequate prenatal care and substance abuse treatment. Plaintiffs also charged that there was a lack of contact visits for incarcerated mothers and their children. The settlement agreement provided more accessible prenatal care, appropriate to the specialized needs of pregnant women and pregnant drug-dependent prisoners.

Fuller v Tidwell (1987) was filed on behalf of both male and female prisoners at the San Bernardino County Jail. Plaintiffs alleged overcrowded conditions, inappropriate diet and exercise, and inadequate visitation opportunities. A settlement established guidelines for proper procedure and adequate pregnancy care.

The fourth lawsuit, *Yeager v Smith* (1987), was filed on behalf of pregnant and postpartum prisoners at the Kern County Jail, a large rural county jail in central California. Comprehensive guidelines and standard procedures for adequate treatment of pregnant prisoners were established by a settlement agreement reached in 1989.

Weeks v Williams (1987) was the fifth class action lawsuit filed involving pre- and postnatal care for incarcerated women. The suit charged poor general conditions at the San Luis Obispo County Jail, and a settlement provided for modifications similar to those in *Harris* and *Fuller*.

In addition to class action suits, individual damage claims and civil rights actions have been filed on the behalf of pregnant prisoners. While these cases have set strong precedents and improved the living conditions for some women, widespread change within the correctional system remains hampered by the lack of national standards specific to the needs of pregnant prisoners.

Several organizations have outlined standards of medical care for pregnant women. Most, however, do not directly and fully address the concerns of pregnant prisoners:

The American College of Obstetricians and Gynecologists (1986) has issued an extensive compilation of standards outlining proper medical treatment for pregnant women. These standards, however, do not address the specialized needs of pregnant prisoners.

The National Commission on Correctional Health Care (1987) and the American Public Health Association (1986) have both issued standards addressing medical care for pregnant prisoners. These standards are extremely general and do not specific guidelines for the care of incarcerated pregnant women.

The California Medical Association Task Force on Pregnant Addicted Inmates (Ryan, 1991) produced one of the more extensive studies and compilation of standards for medical care for pregnant prisoners. The study includes background information on the effects of substance abuse on pregnancy, standards of treatment, sample procedures, California regulations, and medical policy statements.

While such studies have assisted in the development of standards for improved pre- and postnatal care, the conditions for many pregnant prisoners remains the same. Nonetheless, the attempt to establish standards has laid a foundation for advocates to build upon. Indeed, settlements reached through litigation have set vital precedents that provide a means for more widespread change in the future.

Treatment of Pregnant Substance-Dependent Women

Dolores M was sentenced to serve 6 months in a large urban county jail when she was 7 months pregnant. Ordinarily, she would likely have received a lighter sentence for a minor probation violation, but the sentencing judge apparently wanted to ensure that she remained in custody for the duration of her pregnancy. Dolores was addicted to heroin and, prior to her sentencing, had sought methadone treatment at a local community based program. Instead of receiving the treatment she needed, she was forced to withdraw from heroin "cold turkey" when she entered the county jail. She suffered severe withdrawal, with vomiting, headaches, abdominal pain, diarrhea, and other traumatic symptoms. She was not examined by an obstetrician for almost 6 weeks and received no follow up appointment or medical treatment. When she was approximately eight and one half months pregnant, she had severe uterine pain and felt no fetal movement. Three days later, her stillborn daughter was removed by cesarean section.

The vast majority of women in prisons and jails have substance dependency problems: addiction to drugs, alcohol, or, most commonly, polydrug addiction. Research indicates that as many as 70% of incarcerated women have a history of substance dependency (National Commission on AIDS, 1991). The issue of addiction is a critical factor in determining the health care needs of women in prisons and jails. While not always portrayed as such in the mainstream media, alcohol or drug addiction is considered a disease by most thoughtful experts on the subject.

Substance dependence has been shown to be related to various types of early traumatic experiences, including child abuse/neglect and sexual molestation (Davis, 1990; Miller, 1990). One major factor that appears to be related to the high incidence of substance dependency among incarcerated women is the equally high prevalence of childhood sexual or physical abuse among this population (Task Force on the Female Offender, 1990; USDJ, 1993).

Over the past 2 decades, in part because of increasing legal sanctions for drug offenses (Huling, 1995), an increase in involvement by women with crack cocaine (USDJ, 1993), and an increase in the use of women as "drug mules" in trafficking activity (Huling, 1995), the number of women who have been incarcerated for drug possession and sales has risen dramatically. Yet few correctional systems have made any serious attempt to address the issue of drug and alcohol addiction among women. While some model programs do exist they are only available to a small percentage of addicted women.

The legal problems facing pregnant, substance-dependent women are especially difficult. As of 1990, there had been at least 35 instances in which women who were pregnant and substance-dependent had been charged with criminal violations of laws that related to child abuse or drug transportation and trafficking (Paltrow, 1990). In most instances, prosecutors who pursued these indictments relied on interpretations of these statutes that greatly distorted the original intent and language of the laws. In one case that received significant national attention, *State of Florida v Johnson*, Jennifer Johnson, a pregnant woman struggling to deal with her addiction to cocaine, was arrested shortly after she gave birth. She was charged with, and ultimately convicted of, delivery of an illegal substance to a minor. In a completely distorted interpretation of the statutory language and intent, the prosecutor argued that Ms. Johnson was guilty of "delivery" of the cocaine to her infant because the illicit drug passed through the umbilical cord during the birth process.

The Johnson case is not an isolated one (Paltrow, 1990). Prosecutions have occurred in over 20 states and the District of Columbia in the last 10 years, and certain states such as South Carolina have been particularly punitive toward pregnant, substance-dependent women. In some instances, the "charges" lodged against the pregnant woman are less criminal in nature than moralistic. In the case of Pamela Rae Stewart, *State of California v Stewart*, a pregnant woman was charged with "failing to follow her doctor's advice" to stay off her feet, to avoid street drugs and sexual intercourse, and to seek immediate medical attention if she experienced difficulties with her pregnancy.

In another case (*In re J. Jeffrey*, 1987), a judge in a Michigan probate court removed an infant from his mother based on her alleged use of "illegal drugs." The petition claimed that several weeks prior to delivery the mother took nonprescription Valium four times to relieve pain that she was experiencing as a result of an automobile accident. Although the infant evidenced some effects from the drugs, he did not suffer from drug withdrawal after birth. Even though the mother had no previous history of drug addition or child neglect, it took her more than a year to regain custody of her son.

In the debate over whether or not to incarcerate pregnant women who are drug- or alcohol-dependent, one factor that receives little attention is the quality of medical care available to pregnant substance-dependent women who *are* incarcerated. While some of judges who incarcerate pregnant substance-dependent women appear to do so simply to punish these women, many judges are genuinely concerned about ensuring that pregnant substance-dependent women receive adequate prenatal care and do not continue to use drugs or alcohol during their pregnancies (Becker, 1991).

Although there have been significant improvements in perinatal care for prisoners, and corresponding improved perinatal outcomes for pregnant prisoners, especially in larger prisons where these services are provided through contracts with university medical centers (see, e.g., Cordero, Hines, Shibley, & Landon, 1991; Egley, Miller, Granados, & Fogel, 1992), most jail systems and many smaller prison systems do not yet provide good quality perinatal care for the high-risk population they serve. Most local and state correctional systems do not have medical protocols or procedures specifically designed to address the safe detoxification of pregnant women addicted to drugs or alcohol. Few jails and prisons employ medical personnel with expertise in the appropriate treatment of pregnant women addicted to heroin, cocaine, methamphetamines, or alcohol. The experience of Dolores M. described above, is the reality for many pregnant, substance-dependent women who are sentenced to jail "for their own protection" or for the "protection of the fetus." Once an addicted pregnant woman enters the jail or prison system, she may experience the same type of poor medical care received by nonaddicted pregnant women. Thus, sentencing pregnant, substance-dependent women to serve time for the duration of their pregnancies in order to ensure that they receive adequate medical care may not accomplish this goal.

Finally, incarceration does not prevent pregnant, drug- or alcohol-dependent women from having access to drugs or alcohol: drugs and alcohol are readily available in many prisons and jails, for a price, and if a pregnant woman is addicted and given no opportunity to participate in an effective recovery program, she will in all likelihood continue to use. Egley, Miller, Granados, & Fogel (1992), for example, found that the majority of pregnant prisoners they studied continued to use a variety of drugs while incarcerated.

While most prisons and jails have Narcotics Anonymous and Alcoholics Anonymous groups, pregnant, substance-dependent women require more intensive and comprehensive treatment programs to increase the likelihood of successful recovery. Programs like ARC House in Madison, Wisconsin and the Neil J. Houston House in Boston, Massachusetts, offer an effective alternative to incarcerating pregnant substance-dependent women. However, these programs, and programs like them, must be insured sufficient funding and be utilized by sentencing judges, probation departments, and other arms of the criminal justice system if they are to become a part of a comprehensive solution to the treatment of pregnant, substance-dependent women. Unfortunately, one recent study of sentencing judges (Becker & Hora, 1993) indicated that judges often lack knowledge about the *availability* of such effective alternatives to incarceration, as well as accurate *information* about the medical consequences of drug and alcohol addiction. Judicial education must be part of the overall effort to educate the public about the need for a more compassionate response to the treatment of pregnant, substance-dependent women.

As with many women in the general population, incarcerated women were often either medically underinsured or totally uninsured prior to their incarceration. The lack of adequate health insurance plays a major role in the inability of many women to obtain treatment for drug and alcohol dependency; the well-established association between addiction and crime places these women at further risk for arrest and incarceration. Thus, adequate health insurance programs that include drug and alcohol treatment, psychological counseling for recovery from physical and sexual abuse, and basic medical services are an integral part of a long-term solution for reducing the number of pregnant, addicted women who become enmeshed in the criminal justice system.

References

American College of Obstetricians and Gynecologists. (1986). *Standards for obstetric-gynecologic services* (6th ed.), Washington, D.C.: Authors.

American Public Health Association. (1986). *Standards for health services in correctional institutions* (2nd ed.), Washington, D.C.: Authors.

Angel, R., & Tienda, M. (1982). Determinants of extended household structure: Cultural patterns or economic need? *American Journal of Sociology*, 87:1360–1383.

Arizona Rev. Stat. Ann. (1974), §8–533.

Barry, E. (1985). Children of prisoners: Punishing the innocent, *Youth Law News* 6(2):12–16.

Barry, E. (1989). Recent developments. *Harvard Women's Law Journal*, 12:189–205.

Barry, E., Kojimoto, C., Issacs, R., Lujan, G., Kandel, M., et. al. (1993). Women in prison. In C. Lefcourt (Ed.), *Women and the law*. Deerfield, IL: Clark, Boardman & Callahan.

Barry, E., & Reid-Green, C. (1990). The foster care system and the children of incarcerated parents: Summary of concerns. In E. Barry (Ed.), *Custody issues for incarcerated parents: A practitioner's guide*. San Francisco: Legal Services for Prisoners with Children.

Becker, B. L. (1991). Order in the court: Challenging judges who incarcerates pregnant, substance-dependent defendants to protect fetal health. *Hastings Constitutional Law Quarterly*, 19(1):235–259.

Becker, B. L., & Hora, P. (1993). The legal community's response to drug use during pregnancy in the criminal sentencing and dependency context: A survey of judges, prosecuting attorneys and defense attorneys in 10 California counties. *Review of Law and Women's Studies*, 2:301–397.

Beckerman, A. (1994). Mothers in prison: Meeting the prerequisite conditions for permanency planning. *Social Work*, 39(1):9–14.

Blackburn v. Snow, 771 F.2d 556 (1st Cir. 1985).

Bloom, B., & Steinhart, D. (1992). *Why punish the children? A reappraisal of the children of incarcerated mothers in America.* San Francisco: National Council on Crime and Delinquency.

Bush v Dietz, 680 S.W.2d 704, 706 (Ark. 1984).

California Civil Code (1994), §232 (a)(5).

California Welfare and Institutions Code (1994), §366.26 (c)(1).

Call, J. D. (1976). Effects on adults of object loss in the five years. *Journal of the American Psycholoanalytic Association*, 24(3):659–667.

Cordero, L., Hines, S., Shibley, A & Landon, M. B. (1991). Duration of incarceration & perinatal outcome. *Obstetrics & Gynecology*, 78(4):641–645.

Davis, S. K. (1990). Chemical dependency in women. *Journal of Substance Abuse Treatment*, 7: 225–232.

Dressel, P., & Barnhill, S. (1990). *Three generations at risk.* Atlanta: Aid to Imprisoned Mothers.

Editors of the Yale Law Journal. (1978). On prisoners & parenting: preserving the tie that binds. *Yale Law Journal*, 87(2):1408–1429.

Egley, C. C., Miller, D. E., Granados, J. L. & Fogel, C. I. (1992). Outcome of pregnancy during imprisonment. *Journal of Reproductive Medicine*, 37(2):131–134.

Estelle v Gamble, 429 U.S. 97 (1976).

Feeley v Sampson, 570 F.2d 364, 372 (1st Cir. 1978).

Fuller v Tidwell, CV-87030265-SVW, USDC (C.D. Cal., filed May 1987).

Gregg v Georgia, 428 U.S. 153, 173 (1976).

Hairston, C. F. (1989). Men in prison: Family characteristics and family views. *Journal of Offender Counseling, Services, and Rehabilitation*, 14(1):23–30.

Harris v McCarthy, No. 85-6002 JGD (C.D. Cal, filed September 11, 1985).

Huling, T. (1995, Winter). Women drug couriers: Sentencing reform needed for prisoners of war. *Criminal Justice* (Forthcoming).

In re Adoption of Herman, 406 N.E.2d 277 (Ind. Ct. App. 1980).

In re Dolores B., 141 A.D.2d 100 (N.Y. 1988).

In re H.G.B., M.A.B., & D.J.B., 306 N.W.2d 821 (Minn. 1981).

In re J. Jeffrey, No. 99851 (Mich. Ct. App., filed April 9, 1987).

In re Neal, 414 N.W.2d 916 (Mich. App. 1987).

In re Terry E., 180 Cal. App. 3d. 932, at 953 (1986).

Johnston, D. (1991). *Jailed Mothers.* Pasadena, California: Center for Children of Incarcerated Parents.

Johnston, D. (1994). *Caregivers of prisoners' children.* Pasadena, CA: Center for Children of Incarcerated Parents.

Jones v Dyer, No. H-114544-0 (Alameda County Superior Court, California, filed February 25, 1986).

Jordan v Hancock, 508 S.W.2d. 878 (Tex. Civ. App. 1974).

King v McMahon, 186 Cal. App. 3d. 648 (Cal. App. Dist., 1986).

LaPoint, V., Picker, MO & Harris, BF. (1985). Enforced family separation: A descriptive analysis of some experiences of children of black imprisoned mothers. In A. Spencer (Ed.), *Beginnings: The social and affective development of black children.* Washington, DC: Pages 239–255.

Lipscomb v Simmons, 926 F. 2d. 1374 (1990).

Martinez v Mancusi, 443 F. 2d 921–923 (2d Cir. 1970) and 401 U.S. 983 (1971).

Matter of Vernia, 443 N.W. 2d 404 (Mich. App. 1989).

McCall, C., Casteel, J & Shaw, NS. (1985). *Pregnancy in prison: A needs assessment of prenatal outcome in three California penal institutions* (Contract 84-84085). Sacramento: California Department of Health Services.

Michigan Comp. Laws Ann. (1986), §712A.19(a), (d).

Miller, B. (1990). Interrelationships between alcohol and drugs and family violence. In *Drugs and violence: causes, correlates and consequences* (Research Monograph No. 103). Washington, DC: National Institute of Drug Abuse. Pages 177–207.

Miller, E. (1986). *Street woman*. Philadelphia: Temple University Press.

Minkler, M. (1993). *Grandmothers as caregivers: Raising children of the crack cocaine epidemic*. Beverly Hills, CA: Sage.

National Commission on AIDS. (1991). *Report: HIV disease in correctional facilities*. Washington, DC: Author.

National Commission on Correctional Health Care. (1987). *Standards for health services in jails*. Washington, DC: Author.

Newman v Alabama, 503 F. 2d 1320, 1331 (5th Cir. 1974), 506 F.2d 1056 (1975), and 421 U.S. 948 (1975).

Editors of Yale Law Journal. (1978) On prisoners and parenting: Preserving the tie that binds. *Yale Law Journal*, 87(2):1408–1429.

Paltrow, L. M. (1990, Winter–Spring). (1990). When becoming pregnant is a crime. *Criminal Justice Ethics*, p. 42.

Poe, LM. (1992). *Black grandparents as parents*. Unpublished doctoral dissertation, University of California at Berkeley.

Ramos v Lamm, 639 F. 2d 559, 575 (10th Cir. 1980), and 450 U.S. 104 (1981).

Ryan, T. A. (1991). *Pregnant female offenders: profile, problems and programs*. Sacramento: California Medical Association Task Force on Pregnant, Addicted Inmates.

Schoenbauer, L. (1986). Incarcerated parents and their children: Forgotten families. *Law and Inequality*, 4:579–582.

Stack, C. (1974). *All our kin: Strategies for survival in a black community*. New York: Harper Colophon Books.

Standing Committee on Legal Services for Prisoners. (1993). *Pregnant women in California jails and prisons*. Sacramento: California State Bar Association.

State of Florida v Johnson, E89-890-CFA (Fla. Cir. Ct. 1989).

Task Force on the Female Offender. (1990). *The female offender: What does the future hold?* Laurel, MD: American Correctional Association.

Todaro v Ward, 431 F. Suppl. 1129 (S.D.N.Y. 1977) and 565 F.2d 48 (2d Cir. 1977).

U.S. Department of Justice. (1991). *Women in prison* (Report No. NCJ127991). Washington, DC: Bureau of Justice Statistics.

U.S. Department of Justice. (1992). *Correctional populations in the United States, 1990* (Report No. NCJ134946). Washington, DC: Bureau of Justice Statistics.

U.S. Department of Justice. (1993). *Survey of state prisoners*. (Report No. NCJ136949). Washington, DC: Bureau of Justice Statistics.

Weeks v Williams, No. CV 87-4187-WMB (C.D. Cal., filed December 13, 1987).

West v Manson, No. H-83-366 (d-Conn., filed May 9, 1983).

Yeager v Smith, No. CN-F-87-493-R.E.C. (E.D. Cal., filed September 2, 1987).

11
Termination of Parental Rights among Prisoners

A National Perspective

Philip M. Genty

Disruption of families through incarceration of parents has become an increasingly serious problem over the past decade. In addition to growing numbers of parents who are separated from their children by incarceration (U.S. Department of Justice [USDJ], 1991, 1993), increasing sentence lengths mean that these families are being kept apart for longer periods of time. In 1986 approximately one-third of the women sentenced to state prison received maximum sentences of 7 years or more. Almost 93% received sentences with a maximum of 4 years or more (USDJ, 1991). For men, in 1986, the *average* maximum sentence was 7 years (USDJ, 1986).[1] Another measure of the degree of family separation is the length of time actually served, since prisoners are typically paroled prior to the expiration of their maximum sentence. In 1986 women served an average of 16 months in state prisons, ranging from 10 months to 56 months, depending on offense. In 1986 men served an average of 24 months in state prisons, ranging from 14 months to 84 months, depending on offense (USDJ, 1991).

The profound impact of separation upon families of incarcerated parents, and particularly mothers, is illustrated by the fact that in 1986 85% of the mothers of minor children had legal custody of their children before entering prison, and 78% of the mothers lived with their children at that time. Furthermore, more than 85% of the incarcerated mothers intended to resume custody after their release from prison. Among men, approximately one-half of the fathers of minor children had lived with their children prior to their imprisonment, and an almost equal number planned to live with their children after their release (USDJ, 1991).

Thus, particularly with respect to incarcerated mothers, imprisonment of a parent disrupts intact, viable families. The overwhelming majority of incarcerated mothers were active parents to their children prior to their incarceration and intend to continue in that role after their release. The time of parental confinement must therefore be looked at as an interlude, during which parental ties must be nurtured and supported so that, to the greatest extent possible, the parent–child relationship is as strong after the parent's release as it was before (Beckerman, 1989; Hairston & Hess, 1989; Hale, 1987; Kaslow, 1987; Lowenstein, 1986; McGowan & Blumenthal, 1978; Sack, Seidler & Thomas, 1976).

Just the opposite often occurs in practice, however. For incarcerated parents who are confined for significant periods of time, there is an acute danger of dissolution of their families through termination of parental rights and adoption proceedings. This is especially true for incarcerated mothers who are likely to have been the sole caretakers for their children prior to imprisonment, frequently do not have family members available to care for their children, and consequently may have to resort to the foster care system (Hale, 1987; USDJ, 1991, 1993). That the permanent loss of children is a very real possibility for such parents is reflected by the fact that at least 25 states have termination-of-parental-rights or adoption statutes that explicitly pertain to incarcerated parents,[2] and four other states, while not addressing parental incarceration generally, permit termination of parental rights for parents convicted of certain types of crimes against children.[3] Moreover, almost every state has reported cases dealing with these parents.

This permanent loss of parental rights can occur in either of two contexts. First, when a child is in the care and custody of the state, an arrangement that will be referred to as "foster care" throughout this chapter, the state may bring a judicial proceeding to terminate the parent's rights permanently. Typically, once parental rights have been terminated, the parent loses all right to have contact with her[4] child, and the child can thereafter be adopted without the parent's knowledge or consent.

The second context in which parental rights may be lost is through adoption of children who are *not* in foster care. A common way in which such cases arise is that the parent who is not incarcerated has custody of the child and marries or remarries. The new spouse, the child's stepparent, then wishes to adopt the child, but this necessitates terminating the rights of the incarcerated parent. All states have statutes that set out circumstances under which the adoption can proceed even without the consent of one or both parents, as, for example, when the nonconsenting parent has had no contact with the child and has therefore "abandoned" the child.

The states have been unable to adjust adequately to the growing phenomenon of incarcerated parents. State laws pertaining to termination of parental rights and adoption were historically aimed at parents who voluntarily abandoned their children and thereafter failed to play any part in their children's lives.[5] The laws are therefore ill-equipped to deal with the problem of parents who are involuntarily separated from their children through incarceration but who actively strive to continue to be parents to their children. As noted above, 85% of incarcerated mothers fit this description. A result of this inability to grapple directly with the problems presented by parental incarceration is that parent–child relationships are needlessly and harmfully severed in cases where a parent is imprisoned.

Terminating the rights of incarcerated parents implicates fundamental rights basic to American jurisprudence. The Supreme Court has stated:

> The rights to conceive and to raise one's children have been deemed "essential," . . . "basic civil rights of man," . . . and "rights far more precious . . . than property rights.". . . . "It is cardinal with us that the custody, care and nurture of the child reside first in the parents, whose primary function and freedom include preparation for obligations the state can neither supply nor hinder." (*Stanley v Illinois*, 1971)

Thus parents are entitled to raise their children without any interference from the state. Even in situations where a parent has temporarily lost physical or legal custody of her child for a variety of reasons, the state may not *permanently* deprive the parent of all rights to her child unless the state has shown that she is "unfit" (*Santosky v Kramer*, 1971).

The constitutional requirement that parental "unfitness" be proven before rights can be permanently terminated does not answer the question of what amounts to "unfitness." While the term "unfitness" appears to be inherently vague, this apparent vagueness is not inappropriate. A judicial inquiry into parental fitness necessarily involves a court in a complex inquiry into the very nature of family relationships generally and parent–child relationships in particular.

The most obvious aspect of such family relationships are physical and financial: families generally live together; they form a kind of economic unit; spouses support and protect each other; parents support and protect their children; in later years, children may support and protect their parents. Thus, marriage and childrearing are most clearly thought of in terms of the tangible physical and financial responsibilities that the family members owe to one another.

But family relationships and parental rights and responsibilities extend beyond these merely material considerations. Even after the family has lost its corporeal qualities, something of considerable substance remains. Thus, divorces split families apart, often leaving noncustodial parents and children separated by great distances. Yet no one would suggest that the rights of noncustodial parents should be terminated merely because of such physical separation (Garrison, 1983). Similarly, in the public law context, there is a clear distinction between loss of physical custody and termination of parental rights. Custody and parental rights are not coextensive; a parent who has lost physical custody of her child to the state remains a parent unless and until her rights are terminated (*In re Adoption of Children by D.*,

1972; *Interest of Jones*, 1975; *Matter of Bistany*, 1924; *Matter of Ricky Ralph M.*, 1982).

In both the private and the public spheres, then, family relationships survive the demise of their physical qualities. This is true because these family relationships involve intangible aspects that are at least as important as the more obvious physical aspects. Such qualities may include love and affection, religious and/or moral guidance, emotional support, and a sense of "roots" and family identity. These intangible qualities must therefore be closely examined in any case where the state seeks the permanent destruction of parental rights. This is true even in cases where the parent and child have been separated for an extended for an extended period of time. Although such a relationship may be "a troubled and confused one that [has] been adversely affected by the separation from the natural mother and by the intervening formation of a new relationship between the child and her foster parents" (*In re Juvenile Appeal*, 1979), this fact alone does not warrant permanently severing the parent–child relationship.

In discussing this issue, the Supreme Court of Connecticut has noted:

> The fact that the child may have established a loving relationship with someone besides her mother does not prove the absence of a mother–daughter relationship. It is insufficient to prove that the child has developed emotional ties with another person. Certainly children from two-parent homes may have two "psychological parents"; children whose parents are divorced may retain close emotional ties to both, *although the relationship to one is maintained solely through visitation*. (Emphasis added.)[6]

The principle that intangible qualities of love and affection may hold a family together despite physical separation applies fully to situations in which the cause of separation is incarceration. The Supreme Court has recognized this in the context of marriage. In *Turner v Safley* (1987), the Court held that the constitutional right to marry survives incarceration notwithstanding the impossibility of exercising the physical attributes of marriage, that is, establishing a home together and consummating the marriage.

In so deciding, the Court discussed the nonphysical attributes of marriage, including emotional support, public commitment, spiritual significance, and the expectation that most marriages would be fully consummated after release. The Court found these nonphysical attributes of marriage to be sufficiently important, in and of themselves, to warrant constitutional protection. The Court stated that these attributes are "unaffected by the fact of confinement or the pursuit of legitimate corrections goals."

Similarly, the nonphysical, intangible qualities of the parent–child relationship remain intact, albeit strained, after incarceration, and the parent–child relationship is entitled to constitutional protection even after the parent is confined to prison.[7] In a termination-of-parental-rights proceeding involving an incarcerated parent, a court must look beyond the parent's inability to care physically for the child and focus instead upon the "parent's responsibility to provide a nurturing parental relationship" (*In re Daniel C.*, 1984).[8]

The role an incarcerated parent may play in meeting the nonmaterial needs of her child has been summarized as follows:

> [Parental] duty encompasses more than a financial obligation; it requires continuing interest in the child and a genuine effort to maintain communication and association with the child.
>
> Because a child needs more than a benefactor, parental duty requires that a parent "exert himself *to take and maintain a place of importance in the child's life*. (Emphasis added.)" (*In re Adoption of Sabrina*, 1984)

Any judicial examination of parental unfitness must therefore recognize that, as with all cases involving the parent–child relationship, there is a wide variation of circumstances among cases involving incarcerated parents. These individual circumstances must be examined carefully in each case. In *Stanley v Illinois* (1972) the Supreme Court made this point in another context. There the Court rejected the State of Illinois's attempt to adjudicate parental rights solely by a rigid, formalistic focus upon whether the father was married to the mother of the child, without regard to the father's actions subsequent to the birth of his child. The Court cautioned:

> Procedure by presumption is always cheaper and easier than individualized determination. But when . . . the procedure forecloses the determinative issues of competency and care, when it explicitly disdains present realities in deference to past formalities, it needlessly runs roughshod over the important interests of both parent and child.

The requirement of an *individualized* showing of parental unfitness necessitates a thorough, searching inquiry into the circumstances of the particular incarcerated parent and her family; the fact of the parent's crime and the length of her sentence cannot serve as proxies for a finding of unfitness. Two specific principles flow from this. First, the court's inquiry must focus primarily upon the parent's *present* fitness as measured by her relationship with her child and the degree to which she has been rehabilitated while in prison. In evaluating parental fitness, the court may not limit its inquiry to the fact of the parent's past criminal acts. Second, a court must carefully examine the incarcerated parent's ability to provide the child with the "intangibles" of the parent–child relationship. Rights may not be terminated simply because the parent will be confined for an extended period of time and will therefore not be able to perform the material, physical, and financial duties of parenting.

With respect to the first of these principles, a court must examine the parent's conduct subsequent to her incarceration, looking at the "determinative issues of competency and care" in the context of "present realities" (*Stanley v Illinois*, 1972). The court must go beyond the fact of the parent's crime, and determine the extent to which that crime adversely affects the parent–child relationship in the present. Factors relevant to such an inquiry include the parent's participation in rehabilitative programs and her efforts to maintain a meaningful relationship with her children while in prison. The parent's past actions must be "reviewed in the light of subsequent events" to determine the extent of the parent's rehabilitation (*In re Terry E.*, 1986), and whether these past acts continue to render the parent unfit.

The most difficult cases are those in which the parent has been convicted of a crime against a child or another family member. A child whose parent has abused her or her siblings, or has murdered her mother is, to say the least, unlikely ever to trust and accept the parent fully. Crimes of this nature inevitably cause permanent damage to the parent–child relationship. In some cases, the nature of the parent's crime may be so reprehensible that the parent will never be able to provide the child with the intangible qualities of a positive, nurturing family relationship. In such cases, a court would be warranted in concluding that the parent–child relationship is beyond repair and that parental rights should be severed (*Interest of D. S.*, 1985; *In re Frances*, 1986).

However, in other cases, it may be possible to begin to heal the parent–child relationship through therapeutic services and regular visitation. In such cases, even a damaged parent–child relationship is likely to be better than no relationship (Garrison, 1983).

Thus, while certain past conduct may create considerable doubts that a parent will ever be fit to raise her children, that is not a sufficient reason to forgo a full judicial inquiry.[9] As one court has put it:

> It may be true that [the incarcerated parent] will not be able to prevail in [an] action [to terminate parental rights] after evidence and testimony are presented. It may even be true that most [incarcerated] parents . . . would be unable to defeat a proceeding brought to declare their children wards of the court; but that opportunity *must* be afforded. (*Matter of Christina T.*, 1979)

Given the grave consequences of an erroneous termination of rights, constitutional requirements cannot be satisfied by a presumption that parents who have engaged in a type of past misconduct are forever unfit to be parents. Indeed, it is in those extreme cases, where the parent's egregious conduct makes her least sympathetic, that due process protections are most needed to prevent a fact-finder from prejudging the case.

With respect to the second principle—that an inquiry into parental fitness must focus upon the incarcerated parent's ability to provide a child with the "intangibles" of a parent–child relationship—this analysis cannot be merely *quantitative*, for example, by addressing the number of hours the parent is able to spend with her child or the amount of money the parent is able to contribute to her child's support. Rather, the court must look at the *quality* of the parent–child relationship and the extent to which the parent, during her confinement, continues to "maintain a place of importance in the child's life" (*In re Adoption of Sabrina*, 1984).[10] This is, of course, not just an issue of the *parent's* rights; it also concerns the *child's* right to a relationship with her parent.[11]

Permitting rights to be terminated solely or primarily on the basis of long-term parental incarceration and consequent prolonged future physical separation between parent and child may reflect an assumption that such prisoners can no longer play a meaningful role in their children's lives. On the other hand, it may reflect something less principled, a desire not to have to deal with the emotional and logistical difficulties associated with such cases, for example, the time and expense involved in taking children to prison to see their parents, the complications of arranging counseling and other services for parent and child so that they may better cope with the pain of separation, or the expense of keeping a child in foster care for an extended period of time.

Whatever the motivation, however, allowing a blanket termination of rights in such cases ignores a critical reality: the vast majority of incarcerated women are mothers of minor children who were caring for their children immediately prior to their imprisonment, and who intend to resume caring for their children after their release (USDJ, 1991) This is true for the majority of incarcerated men too (USDJ, 1991). Thus, a large number of incarcerated parents have viable, ongoing relationships with their children, relationships that can and should be preserved if possible.

Due process as well as public policy require that *all* aspects of the parent–child relationship be examined in assessing parental fitness. Courts must recognize that even a parent who is confined on a lengthy prison sentence may occupy an essential place in her child's life, a place that cannot be filled by anybody else. Such a parent may therefore be in a unique position to perform the intangible aspects of parenting such as providing the child with nurturing love and a sense of family identity.

As incarceration rates increase, the problems associated with parental incarceration worsen. Parents with no other available childcare resources must turn to the foster care system, and state legislators, judiciaries, and child welfare agencies are forced to deal with complex and emotionally wrenching family situations.

The traditional model of foster care placement is ill-equipped to deal with this growing phenomenon of parental incarceration. That model contemplates that a parent be prepared to resume physical custody of her child within a relatively short period of time, sometimes as little as 1 year after the initial placement in care.[12] Under this model, parents who are unwilling or unable to do this are deemed to be unfit parents with no meaningful relationship with their children, and such parents may have their parental rights terminated.

This time-driven model of foster care placement simply cannot cope with the situation of an incarcerated parent who has an ongoing, viable, positive relationship with her child, but who is unable to resume physical custody of her child for many years. The traditional model does not recognize that parents who cannot meet the tangible, physical responsibilities of parenting, such as providing a dwelling space and financial support, may still be able to offer intangible qualities of parental love and nurturing, which are perhaps of even greater importance to the children and which no one except the parents can provide.

States only add to the problems of parental incarceration by needlessly severing viable parent–child relationships through termination of parental rights proceedings that fail to take full measure of the complexities of such family situations. Such responses grossly simplify and distort what should be a profound, painstaking inquiry into the parent–child relationship and reflect, at the very least, confusion about how to address the problems of parental incarceration. The responses probably reflect frustration as well; these cases are messy, and many legislators, judges, child welfare officials, and caseworkers would undoubtedly like to wish them away.

The unique needs of incarcerated parents and their children require a carefully tailored policy response. Courts, social services officials, and other policymakers must develop means for identifying the families that remain viable despite parental incarceration and working with those families to strengthen the ties between the parents and children and maximize the parents' role in the lives of their children.

This requires, first, that the state make concerted affirmative efforts to support and strengthen the family, for no family can remain stable throughout a parent's incarceration without such assistance. At a minimum, these efforts should include:

1. transporting the children to prisons for visits with their parents on a regular basis;
2. facilitating phone contact between the parent and child, including allowing parents to make free phone calls to their children or reimbursing foster families for collect phone calls made by incarcerated parents;
3. suggesting appropriate rehabilitative services, including therapeutic

counseling and parent training, and assisting the parent in obtaining those services;

4. suggesting and providing appropriate therapeutic services to children to help them deal with their parent's incarceration and absence;
5. suggesting and providing appropriate therapeutic services to parents and children jointly;
6. conducting an investigation to locate relatives of the child who may be able to care for the child during the parent's absence;[13]
7. providing supportive services and financial assistance to extended family members or unrelated foster parents who are caring for the child.[14]

Such affirmative efforts will be futile, however, if the parent is not committed to discharging her parental responsibilities. An incarcerated parent, like any parent, has a duty to communicate with and maintain an interest in her child to the best of her ability, and her rights may appropriately be terminated if she fails to discharge this duty. Thus, an important indicator of parental fitness is the extent to which an incarcerated parent has, through her actions while incarcerated, manifested a continuing interest in being a parent to her children. The Supreme Court of Pennsylvania has stated that an incarcerated parent must "utiliz[e] those resources at his or her command while in prison in continuing a close relationship with the child" (*In re Adoption of McCray*, 1975). The Supreme Court of Minnesota has offered a more concrete description: "If a parental relationship existed prior to a [parent's] imprisonment and he continued this relationship to the best of his ability during incarceration through letters, cards, and visits where possible, and through inquiry as to [the] children's welfare, his parental rights would be preserved, both because of his actions and for the benefit of [the] children" (*Staat v Hennepin County Welfare Board*, 1970).

In evaluating the extent to which an incarcerated parent has satisfied these duties there are two important qualifications. First, a failure to satisfy these parental duties may be excused if the parent can show that the state or another person has thwarted her attempts to maintain a relationship with her child. Second, the incarcerated parent's discharge of her parental responsibilities must be judged by a standard that takes into account the constraints imposed by the parent's imprisonment.

Beyond this determination of the extent to which an incarcerated parent has exhibited an interest in her children, a number of additional factors are relevant to determining whether the family remains viable. These might include the following:

1. the institutional programs in which the parent has participated and the extent of the parent's rehabilitation while in prison;

2. the quality of the parent–child relationship, that is, the extent to which the parent is able to maintain a place of importance in her child's life and to perform the intangible aspects of parenting such as providing the child with nurturing love;

3. the duration of the parent–child relationship;

4. any pattern of repeated incarcerations;

5. any history of especially heinous crimes, such as crimes against children;

6. the age of the children;

7. the evidence of abuse or neglect of the child or siblings of the child by the parent prior to incarceration;

8. the length of the sentence;

9. for minors 10 years of age or older, the minor's attitude toward efforts at family preservation.

Parental unfitness may *not* be found solely on the basis of the parent's inability to resume *physical* custody of her child.[15]

Adopting the guidelines suggested above would satisfy constitutional requirements and amount to sound and farsighted public policy by helping to ensure that a parent's incarceration will not lead to the needless destruction of her family. The mere fact of a parent's incarceration is tragedy enough for her family; a state should not be adding to the family's agony by unnecessarily and permanently severing the bonds between parent and child. In those cases in which a viable parent–child relationship is found to exist, states must work to support, preserve, and strengthen the relationship, complicated as that task may be.

However, even if the guidelines suggested above are followed, the problems associated with parental incarceration will remain; indeed, those problems can probably only be solved by implementing alternatives to incarceration so that parents who are their children's primary caretakers are no longer being imprisoned. Sadly, such a radical rethinking of our criminal justice system is not likely to occur in the near future.

Notes

1. These data underestimate sentence lengths, because they do not include data for mean sentence lengths for sentences of "life without parole," "life plus (additional) years," "life," and "death." Average maximum sentences ranged from four to 28 years, depending on the crime.

2. *Ala. Code* §26-18-7(a)(4), 1986; *Ariz. Rev. Stat. Ann.* §8-533(B)(4), 1989; *Cal. Welf. & Inst. Code* §366.26(c)(1), West Suppl., 1992; *Colo. Rev. Stat.* §19-3-

604(1)(b)(III), Suppl., 1986; *GA Code Ann.* §15-11-81(b)(4)(B)(iii), 1990 & Suppl. 1991; *Idaho Code* §§16-1602(s)(2), 16-1615, 16-2005, Suppl. 1991; *Iowa Code Ann.* §§232.116(1)(i)(2), 232.116(2)(a), West Suppl. 1991; *Kan. Stat. Ann.* §38-1583(b)(5), 1986; *LA Stat. Ann., Children's Code*, art. 1015 (1)(6), West Suppl. 1992; *Miss. Code Ann.* §93-15-103(3)(e), Suppl. 1991; *MO Ann. Stat.* §211.447(3)(6), Vernon Suppl. 1992; *Mont. Code Ann.* §§41-3-609(2)(e), 41-3-609(4)(b), 1991; *Nev. Rev. Stat. Ann.* §§128.105, 128.106(6), Michie Suppl., 1991; *NH Rev. Stat. Ann.* §170-C:5(VI), Suppl., 1991; *NM Stat. Ann.* §§32-1-3(1)(4), 32-1-54(B)(3), 1989; *NY Soc. Serv. Law* §384-b(7),(e),(f). McKinney, 1992; *OK Stat. Ann.*, Tit. 10, §§1130(A)(5),(6),(7), West 1987; *RI Gen. Laws*, §15-7-7(1)(b)(i), 1988; *WI Stat. Ann.* §§48.13(8), 48.415(2), 48.415(5)(a), West 1987; *WY Stat.* §14-2-309(a)(iv), 1986.

The Oregon statute involving the termination of parental rights of parents of children who are in foster care, *OR Rev. Stat.* §109.322, 1991, does not address parental incarceration, while the statute dealing with adoption of children who are not in foster care, *OR Rev. Stat.* §109.322, 1991, permits a child to be adopted without the consent of parent who has been incarcerated for at least 3 years.

3. *IL Ann. Stat.* ch. 40, para 1501(D)(f),(g), Smith-Hurd, 1980; *IN Code Ann.* §31-6-5-4.2(a), Burns Suppl. 1991; *ME Rev. Stat. Ann.*, Tit. 22 §4055(I-A)(B), 1992; *TN Code Ann.* §37-1-147(d)(3) 1991.

4. Feminine pronouns will be used throughout this chapter because of the particular importance of the issue of parental rights to incarcerated women. However, the principles discussed should be understood to apply to incarcerated fathers, as well, unless otherwise specified.

5. For a discussion of the historical development of termination of parental rights proceedings in New York and the creation of standards less stringent than abandonment, see *Matter of Anonymous v Longobardi* (1976).

6. In this case (*In re Juvenile Appeal*, 1979), a mother had hired a full-time babysitter to care for her daughter while she was working. The mother had gone to the doctor because of nervousness and depression. She had been to a psychiatrist who had apparently misdiagnosed her and had her involuntarily committed to a psychiatric hospital, where she stayed for 6 weeks. Her child had been placed into foster care, with the babysitter designated as the foster parent. The mother had spent most of the following 2 years attempting to regain custody of her daughter, maintaining a relationship with her daughter through visitation, letters, and telephone calls. The state had commenced a proceeding to terminated the mother's rights so that the daughter could be adopted by the babysitter/foster mother. The trial court had denied the mother's petition to revoke the foster care placement and had granted the state's petition to terminate the mother's rights, primarily because of the close relationship that the child had developed with the foster mother. The intermediate appellate had affirmed the lower court's determination.

The Supreme Court affirmed the denial of the mother's application to revoke the placement, but reversed the order terminating the mother's rights, holding that the state had failed to satisfy the statutory requirement of "no ongoing parent–child relationship." The Court held that the mother had maintained such a relationship through her efforts to visit, write, and telephone her child, and that it was possible for the child to have close relationships with both her mother and the foster mother.

7. It should be noted that a number of courts have found that the parent's duty to support her child, to the extent that she is financially able to do so, continues during the parent's incarceration. See: *Cardwell v Gwaltney*, 1990; *Division of Child Support Enforcement ex rel. Harper v Barrows*, 1990; *Illinois ex rel. Meyer v Nein*, 1991; *Interest of M.L.K.*, 1991; *Matter of Bradley*, 1982; *Ohler v Ohler*, 1985; *Petition of R.H.N.*, 1985; *Proctor v Proctor*, 1989; *Smith v Alaska Department of Revenue*, 1990. But also see: *Leasure v Leasure*, 1988.

    Arguably, the principle that a prisoner retains a duty to support her child implicitly acknowledges that an incarcerated parent continues to play an important role as a parent.

8. *In re Daniel C.* (1984) held that "under proper circumstances an appropriate parent–child relationship can be developed despite the parent's incarceration and consequent inability physically 'to protect the child from jeopardy.'" However, in that case the father had failed to maintain contact with his child not only while he was incarcerated on two separate sentences, but also during a brief period in between when he was free.

    In *Santosky v Kramer* (1982), the Supreme Court has described the difficult task facing a court in a termination of parental rights proceeding as follows:

    Termination of parental rights proceedings employ precise substantive standards that leave determinations unusually open to subjective values of the judge. . . . In appraising the nature and quality of a complex series of encounters among the agency, the parents and the child, the court possesses unusual discretion to underweigh probative facts that might favor the parent. Because parents subject to termination proceedings are often poor, uneducated, or members of minority groups . . . such proceedings are often vulnerable to judgements based on cultural or class bias. . . .

    Like civil commitment hearings, termination proceedings often require the factfinder to evaluate medical and psychiatric testimony, and to decide issues difficult to prove to a level of absolute certainty, such as lack of parental motive, absence of affection between parent and child, and failure of parental foresight and progress.

9. Cases in which the father has killed the child's mother are probably the most difficult. As discussed elsewhere, some cases have reasoned that by depriving his children permanently of their mother, a father has shown such disregard for their well-being that he does not deserve to retain his parental rights, and this reasoning is not unpersuasive. However, even in these extreme situations, there are exceptional cases where a constructive parent–child relationship can be salvaged; see *In the Interest of H.L.T.* (1982). Without a full judicial inquiry into present circumstances, such exceptional cases may not be identified, and rights may be terminated erroneously. The balancing test articulated in *Matthews v Eldridge* (1976) therefore mandates that full hearings into *present* fitness be conducted in all termination-of-parental-rights proceedings, even those that involve extreme past parental misconduct.

10. See *In re Juvenile Appeal* (1979): "The parent's loss of custody should not . . . be premised solely on 'tangible material benefits to the child at the expense of intangible, non-material advantages which a parent's care can provide even when the parent has limited financial resources.'"

11. The Supreme Court in *Santosky v Kramer* (1982) noted that the parent and the child share an interest in preventing the erroneous termination of parental rights. The Court observed:

    Some losses cannot be measured. In this case, for example, [the child] was removed from his natural parents' custody when he was only three days old; the judge's finding of permanent neglect effectively foreclosed the possibility that the [child] would ever know his natural parents.

12. A number of state statutes provide that children may generally remain in foster care for only a limited period, and that parental rights may be terminated when a child's placement has exceeded this limit. Examples of such statutes are Maryland, 1 year (*MD Fam. Law Code Ann.*, 1991); Michigan, 1 year (*Mich. Comp. Laws Ann.*, 1988 & 1991); and South Dakota, 18 months (*SD Cod. Laws Ann.*, 1984 & 1991).

13. Courts in California and Massachusetts have recognized the duty of child welfare agencies to attempt to locate relatives who can care for children whose parents are unable to do so. See *In re Terry E.* (1986):

    . . . applicable statute "clearly implies that when the juvenile court orders removal of a child from the physical custody of his or her parents, the child should be placed, if at all possible, in the home of a relative, provided only that the relative's home is suitable for the child."

    Also see *Petition of the Department of Child Welfare to Dispense with Consent to Adoption* (1981), which reprimanded the child welfare agency for not having followed up on the mother's suggestion at the time of initial placement and investigated the suitability of relatives to care for the child. The court refused to reverse the order terminating parental rights on this basis; the court reversed on other grounds.

    An Oklahoma court has similarly held that the availability of relatives or friends who might be childcare resources was an important issue in a termination-of-parental-rights proceeding involving an incarcerated parent (*Matter of Christina T.*, 1979).

    New York and Mississippi have dealt with this issue through statute. New York law requires that, prior to accepting a child into foster placement, a child welfare agency attempt to locate relatives of the child who can appropriately care for the child, either as custodians or foster parents (*NY Fam. Law Act*, 1992; *NY Soc. Serv. Law*, 1992). The Mississippi statute mandates that "legal custody and guardianship by persons other than the parent . . . should be considered as alternatives to the termination of parental rights" (*Miss. Code Ann.*, 1992).

14. This list of services is suggested by various New York and California statutes (*Cal. Welf. & Inst. Code*, 1992; *NY Fam. Ct. Act*, 1992; *NY Soc. Serv. Law*, 1992).

15. These factors are derived primarily from three sources: the Oklahoma statute concerning termination of parental rights (*OK Stat. Ann.*, 1987); the California statute (*CA Welf. & Inst. Code*, 1992; and the decision of the New Jersey Supreme Court in *The Matter of the Adoption of the Children by L.A.W.S.*, 1993.

    The New Jersey Supreme court decision is noteworthy for its wise and careful reasoning. The case involved a father serving a life sentence for murder. The court rejected a *per se* finding of unfitness based on sentence length or nature of the crime and instead provided a thoughtful, detailed discussion of the considerations that must be weighed before rights of incarcerated parents may be terminated.

In another case (*In re Terry E.*, 1986), an order terminating parental rights was reversed and the petition dismissed; despite the nature of the mother's crime and the length of her sentence, she had a strong record of rehabilitation and could perform the parental role, even while foster parents continued to act as guardians of the child.

Another court rejected the notion that a mother was unfit simply because she would not be able to care *physically* for her child for an extended period of time (*Petition of Boston Children's Service Association & Review denied*, 1986). The court reversed an order terminating parental rights and remanded for a determination of the mother's current fitness. While the mother's life sentence was "a circumstance which bears upon her fitness because of her long unavailability," the mother's incarceration did not "conclusively render her unfit as a parent." While the mother was unable to obtain physical custody of her child, it was conceivable that she and the father could obtain legal custody, that the father could obtain physical custody, and that the mother would still be capable of assisting in issues concerning her children's health and education. Even if physical custody were to remain with the foster mother, the mother would retain her parental rights and could therefore continue to participate in decision making.

In another case (*Petition of Department of Public Welfare*, 1981) the order terminating parental rights was reversed, despite the foster parent's wish to adopt the child, where the mother had reorganized her life, had participated extensively in educational, vocational, and rehabilitative programs while in prison, and appeared to be a fit mother.

References

Alabama Code §26-18-7(a) (1986).

Arizona Rev. Stat. Ann. §8-533(B)(4) (1986).

Beckerman, A. (1989). Incarcerated mothers and their children in foster care: The dilemma of visitation. *Children and Youth Services Review*, 11:175–183.

California Welf. & Inst. Code §§361.5(e)(1–4), 366.26(c)(1) (West Suppl. 1992).

Cardwell v Gwaltney, 556 N.E. 2d 953 (Ind. Ct. App. 1990).

Division of Child Support Enforcement ex rel. Harper v Barrows, 570 A. 2d 1180 (Del. Sup. Ct. 1990).

Georgia Code Ann. §15-11-81(b)(4)(B)(iii) (1990 & Suppl. 1991).

Garrison, M. (1983). Why terminate parental rights? *Stanford Law Review*, 35:423–496.

Hairston, C. F., & Hess, P. M. (1989). Family ties, maintaining child–parent bonds is important. *Corrections Today*, 51:102.

Hale, D. C. (1987). The impact of mother's incarceration on the family system: Research and recommendations. *Marriage and Family Review*, 12(1/2):143–154.

Idaho Code §§16-1602(s)(2), 16-2005 (Suppl. 1991).

Illinois Ann. Stat. Ch. 40, Para. 1501(D)(f-g) (Smith-Hurd, 1980).

Illinois ex rel. Meyer v Nein, 209 Ill. App. 3d 1087; 568 N.E. 2d 436 (1991).

Indiana Code Ann. §31-6-5-4.2(a) (Burns Suppl. 1991).

In re Adoption of Children by D., 61 N.J. 89; 293 A.2d 171 (1972).

In re Adoption of Sabrina, 325 Pa. Super. 17; 472 A. 2d 624 (Super. Ct. 1984).

In re Daniel C., 480 A. 2d 766 (Maine 1984).

In re Frances, 505 A. 2d 1380 (R.I. Sup. Ct. 1986).

In re Juvenile Appeal, 177 Conn. 648; 420 A. 2d 875 (1979).

In re Terry E., 180 Cal. App. 3d 932; 225 Cal. Rptr. 803 (Ct. App. 1986).

Interest of D. S., 176 Ga. App. 482; 336 S.E. 2d 358 (Ct. App. 1985).

Interest of H.L.T., 164 Ga. App. 517; 298 S.E. 2d 33 (Ct. App. 1982).

Interest of Jones, 34 Ill. App. 3d 603; 340 N.E. 2d 269 (Ill. App. Ct. 1975).

Interest of M.L.K., 804 S.W. 2d 398 (Mo. App. 1991).

Iowa Code Ann. §§232.116(1)(i)(2), 232.116(2)(a) (West Suppl. 1991).

Kansas Stat. Ann. §38-1583(b)(5) (1986).

Kaslow, X. (1987). Couples or family therapy for prisoners and their significant others. *American Journal of Family Therapy*, 15:352–360.

Leasure v Leasure, 378 Pa. Super. 613; 549 A. 2d 225 (Pa. Super. Ct., 1988).

Louisiana Stat. Ann., Children's Code, art. 1015(1), (6) (West Suppl. 1992).

Lowenstein, A. (1986). Temporary single parenthood: The case of prisoners' families. *Family Relations*, 36:79–85.

Maine Rev. Stat. Ann. Title 22, §4055(I-A)(B) (1992).

Maryland Fam. Law Code Ann. Sect. 5-313 (1991).

Matter of Anonymous v Longobardi, 40 N.Y. 2d 96; 351 N.E. 2d 707; 386 N.Y.S. 2d 59 (1976).

Matter of Bradley, 57 N.C. App. 475; 291 S.E. 2d 800 (N.C. Ct. App. 1982).

Matter of Bistany, 239 N.Y. 19; 145 N.E. 70 (1924).

Matter of Christina T., 590 P. 2d 189 (Okla. Sup. Ct. 1979).

Matter of Ricky Ralph M., 56 N.Y. 2d 77; 436 N.E. 2d 491; 451 N.Y.S. 2d 41 (1982).

Matthews v Eldridge, 424 U.S. 319 (1976).

McGowan, B., & Blumenthal, K. (1978). *Why punish the children? A study of the children of women prisoners*. Hackensack, NJ: National Council on Crime and Delinquency.

Matter of the Adoption of Children by L.A.S., 134 N.J. 127 (1993).

Michigan Comp. Laws Ann., Sect. 712A.19a (West 1998 & Suppl. 1991).

Mississippi Code Ann. §§93-15-103(3)(e) (Suppl. 1991), 93-15-103(4) (Suppl. 1992).

Missouri Ann. Stat. §211.447(3)(6) (Vernon Suppl. 1992).

Montana Code Ann. §§41-3-609(2)(e), 41-3-609(4)(b) (1991).

Nevada Rev. Stat. Ann. §§128.105, 128.106(6) (Michie Suppl. 1991).

New Hampshire Rev. Stat. Ann. §170-C:5(VI) (Suppl. 1991).

New Mexico Stat. Ann. §§32-1-3(L)(4), 32-1-54(B)(3) (1989).

New York Fam. Ct. Act §1017 (McKinney Suppl. 1992).

New York Soc. Serv. Law §§384-a(1-a), 384-b(7)(e-f) (McKinney 1992).

Ohler v Ohler, 220 Neb. 272; 369 N.W. 2d 615 (1985).

Oklahoma Stat. Ann., Title 10, §1130 (A)(5–7) (West, 1987).

Oregon Rev. Stat. §§109.322, 419.523 (1991).

Petition of Boston Children's Services Association, 20 Mass. App. 566; 481 N.E.2d 516 (App. Ct.); 396 Mass. 1102; 484 N.E. 2d 102 (1985).

Petition of R.H.N., 710 P. 2d 482 (Colo. Sup. Ct. 1985).

Petition of the Department of Child Welfare to Dispense with Consent to Adoption, 383 Mass. 573; 421 N.E. 2 (1981).

Proctor v Proctor, 773 P. 2d 1389 (Ct. App. Utah, 1989).

Rhode Island Gen. Laws, §15-7-1(1)(b)(i) (1988).

Sack, W, Seidler, T. & Harris, S. (1976). Children of imprisoned parents: A psychosocial exploration. *American Journal of Orthopsychiatry*, 46(4):618–628.

Santosky v Kramer, 455 U.S. 745 (1982).

South Dakota Codified Laws Ann., Sect. 26-8A-26 (1984 & Suppl. 1991).

Smith v Alaska Department of Revenue, 790 P. 2d 1352 (Alaska 1990).

Staat v Hennepin County Welfare Board, 287 Minn. 501,; 178 N.W. 2d 709 (1970).

Stanley v Illinois, 405 U.S. 645 (1971).

Tennessee Code Ann. §37-1-147(d)(3) (1991).

Turner v Safley, 482 U.S. 78 (1987).

U.S. Department of Justice. (1986). *National corrections reporting program* (Report No. NCJ-132291) Washington, D.C.: US Bureau of Justice Statistics.

U.S. Department of Justice. (1991). *Women in prison* (Report No. NCJ-127991). Washington, DC: U.S. Bureau of Justice Statistics.

U.S. Department of Justice. (1993). *Survey of state prisoners* (Report No. NCJ-136949). Washington, DC: U.S. Bureau of Justice Statistics.

Wisconsin Stat. Ann. §§48.13(8), 48.415(2), 48.415(5)(a) (West 1987).

Wyoming Stat. §14-2-309(a)(iv) (1986).

12
Practical Considerations Regarding Termination of Incarcerated Parents' Rights

Gail Smith

The dramatic growth in sentences of imprisonment, increasingly long sentences for relatively minor offenses for women who are single parents, and the subsequent rise in the permanent destruction of families as a result, are social realities that are well documented elsewhere in this book. This chapter will discuss the practical realities that lead to the permanent severance of parent–child relationships, ways in which imprisoned parents and their lawyers or advocates can reduce the likelihood of parental rights termination, and policy changes that would promote the survival of viable families.

The essential nature of being a mother is to be present in your child's daily life and to make small and large decisions about how to raise your child, from schooling, religion, and medical care to the child's bedtime schedule and meals. The very nature of being a prisoner is to be absent from your home, isolated many miles away from your family, with very limited access to telephones, restricted visits, and the most limited power imaginable over the small day-to-day decisions that make up your life: what and when to eat, what to wear, how to spend your time, even when to take a shower and when to go to bed. A mother's parental autonomy, self-determination, and sense of responsibility for her child, and the mother–child relationship itself, inevitably are harmed by even a short period of imprisonment. The majority of imprisoned mothers are serving time for offenses that have little impact on their parenting abilities, and have children who need them. These basic realities have implications that should lead us to question the nationwide policy of imprisonment as the preferred sentence for nonviolent property and drug-related crimes committed by parents who are their children's primary caregivers. This and other policy considerations to preserve families will be outlined in the conclusion of this chapter.

As state legislatures lengthen prison sentences for relatively minor crimes, parents are increasingly faced with termination of parental rights simply due to the length of time their children will be in foster care. In addition, as states expand the legal grounds for parental rights termination and as increasing numbers of petitions for termination of parental rights are brought, more and more parents and children are losing each other regardless of their wishes, past relationships, or ability to reunite as families. This happens in two contexts: the foster care system and private adoption by a stepparent, extended family member, or nonrelated person who was caring for the child in the parent's absence. A number of systemic conditions make it difficult for parents to protect their rights, as the next section will explain.

Factors that Promote the Termination of Parental Rights

Correctional Policies and Parent–Child Contact

Parents with children in foster care are required to show evidence that they have maintained contact with these children during parent–child separation. Nationwide, most state prisons tend to be located in rural or otherwise remote areas, and they usually are inaccessible by inexpensive public transportation and require a long drive by car from greater metropolitan areas. This means that regular, frequent parent–child visits are the exception rather than the rule. It is not unusual for a year or more to pass between visits. The quality of parent–child visits is the major way for foster care agencies to assess a child's bond with the parent and a parent's progress toward reunification. Also, visitation is the primary vehicle for building and maintaining the parent–child relationship. However, even when monthly visits are mandated by state foster care regulations, many parents only see their children every 3 or 4 months. Foster care caseworkers, who often are overburdened with many more cases than they are supposed to be assigned, are unable to take a full day away from their caseload to provide a visit for one family. Relatives who are caring for children often do not have the resources to travel long distances to provide frequent visits; many do not even own cars.

The increase in prison overcrowding, particularly in women's facilities, has led to the transfer of women to facilities that are ever greater in distance from their homes. Prisons that are located far enough away to require an overnight trip pose the additional cost of a hotel stay for caregivers. In some states, the establishment of nonprofit volunteer programs to provide transportation for children's visits and overnight housing near the prisons are a great help to families who otherwise would have no visits at all during the parent's incarceration. However, such programs reach only a fraction of the families in need and can only provide limited visits;

these programs provide few parents and children with weekly, ongoing visits throughout the parent's confinement.

Telephone visits present additional cost-related problems. Since incarcerated parents are only allowed to make collect telephone calls, the expense is greater than that of normal long-distance calls and calling must therefore be strictly limited for most families.

Lack of Prison Programs and Services

Parents whose children are in foster care are required to follow a service plan and complete various tasks before they can regain custody. Lack of communication between overburdened foster care workers and corrections staff may cause the foster care agency to establish a plan that requires participation in a program that is unavailable to the parent. The foster care agency then often blames the parent for failure to make progress in completing the service plan tasks. Such failure, by itself, is a frequently used ground for termination of parental rights. For example, in Illinois, drug treatment is available in only one of the four state prisons that house women, and there is a long waiting list to get into the program. However, if the mother cannot prove that she sought treatment and document the reason why she did not obtain it, the agency may evaluate her progress as unsatisfactory. Similarly, the parent may be required to participate in parenting or child development classes that exist only in a state report and not in reality. In addition to substance abuse treatment and parenting classes, other programs that may be required and should be made available to parents include individual counseling, generally and in relation to such issues as domestic violence and childhood sexual abuse; vocational and educational programs to assist the parent in becoming more employable; and joint family counseling (discussed below). Prison overcrowding further reduces parent's access to programs they are required to attend. While some facilities give priority on waiting lists to parents whose foster care service plan mandates participation in a particular program, transfer to another facility due to prison overcrowding frequently defeats completion of the program.

Lack of Joint Counseling for Parents and Children

Children left behind by a parent's imprisonment almost inevitably will have problems related to the separation. Depending on the age of the child, problems ranging from severe trauma and regression to suicidal tendencies, inability to concentrate in school, and delinquency may occur. If they are to maintain a viable relationship, the parent and child might well need joint counseling is to help both to address their feelings and to assist the parent in dealing wisely with the child's reaction. Such counseling is rarely available. Without this assistance in maintaining and strengthening their relationship, some families are unable to surmount the difficulties of weathering the separation and getting through the adjustments required in reunification. Mothers who love their children may be unable to handle the children's anger at the separation, and may end up losing custody permanently because their feelings of guilt and helplessness prevent them from handling visits well upon their release.

Lack of Adequate Screening, Training, and Support for Caregivers

Yolanda had a 4-year sentence to serve. After an initial foster placement, her two sons, ages 2 and 5, were placed with a private guardian by the juvenile court. When Yolanda refused to consent to the adoption of the children, the guardian refused to care for them any longer and dropped them off at the state foster care agency. The children were placed in a state foster home that was licensed to care for children with special needs. The children soon reported that they had been physically and sexually abused in the home of the guardian; a medical report indicated evidence of severe sexual abuse. When the first mother–child visit was planned, the children reported that their mother also had sexually abused them. The next two visits were extremely tense: the children acted afraid to be near their mother, and she was baffled and hurt by their behavior as well as their false allegations against her. She chose not to pursue regular visits when the foster father convinced her that visits were only upsetting the children and that it was better for them to have time away from her to sort out their confusion. Two years passed. It was then discovered that the foster father had coached the children to make allegations against their mother, threatening them with extreme punishment if they said their lines wrong, and he was charged with forcing another foster child to make similar allegations against her mother to prevent her return home from foster care. The foster parents' license was investigated but not revoked. Six months later, the foster mother revealed that the foster father had regularly battered her, left him and filed for divorce. Yolanda's younger son then revealed that a broken leg he previously maintained was accidental actually was inflicted by the foster father. By then Yolanda's relationship with her sons was so attenuated that she decided to surrender parental rights to the foster mother. The foster mother continued to allow the abusive foster father to visit the children, and they were removed and placed in a series of foster placements. The children began taking out their anger on younger children, and understandably were unable to trust adults. A positive, permanent home for the two boys as they grow into adulthood would require a miracle.

Foster parents and other caregivers generally are not prepared to assume a role that supports the parent–child bond and eventual reunification, nor are they prepared for the tumultuous changes children go through during the separation from their parents. An adversarial relationship between the caregivers and the parent often results. Foster parents may be led to expect that they will be able to obtain permanent custody of the child; this misunderstanding creates conflicts upon the parent's release. If caregivers of prisoners' children were trained to support the child and to nurture the parent–child relationship, much heartache could be spared for all parties and far fewer parents would lose their children permanently. Foster parents are not prepared for the natural acting out of grief that comes at the end of a visit when the child has not seen the parent for a long time, and they often misinterpret the behavior as an indication that visits are bad for the child. Foster parents who expect or hope to adopt the child may subtly or overtly undermine the parent–child relationship by telling the child bad things about the parent.

Lack of Legal Counseling for Incarcerated Parents

> Juana's children were ages 7, 9, and 12 when she was arrested, and they had always been in her care. She had 2 years to serve on a drug-related charge. The paternal grandmother took custody of the children and became their official foster parent through the state child welfare agency. Juana had two visits with her children; then she was transferred to a facility hundreds of miles from her home, and the visits ended. Although she wrote to her children regularly, the foster care agency found the distance too great to bridge, and did not provide visits or include Juana in the plans for her children. When Juana was brought to court for a routine hearing, the caseworker persuaded her to sign custody over to the grandmother "temporarily." In front of the judge, Juana was handed a piece of paper to sign but was not given time to read it. She signed the document, and later discovered that she had signed a permanent surrender of her children, and that her parental rights had been terminated on the next court date on the basis of the surrender.

Grounds for termination of parental rights, such as failure to communicate with the child or agency, failure to plan for the child's future, or failure to make progress toward reunification, are easy to fall into for a parent who is unfamiliar with the law and the workings of the child welfare system. Many parents do not know they have a right to have visits with their children while they are incarcerated. Others may feel so guilty and overwhelmed with depression at being away from their children that they may rationalize their plight by deciding that they will make it all up to them later, but stay out of their lives for the present. Others may be discouraged when their children do not receive their letters, either because they must be sent via an overworked foster care worker or because the caregiver withholds them from the children because she feels threatened by the children's relationship with the parent, and the parent may give up writing to them. Since most foster care agencies do not permit the parent to have the address of the children's foster home, the mother must send letters to the caseworker, who is supposed to deliver them to the child; many incarcerated mothers have felt like giving up when they find out that all their letters from months ago still have not been delivered. If the parent does not have regular contact with the children and the foster care agency, or if she fails to keep records of her contact, she may face termination of her parental rights later. Therefore, it is critical that parents have access to legal counseling and education about the law, so that they can make informed decisions about their children's placement and take steps to preserve their parental rights. Further, parents may be pressured into signing documents they only vaguely understand, with disastrous results.

Systemic Failure to Include Parents in Placement Decisions, Planning, and Case Reviews

> Martha was an accomplice on a robbery in which her codefendant was convicted of felony murder, and she was sentenced to 20 years. Her 5-year-old daughter was placed in foster care. Martha contacted her cousin in another county, who agreed that it would be best for her and her husband to raise Martha's daughter so that she would have a sense of family and would grow up knowing her mother. The cousin's home passed the state adoptive licensing process with flying colors. Martha did not have access to legal advice, and she signed a surrender of custody, intending that her cousin would adopt her daughter. However, a specific consent naming her cousin as the adoptive parent was needed to protect her plan. The agency caseworker opposed the cousin's petition, preferring the nonrelative foster parents. The judge followed the caseworker's recommendation and allowed the unrelated foster parents to adopt the child.

A parent who has been excluded from her child's life, whether because the child welfare system fails to value her opinions or because it is inconvenient to make contact with her in prison, will have a more difficult time resuming responsibility for her child. Conversely, if the agency makes plans for the children that do not take into account the mother's service needs and parole plans, her chances of successfully reuniting her family are severely reduced. However, it is common for foster care agencies to exclude mothers from the planning process and the semiannual agency assessments (often called administrative case reviews) that establish the service plan for the next 6 months. (At the administrative case review, the administrator and the caseworker choose a goal for the child, such as "return home," "long-term placement in relative foster care," "long-term placement in nonrelative foster care," "institutional placement," "independence," "adoption," or "substitute care pending a court decision whether to terminate parental rights.") If state child welfare departments and corrections departments do not coordinate services, they create nearly insurmountable obstacles for parents who wish to preserve their parental rights and reunite their families. In instances in which the length of the parent's sentence will prevent her from regaining custody, she is unable to choose a caregiver who will support an ongoing relationship with her child.

Preventing the Termination of Parental Rights

The Role of the Parent

Whenever possible, parents should plan for their children's placement as soon as they are arrested. State provisions for power of attorney or standby guardianship may protect a placement with a caregiver who will help the parent keep contact with the child. If the child is in the custody of a relative or friend, it is important to keep as cooperative a relationship as possible with the caregiver. While private petitions to adopt are less common than petitions brought in the foster care setting, they can be even more difficult for the parent to defend, since the parent may have no statutory right to counsel and since the caregiver does not have any responsibility to provide reunification services to the parent, as does the state foster care agency in some states.

The parent should be aware of all the grounds that can be used to terminate parental rights in the children's home state, and should be sure not to lose her rights through inaction. No matter whether the child is in foster care or with a private caregiver, the parent should request regular visits and document the visits (or the requests, if not heeded). If necessary, the parent may need to go to court to enforce visitation rights. The parent should maintain frequent contact with the child between visits, and keep copies or records of all letters and telephone visits. A logbook documenting the date and time of telephone calls, and noting the topics discussed, may help the parent's recollection of specifics so that she can present clear evidence of her regular communication with her children in a court hearing, if necessary. Some courts will allow such records to be introduced as evidence.

The parent should make every effort to obtain services to address problems that led to her imprisonment or that affected her children prior to imprisonment, and should keep documentation of successful completion of programs and/or unsuccessful efforts to enroll in programs. For example, if the mother has a substance abuse problem, she should try to get a certificate of completion of a treatment program and a letter describing her participation, or a letter explaining that she made efforts to apply to a program but that none was available, or that she is on a long waiting list, or whatever.

If her children are in foster care, the parent should write to the agency caseworker at least monthly to express any concerns she has about the children, to inform the agency of any progress she has made toward completion of her service plan, and to request visits or confirm the visiting schedule. She should follow the agency service plan to the best of her ability and should document any reasons she is unable to comply with it. She should enclose letters or cards for the children in each correspondence with the agency; a simple drawing with an "I love you" message for her child shows just as much desire to maintain contact as a lengthy letter. Even if she knows that her letters are not being given to her children in a timely manner, she should persist in writing for two reasons: because the children may receive the letters later and then will learn that their mother was thinking about them all along, which will be critical in combating their feelings of abandonment, and because the record of her regular letters, even if undelivered, may prevent an allegation that she failed to maintain contact with her children.

Parents whose children are in foster care should try to be included in the regular administrative case review for the children. In rare instances, an agency may be persuaded to hold the administrative review at the prison so that the parent can participate. More commonly, the parent may be able to participate in the plan via a speaker phone set up in the agency office, with some advance planning in cooperation with corrections staff. If this option is not available, the parent may want to send a relative or other advocate in her place, or at the very least, write a letter to be read at the case review, outlining her concerns, requests, and any progress made on the previous service plan.

Parents whose children are living with an ex-spouse should try hard to stay on good terms with the other parent and to focus on the children's needs rather than any old wounds or anger they may feel. As in other placement settings, they should maintain contact with the child; if possible they should contribute a reasonable amount to the child's support through small gifts, or, if the parent is able to earn money through prison industry, by sending certified checks. Private adoptions often are based on allegations of abandonment and lack of interest in the child; regular communication and making whatever contributions toward the child's support are possible will do much to defeat this allegation. Again, it is critical to keep records.

Finally, parents should participate in programs that can be used as evidence of rehabilitation and should try to keep a clean disciplinary record. States that allow termination of parental rights based on felony conviction or depravity often allow evidence of the parent's rehabilitation to refute the unfitness allegation.

If the parent receives notice of a petition to terminate parental rights, or if a relative or friend sees a publication notice in the newspaper, the parent should seek legal help if at all possible. If necessary, the parent should file a notice of appearance with the court, indicating that the parent wishes to contest the adoption, along with a request for appointment of counsel, and a request to have the court send a writ so that the parent can be present in court. These should be sent even if it is necessary to send a handwritten notice; they may prevent the parent from having a default judgment entered against her. If the petition is brought in the context of the foster care system, it is likely that the parent has a right to be represented by counsel; she should make the best of that representation.

If the petition is being brought in another state, it is unlikely that the parent will be brought to court for the hearing. It is critical to try to get an attorney to represent the parent in court and to provide the attorney with all the necessary information and evidence to defeat the grounds for termination alleged in the petition and to make an argument as to why it is in the children's best interest to maintain their relationship with the parent.

The Role of Legal Practitioners and Advocates

Prevention. Lawyers and other advocates who work with imprisoned parents should make sure that parents understand the grounds for termination of parental rights in their state, or, if different, the state in which the children are living. They should provide forms to assist the parent in keeping records of communication with the children and the foster care agency, and in keeping documentation of participation in programs that are mandated by the foster care service plan or that demonstrate the parent's rehabilitation.

If possible, practitioners should try to meet with parents as early as possible during the parent's period of incarceration. If the parent receives legal advice and assistance regarding the children's placement from the beginning, countless problems may be avoided. If a private guardianship is appropriate, with the consent of the parent, both the parent and the guardian should be advised as to the nature of guardianship, the process for discharging the guardian when the parent is ready to resume custody, the importance of cooperating in the children's best interest, and the importance of visits. The family should be referred to any available services to assist with transportation for the children's visits, and to any available counseling or support groups to help them handle the separation and the transition process of reunification.

Practitioners working with imprisoned parents often walk a fine line between doing social work and providing legal services. Imprisoned parents may need encouragement in pursuing their rights and standing up for themselves; they should be encouraged to be persistent (although polite) in their efforts to obtain visits with their children and services in the corrections system. They should be informed of the potential ramifications of inaction, particularly when they are discouraged by a seemingly insurmountable bureaucracy. Similarly, the parent should be advised not to go along with family secrets in which caregivers keep the children from knowing that the parent is in prison. A mother's willingness to please her relatives by simply disappearing from her children's lives until her release may lead to a termination of her parental rights based on failure to show interest, concern, and responsibility for her children, or failure to communicate with her children.

If feasible, the practitioner should represent the parent not only in court, but at the agency case review if the parent cannot participate. It is much easier to prevent a change in the service goal than to remedy an undesirable change in direction after the fact. At the same time, it is possible to get a goal of "return home" reinstated for a parent who is working toward reunification even if the goal was changed to "long-term foster care" 6 months earlier. An advocate need not be a lawyer in order to represent the parent at an administrative case review; it is only necessary that the advocate be well informed about the case and the parent's concerns, and be able to attest to the efforts the parent has made. The case review is an opportunity to hold the agency to its own standards, and issues such as canceled visits or undelivered mail can be effectively addressed at the review. If the administrator does not direct the caseworker to make improvements, the attorney should consider filing a supplemental petition to enforce the parent's rights under agency regulations.

Defense. First of all, lawyers and advocates should be familiar not only with their state's statutory grounds for termination of parental rights and relevant case law, but also with the procedural protections outlined in Philip Genty's "Termination of Parental Rights" chapter in this volume and any state statutes that further specify or augment those rights. In many cases, grounds for termination of parental rights are alleged that are fairly easily disproved by presenting evidence of and witnesses to the parent's efforts to maintain a relationship with her children. This is especially common in private adoptions, in which the opposing attorney anticipates that the parent will default or will be unrepresented by counsel. It is not uncommon for the petitioners to allege—falsely—that they have not heard from the parent or do not know her whereabouts. Careful compilation of evidence, such as records of outgoing mail and telephone calls, or telephone bills from the children's place of residence, together with careful preparation of the parent for trial, can defeat termination petitions brought on false grounds. Evidence of the parent's efforts toward rehabilitation, together with testimony of prison personnel who have observed the parent's progress, also may defeat termination of rights. In addition, discovery may play a key role in making an argument as to why it is against the child's interest to sever the parent–child relationship and terminate parental rights.

> Judy was serving a 4-year sentence for burglary. Her 6-year-old son Freddy was in foster care. Despite Freddy's frequent requests for visits with his mother, the agency screened the case for adoption and filed a petition to terminate parental rights based on the mother's alleged failure to make reasonable efforts and reasonable progress toward return of the child within 12 months. Freddy

was seeing a psychiatrist, and on one visit with his mother, he told her that when he didn't get visits he thought about killing himself by taking all of his foster mother's pills.

The caseworker unsuccessfully tried to persuade the foster mother, who was elderly and had health problems, to adopt Freddy. The caseworker finally persuaded the paternal grandmother, who had initially placed Freddy with the state foster care agency, to consider adopting him. The agency began overnight weekend visits for Freddy and his grandmother. The agency, the child's guardian ad litem, and the state's attorney all took the position that Freddy would be better off with his grandmother, despite his close relationship with his mother, and a trial date for the termination was set. Judy's lawyer subpoenaed the psychiatrist's records and, after much resistance, finally obtained them. The records revealed that Freddy's grandmother had been beating him during their weekend visits. Armed with this evidence, Judy's lawyer was able to get the termination petition withdrawn and a regular schedule for mother–child visits reinstated.

If at all possible, the lawyer should obtain a writ to have the parent present in court for all substantive hearings. A well-prepared and concerned parent's demeanor goes a long way to debunk stereotypes of parents in prison that even well-intentioned judges may harbor. If the petition is brought by a private party who is related to the mother, it may be a good idea to try to get court-ordered mediation prior to going to trial. If it is possible to reach a reconciliation of sorts and prevent the wrenching emotional battle of a trial, all parties—parent, child, and caregiver—will benefit. However, unless the state has a statute providing for open adoption with enforcement of visitation agreements, the lawyer should advise the parent to be wary of any agreements to have the child adopted but to permit ongoing contact. Such agreements may be impossible to enforce without statutory authority.

Conclusions and Recommendations

In order to avoid needless destruction of families through wrongful termination of parental rights, widespread implementation of the following policies is necessary:

Sentencing

State legislatures should not rely on imprisonment as a sentence for primary caregiver parents who pose no danger to the community (i.e., those convicted of nonviolent offenses and offenses that arguably were made in self-defense against batterers). Parents who pose a real danger to the community, and who must be incarcerated, should be housed in facilities as close as possible to the community where their children live. A range of sanctions should be available for the sentencing of parents who are not a danger to the community; these could include restitution; community service hours; day programs such as substance abuse treatment, counseling, and vocational or educational training; and community-based residential sentencing programs in which parents and children stay together and attend any necessary programming at the center or in nearby community agencies. Such a policy could prevent thousands of viable families from being needlessly destroyed.

Visits

States should allocate funds for parent–child visits whenever a parent who lived with the child prior to incarceration is imprisoned. Ideally, visits for parents and children who are likely to reunite after the parent's release should take place no less than once a week. Visits for parents and children who cannot be reunited (such as parents with life sentences) could take place less frequently, but monthly visits are desirable if the child is to grow up with any real sense of the parent's love and concern.

Placement Issues

Policy should be geared to end adversarial relationships between adults when child custody is at issue, insofar as practicable. For children whose parents are in prison, specialized foster care placements should be available, preferably with a relative who is supportive of the parent. Whether or not the foster parent is related to the child, training and support services should be available to teach the foster parent and birth parent how to coparent the child cooperatively, and to educate them about separation issues and other difficulties the child may be expected to experience. Counseling and support groups should be available for the foster parent, the child, and the parent. Foster parents should be screened for their willingness and ability to be supportive of the parent–child relationship, in addition to regular foster parent screening. While it admittedly takes a courageous and bighearted person to love and care for a child without trying to take permanent custody of that child, that is exactly the sort of person children need as a foster parent, to avoid placing the child in a position of conflict. For the same reason, imprisoned parents should be encouraged to support an ongoing relationship between the child and the foster parent, as an aunt/uncle or grandparent figure, after the parent regains custody of the child, to ease the child's transition and provide the maximal ongoing relationship with all adults who have played an important role in the child's life.

Service Issues

As a matter of policy and practice, states should move toward broad-scale availability of high-quality services inside correctional facilities: parenting classes, classes on family and juvenile law, individual counseling, joint parent–child counseling, substance abuse treatment, counseling for survivors of childhood sexual abuse and domestic violence, and vocational or educational programs to help parents become employable.

Legal Services

Legal counseling and representation should be widely available for imprisoned parents. State statutes should mandate effective representation in defense of *all* petitions to terminate parental rights, whether filed in the context of the foster care system or by private parties. On-site legal services should be provided on a regular basis to make parents aware of the ramifications of putting off dealing with family issues until release. The procedural protections spelled out by the U.S. Supreme Court and by state statutes, as discussed in Philip Genty's "Termination of Parental Rights" chapter should be honored in each and every case.

Open Adoptions

The concept of permanency planning for children was implemented in the 1980s to prevent foster care drift and to assure permanent homes for children whose parents could not care for them. However, in our willingness to address the failures of the foster care system we have instead failed to take into account children's need to maintain a bond with their parents. (See the discussion of intangible support by parents in Philip Genty's "Termination of Parental Rights" chapter). Adoption is seen as a panacea, although it is not what most people would want for themselves, given a choice. When a parent is in prison, the push toward a hasty and perhaps ill-decided adoption is all the more likely. We do not help children by our failure to value the benefit of being raised by their own—albeit imperfect—parents, or at least to give children the opportunity to know that their parents, despite their limitations, love them and never meant to leave them. The widespread passage of statutes to permit parents and adopted children ongoing contact would make it easier for parents with very long sentences to obtain permanency for their children without having to sever their relationship. With the appropriate training and support services, and with the requisite goodwill on the part of the adoptive parents, children could grow up feeling secure in their adoptive homes and loved by their birth parents as well. As other commentators have pointed out, state legislatures and courts strongly support ongoing visits with noncustodial parents in divorce even if those parents live thousands of miles away from the child. We should not assume that children of imprisoned parents deserve any less when it comes to ongoing relationships with their parents.

PART V

Intervention

13
Intervention

Denise Johnston

Historically, the U.S. criminal justice system has focused on the isolated offender and ignored his or her family and community connections. In spite of attention to family issues, the earliest advocates for children of offenders adopted this perspective and developed services that related exclusively to parental incarceration. It is only recently that a child-centered perspective has emerged, one that recognizes that these children live the great majority of their lives with unincarcerated parents and away from correctional facilities.

The Children of Offenders Study and other work by the Center for Children of Incarcerated Parents (Johnston 1991, 1992, 1993d) suggests that there are three factors that characterize these special children: (1) enduring trauma in childhood, (2) parent–child separation, and (3) an inadequate quality of care, largely due to poverty. Effective programs for children of prisoners and other offenders address one or more of these areas. Advocates and other human services professionals should be aware of the types and content of available interventions designed to meet these children's needs.

Interventions that Address Enduring Trauma in Childhood

The new perspective on the needs of children of prisoners and other offenders has led researchers to examine the quality and characteristics of their life experiences. Recent studies have documented enduring trauma—multiple or recurrent traumatic events—as one of these experiences (Johnston, 1992, 1993d). Because this information is new, it is not surprising that very few interventions addressing enduring trauma exist specifically for children of offenders. However, there are services that prevent or treat the effects of childhood trauma in all children and that may be effectively utilized by this population (see Table 13.1).

Table 13.1
Interventions for Children of Offenders: Services Addressing Enduring Trauma

	Client Profile	Goals/Expected Outcomes	Model Programs
Crisis nursery	Ages 0–6 years Family experiencing acute stress/crisis	Prevention of exposure of infants and young children to trauma	Bay Area Crisis Nursery, Concord, California
Therapeutic visitation	Children of long-term prisoners (sentences > 1 year)	Reduction of postrelease domestic discord and violence in the families of formerly incarcerated parents.	Project ImPACT, Las Lunas Correctional Facility, New Mexico
Arrest-related services	All children of arrested parents, with priority given to young children 2–6 years of age	Reduction in the immediate and long-term traumatic effects of parental arrest.	Parental Arrest Policy Group, Center for Children of Incarcerated Parents, Pasadena, California
Therapeutic intervention	Children of offenders, ages 4–10	Decrease in trauma-reactive behaviors and long-term outcomes of trauma.	Early Therapeutic Intervention Project, Center for Children of Incarcerated Parents, Pasadena, California

General Prevention of Trauma in Early Childhood: The Crisis Nursery

There is one intervention that is generally useful in the prevention of the acute effects of many causes of childhood trauma: the crisis nursery.

Recommended Intervention Goals. The primary purpose of crisis nurseries is to prevent the exposure of infants and young children to acute trauma. Parents may place children who are at risk for immediate exposure to crises like parental arrest, sudden homelessness, or episodes of domestic violence into this temporary residential care setting until the crisis is resolved. The goal of adjunct nursery services like parent support groups and respite care is to help families develop adaptive coping patterns for dealing with ongoing stress.

Recommended Client Selection Criteria. Existing crisis nurseries limit clients to infants and children 6 years of age or younger and their parents. Any family meeting this criteria and coming to the nursery in times of stress or crisis is served, as space allows.

Recommended Methods and Activities. The primary service provided is full residential child care for a limited period (usually 1 to 21 days). While children are housed at the nursery, their parents are assisted in developing a plan of action to alleviate the crisis or stressful situation. Other services include parent support groups, referrals, and respite care. Respite care services offer 2- to 4-day stays for children as part of ongoing, follow-up support provided to families who have used the nursery during a crisis.

Recommended Staffing. Like other intensive residential services for high-risk children, crisis nurseries should be directed and supervised by licensed professional persons trained in the area of child development. Parent educators should be child development and family ecology specialists experienced in working with families in crisis. Residential care staff should have a minimal level of training in child health, nutrition, safety, and child development. All paid and volunteer staff must be screened.

Expected Outcomes. This service should prevent the exposure of participating children to traumatic events, or reduce the amount of their exposure in family situations of ongoing stress and trauma. Respite and parent support services should reduce the levels of perceived stress among parents or caregivers and participating children, and should increase participating families' levels of utilization of community resources.

Model Program. The Bay Area Crisis Nursery was opened in 1981 and now provides services for nearly 400 children per year. It serves three counties with 15 beds and has an average daily census of eight children. The average length of stay is slightly more than 6 days for children of families in crisis, and 2 days for children in respite care. Most children of families in crisis are admitted because of parental stress (40%), parental unemployment or homelessness (20%), or parental illness (16%). Children are most often admitted to respite care for situations of ongoing parental stress (56%), substance dependency (20%), or marital problems (15%). The nursery is supported through grants and private donations. Volunteers work in short shifts, providing childcare, office help, or yard work under the supervision of trained and licensed staff. There is no fee for clients.

Prevention of Specific Childhood Traumas: Therapeutic Visitation

One major source of childhood trauma is domestic conflict and violence (Brown, Pelcovitz, & Kaplan, 1983; Hershorn & Rosenbaum, 1985; Kraft, 1984; Silvern & Kaersvang, 1989). Children of offenders may be particularly likely to have this experience. Dutton and Hart (1992) found that incarcerated men are at high risk for perpetrating domestic violence following their release from prison. Studies of incarcerated women have revealed that a large proportion have experienced battering or other forms of domestic abuse (Task Force on the Female Offender, 1990; U.S. Department of Justice [USDJ], 1994).

Interventions that decrease the incidence of domestic violence among the families of offenders would decrease the exposure of their children to this trauma. One such intervention is therapeutic visitation.

Recommended Intervention Goals. The purpose of these services is to reduce the incidence of postrelease domestic violence among the families of formerly incarcerated parents, indirectly reducing the exposure of children of these families to a specific source of trauma.

Recommended Client Selection Criteria. Ideally, these services should be available to all prisoners, with priority given to incarcerated parents and prisoners with a history of domestic violence (either as witness, abuser, or victim) in childhood or as adults.

Recommended Methods and Activities. Regular therapeutic visitation, or counselor-mediated family visits, is the core of this program. Other services may include parent and family life education for incarcerated parents and caregiving parents, parent–child contact visitation, and home-based support services for caregiving parents and children. Aftercare is necessary and may include home-based services, support groups, referrals, placements, and advocacy.

Recommended Staffing. This program should be directed by a trained and licensed professional. Therapeutic visits should be mediated by licensed therapists or social workers. Home-based services also require trained and licensed personnel, but other services may be provided by nonprofessionals or volunteers under trained supervision.

Expected Outcomes. These services should result in a reduced incidence of postrelease domestic violence among participating families of formerly incarcerated parents.

Model Programs. Since 1991, Project ImPACT (Importance of Parents And Children Together) has offered a therapeutic visitation program for the families of men incarcerated at New Mexico's Las Lunas Correctional Facility. Project staff have identified domestic violence as a major source of incidents leading to rearrest and recidivism in that prison population. The project provides mediated family visits for a minimum of 1 year prior to the parent's release, home-based services, support groups, and referrals. In its first 3 years of operation, the project served 97 incarcerated men, 54 spouses, and 191 children. Initial evaluation found a minimal incidence of postrelease domestic violence among participating families, and a corresponding 1-year recidivism rate of 1% among formerly incarcerated participants.

Interventions Following Parental Arrest

Although they share many experiences with other children from highly stressed and/or low-income families and communities, children of offenders are defined and distinguished by the experience of parental arrest. Such experiences are often significant sources of trauma in the lives of these children.

The Jailed Mothers Study (Johnston, 1991) found that about one in five minor children of arrested and detained women are present at their mother's arrest, and that the majority of this group are between of 2 and 6 years of age. No similar data is available for children of incarcerated men. The traumatic effects of parental arrest are well described (McGowan & Blumenthal, 1978; Prison MATCH, 1984). These effects may be particularly difficult to overcome for young children who have the cognitive abilities to understand traumatic events as they occur but do not have the developmental skills to process their emotional responses to trauma.

Early interventions for children of offenders would logically be arrest-related. They would assist parents and law enforcement personnel in minimizing the effects of parental arrest on children, and provide supports for children in the immediate aftermath of this trauma. Such services do not exist. The American Bar Association's (1993) study of children whose primary caretaker is arrested found that law enforcement agencies in several jurisdictions now have written policies addressing the management of parental arrests, but the study identified no crisis services available to assist children who have experienced this event.

Recommended Intervention Goals. The purpose of interventions for children following parental arrest should be to reduce the negative immediate and long-term effects of this traumatic experience.

Recommended Client Selection Criteria. All minor children who experience parental arrest should be eligible for services, but children at the developmentally vulnerable ages of 2 to 6 years should be given priority.

Recommended Methods and Activities. Crisis intervention counseling should be provided for all ages. Other activities should include the provision of information about the arrest, detention, and ajudication processes for older children, and referral to sources of ongoing support for families of offenders. Services that facilitate child placement, increasing parent participation and satisfaction in the selection of emergency caregivers and decreasing the likelihood of multiple placements, will also reduce the traumatic effects of parental arrest and detention.

Recommended Staffing. Crisis counseling, like all therapeutic services, must be provided by trained, licensed, and experienced professionals. Referral and educational components of these services could be provided by trained and screened volunteers.

Expected Outcomes. These services should reduce the effects of trauma on children who experience parental arrest. If placement assistance is provided, services should also improve parental satisfaction with and the long-term stability of placements for children whose parents are incarcerated after arrest.

Model Programs. There are no programs of this type currently in existence. In Los Angeles County, a Parental Arrest and Detention Policy

Group that included participants from Los Angeles City and County law enforcement agencies, the Department of Children's Services, and local advocacy agencies was convened. The group produced recommendations for law enforcement officer training and a brochure for arrested parents (Center for Children of Incarcerated Parents, 1993) that provides information about options for emergency and long-term placement, resources, and crisis counseling.

Therapeutic Interventions

Therapeutic interventions for the most common childhood traumas—domestic conflict/violence, child abuse/neglect, sexual molestation, and exposure to community violence—are available in many communities. Core services in each of these areas usually include individual, group, and/or family counseling (Martin, 1976; Ounstead, Oppenheimer, & Lindsay, 1974; Renshaw, 1982; Sgroi, 1984) and were developed for specific, narrowly defined populations of children who had experienced one type of trauma, rather than for large numbers of children who had experienced many different kinds of trauma throughout their entire lives.

Children who experience multiple traumas or recurrent episodes of the same trauma have traditionally been seen as child welfare system clients, a small population of the severely disadvantaged whose complicated needs are managed by social service caseworkers. Entire communities of such children have just not been envisioned. In fact, millions of children have come to live in conditions of enduring trauma throughout the United States (Garbarino, Dubrow, Kostelny, & Pardo, 1992). This conceptual error has left most trauma-reactive children—including specifically children of offenders—without an accessible source of general services.

The large population of trauma-reactive children—for whom children of offenders are a paradigm—need easily accessible therapeutic interventions. Except where they are offered as part of a larger, more comprehensive program of services for children of offenders, these specific interventions are currently unavailable in the United States.

Recommended Intervention Goals. Traumatized children, regardless of the source of the traumatic experience, need interventions that lead to recovery. The primary goal of these services should be children's mastery of the effects of current and previous traumas. A supplementary goal may be to enhance children's abilities to overcome future trauma by improving their individual coping skills.

Recommended Client Selection Criteria. Childhood trauma and its effects are not well understood. Traumatic experiences clearly effect different individuals in different ways, and there is no clear evidence that all persons exposed to traumatic events sustain emotional injury (Block, Silber & Perry, 1956; Brett, Spitzer & Williams, 1988; Doyle & Bauer, 1989). While the vast majority of children of offenders have probably had traumatic experiences, not all may require intervention for recovery from trauma. At the Center for Children of Incarcerated Parents we recommend that intervention be considered when children display persistent trauma-reactive behaviors, including but not limited to:

- aggression (verbal, physical, and/or sexual);
- withdrawal/depression;
- concentration/attention problems;
- asocial behaviors (lying and stealing); and/or
- anxiety states, including hypervigilance.

These services should also be part of an intervention plan for older children who exhibit fixed patterns of trauma-reactive behaviors like interpersonal or gang violence, sexual misconduct, substance abuse, and/or theft.

Recommended Methods and Activities. Comprehensive behavioral, developmental, family, and medical assessment of children referred for services is required. Children should participate in weekly therapeutic sessions supplemented, if possible, by social activities. As with any therapeutic intervention for children, the participation of parents/caregivers is essential to the success of services (James, 1989; Montgomery, 1982; Pilisuk & Parks, 1986); in addition to regular meetings with the children's therapists, family counseling sessions and support groups for parents/caregivers are recommended.

Recommended Staffing. Therapeutic services for enduring trauma should be directed by a physician or psychologist with specialization in childhood trauma and recovery, and extensive experience in working with offenders and their families. Direct services should be provided by licensed psychotherapists or social workers specially trained to work with children and experienced in the area of trauma and recovery. Support staff should included trained and screened persons. Untrained volunteers are not appropriate in client contact roles. Services will be most effective when staff members have experience in work with families involved in the criminal justice system.

Expected Outcomes. These interventions should eventually result in a decrease in trauma-reactive behaviors and the perceived level of stress among participating children. It is important to recognize that many children will experience increased stress and exhibit an increase in problem behaviors at the beginning of treatment. Long-term outcomes should include a prevention or reduction of the development of maladaptive coping mechanisms associated with delinquency and/or adult crime and incarceration among participating children.

Model Programs. The Early Therapeutic Intervention Project (ETIP) was developed by the Center for Children of Incarcerated Parents in 1991. It provided community-based therapeutic services for young children of prisoners. There were no selection criteria for participation other than caregiver reports of behavioral problems. A sliding-scale fee for service was charged. Children participated in small play therapy (ages 4–6) or counseling (ages 7–10) groups in 16 to 20 week treatment cycles. Cognitive/behavioral methods were used. The focus of intervention was children's reactions to early traumas, specifically parent–child separation. Parents and caregivers of the youngest children were involved in play group sessions, but there was otherwise no structured parent/caregiver involvement. Formal evaluation of this program was not conducted before the program was terminated in 1993.

Interventions that Address Parent–Child Separation

As a result of the early focus of advocates on parental incarceration, parent–child separation was seen as the most critical factor affecting children of offenders (Bakker, Morris & Janus, 1978; Baunach, 1979; Fishman, 1983; Gamer & Gamer, 1983; Rosenkranz & Joshua, 1982). This emphasis on separation directed most programmatic interest toward children who were separated from their parents for the longest periods and the greatest amount of attention to children separated from their sole or primary caregivers. As a result, the earliest services for children of offenders were developed for the children of women prisoners (Cannings, 1990). Today, there are many different types of programs for the children of jailed and imprisoned parents, but the majority are mother–child services directed toward reducing the effects of separation (Table 13.2).

Jail and Prison Nurseries

About 7% of women prisoners give birth while incarcerated (USDJ, 1993). While some jurisdictions delay sentencing of expectant mothers or grant furloughs to allow them to deliver outside of correctional facilities, most of these women deliver while in custody and are separated from their newborn infants at 1 to 3 days after the birth (Sametz, 1980).

Although attention has been focused on this issue (Barry, 1985, 1989; Holt, 1981–1982; McHugh, 1980), negative outcomes on the infants have not been documented. This is not surprising, in light of extensive research

Table 13.2
Interventions for Children of Offenders: Services Addressing
Parent-Child Separation

Type of Service	Client Profile	Goals/Expected Outcomes	Model Programs
Jail and prison nurseries	Infants born to incarcerated mothers, 0–18 months of age.	Improved maternal bonding and infant attachment; stable placement of infant; increased rate of mother–child reunification after release.	Taconic Correctional Facility, Bedford Hills, New York
Community-based mother–infant correctional programs	Pregnant prisoners; incarcerated mothers and their children 0–6 years of age	Improved maternal bonding and infant attachment; stable placement of infants and children; increased rate of mother–child reunification after release.	1) ARC House, Madison, Wisconsin 2) Neil J. Houston House, Roxbury, Massachusetts 3) California Mother-Infant Care [MIC] Program, Department of Corrections, Sacramento, California
Parent–child contact visitation programs	Infants, children, and younger teenagers of incarcerated parents.	Reduction of the traumatic effects of parent–child separation.	Prison MATCH, San Francisco County Jail #7, San Bruno, California
Child custody advocacy services	Parents involved in the criminal justice system at any level; parents in drug treatment.	Increased preservation of the family units of offenders and substance-dependent parents.	Legal Services for Prisoners with Children, San Francisco, California
Support groups for children	Children over 8 years of age.	Improved self-concept and understanding of the justice process; reduced levels of perceived stress.	SKIP (Support for Kids of Incarcerated Parents), Fort Worth FCI, Texas.

documenting the ability of infants who are separated from their natural mothers to form normal attachments if provided with consistent, nurturing caregivers (Bowlby, 1969), and the presumption that most infants born to prisoners go to such homes. It is incarcerated mothers who experience the greater loss, for they do not have an opportunity to consistently meet all material and emotional needs of their totally dependent infants. The achievement of the parental role and a sense of full parental responsibility for their infants is therefore interrupted by separation and becomes more challenging as separation persists.

An intervention that has successfully addressed the need for successful maternal bonding is the prison or jail nursery. There are three such nurseries currently in existence in the United States; all of these are located in the State of New York, one at New York City's Riker's Island Jail. Prison nurseries are available in most women's prisons in Great Britain (Catan, 1992) and widely throughout the rest of the world. They allow women who give birth while incarcerated to live with and care for their infants throughout the first 12 to 18 months of the infant's life. The prison nursery is discussed more thoroughly by Gabel and Girard in Chapter 14.

Recommended Intervention Goals. The purpose of these services is to foster maternal bonding, provide a stable placement throughout infancy for children born in custody, and increase the rate of mother–child reunification after release.

Recommended Client Selection Criteria. Ideally, all women who give birth while incarcerated, are physically and emotionally capable of providing full infant care, are serving sentences with possibility of parole, plan to parent their child from prison, and desire reunification with the child after release should be eligible to utilize jail or prison nurseries. In fact, where these nurseries exist, they are privilege programs and participation is denied to women who have a history of violent offenses, disciplinary problems as prisoners, or charges of child abuse/neglect.

Since criminal charges often do not reflect the women's actual crime, and since child protective laws are disproportionately applied against low-income women of color (Guggenheim, 1983–1984), more just and reasonable priorities in selection of nursery users would include:

- intention to parent the child, regardless of length of sentence;
- intention to reunify with the child after release;
- shorter sentence;
- evidence of other appropriate parental concerns, for example, participation in family reunification activities for other children, parent education, drug treatment, employment preparation, and so on.

Recommended Methods and Activities. Required activities may include prenatal and postpartum education, parent education, child development, and related training for participants. Some programs offer drug education and/or counseling, basic education, and job training. Participants are required to provide most or all care for their infants. For a fuller discussion of prison nursery activities, see Chapter 14.

Recommended Staffing. Catan (1991) noted that many of the problems associated with Great Britain's prison nurseries were related to the lack of professional staffing. All work with infants, but especially work with infants at high risk for multiple problems, requires trained and licensed professional staff. For a fuller discussion of this topic, see Chapter 14.

Expected Outcomes. The immediate expected outcome of this intervention is an improved rate of mother–infant reunification following the mother's release. Measurement of the effectiveness of services in this area is complicated by the fact that many participating mothers are not released at the time their babies are discharged from the nursery, so that these mothers and children experience a separation that is different in quality from both nonparticipating mothers and participating mothers who go home with their children. Another expected outcome is improvement in mother-to-child bonding, as compared to women who give birth while incarcerated and are separated from their infants. Recidivism rates of participating mothers are not a useful or appropriate measure of jail or prison nursery outcomes, since recidivism is related to many factors that are not addressed by nursery services.

Model Programs. New York's Taconic Correctional Facility nursery is described in Chapter 14.

Community-Based Mother–Infant Correctional Programs

Although their outcomes may be of significant benefit to participants and to society, jail and prison nursery programs have a high cost in material and human resources. It is unrealistic to expect a degree of change in current correctional policies and/or the availability of funding sufficient to support the creation of jail and prison nurseries for up to 7,000 incarcerated mothers and their infants each year.

Adaption of the same model in a community setting substantially reduces the costs of services that meet the same needs. Community-based prisoner mother–infant programs recognize these needs as well as the low security requirements for correctional supervision of the majority of women prisoners. These programs, which allow incarcerated mothers to be housed with their infants and young children in community corrections facilities for the period of their entire sentence, are also described elsewhere in this book by several authors.

Recommended Intervention Goals. The primary purposes of community-based mother–infant and mother–child correctional programs are to foster maternal bonding, provide a stable placement throughout infancy or early childhood for participating children, and increase the rate of preservation of the families of participating women prisoners.

Recommended Client Selection Criteria. Like prison and jail nurseries, these programs typically limit participation by offense and child abuse/neglect history. Ideally, selection criteria should give priority to women who intend to parent their children, have no history of escape activities or violent offenses, and show evidence of other appropriate parental concerns, for example, participation in family reunification activities for other children, parent education, drug treatment, and employment preparation. Current programs limit participation by length of the mother's sentence, the common maximum being a balance of 6 years left to serve at time of entry into the program. Such limitations are appropriate in light of increasing costs and stresses on all participants as children grow older.

Recommended Methods and Activities. There are currently at least two models for this type of intervention. Perinatal programs provide services to pregnant prisoners, and to mothers who give birth while incarcerated and their infants. Mother–child programs provide services to any qualifying women prisoners with infants and young children, whether or not these children were born while the mother was in custody.

Like jail and prison nurseries, the focus of these programs is the provision of care for the children by their natural mothers. Programs may include any or all of the following:

1. infant/child nursery and related services, such as a therapeutic nursery, developmentally-appropriate infant activities, and pediatric medical services;
2. parent education;
3. individual, group, and/or family counseling for mothers and children;
4. physical conditioning and nutrition services;
5. emotional/behavioral interventions where appropriate, including services for adult children of addicts/alcoholics, victims of domestic violence, survivors of childhood abuse or exploitation, and codependents;
6. life skills training;
7. substance dependency education, treatment, and/or self-help activities;
8. general education, especially high school equivalency;
9. job training and placement;
10. child custody/placement advocacy; and/or
11. aftercare.

Recommended Staffing. These programs should be planned and directed by trained social service or child development professionals with extensive experience in working with offenders and their families. Services should be provided by trained and licensed social workers, educators, and/or childcare specialists. Specialists in pediatrics, nutrition, and women's health care should provide consultation to staff and regular on-site services. Programs providing perinatal services require consultant medical specialists in high-risk obstetrics and perinatology.

Expected Outcomes. These services should lead to improved maternal–infant bonding, child development, and preservation of mother–child units among participants.

Model Programs. ARC House in Madison, Wisconsin, is a private residential treatment program that serves pregnant prisoners and incarcerated mothers with children under the age of 5 years, as well as other women offenders. ARC House allows women to achieve increasing levels of privileges and decreasing levels of custody while participating in individually designed programs of activities like those listed above. Formal evaluation has been limited to services utilization levels and has not measured long-term preservation of participating families or effects of services on participating children.

Neil J. Houston House, a project of Social Justice for Women in Roxbury, Massachusetts, is a program for pregnant state prisoners with a history of chemical dependency. Participants must be within 18 months of parole. The program is 10 months in length and offers a selection of the above services; aftercare includes a full year of services. A formal evaluation of this program has not been conducted.

The California Prisoner Mother Program, also known as the Mother–Infant Care (MIC) Program, is a unique model of legislatively mandated, statewide intervention. The program is conducted by private agencies, such as Friends Outside and Volunteers of America, under contract to the California Department of Corrections. Programs are located in seven sites throughout the state, and allow pregnant and parenting women who have been sentenced to short terms of incarceration to live with their infants and/or young children in community settings for up to 6 years. Program sites offer various combinations of the above activities and graduated levels of restriction of participants. Other than measurements of utilization, these services have not been evaluated.

Parent–Child Contact Visitation Programs

Virtually all women's prisons allow limited contact visits for most prisoners. Such visits are conducted in "open" visiting areas, like cafeterias or outdoor recreational space, and usually allow prisoners and their families to share a minimal amount of physical contact—like hugs and short embraces—at the beginning and end of visits. These circumstances are extremely restrictive for children, and especially young children, who are usually accustomed to more intensive, repeated physical contacts with their parents. This is particularly true when the incarcerated parent was their primary caregiver before arrest.

Contact visitation programs address the needs of children for extended physical contact with their parents. Such programs are almost always offered in "children's centers," child-oriented environments designed to make visits a more positive experience for children. The earliest of these programs were developed in the mid-1970s; since that time, variations such as parent–child weekend visits and parent–child summer camps have been implemented (see Cannings, 1990, for a comprehensive review of all types of visitation programs). The history of the seminal Prison Mothers

And Their Children (Prison MATCH) visitation program is presented by Weilerstein in Chapter 15.

Recommended Intervention Goals. The purpose of parent–child contact visitation is to ameliorate the effects of separation due to parental incarceration.

Recommended Client Selection Criteria. In most correctional facilities, parent–child contact visitation is a privilege program conducted only on weekends and holidays. Some jail programs have additional limitations on participation, related to the parents' sentencing status. Child participation is limited by age, with many programs excluding older teenagers. Most programs also limit the number of children per parent who may participate at one visit.

Recommended Methods and Activities. The program area is often adjacent to regular visiting sites. Inmate preparation for visits can include site cleaning, arrangement of care and play areas, and planning of structured activities for the children. Many programs include or require prisoners to participate in parent education sessions. The visiting area is decorated for children's use and furnished with child-sized tables, chairs, and cabinets. Toys and games are available. Associated visitation support services, such as transportation to and from the facility, are among the major benefits of these programs.

Recommended Staffing. Ideally, parent–child visitation services should be planned and administered by groups that include correctional staff, prisoners, and community representatives. While parent education or child development training requires a trained instructor, these programs can and have been successfully initiated and conducted by untrained volunteers. Professional staff or consultants should be employed in program design, and an experienced and licensed childcare professional should supervise children's activities.

Expected Outcomes. Parent–child contact visitation programs should reduce the amount of stress experienced by parents and children during jail/prison visitation, and contribute to a greater frequency of successful parent–child reunification following release. Jail and prison visitation may also produce behavioral reactions among children visiting their parents. This is a normal finding; children who are attached to their parent and disturbed by parent–child separation can be expected to act out, withdraw, or otherwise express feelings about their situation when reminded of previous traumas by visitation (Johnston, 1993b). Caregivers and social service workers who are troubled by these reactions may attempt to eliminate them by prohibiting children's visits to the jail or prison. This fundamental misunderstanding of the effects of parent–child separation will not remove the underlying emotional damage that is the source of the reactions, nor will it meet children's critical need for healing contact with their parents.

Model Programs. The Prison MATCH Program is described in Chapter 15.

Children's Support Groups

Children of prisoners lack social support, as a result of the effects of trauma on their own functioning and because their families are often isolated, due to the problems that led to parental incarceration. The majority may have problems expressing their feelings and concerns about their parents. A small but significant number of these children are also stigmatized by their parents' activities (Gabel, 1992; Hannon, Martin & Martin, 1984; Schneller, 1978). Support groups address each of these areas of need.

Recommended Intervention Goals. The goals of a support group for children of prisoners are to address the needs of participating children for social support, to provide a structured setting for expression of their concerns, and to create a mechanism for diffusing a sense of shame that accompanies parental incarceration.

Recommended Client Selection Criteria. Support groups require that participants have the ability to work with peers productively, to obey orders or rules of conduct, to utilize secondary process thinking, and to apply consensual validation. Support groups are therefore only developmentally appropriate for children 8 years of age or older.

Recommended Methods and Activities. Groups for children need to meet at least weekly to produce a continuity of effect. Cognitive/behavioral methods should be utilized to help children achieve a greater sense of control over themselves and the events that effect them. In addition to discussions, a variety of workbooks specially for children of prisoners have been developed (see "Booklist for Children of Prisoners," Center for Children of Incarcerated Parents, 1995).

Recommended Staffing. Adult facilitators should be trained, screened, and licensed to work with children; the use of nonprofessional volunteers is not appropriate.

Expected Outcomes. Support groups should improve measurements of children's self-esteem, increase their internal locus of control, and reduce their perceived level of stress. If the group focuses on parent–child separation, activities should increase or regularize parent–child contact.

Model Programs. The Support for Kids of Incarcerated Parents (SKIP) groups are conducted in the residential communities surrounding Fort

Worth Federal Correctional Facility by the Parents and Children Together (PACT) Program. This program offers a series of groups for children of different ages, and has well-developed group curricula for each age.

Child Custody Advocacy

A major outcome of parental incarceration is the dissolution of the family. Several studies of incarcerated mothers have found that the likelihood of mother–child reunification decreases with each maternal incarceration (McGowan & Blumenthal, 1978; Johnston, 1991) Similarly, a study of children of offenders (Johnston, 1992) in the community found that 25% of women offenders had lost their parental rights to one or more of their children, compared to 4% of male offenders. The incarcerated parents most likely to be unable to reunify their families are those with children in foster care. Beckerman (1994) examined such mothers and found that significant numbers had difficulty working with the child welfare system and understanding their rights and responsibilities.

Child custody advocacy services for incarcerated parents have been provided by a few agencies since 1978. These programs offer legal assistance related to child welfare and dependency issues, and information and referrals to incarcerated parents and their families.

Recommended Intervention Goals. Child custody advocacy services have as their primary goal the maintenance of the family units of parents who are involved in the criminal justice system.

Recommended Client Selection Criteria. These programs usually serve all incarcerated parents and their family members with child custody or placement problems. Some programs, like Chicago Legal Aid to Incarcerated Mothers (CLAIM) serve only women offenders and their families; others, like the Child Custody Advocacy Services (CHICAS) Project of the Center for Children of Incarcerated Parents, serve unincarcerated offenders and parents in drug treatment, as well as prisoners and their families.

Recommended Methods and Activities. These vary with each agency's mission. Most agencies provide legal information and referrals, consultation and training for professionals in the criminal justice system and related areas, and public education. Client services may include class action litigation, actual legal representation of individual clients, expert witness testimony, defense team-building, and the production and distribution of publications.

Recommended Staffing. Agencies that provide legal services require direction and staffing by attorneys and paralegals experienced in family and dependency law. Other agencies may utilize legal advisers. All types of child custody advocacy agencies may need to utilize trained volunteers, since funding is perhaps most limited for this type of services to offenders and their families. Several projects are effectively staffed by former clients.

Expected Outcomes. Direct child custody advocacy services should result in an increased rate of retention of parental rights, or retention of children within their natural families, among participating parents. Other services should result in changes in practice and public policy that lead to improved rates of family reunification among prisoners and other offenders.

Model Programs. Legal Services for Prisoners with Children (LSPC) is the foremost child custody advocacy agency for prisoners in the United States. In addition to the above activities, LSPC has conducted highly effective class action litigation to bring about an improved quality of perinatal services and the expansion of community-based, mother–infant correctional programming in the State of California.

Interventions that Address Quality of Care for Children

Interventions in this category either provide an improved quality of placement and care for children while their parents are incarcerated, or indirectly benefit children of prisoners and other offenders by directly serving their parents and/or caregivers. Interventions in this last group may improve the quality of the children's lives by helping these significant adults to increase their ability to meet children's material and emotional needs (Table 13.3).

Child Placement and Foster Care Services

About 10% of the children of female prisoners and 1 to 2% of the children of male prisoners, or about 42,000 children of incarcerated parents, are in foster care (Johnston, 1993a). Some of these children are in the care of relatives and under the supervision of children's protective services. However, the majority are in the care of strangers in institutions, group homes, or foster families (Baunach, 1979; Hadley, 1981; Rogers & Carey, 1979; Stanton, 1980).

In addition to enduring the typical rigors of foster care (Fanshell & Shinn, 1982; Pike, 1976), children of prisoners may be separated from siblings (Baunach, 1979; Hunter, 1984; Stanton, 1980; Zalba, 1964). Children of women prisoners often experience multiple placements (Hunter, 1980; Stanton, 1980; Zalba, 1964). These children do not receive visits from their parents and may be unable to arrange to visit the jail or prison where the parent is incarcerated. Specialized foster care programs were designed to address these circumstances. These services provide placements for prisoners' children who are unable to live with other family members.

Table 13.3
Interventions for Children of Offenders: Services Addressing Quality of Care

Type of Service	Client Profile	Goals/Expected Outcomes	Model Programs
Child placement and foster care services	Children of prisoners for whom there is no possibility of family placement.	Secure long-term placement that will provide special support for parent–child communication.	1) Bethel Bible Village, Hixson, Tennessee 2) My Mother's House, Catholic Charities, Diocese of Brooklyn, New York
Caregiver and family support services	Caregivers of prisoners' children, with priority given to low- or fixed-income families.	Reduction in the level of caregiver stress; increased access to resources and sources of support.	1) Intergenerational Project, Aid to Imprisoned Mothers, Atlanta, Georgia 2) Grandparents As Parents, Nationwide
Parent empowerment projects	Parents involved in the criminal justice system at any level; substance-dependent parents.	Increased ability to achieve family reunification.	Prison Parents' Education Project [PPEP], Center for Children of Incarcerated Parents, Pasadena, California
Drug treatment for prisoners and other offenders	Substance-dependent parents.	Prevention or reduction of continued substance dependency	1) PROTOTYPES, Pomona, California 2) CHOICES, Men's Unit, Robert Presley Detention Center, Riverside, California 3) Forever Free, California Institution for Women, Frontera, California
Reentry services	Incarcerated and recently released, formerly incarcerated parents.	Reduction or prevention of reentry problems associated with recidivism.	1) Womencare, New York City, New York 2) Phase ReEntry Programs, Los Angeles, California

Recommended Intervention Goals. The purpose of these services is to provide secure long-term placements for children of prisoners in foster care.

Recommended Client Selection Criteria. Children for whom there is no possibility of family placement and/or who cannot be placed in situations that will allow parent–child visits may benefit most from these programs.

Recommended Methods and Activities. These programs should provide special support for parent–child contact and jail/prison visitation, and child counseling, in addition to regular group home activities.

Recommended Staffing. Social work or therapeutic specialists, in addition to trained and screened childcare workers, can address the special trauma- and separation-related issues of prisoners' children.

Expected Outcomes. These should include an improved adjustment of children to long-term foster care placement and an increased rate of family reunification following the parents' release.

Model Programs. Bethel Village in Hixson, Tennessee, is a nondenominational, Christian home for children of prisoners founded in 1954. Children may be placed privately or through the children's protective services. The village houses 64 children in eight cottages; each cottage is supervised by two houseparents. Children attend public schools and participate in a variety of Christian activities, including church services, camps, and recreational programs. The average stay per child is 2 to 3 years. The organization also conducts a prison ministry.

My Mother's House is a long-term foster care program for children of women prisoners. It is located in Long Island City, New York, and is affiliated with the Catholic Charities, Diocese of Brooklyn. The house accepts children of women incarcerated in New York state prisons, and infants born in these institutions. Activities include special support for mother–child communication and visitation; children also take part in the programs offered by the Children's Center at Bedford Hills Prison, including weekend visits and summer camps.

Caregiver and Family Support Services

The majority of the children of male prisoners are cared for by their natural mothers in single-parent, low-income households (USDJ, 1993); the majority of the children of female prisoners are cared for by their maternal grandmothers in households with low, fixed incomes (Bloom & Steinhart, 1993; Dressel & Barnhill, 1990). In both of these situations, the caregivers of prisoners' children live in conditions of low resources and high stress. Interventions for caregivers indirectly provide significant benefits to the children of prisoners.

Recommended Intervention Goals. The purpose of these services is to reduce the level of material and emotional stress and to increase access to sources of support for the caregivers of prisoners' children.

Recommended Client Selection Criteria. Material resources should be targeted to low- and fixed-income caregivers. Isolated caregivers without family or social support networks should be given priority for support services. Other types of services, such as support groups, counseling, and caregiver/parent training, should be made available to all caregivers of prisoners' children on a sliding fee-for-service basis.

Recommended Methods and Activities. Client education, referrals, and placements are critical needs for most caregivers. Some programs offer direct access to resources (e.g., through food and clothing banks). The most commonly offered service is support groups; these regular, informal meetings allow participants to discuss concerns, experiences, and resources, and occasionally to hear guest speakers and take part in educational presentations. The support component of these services may be professionally facilitated or may utilize a self-help format. A few programs offer professional counseling.

Recommended Staffing. Referrals, placements, and family support activities can most effectively be offered by a licensed social worker. Although convened and indirectly supervised by professional staff, the support components of many programs are appropriately conducted as self-help activities.

Expected Outcomes. These programs should produce significant reductions in the level of perceived caregiver and family stress, increasing the ability of participants to meet the emotional and material needs of the children in their care.

Model Programs. The Intergenerational Project of Aid to Imprisoned Mothers, in Atlanta, Georgia, demonstrates the above services for grandmother caregivers. The Grandparents as Parents Support Group, another model program, is described by Poe in Chapter 16.

Parent Education

Traditionally, many interventions for incarcerated parents have been based on two unfounded assumptions: first, that offenders are not "good" parents, and, second, that parent education will make offenders "better" parents.

There is no evidence to support the first assumption, unless circular logic that defines incarceration as bad parenting is applied. Although there has been very little research that compares incarcerated parents with matched, unincarcerated controls, existing studies on incarcerated mothers have found that they have appropriate parental attitudes, behaviors, and concerns (Baunach, 1979; Bonfanti, Felder, Loesch, & Vincent 1974; LeFlore & Holston, 1990)

The second assumption is also unsupported. Cannings (1990) describes in detail the efforts of the earliest programs for children of incarcerated parents, including their parent education components. These programs made extensive efforts at evaluation, but were so highly focused on client and staff satisfaction with services that they usually failed to measure objective outcomes. A few, like the Parents in Prison Program at the Tennessee State Prison in Nashville, actually documented increased knowledge of child development and parent skills among prisoners who received instruction. But none have measured the outcome that parent education programs claim they address: the parenting characteristics of participants either during incarceration or after release. Two recent studies inform discussion of this topic.

Browne (1989) closely examined the well-designed parent education project of The PROGRAM for Female Offenders, Inc. She measured self-evaluation (including scales for locus of control, efficacy, self-esteem, self-control, and self-criticism) and parenting attitudes and knowledge (including scales for developmental expectations, emphathetic awareness of children's needs, belief in corporal punishment, and utilization of the child for parental satisfaction). Browne found only three areas of significant change among program participants. Self-esteem was improved, but belief in corporal punishment and inappropriate parental expectations also increased.

Bayse (1991) documented the outcomes of a Family Life Education program among male prisoners. He measured participants "selfism" (narcissistic responses), and their sense of family adaptability and cohesion. After completing the program, participants showed lower levels of narcissistic responses and perceptions of ideal family functioning that were closer to the norm, although only two-thirds "passed" the course by objective examination.

Parent education of prisoners and other offenders may produce increases in their knowledge about children and families. However, these studies suggest that a primary effect of such courses may be to inculcate ideal parenting goals without providing either a realistic map to those goals or actual experiences in which to apply newly learned parenting skills. In addition, such courses are offered in strongly authoritarian settings where correctional staff are parentified, offenders lack adult power, and desired behavior is obtained by the threat or application of physical force. It seems highly likely that the overcontrolling parental behaviors that have been documented in prisoners (Adalist-Estrin, 1986; Kolman, 1983) arise at least in part because of these circumstances, and highly unlikely that purely cognitive interventions in such a setting would produce a behavioral change.

In addition to these weaknesses, many parent education programs for prisoners are burdened with the expectation that they will rehabilitate or reduce recidivism among participants (TALK, 1989; Bayse, 1991). Glasser (1990) produced the best examination of this outcome in her study of the Niantic Parenting Programs at Connecticut's prison for women. This careful study found that parent education-contact visitation had no effect on recidivism among participating parents.

For these reasons, traditional parent education programs are not recommended by the author for prisoners and other offenders.

Parent Empowerment

Parent empowerment programs for prisoners differ from parent education programs first and most importantly because they are designed and/or taught by formerly incarcerated parents. These programs address the parenting topics of greatest interest to prisoners, including the effects of parental incarceration, parent–child separation, childhood trauma, intergenerational behaviors, child custody and placement issues, and family reunification planning.

Recommended Intervention Goals. The purpose of these services is to provide incarcerated parents with the child-related information they have identified as critical to their needs, and to increase the ability of these parents to meet court-ordered family reunification requirements.

Recommended Client Selection Criteria. Any incarcerated parent who can read and write at a 5th grade level should be able to participate in these services.

Recommended Methods and Activities. These programs should include at least 16 hours of classroom or correspondence instruction and an equal number of hours of parents' discussion group activities conducted in a self-help (prisoner-facilitated) format. Participants should be offered workbooks that include required readings as well as worksheets. Small-group research projects (such as surveys of other incarcerated parents) and creative activities are also recommended.

Recommended Staffing. Correctional facility administrators will require the sponsorship and participation of professionally trained program staff for these programs, but the hallmark of parent empowerment programs is the provision of services by current or former prisoners. Therefore, team-teaching approaches are recommended.

Expected Outcomes. Services will provide participants with increased knowledge about parental incarceration that will enable them to assist themselves and other prisoners in maintaining or regaining relationships with and custody of their children. Certification will assist parents in meeting court-ordered family reunification requirements for children in foster care.

Model Programs. The Prison Parents' Education Project (PPEP), the ExOffender Parent Education Project, the Family Life Education Project, and the Reclaiming Parenthood Project have been offered in state prisons, jails, and drug treatment programs as classroom courses. In addition, PPEP has been offered nationwide as a correspondence course for imprisoned parents. The curricula for these courses were developed by formerly incarcerated parents; classroom sessions are taught by former prisoners. Over 600 prisoners and other offenders have participated in these projects, which are conducted by the Center for Children of Incarcerated Parents.

Drug Treatment for Prisoners

The majority of prisoners and other offenders have substance abuse or dependence problems (Miller, 1984; National Commission on AIDS, 1991; USDJ, 1993). While substance abuse may be a fixed pattern of reaction to early trauma and merely a symptom of underlying problems, addiction itself impairs the ability to parent effectively. Substance-dependent parents are almost always overwhelmed by their own needs and unable to recognize or adequately meet the needs of their children. Treatment for substance dependency is therefore critical for offenders and their children.

Recommended Intervention Goals. The purpose of drug treatment for offenders is to prevent or reduce continued substance dependency among participants.

Recommended Client Selection Criteria. The pervasiveness of alcoholism/addiction and its consequences among this population is so great that drug treatment interventions should be made available, on demand, to *all* offenders.

Recommended Methods and Activities. Effective programs may be conducted in locked or community-based correctional facilities and may offer many or all of the following:

1. drug/alcohol abuse prevention education;
2. self-help programming (e.g., Alcoholics or Narcotics Anonymous groups);
3. professional substance abuse counseling;
4. adjunct physical therapies (e.g., acupuncture, physical conditioning, yoga, Tai Chi);
5. adjunct emotional/behavioral interventions, including those for adult children of addicts/alcoholics, victims of domestic violence, childhood abuse survivors, and codependents;
6. parent activities, including parent education/training, child development education, and parent–child activities;
7. mental health services;
8. general education;
9. life skills training;
10. job training and placement; and
11. aftercare, including relapse prevention.

Recommended Staffing. Programs should be designed and conducted by substance dependency diagnosis and treatment specialists, including both professionals and nonprofessionals, at least some of whom are recovering persons.

Expected Outcomes. These services should reduce the incidence of addiction relapse among participants; individual participants should attain and maintain extended periods of recovery. (It is important to recognize that the defining characteristic of substance dependency is relapse; persons who suffer from addictive disorders often relapse, and it is inappropriate for simple relapse to be tied to criminal or child custody sanctions.) Since substance abuse is so intimately tied to the criminal history of most offenders, decreased recidivism rates may also be expected.

Model Programs. There are several different models for effective programming in this area:

Treatment programs that provide alternatives to incarceration. PROTO-TYPES in Pomona, California, is a residential treatment program for substance-dependent women; clients may participate voluntarily or through court commitments in lieu of incarceration. The program is 9 to 18 months in length and serves pregnant women, other mothers, and their children up to 6 years of age. Activities focus on IV drug abuse, HIV/AIDS, and women's issues, including abuse survivorship and codependency. The staff includes recovering women in both professional and nonprofessional roles. Long-term evaluation of program effectiveness has not been performed.

Education programs in correctional facilities. The CHOICES Program at the Robert Presley Detention Center in Riverside, California, offers a 1-month, residential drug education program for jailed men. CHOICES is a privilege program that serves 15 men per month. In addition to drug education and Alcoholics/Narcotics Anonymous activities, CHOICES offers sessions on HIV/AIDS, job skills training, and an educational course for substance-dependent fathers. Evaluation of this program has not been performed.

Treatment programs in correctional facilities. The Forever Free Program is offered at the California Insitution for Women. Forever Free houses 120 women who are serving the last 5 months of their state prison sentences. It is a privilege program that offers drug education, relapse prevention groups, self-help groups, women's workshops (topics include assertiveness, self-esteem, codependency, and problem solving), and case management services. Early evaluation results suggest that program graduates have significantly lower levels of addiction relapse and recidivism than other prisoners.

Reentry Services

The transition from incarceration to independent living is stressful. Reentering prisoners have identified a variety of immediate postrelease stressors, including lack of transportation, lack of access to services, subsistence needs like clothing and food, problems in reunifying with children, and homelessness (Johnston, 1991; Phase ReEntry Programs, 1991). One strong indicator of the difficulty of reentry is recidivism; one in four former prisoners are rearrested in the first 6 months after release (USDJ, 1989).

Former prisoners who face parent–child reunification issues may experience more immediate postrelease stress than other offenders, in spite of the well-documented association between the maintenance of family ties and lower rates of recidivism (Holt & Miller, 1972; Macdonald, 1980). This is supported by Vachio (1991), who found that interventions that reduced postrelease conflicts in the families of former prisoners also reduced recidivism. Services that allow formerly incarcerated parents to quickly stabilize their lives following release can only benefit their children.

Recommended Intervention Goals. The purpose of these services should be to reduce or prevent reentry problems, including increased levels of stress in the release, domestic violence, substance abuse, failed parent–child reunification, and recidivism.

Recommended Client Selection Criteria. Incarcerated and recently released parents who have demonstrated concern for their children and a commitment to reuniting their families (through participation in parent training, maintenance of parent–child communication, the achievement of family reunification requirements, etc.) should be given priority in client selection, but services should be available to all prisoners at the time of their release.

Recommended Methods and Activities. Effective programs may offer some or all of the following:

1. mentoring;
2. referral and placement services;
3. advocacy in the areas of substance dependency treatment, job training and employment, criminal justice, mental health services, education, social services, and child custody;
4. support groups; and/or
5. self-help activities.

Recommended Staffing. Mentor-advocacy services can be provided by screened and trained volunteer mentors, under the supervision of a trained and licensed social worker or other professional with extensive experience in working with offenders and their families. Former prisoners should be trained by professionals to provide referral, placement, and advocacy services.

Expected Outcomes. Services should lead to increased levels of social support and decreased levels of perceived stress, drug use, incidents of domestic violence, failure to meet child reunification requirements, and rearrest among participating parents.

Model Programs. The Womencare Program in New York City matches newly released, formerly incarcerated mothers with volunteer advocates. Both mothers and advocates undergo training prior to participation and on a monthly basis following the mother's release. Each advocate visits a mother in prison before her release. At and after release, the advocate assists the client in identifying and effectively utilizing community resources. Both advocate and client make a commitment to maintain the mentoring relationship for 1 year. Womencare currently serves more than 30 formerly incarcerated mothers.

Phase ReEntry Programs in Los Angeles County is a self-help collective of formerly incarcerated mothers. Phase provides reentry services for newly released women at three levels of participation. At the first level, clients receive referrals, placement services, and publications. At the second level, women attend bimonthly support groups and participate in the program's parent education, recreation, and social activities. At the third level, women may become advocates and service providers; they may also become members of the collective and participate in program administration. Phase is committed to self-determination for former prisoners and receives no funding from outside sources.

Comprehensive Services

Comprehensive services for children of prisoners and other offenders combine services in two or more of the above areas within a single program. The value of such an approach lies in project designs that recognize the multiple challenges faced by these children and their families, and in the increased accessibility of services. Since there are only two such comprehensive programs in the United States—Project SEEK of the Michigan Department of Mental Health, and the Therapeutic Intervention Project of the Center for Children of Incarcerated Parents—both will be described here.

Project SEEK

Services to Enable and Empower Kids (Project SEEK, 1993) is a demonstration prevention project that is cosponsored by the Michigan Departments of Mental Health, Social Services, and Corrections. The project represents an unprecedented collaboration of state agencies for the purpose of addressing the needs of children of prisoners.

Intervention Goals. The purposes of the project are to promote optimal child development, increase family stability, promote positive parenting, maintain the parent–child relationship, and assist with issues of family reintegration among participating families.

Client Selection. The program is conducted in one Michigan county. Corrections department records are used to identify incarcerated parents with sentences of less than 8 years and children under 11 years of age living in that county. These parents and their families are randomized to experimental and control groups. Families assigned to the experimental group may agree to receive services.

Methods and Activities. The program uses a home-based outreach model to provide "wraparound" services, including case management. Caregivers receive referrals, parent training, and support group services. Children participate in support groups and tutoring. Other activities include parent training for the incarcerated parents and facilitation of communication between children and incarcerated parents. Program staff also advocate for children and caregivers with other agencies.

Staffing. Program services are provided by staff with a minimum of a bachelor's degree in a related field. Children's support groups are conducted by a trained and licensed facilitator. The project is directed by a licensed clinical social worker.

Outcomes. Participating families experience fewer stressors and are more stable, as measured by project staff and self-reports, than control families. Crisis issues related to unmet family needs are resolved within a few months of participation. Participating children are rated less hostile and angry than controls by their teachers. They change schools less often, are promoted more often, score higher on academic self-esteem, and are rated as having a higher level of cognitive skills than control children by their parents.

Therapeutic Intervention Project

The Therapeutic Intervention Project (TIP) (Johnston, 1993c) provides school-based services for children of offenders in a high-crime, low-income community of African-American and Hispanic families in southeast Los Angeles County. TIP is a demonstration project that has been conducted by the Center for Children of Incarcerated Parents since 1991. It has been funded by a variety of private foundations and public agencies.

Intervention Goals. The purpose of TIP is to reduce the trauma-reactive behaviors of participating children of offenders, including the fixed, maladaptive behavior patterns of adolescents that lead to crime and incarceration.

Client Selection. Teachers at participating elementary and middle schools are asked to refer to the project any children with classroom behavior or disciplinary problems that appear to be leading them toward early entry into the criminal justice system. There are no other referral criteria.

Children are interviewed by a child psychologist or psychiatrist. Caregivers and parents are interviewed by a maternal/child health specialist and complete developmental, medical, and behavioral histories of the children are taken. Measurements of children's home and classroom behavior, including independent observations, are taken. Children who are assessed as having trauma-reactive behavioral problems, and who have been raised with an adult offender in the household, are accepted for services.

Methods and Activities. Services are provided for participating children, their caregivers and families, and their teachers:

Services for children include weekly therapeutic groups. Younger children participate in play therapy groups; older children and adolescents receive group counseling with a support group component. Cognitive-behavioral methods are employed. Groups for older children focus on issues of self-esteem, survivor guilt, behavior modification, and conflict mediation. Project staff also develop individualized classroom behavior modification programs with children, caregivers, and teachers.

Services for caregivers include referrals and bimonthly support groups. Parents or caregivers of participating children are required to attend a parent training institute at the beginning of each school year. Caregivers may also participate in monthly parent advocacy meetings.

Services for other family members include referrals and placements. Contact between children and incarcerated parents is facilitated when requested. Incarcerated parents may participate in the center's Prison Parent's Education Project course, and utilize center advocacy services.

Services for teachers include continuing education credits for training in childhood trauma and recovery, and support groups. Support groups address issues of burnout, compassion fatigue, and secondary trauma.

Staffing. The project is directed by a physician who is a specialist in children of offenders and maternal/child health. The clinical staff includes licensed child psychologists, clinical social workers, and psychotherapists. Family support services are provided by a licensed social worker. The staff is comprised of persons who reflect the cultural, racial, and ethnic background of clients. No volunteers are utilized in this project.

Outcomes. Project outcomes have been measured in two areas:

Children's outcomes included dramatic reductions in all forms of aggressive behavior. Other significant reductions were seen in the areas of post-traumatic stress symptoms and asocial behaviors like lying and stealing. Decreases in gang-related activity was seen in children with a history of parental gang involvement, but not in children who were themselves involved in gangs. There was no first-time delinquent activity among children in the project; repeat juvenile crime activities among participants with previous histories of delinquency were low (less than 3%).

Caregiver outcomes included an increase in utilization of community resources among 74% of participating families. Over 70% of participating caregivers reported that their level of stress had declined while the children in their care participated in TIP.

Working with Children of Offenders and Their Families

While it is important for advocates and service providers to have knowledge and understanding of the types and content of appropriate interventions for children of offenders and their families, it is more important that they be properly prepared to work with this special population. Unlike other groups of persons that require a large number and a wide range of services, offenders actively contributed to creating their needs and, in doing so, may have directly or indirectly harmed others, including their children. Other factors that make work with this type of clients and their families especially challenging include:

Compulsive behaviors among offenders. The great majority of offenders have compulsive behavior problems, including substance abuse, asocial activities, sexual misconduct, and/or aggression. Their families of origin may have multiple members with such problems, and their partners and children exhibit the typical outcomes of living in circumstances that include crime, arrest, and incarceration. Professionals working in this arena often suffer from stress and its outcomes, including burnout and compassion fatigue, at least in part because of lower rates of successful outcomes of service with these clients (Figley, 1982).

Workers' personal experiences. Most people, including human services workers, find criminal behavior repellent. For some persons, this feeling is intense as the result of personal experiences with criminal victimization, child abuse/neglect, sexual molestation, family violence, or a substance-dependent relative. Such experiences intensify feelings of stress in working with offenders and their families.

Cultural differences. The majority of human services professionals are middle class and white, while the majority of offenders and their families are low-income persons of color. Such differences often impede communication between providers and clients (Green, 1982; Randall-David, 1989).

Client resistance. In spite of their high level of need, offenders are often involuntary clients (Harris, 1991). They may have many reasons for resistance to intervention, including legitimate concerns about confidentiality and how current interventions may affect child custody, public assistance, or criminal liability in related matters.

All of these factors challenge the abilities of workers to provide high-quality services to offenders and their families. Interpersonal approaches that address these limitations include nonjudgmental attitudes, cultural competence in practice, identification of personal issues that effect service delivery, and maintenance of a professional standard of practice.

Nonjudgmental Attitudes

The justice process is designed to assess culpability and apply measured sanctions. It is inappropriate for helping professionals to assume either of these two tasks in their work with offenders and their families.

However, it is particularly difficult to avoid the expression of personal values when working with persons who have committed crimes. Human services professionals may be challenged in their efforts to provide care and assistance without suggesting approval of what a client has done. In working with relatives of offenders, providers may find themselves discouraging further family involvement in crime while offering needed services that have only become available as a result of a family member's arrest/incarceration. Workers in these circumstances may feel compelled to continually express their disapproval of an offender's actions and the actions of the offender's family that may have supported or contributed to criminal activities. As a result, services for offenders and their families are often provided with judgmental attitudes that lead to less successful service outcomes.

Judgmental attitudes in providers may contribute to adversarial relationships with offenders and their families, and may cause these clients to identify providers as part of the criminal justice and correctional systems they perceive as punitive. Clients who feel "judged" by providers are less likely to accept those workers' professional advice.

Effective work with this population requires that providers focus on the competencies rather than the deficiencies that clients possess. The following Case Examples illustrate this process:

> A-31-year-old mother has four children in foster care as a result of repeated incarcerations for shoplifting. She has persistently, if unsuccessfully, pursued reunification with her children who appear to remain strongly attached to her. Intervention should assist this mother in utilizing her close bond with her children and her strong sense of family as motivators and supports in her attempts to overcome her compulsive substance abuse and theft behaviors, rather than on her criminal behavior and its effects on her children.

> The 15-year-old son of a veteran gang member is on probation for his own activities with the same neighborhood gang. Interventions should not focus on the child's risk of incarceration or "following in his father's footsteps," but rather should help the child utilize his strong identification with his family and

his sense of loyalty to develop alternative ways to organize the reactive behaviors that he currently expresses through gang involvement.

A 71-year-old grandmother is caring for three children of incarcerated parents. Two of the children have school behavior problems and one is delinquent. Intervention should focus on sustaining this grandmother's commitment to her family by increasing her resources and level of support, rather than on identifying deficiencies in her parenting skills that may have produced two generations of offenders.

Competency-based approaches allow workers to focus on their clients' positive characteristics and thereby promote nonjudgmental attitudes in service delivery.

Identification of Personal Issues

Workers who have had significant personal experiences with criminal victimization, child abuse/neglect, sexual molestation, family violence, or a substance-dependent relative may be unable to objectively assess and provide services for offenders and their families. The dysfunctional provided–client relationship that results in these cases can be damaging to both the client and the human services worker.

The risks of subjectivity or bias in practice are recognized and guarded against by policies which, for example, prohibit physicians from taking family members as patients, bar judges from hearing cases on subjects in which they have a personal involvement, or restrict codependent relatives of alcoholics from providing direct services to alcoholics in treatment. Where such policies do not exist, it is important for human services professionals to carefully consider their personal histories, experiences, and biases before entering into work with offenders and their families.

Cultural Competence

Cross-cultural competence is the ability to work effectively with clients from a different culture. The three major components of cross-cultural competence include (1) self-awareness, (2) knowledge of specific information about clients' cultures, and (3) skills that allow successful cross-cultural interactions (Chan, 1990; Hanson, Lynch & Wayman, 1990).

Self-Awareness. This includes clarification of one's own values and assumptions. Only by examination of their own heritage can service workers become aware of how their values, beliefs, and behaviors are shaped by their culture. An understanding of the effects of their own culture on their practice allows professionals to distinguish objective or culturally neutral

230 • *Children of Incarcerated Parents*

standards from those that may not be equally applicable to persons and groups from all cultures.

Culture-Specific Information. This is acquired by studying and reading about another culture, talking or working with "cultural guides" or mediators, and participating in the daily life of another culture, including learning that culture's language. Additionally, in the case of human services professionals who will work with families, it is important to understand a culture's views of children, family roles and structures, and childrearing practices.

Cross-Cultural Skills. These allow workers to interact with members of different cultures, rather than to act upon them. The primary cross-cultural skill is communication. Like all communication, cross-cultural communication can be both verbal and nonverbal. While some cultures concentrate strongly on verbal communication, many other cultures communicate through the context of situations, the relationship of the communicators, and physical cues. Since most of the communication between human services workers and their clients is verbal, workers need to pay attention to the physical behaviors that are important as communication cues in their clients' cultures. Examples of important physical cues in cross-cultural communication are eye contact, facial expressions, proximity and touching, gestures, and other forms of body language.

Professional Standard of Practice

Professionals are characterised not only by their credentials and level of training, but also by their attitudes, skills, and standards of practice. Nonjudgmental, objective attitudes and cross-cultural competence are integral components of professional practice. Professional standards address a broad range of activities, and include the ability of the practitioner to recognize the extent and limitations of his or her expertise.

This is important for professionals working with special groups such as offenders and their families. The amount of valid demographic information and empirical research on this population is limited. The lack of a substantive body of documentation increases the weight given to authoritative statements by those who work with these families. Professionals in this position must therefore adhere to the strictest standards of practice.

The training and credentials for practice in the fields of social work, law, medicine, or other professions do not qualify practitioners as experts on offenders and their families. In fact, there is no one discipline that does. Expertise in this field is acquired by interdisciplinary training, service, and research experiences. Therefore professionals who work with this special population, and make authoritative presentations, sworn testimony, or other statements on their status and needs, must qualify these statements, as the following Case Examples demonstrate:

A social worker for the infant of a prisoner will not allow the parent to have visits with the child. In presenting her position in reports to the court, she must qualify herself with statements such as "I am a licensed MSW with 5 years of casework experience, I have completed 6 units of college coursework in child development, and I have had 15 children of prisoners as clients. I have visited the state prison twice and observed the visiting area. Based on my training and experience, I recommend that parent–child prison visits be prohibited because of the detrimental effects of the prison environment on the infant."

A counselor who conducts a support group for imprisoned mothers will advocate for the mother of the above infant. In presenting her position, she must also qualify her testimony with a statement such as, "I am an LCSW with 5 years of experience in working with women offenders. I have completed 6 units of college coursework in child development. I have worked with over 200 incarcerated mothers in my current position with the Department of Corrections. I helped to develop the prison's children's center and parent education program. I have conducted an extensive review of the child development and child welfare literature and can find no reports of negative effects of prison visitation on infants or children, and two reports that conclude that the prison environment has no negative effects on visiting children. Based on my training, experience, and review of the relevant literature, I believe that prison visitation would be beneficial for this baby and mother."

Statements of qualification help the listener weigh the opinions of professionals who currently provide much of the information about offenders and their families used in social service reports, criminal courts, and dependency hearings.

Delivery of services to offenders and their families has often been characterized by a nonprofessional standard of practice. Until recently, the population of offenders has been so small and behaviors involved in crime so uncommon that this work was considered undesirable employment or a charitable activity. The increasing proportion of human, social, and economic resources devoted to crime and its consequences in the United States demands a more professional standard of practice from those who work with offenders and their families. Over time, such standards will appropriately shift the burden for provision of a professional quality of services from the individuals who now bear it to the agencies and institutions that employ them.

CONCLUSIONS

Developing and providing interventions for children of offenders and their families is challenging, but the intergenerational nature and increasing rates of crime and incarceration in the United States require that our society pursue the highest standards of professional practice in providing services for this population. In addition to familiarity with the types and content of interventions that are appropriate for these children, practice in this interdisciplinary field requires nonjudgmental attitudes, cross-cultural competence, a broad range of background knowledge, in-depth knowledge of specific topics and resources, and special skills in assessment, advocacy, counseling, and working with children.

References

Adalist-Estrin, A. (1986). Parenting . . . from behind bars. *Family Resource Coalition Report*, 5(1):12–13.
American Bar Association. (1993). *Children on hold*. Washington, DC: Author.
ARC Community Services. (1993). *Brochure*. Madison, WI: Author.
Bakker, L. J., Morris, B. A., & Janus, L. M. (1978). Hidden victims of crime. *Social Work*, 23:143–148.
Barry, E. (1985). Quality of prenatal care for incarcerated women challenged. *Youth Law News*, 6(6):1–4.
Barry, E. (1989). Recent developments: Pregnant prisoners. *Harvard Women's Law Journal*, 12:189–205.
Barry, E. (1990). Women in prison. In C. Lefcourt (Ed.), *Women and the law* (6:18.01–18.35). Deerfield, Illinois: Clark, Boardman & Callahan.
Baunach, P. J. (1979, November). *Mothering from behind prison walls*. Paper presented at the meeting of the American Society of Criminology, Philadelphia.
Bay Area Crisis Nursery. (1992). *Brochure*. Concord, CA: Author.
Bayse, D. (1991). Family life education: An effective tool for prisoner rehabilitation. *Family Relations*, 40:254–257.
Becker, B. L. (1991). Order in the court: Challenging judges who incarcerate pregnant, substance-dependent defendants to protect fetal health. *Hastings Constitutional Law Quarterly*, 19:235–259.
Beckerman, A. (1994). Mothers in prison: Meeting the prerequisite conditions for permanency planning. *Social Work*, 39(1):9–14.
Bethel Bible Village. (1992). *Brochure*. Hixson, TN: Author.
Block, D., Silber, E., & Perry, S. E. (1956). Some factors in the emotional reactions of children to disaster. *American Journal of Psychiatry*, 113:416–422.
Bloom, B., & Steinhart, D. (1993). *Why punish the children? A reappraisal of the children of incarcerated mothers in the United States*. San Francisco: National Council on Crime and Delinquency.
Bonfanti, M. A., Felter, S. S., Loesch, M. L., & Vincent, N. J. (1974). *Enactment and perception of maternal role of incarcerated mothers*. Unpublished master's thesis, Louisiana State University.
Bowlby, J. (1969). *Attachment and loss*. New York: Basic Books.
Breier, A., Kersoe, J. R., Kirwin, P. D., Beller, S. A., Wolkowitz, O. M., & Pickar, D. (1988). Early parental loss and development of adult psychology. *Archives of General Psychiatry*, 45:987–493.
Brett, E., Spitzer, R. L., & Williams, J. B. W. (1988). DSM-III-R criteria for posttraumatic stress disorder. *American Journal of Psychiatry*, 145(10):1232–1236.

Brown, A. J., Pelcovitz, D., & Kaplau, S. (1983, August). *Child witnesses of family violence: A study of psychological correlates.* Paper presented at the annual meeting of the American Psychological Association, Anaheim, CA.

Browne, D. (1989). Incarcerated mothers and parenting. *Journal of Family Violence,* 4(2):211–221.

California Department of Corrections. (1989). *Mother–Infant Care Program information sheet.* Sacramento: Author.

Cannings, K. (1990). *Bridging the gap: Programs and services to facilitate contact between inmate parents and their children.* Ottawa: Ministry of the Solicitor General of Canada.

Catan, L. (1992). Infants with mothers in prison. In R. Shaw (Ed.), *Prisoners' children.* London: Routledge.

Catholic Charities. (1989). *My Mother's House brochure.* Long Island, NY: Author.

Center for Children of Incarcerated Parents. (1991). *Reclaiming Parenthood Project information sheet.* Pasadena, CA: Author.

Center for Children of Incarcerated Parents. (1992). *Family Life Education Project information sheet.* Pasadena, CA: Author.

Center for Children of Incarcerated Parents. (1993). *What about the kids? A planning guide for arrested parents.* Pasadena, CA: Author.

Center for Children of Incarcerated Parents. (1995). *Booklist for children of prisoners.* Pasadena, CA: Author.

Chan, S. Q. (1990). Early intervention with culturally diverse families. *Infants and Young Children,* 3(2):78–87.

Doyle, J. S., & Bauer, S. K. (1989). Post-traumatic stress disorder in children. *Journal of Traumatic Stress,* 2(3):275–288.

Dressel, P., & Barnhill, S. (1990). *Three generations at risk.* Atlanta, GA: Aid to Imprisoned Mothers.

Dunst, C., Trivette, C., & Deal, A. (1988). *Enabling and empowering families.* Cambridge, MA: Brookline Books.

Dutton, D. G., & Hart, S. D. (1992). Risk markers for family violence in a federally incarcerated population. *International Journal of Law and Psychiatry,* 15:101–112.

Fanshell, D., & Shinn, E. B. (1982). *Children in foster care.* New York: Columbia University Press.

Figley, C. (1982). *The traumatized therapist.* Paper presented at the annual conference of the American Association of Marriage and Family Therapists, Chicago.

Fishman, S. H. (1983). Impact of incarceration on children of offenders. In *Children of exceptional parents.* Hartford, CT: Haworth Press. Pages 89–99.

Gabel, S. (1992) Behavioral problems in sons of incarcerated or otherwise absent fathers: The issue of separation. *Family Process,* 31:303–314.

Gamer, E., & Gamer, C. P. (April 12, 1983). *There is no solitary confinement: A look at the impact of incarceration upon the family.* Paper presented at the annual conference of the Association for Professional Treatment of Offenders, Chestnut Hill, MA.

Garbarino, J., Dubrow, N., Kostelny, K., & Pardo, C. (1992). *Children in danger.* San Francisco: Jossey-Bass.

Glasser, I. (1990). *Maintaining the bond: The Niantic Parenting Programs.* Niantic, CT: Families in Crisis.

Green, J. W. (1982). *Cultural awareness in the human services*. Englewood Cliffs, NJ: Prentice-Hall.

Guggenheim, M. (1983–1984). The political and legal implications of the psychological parenting theory. *Review of Law and Social Change*, 12:549–555.

Hadley, J. G. (1981). *Georgia women's prison inmates and their families*. Atlanta: Georgia Department of Offender Rehabilitation.

Hannon, G., Martin, D., & Martin, M. (1984) Incarceration in the family: adjustment to change. *Family Therapy*, 11:253–260.

Hanson, M. J., Lynch, E. W., & Waymou, K. I. (1990). Honoring the cultural diversity of families when gathering data. *Topics in Early Childhood Special Education*, 10(1):112–131.

Harris, G. (1991). *Tough customers: Counseling unwilling clients*. Laurel, MD: American Correctional Association.

Henriques, Z. W. (1981). *Imprisoned mothers and their Children*. Washington, DC: University Press of America.

Hershorn, M., & Rosenbaum, A. (1985). Children of marital violence. *American Journal of Orthopsychiatry*, 55:260–266.

Holt, KE. (1981–1982). Nine months to life: The law and the pregnant inmate. *Journal of Family Law*, 20(3):523–543.

Holt, N., & Miller, D. (1972). *Explorations in inmate–family relationships*. Sacramento, CA: Department of Corrections.

Hunter, S. M. (1984). The relationship between women offenders and their children. *Dissertation Abstracts International*. (University Microfilms No. 8424436.)

James, B. (1989). *Treating traumatized children*. Lexington, MA: Lexington Books.

Johnston, D. (1991). *Jailed mothers*. Pasadena, CA: Pacific Oaks Center for Children of Incarcerated Parents.

Johnston, D. (1992). *Children of offenders*. Pasadena, CA: Pacific Oaks Center for Children of Incarcerated Parents.

Johnston, D. (1993a). *Caregivers of prisoners' children*. Pasadena, CA: Center for Children of Incarcerated Parents.

Johnston, D. (1993b). *Children's reactions to visitation in the prison*. Pasadena, CA: Center for Children of Incarcerated Parents.

Johnston, D. (1993c). Helping children of offenders through intervention programs. In *The state of corrections*. Laurel, MD: American Correctional Association. Pages 238–244.

Johnston, D. (1993d). *The Therapeutic Intervention Project: A report to funders*. Pasadena, CA: Pacific Oaks Center for Children of Incarcerated Parents.

Kolman, A. S. (1983). Support and control patterns of inmate mothers: A pilot study. *The Prison Journal*, 63(2):155–166.

Kraft, S. P., (1984, August). *Spouse abuse: Its impact on children's psychological adjustment*. Paper presented at the annual meeting of the American Psychological Association, Toronto, Canada.

LeFlore, L., & Holston, M. A. (1990). Perceived importance of parenting behaviors as reported by inmate mothers: An exploratory study. *Journal of Offender Counseling, Services and Rehabilitation*, 14(1):5–21.

Legal Services for Prisoners with Children. (1993). *Information sheet*. San Francisco: Author.

Macdonald, D. (1980). *Follow-up survey of post-release criminal behavior of par-*

ticipants in a family reunion program. Albany, NY: Department of Correctional Services.

Martin, H. P. (1976). *The abused child: A multidisciplinary approach to developmental issues and treatment*. Cambridge: Ballinger.

McCall, C., & Shaw, N. (1985). *Pregnancy in prison: A needs assessment of prenatal outcome in three California penal institutions* (Contract No. 84-84085). Sacramento, CA: Department of Health Services, Maternal and Child Health Branch.

McGowan, B. G., & Blumenthal, K. L. (1978). *Why punish the children?* Hackensack, NJ: National Council on Crime and Delinquency.

McHugh, G. A. (1980). Protection of the rights of pregnant women in prisons and detention facilities. *New England Journal of Prison Law*, 6(12):231–263.

Miller, R. E. (1984). Nationwide profile of female inmate substance involvement. *Journal of Psychoactive Drugs*, 16:319.

Montgomery, B. (1982). *Family crisis as process: Persistence and change*. Washington, DC: University Press of America.

National Commission on AIDS. (1991). *HIV disease in correctional facilities*. Washington, DC: Author.

Ounstead, C., Oppenheimer, R., & Lindsay, J. (1974). Aspects of bonding failure: The psychotherapeutic treatment of families of battered children. *Developmental Medicine and Child Neurology*, 16:446–456.2

Phase ReEntry Programs. (1991). *StreetReady: A release-planning handbook for jailed women*. Pasadena, CA: Pacific Oaks Center for Children of Incarcerated Parents.

Pike, V. (1976). Permanent planning for foster children. *Children Today*, 5(6):22–25.

Pilisuk, M., & Parks, S. H. (1986). *The healing web: Social networks and human survival*. Hanover, NH: University Press of New England.

Prison MATCH. (1984). *I know how you feel, because this happened to me*. Berkeley, CA: Author.

Project ImPACT. (1992). *Brochure*. Las Lunas, NM: Peanut Butter and Jelly Programs.

Project SEEK. (1993). *Progress report*. Flint: Michigan Departments of Mental Health.

PROTOTYPES. (1993). *Brochure*. Pomona, CA: Author.

Randall-David, E. (1989). *Strategies for working with culturally diverse communities and clients*. Washington, DC: Associate for the Care of Children's Health.

Renshaw, D. (1982). *Incest: Understanding and treatment*. Boston: Little, Brown.

Rogers, S., & Carey, C. (1979). *Childcare needs of female offenders*. Toronto: Ontario Ministry of Correctional Service.

Rosenkrantz, L., & Joshua, V. (1982). Children of incarcerated parents: A hidden population. *Children Today*, 11:2–6.

Sametz, L. (1980). Children of incarcerated women. *Social Work*, 25(4):298–303.

Schneller, D. P. (1978). *The prisoner's family*. San Francisco: R & E Research Associates.

Sgroi, S. (1984). *Clinical handbook of intervention in child sexual abuse*. Lexington, MA: Lexington Books.

Shelton, B., Armstrong, F., & Cochran, S. E. (1983). Childbearing while incarcerated. *American Journal of Maternal Child Nursing*, 8:23.

Silvern, L., & Kaersvang, L. (1989). Traumatized children of violent marriages. *Child Welfare*, 68(4):421–436.

Social Justice for Women. (1993). *Neil J. Houston House information sheet.* Boston: Author.

Stanton, A. (1980). *When mothers go to jail.* Lexington, MA: Lexington Books.

Task Force on the Female Offender. (1990). *The female offender: What does the future hold?* Laurel, MD: American Correctional Association.

TALK: Teaching & Loving Kids. (1989). *Program brochure.* Los Angeles: Los Angeles County Jails.

U.S. Department of Justice. (1989). *Recidivism among prisoners released in 1983* (Report No. NCJ-116261): Washington, DC: Bureau of Justice Statistics.

U.S. Department of Justice. (1993). *Survey of state prison inmates* (Report No. NCJ-136949). Washington, DC: Bureau of Justice Statistics.

U.S. Department of Justice. (1994). *Women in prison* (Report No. NCJ-145321). Washington, DC: Bureau of Justice Statistics.

Vachio, A. (1991, November 16). *How we work with families.* Paper presented at the Conference of the New Mexico Corrections Department, Santa Fe, NM.

Wayman, K. I., Lynch, E. W., & Hanson, M. J. (1990). Home-based early childhood services: Cultural sensitivity in a family systems approach. *Topics in Early Childhood Special Education*, 10(4):56–75.

Womencare. (1993). *Brochure.* New York City: Author.

Zalba, S. (1964). *Women prisoners and their families.* Sacramento, CA: Department of Social Welfare and Department of Corrections.

14
Long-Term Care Nurseries in Prisons: A Descriptive Study

Katherine Gabel
Kathryn Girard

Prison nurseries have the potential to address two problems faced by children of incarcerated mothers: the trauma of early separation and the inconsistent quality and stability often associated with placement care. Unfortunately, a lack of research on prison nursery programs makes it difficult to argue a case for or against such programs. As the number of women in jails and prisons grows, efforts are needed to document the nature of existing prison nurseries, to examine the effects of nursery programs on babies and their mothers, and to explore the advantages and disadvantages of such programs for prisoner mothers, their infants, correctional facilities, and the state.

This chapter presents the findings of a descriptive study conducted at two State of New York prison nurseries in June 1992. The study represents a first, small step toward documenting the prison nursery alternative. Longitudinal studies and controlled research studies examining potential effects related to child development and maternal recidivism are needed to provide the type of information the child advocacy and corrections communities require to reach sound recommendations and decisions.

Background

During this century, the State of New York has led the movement to provide long-term nursery care for children born to incarcerated women. While pediatric studies emphasize the importance of mother–child bonding during the first year, we still lack enough evidence to answer a key question: Is it beneficial for a mother and child to be kept together during the first year within the confines of a correctional institution? Although several other states, namely, Wyoming, Massachusetts, Virginia, and Florida, have at some time run prison nursery programs, only the State of

New York has provided long-term nursery care within their women's prisons for some 90 years.

Long-term nursery programs allow children to stay with their incarcerated mothers from birth until age 1 year or 18 months. Interim nurseries, where infants can return to the prison infirmary with their mothers for anywhere from 2 days to 6 weeks, are available in a number of states. The intent of interim programs is to provide for the temporary care of infants by their incarcerated mothers until outside care arrangements are made. In past years interim nurseries were utilized in Virginia, Pennsylvania, South Dakota, Minnesota, California, North Carolina, and Ohio (Cannings, 1990; Grossman, 1982).

According to internal state prison documents, New York established its first long-term nursery in 1901 with the opening of what was then called Westfield Farms, a correctional home for maladjusted girls, at a time when women could be prosecuted for immoral conduct. It was later renamed the New York State Reformatory for Women. In 1930 Auburn Prison for Women was moved to Bedford Hills across from the reformatory, and in that same year Dr. Ellen Polter, with the assistance of the National Commission on Prisons and Prison Labor, drafted legislation to allow women in the New York prisons and reformatories to keep their babies with them for 1 year. That bill was signed into law in 1930 by Governor Franklin D. Roosevelt. It is still on the books over 60 years later as the New York Corrections Law bill.

From 1930 until 1972 the women's prison and the reformatory were kept separate, although headed by one superintendent. A nursery was operated in the reformatory, with babies from both facilities. Mothers from the prison were allowed to visit their infants twice a week. In 1972 the prison and the reformatory were combined and named the Bedford Hills Correctional Facility, which operates today as a medium and maximum security prison for women.

The nursery program continues to operate within the prison with approximately 25 beds. Babies are born in a local hospital outside the prison grounds and are returned with their mothers to the nursery floor of the prison hospital. Mothers and babies live together in single or double rooms. Since most women at Bedford Hills are serving sentences that are longer than 18 months, babies are placed with relatives or foster parents at the end of their first year in the nursery. For those women whose babies are placed nearby, or whose families can manage visits, Bedford Hills provides a developmentally appropriate visiting area through its Children's Center.

The female prison population in the State of New York, as elsewhere in the United States, has grown dramatically over the last 15 years. The number of women incarcerated in New York grew from 568 in 1979 to 2,711 in 1990 (U.S. Department of Justice [USDJ], 1988, 1992). The minimum custody Taconic Correctional Facility was established in 1990 across the road from the Bedford Hills prison.

The Taconic nursery program, initiated by Governor Cuomo, opened with 23 beds. Financed under a federal grant and supplemented by State of New York funds, the nursery has been full since its opening. During the first year of operation 20 women with babies completed the program. Since sentences for women at Taconic are typically shorter than those at Bedford Hills, most mothers are able to leave with their babies. Sixteen women were paroled with their infants and four remained in prison while their babies were placed temporarily with relatives. Three mothers who did not complete the program were removed for disciplinary reasons.

The Taconic nursery is located on the second floor of one of the traditional prison buildings. Mothers and babies live together in double rooms or larger dormitory-type housing. Adjacent to the building is a large, grassy, enclosed yard furnished with chairs, tables, and play equipment for the babies.

Both the Bedford Hills and Taconic nursery programs have strict guidelines for participation. At Taconic, for example, the nursery counselor investigates the mother's background, reads the presentencing report, interviews the mother, interviews those providing care for the mother's other children, contacts the mother's family, and contacts corrections staff working with the mother. In some cases a psychiatric evaluation may be conducted. The nursery counselor's report and recommendation is submitted to the senior counselor for review and recommendation. The deputy superintendent determines admission to the program. The mother's social history, parenting history, reasons for wanting to keep the baby in prison, disciplinary record, and relationship with staff and other inmates are all considered. At both Bedford Hills and Taconic, any history of violence, child abuse, or child neglect prevents admission to the nursery program. At both facilities, participation is viewed as a privilege that mothers must earn and maintain.

Methods

The purpose of this study was to provide an overview of the Bedford Hills and Taconic nursery programs. Interviews were conducted with prisoners, officers, and staff to obtain perceptions of the nursery program as it affects the mothers, babies, and the institution.

The total number of women participating in the nursery programs at Bedford Hills and Taconic during the month of June 1992 was 49, with 27 in the Bedford Hills program and 22 in Taconic's nursery. Fifty-three percent of the women in the nursery programs were interviewed ($N = 26$); 22% of the Bedford Hills nursery mothers ($N = 6$) and 91% of the

Taconic mothers ($N = 20$). Fewer women were interviewed at Bedford Hills because of limited access granted to the interviewers. Since one-fourth of the women interviewed at Taconic had been at Bedford Hills previously, it was decided that the uneven distribution of subjects between the two institutions need not preclude examination of the data as if it derived from a single population. Where patterns of difference exist between the Bedford Hills and Taconic populations, the data will be presented separately.

Interviews were conducted during the morning when all prisoners were on the nursery unit and in the afternoon when some were off-unit in programs. Interviews were conducted in prisoners' rooms and in the outdoor recreation area for babies. Interviews were also conducted with prison staff associated with the nursery program at Taconic. The superintendent, nursery manager, staff psychologist, nurse, and main officer in charge of the unit were all interviewed jointly by the authors.

Findings

Findings are presented in three sections: first, a detailed description of the prison nursery facility and schedule; second, a description of the incarcerated mothers; and third, a summary of the mothers', officers', and staff's perceptions of the program.

The Prison Nursery Program

Expectant mothers at Taconic receive prenatal care that includes obstetrical exams and a series of classes on fetal growth and development, nutrition during pregnancy, labor and delivery, and breast and bottle feeding. These classes are required for all inmates who expect to participate in the nursery program. For each set of classes completed, the mother receives a certificate.

Taconic also brings in a public health nurse to offer required postpartum classes to nursery program participants. Topics in these classes include infant nutrition, immunizations, childhood diseases, contraceptives, postpartum, exercises, breast examination, sexually transmitted diseases, and an overview of infant development. Pediatricians affiliated with a local hospital hold clinics at the nursery every other week, in addition to being on call 24 hours a day. A registered nurse who specializes in maternal–child health is on call 24 hours a day, and also holds a screening clinic each week. Taconic staff nurses are in the nursery all morning, every day, to administer any special medications and to provide other assistance. A nursery manager with child development expertise has an office on the unit and is there every day.

Babysitters at Taconic come from the general prison population and are carefully screened by the prison administration and the nursery manager. They are trained and supervised by the nursery manager and may only watch two children at a time, just as mothers may only watch their own child and one other child at any time. Mother's are encouraged to help each other out by taking turns babysitting so that the maximum number of mothers can participate in academic, self-help, and other off-unit activities.

Because Taconic specializes in serving a prisoner population with drug- and alcohol-related problems, a substance abuse treatment program is offered. Mothers spend their mornings in parenting classes and their afternoons in the required recovery program or, when that has been completed, in optional academic studies or self-help groups. The morning parenting program includes sewing and crafts for babies (clothing, toys, baby books, etc.); baby development, where mothers are separated into groups to learn about motor, cognitive, and social developmental expectations and stimulation activities; mothers' groups, where small groups discuss issues and problems related to self-awareness, self-improvement, and appropriate parenting; health issues, including prenatal and postpartum classes; and community living, including topics raised by mothers and nursery staff.

An average day at the Taconic nursery has the following schedule:

6:00 A.M.	Count
7:00 A.M.	Breakfast (feeding of infants, cleaning of rooms)
8:15 A.M.	Parenting/baby care program
11:30 A.M.	Lunch
12:30 P.M.	Count
12:50 P.M.	Afternoon programs
	Outdoor recreation for babies
4:00 P.M.	Count
4:30 P.M.	Dinner
5:30 P.M.	Evening programs
6:00 P.M.	Optional outdoor baby recreation during Daylight Savings Time only
10:00 P.M.	Count—all mothers in rooms with babies

Mothers take turns going to the mess hall, with one group watching the babies while the others eat. When children are ready to eat regular foods, as authorized by the pediatrician or nursery staff, special trays are sent to the nursery for the children. Mothers are required to hold their babies for feeding or to feed them in a highchair when old enough. Formula and baby food is dispensed weekly at Taconic, as are diapers and other baby items.

Donated baby clothing is distributed by the nursery manager as needed and available. Cribs are provided for each baby and are located in each mother's room. Nursery guidelines recommend that mothers hang a mobile over the crib and only keep one toy at a time in the crib.

The nurseries and the living quarters for the mothers and babies are far from luxurious. At Bedford Hills, the women complained about the peeling paint and cockroaches. At both Bedford Hills and Taconic, the women complained about having to share rooms with other women and their babies. Differing sleep and feeding patterns, accompanied by predictable nighttime crying, can be a source of friction in cramped rooms. Kitchens, common rooms with rugs, soft chairs and sofas, and laundry areas within the nursery provide opportunities for mothers to take care of their babies' needs and places for both mothers and babies to socialize.

The prison nurseries are structured to assure that infants have sufficient and appropriate food, clothing, medical attention, and social stimulation. They also provide activities that promote maternal attention to infant needs, bonding, and the development of other parenting skills. Bonding and parenting are the focus every day in the nursery.

The Mothers and Their Children

Age, Ethnicity, and Education. The average age of the women participating in the nursery programs was 28. Eighty-one percent of the women were African-American, 12% were Caucasian, and 7% were Hispanic.

Twenty-three percent of the mothers (6) had completed 2 years of college, although only two of the six women had actually attained an A.A. degree. Thirty-five percent of the mothers had completed high school, seven through the GED. Forty-two percent of the mothers had dropped out of school before high school graduation and had not continued their educations; 24% dropped out before 10th grade.

Patterns of Drug Use and Addiction. Fifty-eight percent of the women reported that they were alcohol- or drug-addicted at the time of their arrest. Heroin, crack, and cocaine were the drugs cited. Two women noted that they had been drug-addicted at the time of previous arrests, but not at the most recent one. Less than half of the women who were addicted at the time of arrest reported that their baby had been exposed to drugs before birth.

Of the 15 women reporting substance dependency, eight had been incarcerated long enough to be drug-free for 6 or more months at the time of delivery, and one reported that she had begun recovery from alcohol addiction before becoming pregnant. Four mothers had been drug-free for 2 months or less at the time they gave birth.

Criminal Justice Histories. Thirty-nine percent of the women reported their age at first arrest was under 21. Two women reported a first arrest after age 35. The average age of reported first arrest for the group was 24. The average number of arrests for the whole group was five. However, for women first arrested under the age of 21, the average was nine. All of the mothers from Bedford Hills had been previously arrested. Fifty percent of the Taconic mothers (39% of the total group) were serving a sentence for their first arrest. Only two of these women were under 21 at the time of arrest; the rest ranged in age from 26 to 38, with an average age of 28.

About two-thirds of the women had been sentenced for drug felony, drug possession, and/or drug sale offenses. Only one-third of the women from Bedford Hills had served sentences for drug-related charges, while 62% of the women in the Taconic program had served sentences on such charges. Since the nursery program screens out prisoners who have been involved in violence, none of the women interviewed had served time for charges involving violence. In addition to the drug charges, other charges for which women had been previously sentenced included grand larceny, forgery, robbery, other major felonies, parole violation, and prostitution.

For those women who had been arrested more than once, the average number of arrests was seven (range 2 to 30). Total years incarcerated following these arrests averaged 2.2 years, with a range of 7 months to 8 years.

Current Charges and Sentences. Sixty-nine percent of the current charges for which the women were serving sentences were drug-related. Of the 10 women at Taconic who were serving time following a first arrest, nine had drug-related charges. Other charges included parole violations, forgery, grand larceny, and robbery. Current charges reflected patterns of past convictions. Of the 16 women who had previously been incarcerated, 13 were currently sentenced for the same category of offense.

The sentences women were currently serving ranged from 3 months to 4-Life (4 years to life). Half the sample were serving sentences with a minimum of 1 year or less. The longest sentences were 3-Life and 4-Life; six women had received sentences in these categories.

Family Characteristics. Sixty-five percent of the women in the nursery program report having family members who have been in jail or prison; the majority (54%) had a brother or sister who had been jailed or imprisoned. Only two women reported intergenerational patterns of incarceration: one with a mother, father, and aunt, and one with a mother, sister, and grandmother, who had been incarcerated.

Almost a third of the women had been living with an adult family member at the time of their arrests, most with a parent. Another third had been living with a current partner or the natural father of one or more of their children.

Children. In addition to the babies with them in the prison nurseries, these women had a total of 42 children. Eighty-five percent of their children on the outside were under 6 years of age. The average number of children for these mothers was 2.7, with a range of 1 to 7.

The primary reason for separations between mothers and children was incarceration. Nineteen women had children in addition to their new babies. Of these, nine reported that they had custody of all their children at the time of arrest; eight of the nine were living with all of their children, and one woman was not living with any of her children. Four women had custody of some of their children; three were living with those children, and one was not living with any of her children. Six of the women did not have custody of any children. Overall, 42% of the mothers with other children were living with all their children at the time of arrest, 16% were living apart from some of their children at the time of arrest, and 42% were living with none of their children when they were arrested.

Of the 42 children, only 12 (29%) were living with their mother and all their siblings at the time of the mother's arrest.

Of the 19 women who had children on the outside when they were incarcerated on their current charge, more than a third (7) have not seen any of their children. Five of the seven mothers in this group had been living with all of their children prior to arrest, one of the mothers had been living with some of her children, and one had not been living with any of her children. There were three basic reasons given for the lack of visits with children: the distance is too great, the caretaker does not want the children to visit, or the mother does not want the children to visit her in prison.

Two women who have not seen their children in prison have had some contact with them in other settings. One is able to see her children when she goes to court. Her mother brings her daughter to see her in the court because the handcuffs are removed then. Another woman has seen her children, who are in separate foster care homes, while on furloughs. In this instance the caregivers and social worker do not want the children visiting at the prison.

Two other inmates have had contact with some children and no contact with others. In one case, the mother reports that her son does not wish to have contact with her. In another case, the courts have forbidden contact with a child.

The remaining mothers who entered prison leaving children on the outside report visiting patterns ranging from once every 1 or 2 weeks to less than once a month. One mother whose baby had reached the 12-month age limit and been sent to outside care reported receiving visits from this child every week.

Including the mother whose baby had left the program at 12 months, there were 20 women with children in the care of others. Eight of those women were able to see the caregivers at the prison. Most communicated by phone or letter, and only three indicated that they had no contact with their children's caregivers.

Plans for Placement. Half the sample were serving sentences of 1 year or less. Accordingly, all but two of the mothers in this group anticipated being released from prison with their babies. The other two were seeking 6-month extensions for their babies so that they could remain with the child until their release.

All of the women planning to be released with their child expect to care for the baby themselves on the outside. Nine of these mothers have other children; five had been living with all their children prior to incarceration, and four had not been living with any of their children.

Of the remaining 13 mothers who do not expect their release date to coincide with the date when the baby must leave the nursery, three are seeking to extend the child's stay from 3 to 6 months so that they can leave together. Four of the mothers are seeking extensions so that the child can stay with them until 18 months of age, so that the gap between the child's leaving and the mother's release will be minimized. If extensions are allowed, the time of separation would be from 2 weeks to 4 months.

Most of the women who cannot count on leaving with their babies, or who know that they will not do so, have made arrangements for the father or another family member (usually the inmate's mother) to care for the child. For the remaining mothers, two will place their child in a foster home, one will have her baby placed nearby in a special "bridge" program that facilitates child–parent contact, and one is considering a range of options from adoption to placement with a family member. This inmate is the only one who reported that she did not want to have children.

Goals. The women's goals for their babies are simple and straightforward: these mothers want "the best" for their babies. This means very basic things: happiness (12), education (5), a stable family (4), good social and physical environments (4), good character and positive qualities as a person (3). The mothers also want their children to avoid drugs, prison, and all the mistakes they had made (8).

The women's goals for themselves are similarly basic. They want a job when they get out (14). They want education (10). They want to make a family, to parent, and to teach their children (10). They want to overcome the past (9). They want a place to live (7). They want security (2) and a decent relationship (2). They want to act responsibly and with character. The phrasing of these women's goals for themselves reflects their sense of the tenuousness of the future: "I want strength in places where I'm weak. I pray, 'Don't let me just talk—no more drugs, no more street life.' I want to go forward."

Mothers' Perceptions of the Nursery Program

Advantages. Overall, the mothers perceive the program to be highly valuable and important to them. Nine categories of benefits were identified from their responses to open-ended questions. Five of these categories can be viewed as benefits to the women as prisoners and four as benefits to the women as parents and to their infants. A total of 74 responses were coded and categorized; responses were evenly divided between the two types of benefits.

The categories of responses suggesting benefits to participating women as prisoners included: education, comparison with doing time in the general population, help from other nursery mothers and staff, self-respect, and assistance with addiction problems. The categories suggesting benefits to the women as mothers and to their infants included: bonding, parenting skills, socialization of the babies, and services and supplies provided for the babies.

Opportunities for Education. Ten of the inmates identified opportunities to learn, to go to school, or to obtain specialized training as a major benefit of the program. The focus of their pride in learning is different for each of the 10 women in this category. One is taking college classes. One is working on her GED. Two have obtained certificates in child health and parenting. One has completed two diplomas. The rest speak about attending all the classes and programs that are offered.

Better Conditions of Confinement. Ten women noted that being in the nursery program was easier in some respects than serving time in the general population. Women reported that the program allowed them to avoid the negative behavior common in the latter setting, and helped them to get through their time positively. One woman who had previously served both jail and prison time noted: "Without [her baby] I'd be in the SHU (special housing or control unit). I'd be fighting 'cause I don't want to be someone's girlfriend." Concern about fighting and attitude (their own and others) in the general population was a clear theme. Another inmate, speaking about the benefits of the nursery program, stated: "[It] helps me deal with being in jail. It relaxes me to have someone else to take care of and keeps my spirits up . . . waking up every day and seeing (her baby) here."

Drug Education and Treatment. Seven of the 26 women specifically cited participation in the drug program as a major benefit. Three of these women noted that the completion of the drug program with certification would enable them to begin school. Since the Taconic facility specializes in providing drug abuse treatment, women incarcerated there may not have cited this as a benefit of the nursery program due to seeing it as part of the general program at Taconic.

Help from Other Inmates. Comments in this category addressed the help women receive from each other and the help they receive from staff. One woman pointed out that roommates help each other with parenting and gave, as an example, getting up to feed her roommate's baby when the roommate didn't awaken at the baby's crying. The sharing of parenting responsibilities—for example, women watching each other's children—was something observed repeatedly during the study. Other comments in this category spoke to the help women received from the nursery manager, who they described as compassionate, "like a grandmother," understanding, and knowledgeable. The idea that help was available, whether in classes or in conversations, was very important to these women.

Self-Respect. Four women identified the development of greater self-respect as a benefit of participation in the program. Two felt that the focus on parenting and bonding with their baby had changed how they saw themselves. In one woman's words, being with her baby had "turned her life around." The other woman remarked, "I learned really how to love my child. That gave me more respect for myself." Another comment suggests that some benefits in the arena of self-respect may come from the drug program. This woman identified both the learning about parenting and the drug program with building her sense of self: "The ASAT program has helped me. I've come to know myself better. Now I can do a lot of things, I can do things on my own. I've learned a lot from Pat [the nursery manager]. She has a lot of patience. I learned I could do that too."

Improved Bonding with Infant. Twenty-one women identified bonding as a major benefit of the program in their open-ended responses. Several women pointed to the difference between being on the outside with the baby versus being on the inside with her. Said one:

> "The major advantage is time with my baby. There's a focus on material things outside. I'm not out on the streets, not using cocaine. I have a clear head. I notice things. I see what [my children] mean to me. Now I'm going to be the mother they need."

Another women, the mother of four, noted:

> "You come to realize what parenting means, how much we're needed. You develop maternal instincts because the child is the focus. You can feel when something is wrong with child. I get the feeling she's going to miss me. I feel more like a parent. Though I had four children, I learned really how to love this child."

Another, whose baby had recently been released and who had kept the child with her in the prison nursery despite her family's objections, identified what are hoped to be long-term outcomes of the bonding that occurs in the program:

> "I wanted to bond with her since I would be away for 3 years. My daughter knows me. Talks to me on the phone. When she came to visit 3 weeks after release she knew me and she cried at the end of the visit."

Development of Parenting Skills. More than a third of the respondents cited learning parenting skills as an important advantage to the program. Giving credit to the parenting classes, one woman noted: "All the parenting classes teach us what we didn't learn on the outside. [The program] gives me a chance to take care of him, to know that I can take care of both my children for the rest of my life." While some mothers spoke to the advantage of learning about child development, another described parenting skills learned in the unit through activities for the babies: "Every holiday is something nice for children. The program shows you there are certain things you have to do with your child—birthdays, Halloween, Easter. They show you how to make things instead of buying it."

Infant Services and Supplies. Six women specifically mentioned the services and supplies provided as advantages. These included: Pampers, formula, milk, food, clothes, babysitters, and medical attention. As one mother noted: "No one's going to give me anything on the outside. I'll miss that."

Disadvantages and Difficulties. While five of the mothers participanting in the nursery program cited no disadvantages or difficulties in the program, others spoke to a range of concerns from cleanliness (1) and an insufficient supply of the right things (1), to pressures created by overcrowding and high demands and expectations. There were fewer responses and less agreement to the questions concerning disadvantages and problems. Only one category of response had a significant level of agreement.

Crowded Conditions. Fifteen inmates identified problems related to overcrowding, cramped quarters, the mix of personalities in a confined space, and noise. One woman noted, "Because you want the children to be out and around with the other children and in the play areas, you have to be out and about. It's hard to be with all the personalities." Women are assigned rooms based on the age of the babies. When babies are younger, mothers and infants are housed in double rooms with space for two beds, two cribs, and two dressers. There is also a large triple room. As the babies age, women can go on the list for single rooms. In small double rooms, the problems of babies' differing sleep patterns and crying, coupled with the lack of privacy, create substantial stress. A related concern cited by two women, but undoubtedly a part of the stress of overcrowding cited by others, is that of noise. On the one hand, there is the stress of trying to prevent one's baby from crying and disturbing others. On the other hand, there is the shouting of officers during count, which tends to awaken the babies and cause them to cry. Given the differences in temperament among the women, it is no surprise that some of the women were "loud and rowdy with no respect for the babies. There's just too much loud noise and talking."

Negative Interactions with Officers and Staff. One woman at Bedford Hills cited as a problem that "every officer wants to run the nursery differently." She went on to give examples of memos on rules that different officers variously contradicted or enforced. Another Bedford Hills prisoner, one who felt that there were no problems with the nursery program, did note that whatever problems existed were related to the administration of the correctional facility as a whole. No similar comments were made by the prisoners at Taconic. The fact that this did not emerge as a response among the Taconic women may relate to the consistency of personnel assigned to the nursery and the main officer's approach to his work with the mothers, as described under staff perceptions. The only negative comment in this category from a Taconic mother concerned her wish "that the nurses were more compassionate."

High Expectations and Demands. Six women commented on the pressures caused by program expectations and demands as a disadvantage or difficulty in the program. One woman from Bedford Hills noted: "It takes three times the effort to care for a baby here. There are expectations from everyone on a daily basis. It's hard work." Comments from mothers in the Taconic facility identified a variety of sub themes related to the constant expectations around caring for the baby. These included: being told when to go out and when to come in, when and what to feed the baby, and being constantly in demand.

Other Problems. Two inmates identified problems with sleep. Although sleep is a problem for most parents of infants, these problems are exacerbated in the prison nursery by the sharing of rooms. While some women cited the positive aspect of this situation, such as helping one another by feeding a roommate's baby for her if she doesn't awaken immediately upon the baby's crying, others cite the distrubance of being awakened by another baby's crying when her own is finally asleep. And, of course, the prison nursery schedule is not altered for mothers who are up all night with their babies. As one woman summarized it, "I can be up all night, but I still have to get up on time." Two women cited the waiting list for entry into school programs (1) and the lack of babysitters necessary for attending a college program (1) as additional problems. Finally, one woman noted that there are too few things for older babies to do.

Correctional and Program Staff Perceptions

Staff interviews were conducted at Taconic. The superintendent, psychologist, nursery manager, and nurse all view the program very positively. The superintendent talked about the women from the program with whom she was still in touch, who are struggling to make it on the outside. She believes that the relationship built between the mother and child during the baby's first year serves as a powerful incentive for the mother to pull her life together upon release.

The presence of this bond was noted by both the psychologist and the nursery manager. Both spoke of observing the babies' faces "light up" at the sight of their mothers. Both also spoke of the softening of the mothers' faces and voices when returning to their babies. Through her experience at the Bedford Hills Children's Center, the nursery manager could describe evidence of bonding between mothers and babies that persisted once the babies had left the program and were only able to see their mothers during visits at the Children's Center.

The psychologist, who sees all mothers in mandatory monthly appointments and runs a group for mothers, noted that the babies are born healthy. The Taconic nursery manager, who had previously worked at the Bedford Hills nursery, noted that in 8 years only one baby born to an inmate at Bedford Hills had shown any developmental delays; that infant had been born with a congenital heart problem.

The nurse concurred with this opinion of the overall health and normal development of the babies in the nursery. Her concerns focused on what happens to mothers who are not released at the time the babies must leave. She would like to see a structured and supported transition for the mother who is abruptly separated from her baby and and sent back to the general prison population. She did note that some women who must return to the general population serve as babysitters for the nursery and this gives them some continuing contact with children. For others, however, working with babies is too painful a reminder of their recent loss.

The psychologist indicated that her observations and sessions with the inmate mothers led her to conclude that all of them are "good enough" mothers and that some are truly excellent mothers. She also felt that the structure of the program promoted better parenting skills.

The main officer in charge of the unit was not sure that he supported the idea of a prison nursery, on "general principles," but in going through the list of participants, on a case-by-case basis, he noted that the majority of women seemed to be having meaningful experiences. Overall, he liked working on the unit, although he was subjected to substantial kidding from fellow officers. He noted that he sits the mothers down and explains that everything can be handled in a soft voice. As a father, he feels he's able to block out the children's noise and, if a woman has to do something quickly, he'll watch her baby. During the study, the officer was observed going over to a crying baby and helping to settle her down. He pointed out that he rarely writes up women for rule infractions; instead he prefers to talk things through.

The officer liked the size and feel of the unit. He liked knowing all the women, their names and numbers, their babies, and where they are at all times. He remembers the women and their babies when they leave. He has been surprised by who does well on the outside and who doesn't.

Discussion

Obtaining reliable information from interviews with incarcerated mothers is difficult. For example, it is quite likely that use of drugs during pregnancy was underreported by the women we interviewed. There seemed to be great reluctance to discuss this topic, possibly due to the education the mothers have received in the prison program on the effects of neonatal drug exposure. Also, many women had been in prison long enough to have been drug-free by the time they gave birth and responded to the question from that perspective. For example, one mother who reported being addicted to crack and 7 months pregnant at the time of her arrest also reported that her baby had not been exposed to drugs before birth. Separation from children is another area in which self-reports may not be reliable. For example, all seven of the respondents who indicated that they had never been separated from their children had previously served sentences ranging from 3 months to 3 years.

Women participating in the nursery program have a great incentive to present themselves as good mothers who understand the importance of bonding and consistency in care giving. Reports of separations from their children, especially during their early years, would not be consistent with their current values and situation and could seem threatening—either to their position in the program or to their view of themselves as mothers. Also, many women responded accurately that they had not been physically separated, except for periods of incarceration, but noted in passing that their parent or sibling or some other family member has really functioned as their children's primary caregiver.

A growing sense of pride in themselves as people and as parents may have compromised some of the self-reports, but may also be an important outcome of the program. Many women identified educational opportunities as a program advantage. The tone in which these reports were made was consistently one of pride. It is quite possible that for some of the women, the nursery program afforded their first opportunity to learn in a classroom and then observe and engage in the immediate and successful application of that learning. Many addicts share a pattern of interrupted and unfinished commitments. The structure of learning opportunities, from the parenting classes through the alcohol and substance abuse program, is one that supports completion. Certificates mark the successful conclusion of each program. The experience of such achievements may be an important dimension of the program.

Key questions about prison nurseries concern consequences for child development. While these questions go beyond what could be observed and reported in the context of this descriptive study, our observations, when combined with reports in the literature, do suggest areas for further hypothesis, investigation, and program review.

For example, the confinement of infants in the restricted and impoverished environment of a prison would seem to suggest some negative effect on infant development. The only controlled study examining development in infants placed with others and infants kept with the mothers in a prison nursery was conducted in England by Lisa Catan (1992). This study followed 74 babies residing in prison nursery units and 33 similarly aged children born in prison but placed with extended family members or foster parents. Catan found that both groups of babies followed normal developmental patterns in relation to a larger group of contemporary Bristish babies. There were no differences between the two groups of babies being studied; no generalized developmental delays were found in either group.

Catan did find a gradual decline in both locomotor and cognitive development in the prison nursery babies, declines she attributed to the regimes and environmental limitations of the facilities and to the lack of child development knowledge of prison staff. Indeed, in the programs studied by Catan, babies spent long hours strapped in strollers, bouncers, and chairs. These physical restrictions gradually had a short-term impact on locomotor development. Catan also noted that there were few educational toys in the units, no action singalongs, and no "messy exploration" play. The units were managed by medical nurses and uniformed prison staff. Catan suspected these conditions as factors in the slight decline in cognitive scores compared to the outside group. The developmental decrements that appeared among the unit babies seemed to be only temporary, however, disappearing when the children moved into the community. But, since the prisoners and babies studied by Catan had relatively short stays (13 to 19 weeks) in the nurseries, her findings bear serious consideration in the planning and conducting of long-term nursery programs.

Catan's research also pointed to the lack of stability and continuity in the care of the children placed outside. Half the babies living outside experienced a change in caregiver. Almost three-quarters had their care shared by two or more women, simultaneously or serially. Just under half the babies changed homes from two to four times in less than 1 year. Seventy percent of the babies visited their mothers once a month or less. While all the mothers keeping their children on the prison unit expected to remain with their babies when released, only 18 out of the 33 separated mothers had plans for reuniting with their babies. These findings appear to constitute a strong argument for expanding jail and prison nursery services.

Other arguments in support of long-term nurseries relate to the development of infant attachment and maternal bonding. The literature on associations between attachment problems and later maladaptive social behavior coupled with the literature on the development of attachment in at-risk infant–mother pairs suggests that any intervention supporting healthy mother–infant attachment patterns could benefit infants directly and prevent later behavior problems among these children (Lyons-Ruth, Alpern, & Repacholi, 1993; Jacobson & Frye, 1991). Lyons-Ruth, Alpern, and Repacholi (1993) found, in their study of 62 low-income preschool children, that the strongest predictor of serious hostile behaviors toward peers in the classroom was a disorganized attachment relationship in infancy. The findings from Jacobson and Frye's (1991) experimental study of attachment in 46 infants whose mothers participated in the federal Women, Infants, and Children (WIC) supplemental food program provide evidence of the importance of social support on infant attachment.

While such data might not apply to prison-born infants who develop normal attachment behavior in the continuous care of nurturing outside caregivers (Bowlby, 1966, 1973), Catan found that a significant number of babies born in prison but placed with outside caregivers do not experience continuity of care throughout infancy. In the study reported here, informal observations of the babies' exploratory and proximity behaviors during play and of babies' responses when seeking comforting and reassurance suggested that strong, healthy attachment patterns were operating between mothers and infants in the prison nursery. Similarly, major improvements in the well-being of unborn and newborn infants of prisoners when compared to infants born outside of prison to matched controls (Cordero, Hines, Shibley & Lauton, 1991; Egley, Miller, Granatos, & Fogel, 1992) suggests that the stability, adequate nutrition, and health care resources of the structured prison environment may also present advantages to the older infants of women offenders. The chaotic and dangerous outside lives reported by the nursery mothers in this study supports that impression. These findings, coupled with prisoners' descriptions of their relationships with previous children, suggest that the development of normal attachment among the babies born to incarcerated mothers may be most likely to be achieved in long-term prison nurseries.

Conclusions

The two existing prison nursery programs in the United States are described. Results of interviews with nursery participants and staff suggest that there are significant benefits to participating mothers. Observations and a review of the relevant literature suggest that the development of normal attachment among the infants of women prisoners may be most likely to occur in prison nursery settings. Developmental studies of infant graduates of British prison nurseries suggest that future research in American prisons pursue this topic as groundwork for further evaluation of the outcomes of prison nursery services.

254 • Children of Incarcerated Parents

References

Bowlby, J. (1966). *Maternal care and mental health*. New York: Schocken Books.

Bowlby, J. (1973). *Attachment and loss, volume 2: separation*. New York: Basic Books.

Cannings, K. (1990). *Bridging the gap: Programs to facilitate contact between inmate parents and their children*. Ottawa: Ministry of the Solicitor General of Canada.

Catan, L. (1992). Infants with mothers in prison. In R. Shaw (Ed.), *Prisoners' children*. London: Routledge.

Cordero, L., Hines, S., Shibley, A., & Lauton, M. B. (1991). Duration of incarceration and perinatal outcome. *Obstetrics and Gynecology*, 78:641–645.

Egley, C. C., Miller, D. E., Granatos, J. L., & Fogel, C. I. (1992). Outcome of pregnancy during imprisonment. *Journal of Reproductive Medicine*, 37(2):131–134.

Grossman, J. E. (1982). *Survey of nursery programs in ten states*. Albany, NY: Department of Correctional Services.

Jacobson, S. W., & Frye, K. F. (1991). Effect of maternal social support on attachment: Experimental evidence. *Child Development*, 62:572–582.

Lyons-Ruth, K., Alpern, L., & Repacholi, B. (1993). Disorganized infant attachment classification and maternal psychosocial problems as predictors of hostile-aggressive behavior in the preschool classroom. *Child Development*, 64:572–585.

U.S. Department of Justice. (1988). *Historical statistics on prisoners in state and federal correctional institutions, yearend 1925–1986* (Report No. NCJ-111098). Washington, DC: Bureau of Justice Statistics.

U.S. Department of Justice. (1992). *Correctional populations in the United States, 1990* (Report No. NCJ-134946). Washington, DC: Bureau of Justice Statistics.

15
The Prison MATCH Program

Rose Weilerstein

In the jails and prisons of this country there are many mothers and fathers whose children have been left in the care of others. These children and their parents share something that is of great importance to their lives. All are victims of the trauma of parent–child separation. What becomes of these children? What problems do they and their parents share? Most important, what should and can be done to address these problems? Prison MATCH is dedicated to alleviating these problems. Incarcerated parents' contact with their children can help to maintain family relationships.

The Experience of Parental Incarceration

From years of working with incarcerated parents, we know that separation can be the hardest part of the experience, for both parents and children. Mothers and fathers are not really able to parent while inside, for prisoners often lose track of their children's daily development and all the experiences that parents on the outside deal with each day. When crises come up for children, as they often do during these stressful times, the lack of connection between parent and child and the helplessness the former feels can be even more painful. Incarcerated parents also have to worry about what will happen when they are released. The vast majority will return home to care for their children again. They must plan how to resume vital relationships that have been interrupted and perhaps seriously damaged. Yet it is almost impossible to plan anything well from jail or prison. The daily guilt and anguish about leaving their children that some parents experience causes many to refuse to have contact with their children and bury the pain inside, so that they can do their time and feel they are getting home as quickly as possible.

Research on female prisoners points to their special problems and needs concerning their children. They are, on the average, young and unmarried women of color. More than two-thirds are under 30 and as many as 80%

have dependent children. Studies of the effects of maternal incarceration consistently emphasize common issues, including:

1. the trauma of abrupt separation from children at the time of arrest;
2. the difficulties in finding and maintaining secure alternative care arrangements for children;
3. the social and emotional stress experienced by both mothers and children during their separation; and
4. the pregnant inmate's unique problems of inadequate pre- and postnatal care and inability to bond with her infant.

Children can experience difficult and confusing feelings, depending on their developmental stage. For the infant, disruption of critical bonding with the mother may be the end of the only security the child knows and may affect the rest of his or her life. A toddler has no way of knowing whether a parent will ever return and may be haunted by the fear that the separation is his or her fault. The school-aged child, who often has only TV images of prison life, can be terrified about his or her parent's safety. And the adolescent must deal with self-image as well as with dependence on peer relations, suffering the stigma of the parent's imprisonment, often with no one to talk with or to help.

Working with incarcerated parents has clarified for us three critical needs. These must be addressed in order to help ensure the children's welfare and to help maintain parent–child bonds.

1. *Supportive contact visiting between incarcerated parents and their children is essential for maintaining their relationships.* Prisons do not provide supportive environments for prisoners and their children. Regular visiting rooms are not set up for family visiting. In many institutions, visitors, even children, may not touch the person they have come to visit. Parents and their children need special settings, oriented to children, so that they may renew and strengthen their ties.

2. *Children need help in the community, especially with social services, to ensure their welfare during their parents' absence.* Even the best alternative care situation for children can have problems: siblings often are separated; children sometimes are moved from home to home; and there are often crises—at home, in school, or with their own feelings—that need to be addressed with supportive services. Parents, too, need such services to maintain involvement in their children's lives.

3. *Parents need assistance in better understanding their children and in learning to be better parents.* Faced with the pain of separation from their children and all the problems that can emerge, incarcerated parents need and want to be more knowledgeable and skillful parents. Supportive

programs that will help them learn and grow in these critical roles should be available for them.

The History of Prison MATCH

Prison MATCH (Mothers, Fathers and Their Children) started as a "Prison Mothers and Their Children" program in 1978 at the Federal Correctional Institution at Pleasanton, California. The history of the first 5 years of this program has best been summarized by Cannings (1990) in *Bridging the Gap: Programs and Services to Facilitate Contact Between Inmate Parents and Their Children*:

> In 1977, Yvette Lehman, a professor of child development at Chabot Community College in California, asked herself, "What happens to children of incarcerated parents?" Through friends, this query brought her together with sociologist Carolyn McCall who was then working under contract with the National Council on Crime and Delinquency. The two women began to research the types of programs available within North American correctional facilities that pertained to maintaining family ties between inmate parents and their children.
>
> Out of this work a program model, which was based in part on the Preschool in Prison Project at the Washington State Reformatory in Monroe, began to take shape. They then approached the warden at FCI-Pleasanton with their proposal for a child visitation program to be offered daily at the the institution. The warden agreed to one that could be run on weekends.
>
> Working in cooperation and consultation with institutional staff and inmates at FCI-Pleasanton, in the Spring of 1977, McCall and Lehman began to plan the first in-prison children's center. The fruition of their initial plans occurred with the opening of the Children's Center at FCI-Pleasanton on Mother's Day, 1978.
>
> Prison MATCH began under the administrative umbrella of the National Council on Crime and Delinquency [NCCD] and it remained there until 1983 when it became a separate, non-profit organization with its own Board of Directors. Prior to this transition, an Advisory Board, which was composed of prison administrators (including the warden), representatives from the community and inmates, met monthly.
>
> Considerable emphasis was given to developing, through appropriate play and learning activities, the bonds between parents and children and from the start Prison MATCH has borne a resemblance to parent-cooperative schools in the community.
>
> Providing parenting educational opportunities was the first step. The initial classes were part of a parenting course which ran from the Fall of 1977 to the Spring of 1978. Through advertising within the institution 16 inmates became the first students.
>
> Not only were the initial classes used to teach parenting and child care,

they were a vehicle for developing the Children's Center program. The first planning committee consisted of Lehman, McCall and the class participants. This group was responsible for engaging Louise Rosenkrantz, the first Director for the Children's Center. She also became a member of this nucleus. By the end of the second year this group was formally established as the Steering Committee, responsible for program operations and the hiring of program personnel. While this committee provided the structure for internal decision making for program operation and planning, ultimate authority rested with the warden, his representatives and the president of the parent NCCD.

In keeping with the emphasis on inmate involvement, incarcerated parents assumed ever increasing responsibilities. As noted above, while they began as students in the first parenting classes, this led to their involvement with the initial planning committee and, eventually, to their membership on the Steering Committee. When the Children's Center opened they became its first volunteer caregivers. Subsequent to the establishment of the Steering Committee, they were hired and paid by Prison MATCH as program personnel.

Since its inception in the late '70's Prison MATCH has developed into a community-based organization with a multifaceted program—both aspects of which have served as inspiration for others. From the outset members have been proactive in sharing their experiences, observations and insights and urging others to consider the needs of incarcerated parents and their children.

The Prison MATCH Children's Center operated at the Pleasanton Federal Correctional Institution until 1988 on a contract basis with the U.S. Bureau of Prisons. During this period (1978–1988) an outreach effort was maintained to let other institutions know about this program. Prison MATCH became a model for similar programs in other prisons and jails. Dr. Carolyn McCall traveled to many parts of the country, speaking to groups interested in establishing similar programs; as a result, programs were instituted in a number of other facilities throughout the United States.

In 1988 Prison MATCH was unsuccessful in its bid for renewal of its contract. Another group had submitted a lower bid and the pattern of operation established by Prison MATCH was not followed. There was no longer a steering committee or prisoner involvement in the administration of the program. Simultaneously, other institutions had expressed an interest in hosting Prison MATCH. In 1989 the activities of Prison MATCH were moved from Pleasanton to the San Francisco County Jail, which had a reputation for having a fine set of programs already in operation, including parenting classes, and a modern building with classroom space that could be dedicated for children's center use. In 1989, with the assistance of San Francisco Sheriff Michael Hennessey, the new Children's Center was established at County Jail #7 and is still operating every Sunday from 9:30 A.M. to 2:00 P.M.

The Prison MATCH Model

The Prison MATCH model has changed slightly over the years. Today only prisoners who are parents of children currently attending the Children's Center are permitted to participate. The current practice is to encourage the children to be with the incarcerated parent for at least 4 hours once a week in an enriched recreational setting. The Children's Center is located within the walls of the institution and staffed by competent early childhood educators, social workers, and other professional people as volunteer core staff. Due to financial constraints, there is only one part-time paid teacher.

PRISON MATCH and the Children's Center demonstrate that something can be done for these families to help them maintain their relationships and give them tools for survival and growth. This new model has four interwoven components: the Children's Center itself, supportive social services, parenting skills and child development training for inmates, and a program to break the intergenerational cycle of addiction.

The Children's Center

The Children's Center is a warm, child-centered setting inside the jail where prisoners and their children from infancy through age 15 years can spend Sundays working to reestablish and strengthen their relationships. Run like successful parent–child cooperatives in the community, the Children's Center emphasizes developing parent–child bonds through appropriate play and learning activities.

All prisoners are told about Prison MATCH at their orientation sessions and given an opportunity to apply for participation. When the applications of incarcerated parents are accepted by jail administrators, Prison MATCH is notified and a list of the eligible parents is made available to Prison MATCH staff. The Prison MATCH director then visits the parents in their dormitories to help resolve problems in having the children come to the Children's Center, and assist with other family matters requiring legal or social service intervention. Parents may then notify caregivers to bring their children for Sunday visits.

The children are brought to the facility at 9:00 A.M. by a parent or relative, foster parent, or social worker. They are registered at the gate, and then come as a group to the visiting area where they are inspected by the staff. Prison MATCH volunteers meet the children in the visiting room and lead them to a classroom that has been transformed into a children's recreational area. For the older children, there are a Ping-Pong table, an air hockey game, music, and many arts and crafts. For the younger children, there is climbing equipment and many toys suitable for different ages.

After the children arrive, the parents are notified and allowed to enter the Children's Center. Staff assist with arts and crafts projects, and provide gentle parenting instruction in a positive, nonpunitive manner. Lunch is provided by the sheriff's staff, and snacks are provided by Prison MATCH. Birthdays are celebrated with birthday cakes and a party for the children. Eggs are decorated for Easter, and at Christmas toys are donated by local churches and groups. Teddy bears are provided by the organization "Caring for Children." Prison MATCH takes Polaroid pictures of each inmate and child and gives a picture of the child to the parent and vice versa; everyone cherishes these pictures. Because of space and staff limitations, a maximum of 15 children are permitted in the Children's Center, and these are selected on a first come, first in, basis.

At the end of the day, about 1:30 P.M., cleanup begins and the Children's Center room is restored to its normal classroom state with help from everyone. After cleanup the staff runs children's videos and provides parents with books to read to their children until it is time to depart. The persons transporting the children register again at the gate and come up as a group. Children are then called to the regular visiting area after saying their farewell to their parents. The parents return to their dormitories.

Supportive Social Services

These services help families find the support they need "inside" and "outside" to ensure their children's welfare. The volunteer director provides referrals to services that include foster care assistance, help with child custody issues, and crisis intervention.

Training for Inmates in Parenting and Child Development

Parents can learn just by being in the Children's Center and observing interactions between staff and children and other parents and children. Training materials, booklets, and articles on child development and parenting are available and are discussed by parents and staff. Formal parenting classes are available through the jail.

Breaking the Intergenerational Cycle of Addiction

Prison MATCH has undergone several periods of expansion and contraction during its 15-year year existence. The Robert Wood Johnson Foundation afforded Prison MATCH a 1-year opportunity to develop a program to "Break the Intergenerational Cycle of Addiction." Over 80% of the inmates at San Francisco County Jail #7 are involved in some way with illicit drugs. The foundation gave Prison MATCH a chance to see if building family bonds between children and their jailed parents could provide an incentive for these parents to achieve recovery from addiction. A social worker was hired as a case manager and instructor. Over 55 prisoners and their families—a total of 135 individuals—received supportive services through this program, including individual and family counseling, postrelease planning, referrals, and follow-up.

Planning a Children's Center Program

Although 17 years have passed since it was founded, the Prison MATCH model remains the standard for developing parent–child programming in correctional facilities.

Getting Started

Planning a children's program inside a jail or prison requires diplomacy, for you must bring together two groups traditionally unused to working together: correctional administrators and community professionals. You will never get "inside" to plan unless you make a good contact with someone in the prison's administration. A facility's warden or superintendent has absolute control over entry to the jail or prison and over any programming conducted there. She or he will want to meet you to discuss your plans and what you will require of the institution. Being careful and responsible at these early stages can make things far easier later. As a new program is being developed, conflicts involving prison procedures inevitably arise. A good working relationship with the administration can make your program development go more smoothly.

The participation of community professionals in disciplines concerned with children and family services is crucial. These professionals will be able to get beyond the facility's daily routines to really understand the needs of incarcerated parents and their children. They will have the skills to be effective advocates for children in this restrictive adult environment. The prison staff will appreciate the added resources such professionals can bring to bear in addressing the family needs of prisoners. Conferences between the prison administration and community advocates allow participants to set goals and work out how to begin. Ideally, such conferences result in the formation of task forces to guide program development efforts.

Steps to Starting a Parent–Child Program

- Recruit community professionals with expertise in child and family services as advocates for the program.
- Establish positive communication with the facility's warden or superintendent.

- Enlist the support of one or two key correctional staff members, volunteers, and/or contract workers.
- Hold a conference with facility administrators and advocates to discuss development of the program.
- Form a task force to guide program development.
- Enlist local community leaders and public officials to serve as members of the program's governing board.
- Expect and deal carefully with correctional staff concerns about security issues.

Facility and Procedures

To design your program you first will need to observe the existing visiting program at the institution and then answer this question: "What are the needs of the children and parents who will use this program?"

When our Children's Center was in the planning stage, community planners envisioned a program for infants and preschoolers only. Incarcerated parents quickly pointed out, however, that they needed a supportive program for children of all ages—from newborns to 15-year-olds. It would not make sense and would be too painful to leave out their older children, they said.

Prison visiting conditions and procedures will also influence program design. Visitors to a Children's Center will have to be screened by the same staff that screens regular visitors and the Children's Center will have to operate within the time constraints of visiting room staff. It is important to stay flexible. Administrative procedures will change and the program will have to be able to conform to survive.

Negotiating with the institution for space is an important part of designing a program. Space will be limited to what can be made available. Our present space is a classroom, with one corner devoted to storage of our toys and equipment. Our lockers and closets are designed to hold a maximum amount of materials in a small space. Designers of new programs will need to consider location, space (dedicated or otherwise), and availability of access to bathrooms, water fountains, and offices. Ideally, both indoor and outdoor space would be available, with adjacent bathrooms and nearby office equipment to permit preparation of the necessary documents required by the jail or prison administration at each session. Ideally, no additional correctional supervision will need to be arranged because the space would be under the supervision of nearby staff. Such ideal arrangements may not be possible, so flexibility and ingenuity are required to fit the Children's Center into existing facilities.

The staff for the Children's Center should clearly be differentiated from prison staff. While they are responsible for reporting serious infractions of institution rules, they should not be expected to perform any function not directly related to the Children's Center. To work effectively with incarcerated parents and their children, a program must provide an atmosphere of trust and rapport, as well as the expertise gained through professional training in work with children.

Children's Activities

Age-appropriate activities should be provided. We furnish a stimulating environment of sensory and motor toys as well as space for rest, diaper changing, rocking, and cuddling. Since parent–infant bonding is so critical, we always provide at least a small space where parents can be private and quiet, and are able to play with their babies out of the way of the activities of older children.

The preschooler and his or her parent need a variety of materials and activities: art materials such as crayons, markers, and Playdough; manipulative activities such as puzzles, Legos, and table blocks; dramatic play materials, such as dolls, trucks, costumes, and puppets; and, of course, books and records. Not all materials can or should be available at all times, but a well-rounded program can develop activities for young children and parents in these areas. Through such creative and dramatic play, children have worked out meaningful ways to deal with what is happening to their parents and their own feelings about the separation.

School-aged children and their parents enjoy playing games and doing crafts together. Leather crafts, enameling, and sewing projects have been used effectively in our program. For teenagers, many of these projects have served as backdrops for important parent–child conversations. As a child and parent toss the Nerf football, make hand puppets, or do 500-piece jigsaw puzzles, they talk about the child's home and school situations, when the parent will return, and many related concerns.

We especially recommend activities in which parent and child work together to create something that the child can take home, such as a painting or a crafts project. The parents can also return to their dorms with products of the children's art activities.

Social Services

Ideally, a separate staff member should be assigned to provide referrals and information to parents and families. In the absence of such resources, it is important to establish links with public social service agencies and support services. Identify and cooperate with organizations that provide legal services for prisoners with children, and organizations that provide services for prisoners' other family-related needs.

Conclusion: Prison MATCH Today

Since its founding the Prison MATCH Children's Center has been the site of over 5,000 family visits. In 1991 with one part-time child care professional and 16 volunteers, Prison MATCH served 90 families including 147 children. The Prison MATCH Children's Center is a model program that has been replicated in 11 state prisons and jails and three federal women's prisons in Alderson, West Virginia, Forth Worth, Texas, and Lexington, Kentucky. In addition, Prison MATCH receives approximately 50 requests per year for assistance from other institutions concerned with parental incarceration, family stability, and child development. The Prison MATCH archives are maintained in The Clearinghouse at Pacific Oaks. Seven Prison MATCH publications, including "The Prison MATCH Parenting Series" for prisoners and the children's booklet, *I Know How You Feel, Because This Happened to Me*, are distributed through The Clearinghouse, which is a project of the Center for Children of Incarcerated Parents. The Clearinghouse's unique information service for prisoners and their families was originally developed as collaborative effort of Prison MATCH and Pacific Oaks. For 17 years, Prison MATCH has been a leader in developing services for incarcerated parents and their children.

Reference

Cannings, K. (1990). *Bridging the gap: programs and services to facilitate contact between inmate parents and their children*. Ottawa: Ministry of the Solicitor General of Canada.

16
A Program for Grandparent Caregivers

Leonora Poe

Families are usually thought to consist of a father, a mother, and their children. However, in many of today's households, there is no father, no mother, and the children live with their grandparents. Obviously, the family structure in these homes differs from that in "traditional" families.

Although grandparents have typically been involved to some degree in the lives of their grandchildren, recent social changes have intensified that involvement for many. These changes are the result of the drug epidemic that has significantly increased the number of children whose substance-dependent parents are unable to adequately care for them. Drugs have attacked the American family structure, particularly in poor urban areas, and as a consequence more and more grandparents are becoming primary caregivers for their grandchildren. According to the 1990 California census, approximately 672,000 of the four million children in the state are currently living with grandparents or other relatives.

While the media has focused plenty of attention on drug-using parents who end up in jail, they have paid little attention to the families drug addicts leave behind. The children of drug-dependent parents are subject to many traumas and are at risk for forced separations from their parents and/or abandonment. Grandparents must quietly pick up the pieces left behind by their addicted children, and attempt to provide stable homes for their grandchildren. Many of these grandparents feel that they have no choice, because otherwise their grandchildren would be placed with unrelated foster parents and perhaps be lost to them forever.

Grandparents generally look forward to their retirement years as a period in which they can finally enjoy their leisure time, return to school, pursue sports and hobbies, and so on. As grandparents increasingly take on the role of parenting their grandchildren, they put their own plans on hold. Because they are once again the primary caregivers for young children, they are deprived of their own developmental age- and stage-appropriate activities. Many experience significant emotional and social intrusions into their lives. All of them wanted to be *grand*parents, not parents, to their grandchildren.

265

In addition to bearing the often difficult role of primary caregiver, these grandparents must also cope with the resulting nontraditional family structures. Grandparents who become parents to their grandchildren are deprived of a positive grandparent–grandchild relationship. Needless to say, they are also deprived of a positive and nurturing relationship with their own adult children. While many grandparents feel punished and put out because of this deprivation, they also feel guilty for not providing a home for their drug-addicted adult children. Besides being detrimental to family structure, this conflict effectively diverts emotional focus away from the grandchildren at a time when their need for care and attention is greatest.

In some cases there is a multigenerational family structure in which grandparents, parent, and grandchildren all live together in the grandparents' home. This arrangement can create a blurred line of authority that may have a negative effect on the grandchildren. Children in these circumstances often develop divided loyalties between their parents and their grandparents, as parents and grandparents frequently undermine each other's authority. In many instances, conflicts may be related to the grandparents' natural difficulty in coping with a new generation and new ideas of childrearing.

These major adjustments in the lives of grandparents frequently contribute to their age-related health problems. This is especially so in the case of disorders, like hypertension and back problems, that are exacerbated by increased stress. Grandparents often neglect their own medical needs to concentrate on the health needs of their grandchildren.

While the psychological impact of such circumstances on both the grandparents and the children is less than ideal, the practical difficulties may be worse. In addition to sacrificing their privacy and independence, many grandparents are forced to move into larger living spaces, to purchase additional furnishings, and to accommodate themselves to the schedules of social workers, court officials, attorneys, teachers, therapists, and especially the children themselves.

Those grandparents who rescue their grandchildren from abandonment and neglect have legal issues to deal with in addition to all their other problems. When the biological parents have died, the grandparents most often legally adopt their grandchildren. These grandparents do not have to fear that the children will be taken away from them or that someone will interfere with their caregiving role. However, when the biological parents are still living and do not give up their parental rights, grandparents may live in uncertainty about their future with their grandchildren.

Grandparents often turn to their religious beliefs, their fellow church members, and extended family members for support. However, the complexity of the issues and the stigma attached to many situations that require grandparents to parent may keep them from seeking help from these sources.

A new approach to addressing these problems is the Grandparents As Parents [GAP] program of support groups. Most grandparents come into these groups feeling isolated not only from their families but also from their peers. GAP groups provide safe places for grandparents to express their feelings and talk about their experiences. The support groups serve, in effect, as surrogate families.

Bananas, a child care referral agency in Oakland, California, started such a group in 1989. People who showed up at the first meeting ranged in age from 35 to 70. All of them were initially ashamed of their situations and reluctant to expose their feelings. It was a challenge for program staff to find the right balance between empathizing with the grandparents' problems and keeping enough emotional distance to be able to help them.

In order to balance emotional and psychological support with practical assistance, outside experts were invited to address the group on important issues. For example, a pediatric neurologist described the medical symptoms of crack-exposed babies. A nurse talked to the group about diet and health care for both grandchildren and grandparents. An attorney discussed ways to find affordable assistance when trying to obtain legal custody of the children. A director of social services gave advice on obtaining Aid to Families with Dependent Children. A school counselor spoke about social problems that grandparented children may have in school.

A number of similar groups have sprung into existence across the nation, helping to support grandparents and grandchildren. In addition to support groups and education, many GAP programs also provided referrals, actual resources (like clothing and emergency groceries), and respite care that allows grandparents to have some time to themselves without the burdens of childcare. According to Syl de Toledo, founder of the GAP Program in Long Beach, "It's not who births the baby, it's who takes care of the child."

PART VI

Policy Issues

17
Public Policy and the Children of Incarcerated Parents

Barbara Bloom

Disruption of families due to parental incarceration is becoming an increasingly serious problem. As the United States continues to imprison increasing numbers of persons convicted of crimes, growing numbers of our nation's children are being impacted by their parent's incarceration. In the past, these children have tended to be ignored by the criminal justice and social services systems and yet their well-being is critically tied to the future of our society.

There are now an estimated 1.5 million children of incarcerated parents in the United States (Center for Children of Incarcerated Parents, 1991). There has been a glaring shortage of current information regarding these children. Systemwide data is not routinely maintained, and researchers are therefore often forced to speculate about the numbers, ages, living situations, and problems they face. Nonetheless, advocacy efforts and programs geared toward helping the children of prisoners are developing throughout the United States. States as diverse as California and Virginia are addressing the unique issues relating to children of incarcerated parents through legislative and program initiatives. But clearly much more needs to be done to assist these children and to make their issues more visible on a national level.

Major Trends in Public Policy

The status of children of incarcerated parents has been determined by several interrelated trends: (1) establishment of criminal justice and corrections policies in response to public perceptions of crime, (2) a focus on the isolated offender, and (3) overreliance on incarceration.

The Creation of Policy in Response to Public Perceptions of Crime

In 1992, there were over 14 million arrests in the United States (Federal Bureau of Investigation [FBI], 1993). While arrest, conviction, and incarceration rates have risen steadily over the past 30 years, crime reports, victimization surveys, and self-reported criminal behavior studies indicate that crime rates in all categories have remained fairly stable during that period or have decreased (National Crime Survey, 1992; FBI, 1993).

However, the public perception is that crime has increased. A recent national public survey (Braun & Pasternak, 1993) found that the percentage of respondents believing that crime is the major issue facing U.S. society recently doubled, from 21% in mid-1993 to 43% at the beginning of 1994. Two-thirds of those surveyed cited media reports as the basis for their opinions. Meanwhile, more than eight out of 10 respondents feel that their own neighborhoods are safe, and this number has not changed significantly since 1981. Significant changes that have occurred, and that have influenced public perception of crime, are minor increases in murder and other violent crime rates in small towns and small-to-medium-sized cities (FBI, 1993).

The public cannot be expected to be familiar with these studies, or to use such objective data in their analysis of what is presented to them by the news/entertainment media. The creators of public policy should be held to a different standard. Yet, over the past decade, U.S. public policy has included law enforcement/interdiction ("War on Drugs"), criminal justice (mandatory minimum sentences), and correctional ("Three Strikes" initiatives) policies created specifically in response to public perception of a nonexistent crime wave. Each of these policies has contributed to dramatically increased numbers of arrests and incarcerations, without producing a corresponding effect on actual crime rates.

Focus on the Isolated Offender

Historically, public policy in this country has considered offenders in isolation, ignoring their families and communities. At almost all stages of the justice process, offenders' family relationships and status within their communities are held to be meaningless. The significant exception concerns the sentencing of convicted offenders, where family responsibilities have produced some differentials (Daly, 1989).

This focus has allowed our criminal justice and corrections systems to process millions of persons without collecting critical data that might contribute to our understanding of the causes of crime and how to prevent it. More importantly, it has thoughtlessly allowed millions of families to be subjected to the unmeasured, direct and indirect effects of the practices of these systems. For example, children of offenders and their parents are consistently, repeatedly, and often traumatically separated throughout the justice process, even when such practices are not required for efficiency, cost-effectiveness, correctional security, or public safety.

Research showing that consideration of their children and families at every stage of the justice process may produce better outcomes for offenders has long been available (Holt & Miller, 1972; Macdonald, 1980). Recent studies of these children and their parents suggests that the pursuit of the focus on isolated offenders in public policy, without examination of its effects, may actually be contributing to the growth of intergenerational behaviors leading to crime and incarceration (Johnston, 1992, 1993).

Overreliance on Incarceration

Over the past 3 decades there has been an explosive growth in the numbers of people going to jail or prison. The number of U.S. state and federal prisoners has grown by more than 150% in the past 10 years; in 1992, the state prison population grew by 7.2%, and eight states reported prison population increases of greater than 10% (U.S. Department of Justice [USDJ], 1993).

These increases in the prison population are the result of three factors (USDJ, 1993):

Increased numbers of conditional release (parole) violators returning to prison. Since 1977, the percentage of incarcerated parole violators has increased from 14.5 to 30.5% of all prison admissions. Incarcerated parole violators account for more than one-third of the growth of total annual prison admissions.

Increased numbers of drug offenders. Persons convicted of drug offenses now make up the largest proportion of U.S. prisoners. Since 1977, new court commitments to prison for drug offenses have increased from 11.5 to 32.1%, accounting for more than 40% of the total growth of prison admissions. The largest proportion of these prisoners have been convicted of simple drug possession or driving to endanger.

Increased probability of incarceration following arrest. The rate of incarceration following arrest has increased for all crimes since 1977.

Increased spending on jails and especially prisons has not produced corresponding increases in spending on other areas of corrections or significant decreases in the rate of crime. One of the major effects of the overreliance of the U.S. criminal justice and corrections systems on incarceration has been a corresponding limitation on development of prevention/early intervention services and alternative sanctions.

Policy Remedies

By getting tough on crime, the United States has also gotten tougher on its children and the most disenfranchised segments of its communities. The policy trends just discussed have disproportionately affected African-Americans, Hispanics, and women. Nationwide, state and local governments are spending billions of dollars on building new prisons and jails, at the expense of funding for essential programs that promote crime prevention, such as education, vocational training, drug treatment, health care, and other services that could help families rise out of poverty.

Nevertheless, remedies for harmful public policies affecting children of offenders do exist. These include legislation, and changes in the policies and practices of law enforcement, child welfare, and correctional systems.

Legislation in the Interest of Children of Incarcerated Parents

Advocacy efforts such as those by the American Bar Association Center on Children and the Law (1993) and others (see Chapter 19 by Peter Breen) promote the theme that strong family ties should be maintained as support to offenders and their children both during parental incarceration and after parents' release. Advocates recommend legal remedies in the areas of criminal sentencing, corrections, and child welfare law.

Sentencing Reform. Public misperceptions of an increased rate of crime have produced the mandatory minimum sentencing legislation that forms the statutory basis for increased rates of incarceration. Mandatory minimum sentences have been applied primarily in the area of drug offenses. Women offenders have higher rates of drug use, drug addiction, and drug-related crime; mandatory minimum sentencing has therefore had a disproportionate effect on women prisoners and their children. While recent attempts at reversal of such federal sentencing guidelines have failed (*Mistretta US*, 1989), it is clear that legislation repealing mandatory minimum sentences would reduce current incarceration rates and increase the amount of public resources that could be diverted from prisons and jails to preventive strategies and intermediate sanctions.

Corrections. Early in the 20th century only a few institutions in the United States allowed women to keep their infants with them, but by 1950 13 states had created statutes that allowed mothers to retain infants with them in prison (Reeves, 1929; Smith, 1962). The intent of such legislation and subsequent correctional programming was to preserve the relationship between the incarcerated mother and her child.

Throughout the 1960s and 1970s states began to repeal legislation that permitted mothers to retain their children in prison. The most common reasons cited for this revocation related to security risks, management problems, liability insurance, and the adverse effects of prison on normal childhood development (Radosh, 1988).

The fact that there is existing state legislation allowing mothers to retain infants or young children does not necessarily mean that programs for implementing the law are in place. States such as California, Minnesota, New Jersey, New York, and Wisconsin have statutory provisions for mothers' retention of their infants, but only New York has nurseries in correctional facilities that enable newborns to remain with their incarcerated mothers for a limited period of time (usually 1 year, or up to 18 months if the mother's release is imminent). New York has two state prison nurseries and a nursery for long-term prisoners who give birth while incarcerated at Riker's Island Jail outside of New York City.

Some states, such as North Carolina, have enacted legislation that allows a judge to defer incarceration of a pregnant women convicted of a nonviolent crime until 6 weeks after the birth of her child. This provision allows the child to experience some bonding with her or his mother, as well as provides the mother with an opportunity to establish adequate placement for her child.

Only a small number of the 50 states specifically address the issue of the birth of babies to incarcerated women, or the fact that incarcerated women are mothers of infants or young children. The vast majority of states make no mention in their legislative codes of either providing services to inmate mothers or securing the placement of children of women prisoners at the time of their incarceration. Even in those states that have significant populations of female prisoners, no provisions for the placement of inmate's children are specified in the legislative codes. In the absence of any legislation mandating or preventing prisoners' custody of their children, many states have adopted regulatory policies. North Carolina, Ohio, and Pennsylvania allow infants to remain with their mothers until proper placement may be secured.

States such as California, Connecticut, Massachusetts, Michigan, Minnesota, New Jersey, New York, North Carolina, Pennsylvania, Texas, and Wisconsin offer community-based alternatives to incarceration for eligible pregnant offenders and prisoners with young children. California was a pioneer in terms of its legislatively mandated Community Prisoner Mother (Mother–Infant Care) Program, which currently exists in seven California counties. To qualify for this program women prisoners must be sentenced to 6 years or less in state prison and be pregnant or have children under 6 years of age.

The fact that only a handful of states have legislation that recognizes the unique problems associated with the imprisonment of parents, particularly primary caretakers of children, is a national failing. While individual Departments of Correction have established visitation policies regarding incarcerated parents and their children, the disparities from one institution to another and from one state to another are glaring. For example, only eight states allow overnight visits of prisoners and their immediate family members, and fewer than 20 states have community-based alternatives to incarceration for parents who are primary caretakers and their children (Radosh, 1988).

Legislation that addresses the needs of incarcerated parents and their children throughout the country warrants serious consideration. On the federal level, HCR 33, also known as the Family Unit Act, is the kind of legislation that recognizes the importance of maintaining prisoner family relationships. This law would provide for demonstration parent–child community corrections programs at several sites across the nation.

Child Welfare. The Adoption Assistance and Child Welfare Reform Act of 1980 established priorities, procedures, and services for children at risk of removal from the parental home. The law requires state agencies to make "reasonable efforts" to prevent the need for removal of the children from the home and to reunify families if a child is placed in foster care. Its goal is to avoid the needless "drift" of children through many years of and multiple placements in foster care.

In theory, the children of incarcerated parents would seem to be ideal candidates for the benign intervention of children welfare agency delivery of family reunification services, as prescribed by federal and state child welfare reform laws. In practice, the child welfare system does not respond in any routine manner when a parent is incarcerated. Even when child welfare workers do intervene, their response may be unhelpful to the parent or to the children.

Parents whose children are placed in foster care are entitled to reunification services unless provision of these services would be detrimental to the children. Services may include assistance in maintaining contact between parent and child through letters, telephone calls, and transportation services; visitation services to family members and foster parents; counseling; and parenting education.

Although the federal legislation was designed to reunify families whenever possible, the 12- to 18-month limit on the time children may remain in foster care places some incarcerated parents in a troubling position, especially if they are serving lengthy sentences. When the child welfare agency does assume jurisdiction of a child whose parent is incarcerated, it is required to make reasonable efforts to provide services that will promote the reunification of the incarcerated parent, which is usually the mother, and her child(ren). Incarcerated parents often do not receive court-mandated services (Beckerman, 1994), but even if they do, they often find it difficult to meet the legal requirements for reunification. Failure to meet these requirements and/or lengthy sentences can result in termination of their parental rights.

Several states have addressed the issue of parental rehabilitation by statute. The New York statute explicitly requires that agencies make diligent efforts on behalf of incarcerated parents to strengthen and improve the parental relationship, even in cases involving severe or repeated child abuse. The statute defines "diligent efforts" to include the provision of child visitation at the prison and other social services As in New York, the

California statute sets out requirements for providing reunification services to incarcerated parents. Reasonable reunification efforts are mandated unless such services would be detrimental to the child (Genty, 1991).

Under the California statute, reunification services to incarcerated parents may include: collect phone calls between parent and child, transportation services, visitation services, and services to extended family members or foster parents providing care to the children. In addition, the incarcerated parent may be required and therefore assisted to attend counseling, parenting classes, and/or vocational training programs as part of the reunification plan.

Oklahoma's statute is the most explicit in the country in the guidance it gives to judges in determining whether an incarcerated parent separated from her child for an extended period of time is "unfit." The Oklahoma statute further provides that incarceration of the parent is not sufficient grounds to terminate parental rights (Genty, 1991).

Applications of Policy in the Interest of Children of Prisoners

The procedures followed by law enforcement, social service, and correctional agencies in dealing with children of offenders vary from jurisdiction to jurisdiction. Because there are no consistent statewide standards directing how these agencies should coordinate their efforts to ensure the best care of dependent children of parents who are arrested and incarcerated, children are separated from their parents with varying degrees of sensitivity to the impact that a parent's passage through the justice process has on a child.

Law Enforcement Practices. The American Bar Association (ABA) recently conducted a survey entitled *Children on Hold: What Happens When Their Primary Caretaker Is Arrested?* (1993). This landmark study found that only one U.S. jurisdiction among those studied has a specific policy on parental arrest procedures. The survey focused on what is being done nationwide to meet the needs of children when their sole caregiver is arrested. The complete study will consider parental arrest, emergency placement of the children, parental incarceration and foster care placement of the children, parental release and reunification of the family. Project researchers found that most social workers and law enforcement officers interviewed cited an increase in drug abuse as the primary reason for an increase in the numbers of children referred to their agencies as "children in need of services" due to parental arrest.

When the parents of minor children are arrested, the local law enforcement and social service agencies become involved in the temporary care of the children. In many jurisdictions, law enforcement officers have de facto discretion to make child placement arrangements. Most jurisdictions do not have a specific policy for law enforcement officers to follow in making such emergency placement decisions. Law enforcement officials who were interviewed consistently expressed concerns about their role in responding to the urgent needs of children when their parents are arrested; one concern of officers was that many children will never be referred to social service agencies as a result of their parents' arrest.

However, a few jurisdictions have addressed these issues with written policies for management of child placement after parental arrest. Some have shown great sensitivity to the needs of the families involved, ranking parents as the primary decision makers in all placement decisions from the time of arrest through release from custody (Chesterfield Police Department, 1992). Others have suggested the creation of highly formal, statewide systems that would require documentation and follow-up on every informal child placement made in the field by police officers when a sole caregiver of minors is arrested (Commonwealth of Virginia, 1994). In some communities increased reporting requirements and better cooperation between law enforcement and child protective services (CPS) has resulted in an increasing number of children of arrested parents coming to the attention of social service agencies.

Before they are widely implemented, these forms of agency-to-agency liaisons will need to be examined to determine if they produce primary benefits for the children of arrested parents or merely increase the degree of CPS supervision of these children. Client-centered interventions for parental arrest, such as those produced by the Parental Arrest Policy Group in Los Angeles County (see Chapter 13), should receive similar scrutiny.

Child Protective Services Practices. At least 10% of the children of women prisoners and about 2% of the children of male prisoners, or more than 42,000 children of incarcerated parents, are in foster care (Johnston, 1993). Although there has been no large-scale research on offenders with children in these placements, smaller studies have identified those CPS practices that are helpful to these families and those that are not (Beckerman, 1994; Johnston, 1994).

Drug-Exposed Infants. While the incidence of prenatal drug use appears to be similar among all income and cultural groups, reports of positive maternal drug tests are more commonly made on low-income women of color; corresponding data for newborn infants suggests that such reports are primarily made by public hospitals serving low-income clients (Chasnoff, Lantress & Barrett, 1990). The report of the first 5 years of child custody advocacy services provided by the CHICAS Project found that the children of the majority of clients had entered foster care as the result of a positive newborn drug test or a positive test in a newborn sibling (Johnston, 1994).

The most harmful CPS practice in these cases appears to be the linking of the mother's parental rights with her ability to maintain sobriety. Among CHICAS clients, terminations of parental rights and adoptions of infants in placement were attempted far more often with infants placed in foster care with strangers; where infants were placed with relatives, the mother's parental rights were less often jeopardized by her continued substance dependency, and caregivers were more likely to seek long-term foster care or guardianships for the children (Johnston, 1994). The most helpful CPS practices identified by mothers included: (1) educating mothers about timelines for meeting family reunification requirements and the consequences of failure to meet those timelines; (2) informing mothers of the greater risks of out-of-family foster care before placement and assisting them in arranging family placements; and (3) assisting mothers in entering residential, mother–child drug treatment programs.

At Arrest. Child protective services may become involved in several ways with the children of arrested parents. Workers may respond to the site of parental arrests and merely supervise the transition of care from the arrested parent to the parent-designated caregiver or arrange an immediate transfer of temporary care. These circumstances are most likely when there is another caregiver residing with the children. When such placements cannot be arranged, the children are taken into CPS custody.

When children are taken into the care of county social service agencies, they are typically placed in temporary shelters, often causing separation of siblings. All children in these circumstances will experience at least two placements. At this point, social workers are assigned to these cases to provide reasonable services to arrested parents to assist them in reunifying with their children upon release. Their work includes responsibility for contacting the arrested parent to get him or her involved in decisions about child placement, and for attempting to locate relatives with whom the child might be placed.

Social worker respondents in the ABA survey tended to view the children of arrested parents as being at far less risk than physically or sexually abused or neglected children, and exhibiting fewer behavioral or emotional problems. However, some social workers believe that parental arrest, in itself, is a form of neglect. Only 13% of the agencies surveyed had any policies specific to the plight of children thrust into the social services system because of parental arrest or incarceration.

In the Reunification Period. The ABA study (1993) found that most social service agencies prefer to place children of imprisoned parents with relatives. In cases of relative placement at the time of arrest, there is often no assessment done concerning the suitability of the caregiver. When an assessment is done, it is most likely cursory, consisting of an interview with the person to see if she or he is willing to take the child. Placements arranged after the child has been placed in a shelter and court-ordered placements generally require a more thorough evaluation of the prospective caretaker. According to ABA interviews with CPS workers, there is a severe shortage of quality foster homes, particularly for adolescents, children of color, and groups of siblings. In some instances, group homes are preferred over foster homes because CPS workers consider them to be "less intimidating than going to live in a strange home with a strange family" (ABA, 1993).

Incarcerated parents with children in foster care must depend upon CPS workers to assist them in reunifying with their children. This requires involving the parent in making a plan for reunification, and assisting the parent in meeting the requirements of that plan. Although visitation is mandated as a part of all family reunification plans, CPS workers may believe that jail or prison visits are not appropriate for children (Johnston, 1994). Even when workers allow visitation, factors such as the social worker's caseload, the availability of funds for visit transportation and housing, and the willingness of workers or foster parents to transport the children influence how often visits take place.

Arrangement of visits and all other family reunification activities necessitate written or verbal communication between CPS workers and incarcerated parents. However, Beckerman (1994) recently found that most incarcerated mothers with children in foster care received no correspondence from the CPS caseworker, and only two-thirds of these mothers received notification of their child custody hearings. In addition to failing to make efforts to assist in reunification, CPS workers may occasionally assume adversarial positions in their work with incarcerated and other offenders. More than one-third of CHICAS Project clients with children in foster care believed that their child's CPS worker had been opposed to reunification from the beginning of the case; in approximately half of that group, these circumstances could be documented by advocates (Johnston, 1994). Where workers objected to reuniting parent and child in spite of their mandated responsibility to assist in family reunification, the most common considerations were the mother's previous child welfare history and/or the mother's previous relapses into substance dependency.

Helpful CPS practices included frequent telephone communications between workers and incarcerated parents, active worker referrals and (especially drug treatment) placements for the parents, worker arrangements for transportation of children to visit the prison, and worker involvement in the parent's prerelease and reentry activities. CPS workers who are familiar with offenders, who have a thorough understanding of substance dependency, and who believe that prisoners can maintain a parental role during incarceration are best able to serve their clients well (Johnston, 1994).

Correctional Practices. When a woman is booked into county jail, she is given limited access to the telephone and then can place only collect calls, making it very difficult for her to locate her children and to arrange for their care. Jail visitation is often difficult too because many jails require mothers to be separated from their children by a glass partition and to speak using phones. Of the correctional facilities that allow children to visit, only a minority routinely allow limited contact visits (ABA, 1993). In many of the others, mother–child contact visits are allowed under special circumstances, such as a request by a relative traveling a long distance with a child, a request by CPS, or a request by a prisoner-mother who may be transferring to another facility.

Although visitation is acknowledged to be critical to a family's reunification, many factors prevent incarcerated mothers from receiving regular visits with their children. Many state departments of correction emphasize placing prisoners in institutions closest to their homes and families, but this goal is difficult to accomplish. Most prisons are located in rural areas far from the urban centers where most prisoners' family members reside. Distance from the institution is often cited as the primary reason for lack of contact between incarcerated parents and their children. This is particularly true for incarcerated mothers, who are often placed farther from their homes than their male counterparts because there are fewer prisons for women in most states. Bloom and Steinhart (1993) found that over 60% of the children of women prisoners lived over 100 miles from the mother's place of incarceration. This has serious implications in terms of visitation.

When children do visit their incarcerated parents, contact may be quite limited. For example, some prisons offer minimal visiting opportunities or have stringent rules that only allow children to visit in the company of a legal guardian. The latter restrictions are especially difficult for imprisoned mothers, since only a small percentage of their children reside with the other natural parent; the large majority of their children are in informal, family placements. While about half of all incarcerated parents of both sexes do not receive visits from their children, lack of visitation is most often due to structural barriers in the case of women prisoners (Bloom & Steinhart, 1993). Incarcerated fathers are less likely to have had a close relationship with their children prior to imprisonment, and do not receive visits largely due to their lack of ongoing relationships with their children's mothers (Hairston, 1989; Koban, 1983).

Any correctional practices that allow increased contact or communication between incarcerated parents and their children benefit these families. Basic services provided by correctional facilities include institution-wide "open" or limited contact visitation, family visits, home furlough programs, visitor transportation and hospitality services, and pay telephones within the jail or prison. More specialized services, often offered through partnerships between correctional facilities and community agencies, include the full range of programs documented elsewhere in this book, for example, prison nurseries, mother–infant and mother–child community corrections programs, and extended contact visitation programs.

Other correctional practices which are indirectly in the interest of children of incarcerated parents include release-preparation services for prisoners like job training and placement, counseling, therapeutic visitation, anger management/conflict resolution training, and drug treatment. Each of these help former prisoners to prevent, reduce, or adapt to the stresses they experience after release, and therefore benefit the children in their care.

Conclusions

Recent trends in public policy, including the development of policy in response to public misperceptions about crime, a focus on the isolated offender, and an overreliance on incarceration as a means to prevent or reduce crime, have had a significant influence on the status of children of offenders. At almost all stages of the justice process, their existence and their needs remain unrecognized. Remedies to this situation include legislation and practical applications of policy in the areas of law enforcement, sentencing, child welfare, and corrections.

Legislation can place children of offenders squarely within the public policy arena, while permitting or mandating the development of specific programs for their assistance. Sentencing reform would reduce the rate of parental incarceration, perhaps freeing funds for the development of community-based intermediate sanctions and prevention services like drug treatment. Legislation in the area of corrections has allowed the development of innovative programs to help maintain parent–child relationships. National child welfare law reform has produced circumstances that work against incarcerated parents and their children; however, state statutes have redressed some of the imbalances that occur in practice.

Changes in practical applications of public policy in the areas of law enforcement, child welfare, and corrections will have a greater immediate effect on prisoners and their children. The beneficial practices that are described in this chapter and that have been implemented in one jurisdiction can be easily implemented elsewhere in a more timely manner than changes in practice resulting from new legislation.

References

American Bar Association Center on Children and the Law. (1993). *Children on hold: What happens when their primary caretaker is arrested? Results of the national survey.* Washington, DC: Authors.

Baunach, P. J. (1982). You can't be a mother and be in prison . . . can you? Impacts of the mother–child separation. In B. R. Price & N. J. Sokoloff (Eds.), *The criminal justice system and women.* New York: Clark Boardman.

Beckerman, A. (1994). Mothers in prison: Meeting the prerequisite conditions for permanency planning. *Social Work*, 39(1):9–14.

Bloom, B., & Steinhart, D. (1993). *Why punish the children? A reappraisal of the children of incarcerated mothers in America*. San Francisco: National Council on Crime and Delinquency.

Braun, S., & Pasternak, J. (1993, February 13). A nation with peril on its mind. *Los Angeles Times*, Sec. 1A, pp. 1, 16–17.

Center for Children of Incarcerated Parents. (1991). *Data sheets on children of incarcerated parents*. Pasadena, CA: Author.

Chasnoff, I. J., Lantress, H. J. & Barrett, M. E. (1990). Prevalence of illicit drug or alcohol use in pregnancy. *New England Journal of Medicine*, 322(17):1202–1206.

Chesterfield Police Department. (1992). Memorandum on HJR 218. In *Senate Document No. 10: Addressing issues relating to children of incarcerated parents*. Richmond, VA: General Assembly of Virginia.

Daly, K. (1989). Neither conflict nor labelling nor paternalism will suffice: Intersections of race, ethnicity, gender and family in criminal court decisions. *Crime and Delinquency*, 35(1):136–168.

Federal Bureau of Investigation. (1993). *Uniform crime reports*. Washington, D.C.: U.S. Government Printing Office.

Genty, P. M. (1991). Procedural due process rights of incarcerated parents in termination of parental rights proceedings: A fifty state analysis. *Journal of Family Law*, 30(4):757–846.

Glick, R. M., & Neto, V. (1977). *National study of women's correctional programs*. Washington, D.C.: National Institute of Law Enforcement & Criminal Justice.

Hairston, C. F. (1989). Men in prison: Family characteristics and family views. *Journal of Offender Counseling, Services and Rehabilitation*, 14(1):23–30.

Holt, N., & Miller, D. (1972) *Explorations in inmate–family relationships*. Sacramento, CA: Department of Corrections.

Inter-University Consortium for Political and Social Research. (1991). *Survey of inmates in local jails, 1989*. Ann Arbor, MI: Authors.

Johnston, D. (1992). *Children of offenders*. Pasadena, CA: Center for Children of Incarcerated Parents.

Johnston, D. (1993). *Caregivers of prisoners' children*. Pasadena, CA: Center for Children of Incarcerated Parents.

Johnston, D. (1994). *Child custody issues of offenders: A preliminary report of the CHICAS Project*. Pasadena, CA: Center for Children of Incarcerated Parents.

Koban, L. (1983). Parents in prison: A comparative analysis of the effects of incarceration on the families of men and women. *Research in Law, Deviance and Social Control*, 5:171–183.

Macdonald, D. (1980). *Follow-up survey of post-release criminal behavior of participants in family reunion program*. Albany, NY: Department of Correctional Services.

McGowan, B., & Blumenthal, K. (1978). *Why punish the children?* Hackensack, NJ: National Council on Crime and Delinquency.

National Crime Survey. (1992). *Criminal victimization in the United States*. Washington, DC: U.S. Government Printing Office.

Radosh, P. F. (1988). Inmate mothers: Legislative solutions to a difficult problem. *Journal of Crime and Justice*, 11:61–68.

Reeves, M. (1929). *Training schools for delinquent girls.* New York: Russel Sage Foundation.

Smith, A. D. (1962). *Women in prison: A study in penal methods.* New York: Stevens & Sons.

Stanton, A. (1980). *When mothers go to jail.* Lexington, MA: Lexington Books.

U.S. Department of Justice. (1992). *Survey of state prison inmates, 1991* (Report No. NCJ-136949). Washington, DC: Bureau of Justice Statistics.

U.S. Department of Justice. (1993). *Prisoners in 1992* (Report No. NCJ-141874). Washington, DC: Bureau of Justice Statistics.

18
Child Welfare System Policies and the Children of Incarcerated Parents

Shirley E. Marcus

Child welfare agencies should be in the forefront of promoting children's development and support for parents who need help caring for their children. Child welfare agencies must take the initiative in promoting public policies that will lead to the reduction of the problems that cause children to need child welfare services. It means recognizing changing family life-styles, assisting parents to reconnect with informal supports, and advocating for the creation and expansion of early intervention and developmental services that can support families before a severe problem or crisis develops.

In addition to advocating for the basic supports for families, child welfare agencies need to expand their array of child welfare services for those children experiencing a crisis or requiring protective or rehabilitative support. This proactive, child-centered, family-focused approach to child welfare practice requires child welfare agencies to be increasingly involved with other community agencies and institutions that support children and their families. It calls upon child welfare agencies to marshall the support of mental and physical health care providers; employment, housing, and income support systems; correctional institutions and law enforcement agencies; recreational groups; volunteer organizations; and more. A mobilization of community resources in behalf of strengthening and preserving families will not occur by chance. Child welfare agencies should galvanize the relevant agencies in the community to work together toward the common goal of assuring a comprehensive system of service for supporting all parents in caring for their children, including incarcerated parents and their children.

The provision of any service to strengthen and preserve families with children should be based on the following values and assumptions:

- All families need support at some time, although the type and degree of support needed may vary.

- A child's development and ability to cope with life situations are enhanced by a healthy parent–child relationship and the positive functioning of the entire family unit.

- Most parents want to be successful and effective parents, and to help their children grow into healthy, fully functioning adults.

- Families are influenced by their cultural and ethnic values, as well as by the societal pressures in their community.

- Parents are likely to become better parents if they feel good about themselves and thereby can feel competent in other important areas of their lives, such as jobs, schools, and social relationships.

The Adoption Assistance and Child Welfare Act of 1980, P.L. 96-272, the culmination of years of effort on the part of advocates for children and families, mandated sweeping changes in the foster care system that were designed to rectify serious problems. One of the primary mandates of the statute is that children remain with their families wherever possible, and that families be provided with preplacement preventive services in order to keep the family intact and minimize the potential trauma of separation for the child. If the child must be placed in foster care, either because it is not possible to protect the child within the home or because the parent is unable to care for the child—as is the case when a parent is incarcerated— the federal law requires that reunification services be provided to families, and that return of the child to his or her natural parents be the primary goal of foster placement.

Family reunification is defined as the planned process of reconnecting children in out-of-home care with their families by means of a variety of services and supports for the children, their families, and their foster parents or other service providers. It aims to help each child and family to achieve and maintain, at any given time, their optional level of reconnection—from full reentry of the child into the family system to other forms of contact, such as visiting, that affirm the child's membership in the family. Family reunification should be systematically considered and planned for by the child welfare and legal systems as early as possible in a child's placement in out-of-home care. However, the effective delivery of reunification programs and services to meet the needs of incarcerated parents and children is complicated by the fact that several different bureaucratic agencies are involved in the lives of these families: a state department of corrections or a county jail system, a department of social services or public welfare, and the criminal as well as the juvenile court systems. Moreover, the availability of services and programs for incarcerated parents and their children varies depending on the political climate in the particular state or county, the sympathies of corrections and social services officials, the presence or absence of community support, and increasingly, the role of the media in shaping community attitudes toward prisoners.

All states that receive federal funding under P.L. 96-272 are required to enact legislation conforming with the federal law. Specifically, states must design and implement programs providing reunification services to families in which children are placed in foster care.

In 1993, over 430,000 children were in out-of-home care in this country. It is projected that by 1995 well over one-half million children will be in out-of-home care. Based on the 1991 Survey of State Prison Inmates:

- Male and female inmates were parents to more than 826,000 children under age 18.

- Forty-two percent of the women and 32% of the men had two or more children under age 18.

- One-fourth of female inmates reported having minor children who were living with their father, while more than half said that the children were being cared for by their grandparents. About 24% said that their children now lived with other relatives or friends.

- Ten percent of the women and 2% of the men said that their children were in a foster home, children's agency, or institution.

Over the past 2 years the Child Welfare League of America (CWLA) has sponsored the North American Kinship Care Policy and Practice Committee, with representatives from public and voluntary child welfare institutions from throughout the country. The committee worked to: (1) define kinship care and its appropriate role in child protective services; (2) develop policy recommendations to support that role; (3) develop commensurate program and practice guidelines; and (4) recommend public education and public responsibility strategies to strengthen the delivery and support of kinship care. The results of their deliberations have been presented in a report published recently by CWLA entitled *Kinship Care: A Natural Bridge* (1994a). Philosophically and practically, kinship care is a part of family preservation. When families come to the attention of public agencies, special consideration should be given to supporting the family through its kinship network. When children must be separated from their parents, whether because of the parent's incarceration or for other reasons, the extended family should be the first resource to be assessed, fitted to a plan, and supported through the array of services offered to the child. Arrangements should be selected based on a careful, culturally responsive assessment of the strengths and needs of the child and family. Services should be made available to support the kinship care provider, where possible, in her or his efforts to meet the needs of children while attending to the children's safety and the resolution of family status.

It is clear that as we explore the issue of kinship care a number of rather complicated issues surface. For example, the term *permanency* in relation to kinship parenting needs to be redefined. If the kinship network is family, and long-term kinship care is a reunification, then it also must be considered permanent. The psychological permanence and commitment that a kinship network offers must be recognized and respected. States and the federal government must be flexible, and need to recognize that the traditional forms of permanency such as adoption and guardianship, as currently structured, may not reflect the child and kin's needs and realities. To truly implement a system of kinship parenting that will optimally serve children and families, new laws and regulations, at both the state and federal level, are needed. The reason for this is simple: existing laws and regulations were designed almost entirely with nonrelative family foster care placements in mind. In kinship care cases, we are now, all too often, trying to force "square pegs into round holes." Kinship care supports family identity, connections, and roots. It acknowledges the value of continuity of culture and heritage. Kinship care enhances the child's sense of belonging and promotes connections to siblings.

The context of permanency planning for children in kinship arrangements is quite different from that of children who are being cared for by unrelated foster parents. For children within the extended family context, permanency still means security and continuity, but with a greater degree of flexibility, communication, and sharing of responsibility over time.

Several alternatives could create more positive permanency options for kinship parenting. Since guardianship does provide a means for a family member to assume parental responsibility and authority without permanently severing the parent–child bond, the provision of guardianship subsidies in appropriate cases would remove an unnecessary financial barrier to this family-sensitive option. Another possible option might be kinship adoption, which involves the permanent termination of a parent's custodial rights, while leaving in effect the parent's other rights. Kinship adoption would allow the relative caregiver to become the child's permanent legal parent, while the natural parent, although incarcerated, would retain a valued relationship with the child in a legally defined role. This would formalize and protect the emotional reality in the common case in which the kinship parent must assume the permanent parental role, but parents remain important to the child even with significant limitation.

Child welfare agencies should request courts to act in the interest of the child regarding involuntary termination of parental rights, when it has been determined that in all probability the parents will be unable to fulfill their parental responsibilities by providing their child with the security of a permanent home, but are unable or unwilling to transfer the rights of the child voluntarily. To date, there has been no comprehensive state-by-state review of statutes to determine if termination of parental rights occur more often for parents in prison, although a study by the National Black Child Development Institute (1989) suggests that a very significant number of terminations occur among this group.

There are two other rather significant issues related to kinship care: visitation and support services for the kinship family. In a recent National Council on Crime and Delinquency report (Bloom & Steinhart, 1993), mothers and children living together before arrest had an overall no-visit rate that was uncomfortably high at 46.7%, and mothers separated from their children before arrest had a disturbing no-visit rate of 72%. The main reason cited by the mothers for infrequent visitation or nonvisitation by their children was the distance between the child's residence and the correctional facility. Reluctance of the child's caretaker to let the children visit was cited as another main reason by 12% of the mothers.

Child welfare agencies must work with the correctional system to establish protocols for visitation. In most cases, it is healthy for a child to see his or her parents while incarcerated. Providers must deal with their own prejudices, biases, and fears as they confront this critical developmental issue for children. Additional funding and legislative support for children's center programs, transportation programs, and other community services are needed in order to alleviate this problem.

In terms of services to kinship families, state regulations and agency policies should specify the caseworkers' responsibility to explore extended family resources and include reference to them in the service plan. Agency policies should also appropriately provide that, when a relative wishes to help but faces difficulties in doing so, workers should develop assistance plans to enable relatives to help, rather than unnecessarily purchasing those same services from others. Transportation assistance, purchase of a bed so a child may live with a relative, or compensation for wages lost by a relative when care is provided are all services the kinship care provider may need, especially in low-income families. Providing and funding these modest services is far preferable to allowing the family to fall apart for the lack of them.

According to a recent University of California study (Barth, Berrick & Needle, 1993) that compared kinship foster homes and foster family homes, kinship families received fewer services and less time with social workers than foster care providers. Additionally, the study indicated that kin not only received fewer services, but they also received less money to care for children. The study also found that while 48% of the children in foster care with nonrelatives were receiving mental health services at the time of the study, only 28% of the children living in kinship care were receiving such assistance. From a public policy perspective, we need to ask ourselves why does the differential in practice really exist? Is the difference worker-driven, provider-driven, or a combination of the two?

However you answer the question, we know that children of color are disproportionately represented in all of the child-serving systems. A disproportionate number of incarcerated mothers are minority women. Today, African-American and Latino women comprise over half of the approximately 90,000 women incarcerated in the United States. We need to examine the program philosophies, values, and attitudes underlying the delivery of all services, and especially services to children with incarcerated parents, to ensure that they are culturally sensitive. A series of simple questions can be asked: Why are we investing in building new prisons for women versus providing more of an investment in family support or job education? What assumptions do we make about incarcerated parents? Do we routinely involve the incarcerated parent while services are being planned for the child? Are parents truly considered partners in our service efforts? Do offenders view us as helpers in their struggle to provide for their child? Do offenders see us as we see ourselves? Are we honoring the child's needs to have a connection with his or her parent? Are we giving children voices, allowing them to express anger, grief, and embarrassment regarding parental incarceration? These are but a few of the critical questions we must ask our respective systems if we are to go about the business of making services to incarcerated parents and their children "family-friendly." We must help prisons begin to view inmates differently and encourage collaboration between child welfare and correctional systems. We must work to make the separation of parent and child less separate.

References

Barry, E. (1985). Reunification difficult for incarcerated parents and their children. *Youth Law News*, 6(4):14–16.

Barth, R., Berrick, J. & Needle, B. (1993). A comparison of kinship foster homes and family foster homes. In J. D. Barth, J. D. Berrick & N. Gilbert (Eds), *Child welfare research review*. New York: Columbia University Press.

Bloom, B., & Steinhart, D. (1993). *Why punish the children?* San Francisco: National Council on Crime and Delinquency.

Child Welfare League of America. (1974). *Standards for foster family services*. Washington, DC: Author.

Child Welfare League of America. (1988). *Standards for adoption services*. Washington, DC: Author.

Child Welfare League of America. (1994a). *Kinship care: A natural bridge*. Washington, DC: Author.

Child Welfare League of America. (1994b). *Standards for services to strengthen and preserve families with children*. Washington, DC: Author.

National Black Child Development Institute. (1989). *Who will care when parents can't?* A study of black children in foster care. Washington, DC: Authors.

Nelson, J. (1994, May). Doing time: Our women in prison. *ESSENCE Magazine*, pp. 83–86, 158–159.

Warsh, R., Maluccio, A. & Pine, B. (1994). *Teaching family reunification*. Washington, DC: Child Welfare League of America.

U.S. Department of Justice. (1993). *Survey of state prison inmates* (Report No. NCJ-136949). Washington, DC: Bureau of Justice Statistics.

19

Advocacy Efforts on Behalf of the Children of Incarcerated Parents

Peter Breen

As the United States heads into the 21st century, we are confronted with a wide array of emerging population groups that will challenge the relevance and viability of the existing health and social service systems and structures. One of these emerging at-risk populations is the children of incarcerated parents who are serving time in local, state, and federal institutions across the United States. Until recently, knowledge about these children and the issues that confront them has been marginal and anecdotal at best. But what we do know is that they find themselves in a life situation about which they have no say.

Very little attention has been paid to the methods and the cost of methods for beginning to address the needs of these children. In 1991 the National Commission of Children, established under Public Law 100–203, published *Beyond Rhetoric: A New American Agenda for Children and Families*. Better known as the Rockefeller Report, this document sets forth major issues confronting America's families and children. The commission's task was to "serve as a forum on behalf of the children of the nation." The report, 520 pages in length, recounts the testimony, discussions, and recommendations arising from a series of field hearings, town meetings, and roundtables held across the country over the period October 1990 to October 1991. The report has been characterized as the "blueprint" for strengthening families and promoting healthy development of all the nation's children.

However, the 1,500,000 children of incarcerated parents were not even casually mentioned in this comprehensive document. Direct references were made to the fact that children of single-parent families have a tough time growing up on our mean streets. Gangs and gang activity were discussed as issues that need to be addressed in order for our nation's children to grow up as productive citizens. Yet the children of prisoners who during incarceration of a parent (1) reside in a single-parent family, (2) suffer severe economic deprivation, (3) tend to reside within gang- and crime-

292

dominated social environs, and (4) exhibit incipient behavior disorders, are not recognized or acknowledged as an at-risk group.

Why are these children at risk? There are a number of conditions, some of them interrelated, that place the child of an incarcerated person at risk. It is useful to examine these conditions and, to the extent possible, their underlying causes. Kemper and Rivara (1993) reported on the characteristics of incarcerated parents and their criminal behavior. They concluded that the impact on the child of an incarcerated parent is not short term and cited a longitudinal study reported in St. Louis that showed that arrested parents tended to have arrested children and that the records of the parents and their children were similar. Additionally, the authors cite a series of studies that suggest a possible high-risk health status of the children of incarcerated parents. Children who suffer the loss of a parent to prison experience multiple dangers and losses.

McGowen and Blumenthal (1978) reported that the children of female prisoners experience emotional, psychological, and physical problems. Behavioral problems included a marked decline in school performance accompanied by aggressive and antisocial acting out. Bloom and Steinhart (1993) note that the criminal justice system deals almost exclusively with the convicted parent, while generally ignoring the children. The incarceration of a parent leads to severe disruption in the child's life and often begins a process that includes multiple foster care placements, sibling separation, and the ultimate dissolution of the child's family support system. The cost to the child and his or her family are just beginning when the custodial parent is arrested. What is the cost to society?

Children of Incarcerated Parents and Associated Welfare Cost

In 1992 Centerforce, the network of California state prison visitor hospitality centers, undertook a study of welfare-related costs associated with the care of children of incarcerated mothers in California's state prisons. During the study inquiries were made of both the State Department of Social Services and the Department of Corrections to determine from their records the numbers of children impacted by parental absence due to incarceration in the states prisons. Local inquiries of California's 58 counties were not considered due to the fact that many county welfare departments or sheriffs offices do not keep computerized records.

Unfortunately, neither state department could shed any light on either the numbers or the costs that might be involved in this issue. County welfare departments no longer track the reasons for a child's entry into their system. Verification of parental absence from the home is sufficient to start the flow of monies needed for AFDC, foster care, or institutional payments under Public Law 96–272.

Table 19.1

Estimated Social Service Costs* for Children of Women in California Prisons

Placement	% of Children[1]	Estimated No. of Children	% Receiving AFDC[2] or Foster Care Funds	Monthly Cost per Child[3]	Statewide Monthly Cost	Statewide Annual Cost
Grandparents	53.0	5,463	75%[2]	$ 535	$2,191,895	$26,302,740
Other relatives or friends	25.0	2,577	75%[2]	535	1,034,155	12,409,860
Foster families	9.0	927	100%	540	500,580	6,006,960
Group homes	1.6	164	100%	2,765	453,460	5,441,520
Other placements	11.4	1,272	75%[2]	535	510,390	6,124,680
Totals	100.0	10,403			$4,690,480	$56,285,760

*Excluding Medi-Cal, local social service department costs, shelter care, juvenile court costs.

Calculation of Population Size

~There are approximately 6000 female inmates in California state prisons (CA Department of Corrections, 1993).

~Approximately 75% of women prisoners have dependent children (McGowan & Blumenthal, 1978; Stanton, 1980).

~The US Department of Justice (1991) estimates the number of dependent children per imprisoned mother as:

	# of children
31% of women have one child	1395
28% of women have two children	2520
29% have three or four children	3915
8.5% have five or six children	1912
2.1% have seven or more children	661
TOTAL	10,403

1 USDJ (1991)

2 Henriques (1982); Stanton (1980)

3 California State Department of Social Services (1990)

Table 19.2
Estimated U.S. Foster Care Costs for Children of Women Prisoners

Women Prisoners in the US, 12/31/91[1]

Local jails	39,501
State and federal prisons	47,583
Total	87,084

Incarcerated Mothers of Dependent Children in the United States, 1986[2]

67.5% of 87,084	58,781

Number of Children of Female Prisoners in the United States, 1986[2]

# of children	% of mothers	# Children
Mothers with 1 child	31.7	18,633
Mothers with 2 children	28.7	33,740
Mothers with 3 children	24.1	51,315
Total		103,688

Children of Women Prisoners in Foster or Institutional Care[2]

10.5% of 103,688	10,887

Estimated Costs

Cost of care per child per month	$300
Overhead costs (courts, supervision, etc.) per months	300
Total cost per month	$600
ANNUAL COSTS	$ 7,386,400
10,887 children × $600/month × 12 months/year)	

[1]USDJ, 1991a.
[2]USDJ, 1991b.

Accordingly, the author conducted an informal survey in several local school districts in northern California. It was found that, in preparation for entering into classroom instruction as a certified elementary teacher, no courses, subcourses, lectures, or discussions regarding these issues are formally conducted. Although designed to strengthen families through family maintenance, preservation activities, reunification, and permanent planning services, the social services and other "helping professions" have consistently, if unintentionally, overlooked children of offenders.

The estimated tax dollar costs of providing Aid to Families with Dependent Children [AFDC] and foster care funds for children of women in California state prisons exceeds $56 million each year (see Table 19.1). Excluding AFDC, the annual US costs for the over 10,500 children currently in foster family or group care due to maternal incarceration are approximately $78 million (see Table 19.2). When welfare costs are included, estimated annual expenditures for all children of incarcerated mothers in the US may approach half a billion dollars.

The Centerforce Approach to the Problem

The evidence is compelling: little or nothing has been done at the state or local level to coordinate the services for this growing, but hidden population of children. To bring the children's agenda to an open public forum, the Centerforce Board of Directors developed a legislative initiative that was intended to accomplish two goals:

1. The children of incarcerated parents would be acknowledged as being "at risk" in order to make them eligible for various programs.
2. All state departments working with children's issues would be required to recognize the special needs of these children.

The initiative was purposely kept simple and without any direct costs to any state agency. The proposed legislation was approved by the board and presented to the late assemblyman William Filante, M.D., Centerforce's legislative representative in the state assembly. The assemblyman agreed with the initiative and was joined by Assemblyman John Vasconcellos and State Senator Milton Marks in introducing it as Assembly Concurrent Resolution No. 38 (ACR38) on March 19, 1991.

The resolution, most likely because it dealt with the issues of at-risk children and involved no new costs, moved quickly through both houses of the legislature, and was adopted by the assembly on June 5, 1991, and by the Senate on August 10, 1991. The final resolution was signed by the secretary of state in early September 1991. During its quick passage through both chambers, an amendment was added that directed the Assembly Office of Research to "conduct a comprehensive study of the problems faced by and associated with children of incarcerated parents," and to report its findings to the legislature. In addition to recognizing the at-risk nature of the children, the resolution required the "special consideration of each state agency and department in the development of programs serving children such as child welfare, public assistance, mental health, medical, and educational programs." Copies of the resolution were transmitted to all the involved state agency secretaries and appointed directors.

In response to the legislation, the Assembly Office of Research conducted a review of the literature and a survey of existing service providers to assess the problems and issues of the children of incarcerated parents. The office conducted no primary research into the issues. The results of the Assembly Office of Research study required by the resolution were released in May 1992 (Lawhorn, 1992). The conclusions are printed here in their entirety:

> Data is inadequate to determine the number, identity, and status of children of incarcerated parents. At the present time, none of the state agencies in California collects this information.

We did not find any significant large-scale studies conducted during the past decade on the effects of incarceration on children. The smaller studies involve few children and are not reflective of California's diverse population. Needs may vary according to ethnic populations. The studies also do not consider the effects of today's extensive drug use among female offenders. Without better data, it is impossible to accurately identify these children or the services they may need.

A variety of programs scattered throughout California appears to provide needed services to a small number of children. The services provided by these programs, however, appear fragmented and limited in scope. The effectiveness of the programs cannot be determined without basic data on needs and objective program evaluations.

Several comprehensive studies are currently gathering much of the needed information of children of incarcerated parents. Until these studies are completed, any recommendations of services to children of incarcerated parents are premature.

Clearly, the study did not explore new ground nor did it provide new information. The children's advocates who worked long and hard to move the resolution through the legislature were disappointed by the Office of Research study results. The study reiterated only what was already known throughout the children's services community. Unfortunately, Assemblyman Filante, a particularly strong advocate of children, died during the congressional campaign in 1992, and could not fulfill the commitment he had made to move the children's agenda to national prominence.

Advocacy Efforts for Children of Incarcerated Parents

Advocacy by its very nature is not a one-time type of activity. Change comes very slowly, especially when it concerns a population of children living in the dark shadow of the wave of "Get Tough on Crime" legislation sweeping across the country today. Most advocates do not believe that the current trend of harsh punishment is directed toward the families and children of incarcerated parents. The children are simply forgotten or viewed as insignificant.

Children's advocates are working to increase awareness of the issues of children of incarcerated parents. Acknowledgment of these children will lead to alternatives that may reduce the risk of this current generation of prisoners' children becoming the next generation of prisoners.

California ACR38 has been redrafted and is under review by several members of the U.S. Congress and a national children's organization. The advocates who initiated the resolution plan to introduce follow-up legislation. We are cheered by similar efforts in Pennsylvania and Illinois, and by the greater success of a statewide initiative in the Commonwealth of Virginia.

The lives of many children have been clouded with self-doubt, despair, and great loss due to parental incarceration. Although progress seems slow, change is taking place on many levels throughout the country. Through these and other advocacy efforts, children of incarcerated parents may soon take a place on our national children's policy agenda.

References

Bloom, B., & Steinhart, D. (1993). *Why punish the children? A reappraisal of the children of incarcerated mothers in America.* San Francisco: National Council on Crime and Delinquency.

California Department of Corrections (1993). *Annual Report.* Sacramento: Authors.

California Department of Social Services. (1991, September). *Report.* Sacramento: Authors.

Henriques, Z.W. (1982). *Imprisoned women and their children.* Washington, D.C.: University Press of America.

Kemper, K., & Rivara, J. (1993). Parents in jail. *Pediatrics*, 92:261–264.

Lawhorn, S. (1992). *Children of incarcerated parents: A report to the legislature pursuant to ACR 38.* Resolution Chpater 89, Statutes of 1991, Filante. Sacramento: California Assembly Office of Research.

McGowan, B., & Blumenthal, K. (1978). *Why punish the children?* Hackensack, NJ: National Council on Crime and Delinquency.

National Commission on Children. (1991). *Beyond rhetoric: A new American agenda for children and families.* Washington, D.C.: Authors.

Stanton, A. (1980). *When mothers go to jail.* Boston, Massachusetts: Lexington Books.

U.S. Department of Justice. (1991a). *Correctional populations in the United States.* Report No. NCJ142729. Washington, D.C.: Bureau of Justice Statistics.

U.S. Department of Justice. (1991b). *Women in prison.* Report No. NCJ127991. Washington, D.C.: Bureau of Justice Statistics.

20
Alternatives to Women's Incarceration

Meda Chesney-Lind
Russ Immarigeon

In just the last decade the number of women imprisoned in the United States has tripled. Now, on any given day, over 80,000 women are locked up in American jails and prisons (U.S. Department of Justice [USDJ], 1991a, 1991b). In addition, percentage increases in the number of women incarcerated have surpassed male rates of increase for every year in the 1980s.

As a result of this surge in women's imprisonment, our country has gone on a building binge where women's prisons are concerned. Prison historian Nicole Hahn Rafter (1990) observes that between 1930 and 1950 roughly two or three prisons were built or created for women each decade. In the 1960s, the pace of prison construction picked up slightly with seven units opening, largely in southern and western states. During the 1970s, 17 prisons opened, including units in states such as Rhode Island and Vermont that once relied on transferring women prisoners out of state. In the 1980s, 34 women's units or prisons were established, a number 10 times larger than the figures for earlier decades.

Was this the only response possible? Are we confronting a women's crime wave so serious that building new women's prisons is our only alternative? A look at the pattern of women's arrests provides little evidence of this.

The Character of Women's Crime

In 1980 there were 12,331 women in our nation's prisons. By 1990 that number had grown to 43,845, an increase of 256% (USDJ, 1991, p. 1). By contrast, total arrests of women (which might be seen as a measure of women's criminal activity) increased by only 60% during the last decade.

Arrests of women for Part One offenses (including murder, rape, aggravated assault, robbery, burglary, larceny-theft, motor vehicle theft, and arson) increased by about 46% during the same time period (Federal Bureau of Investigation, 1991). While these trends in women's crime may appear to be serious, it should be noted that most of the increase in women's arrests is accounted for by more arrests of women for nonviolent property offenses such as shoplifting, check forgery, and welfare fraud, as well as for substance abuse offenses such as driving under the influence of alcohol and possession or sale of illegal drugs.

Looking at these same Part One Offenses differently, women's share of these arrests (as a proportion of all those arrested for this offense) rose from 21 to 23% over the last decade—hardly anything to get excited about. Women's share of arrests for serious violent offenses moved from 10.0 to 11.3% during the same decade, displaying, if anything, the remarkable stability of women's offending (Federal Bureau of Investigation, 1991). Clearly, dramatic increases in women's imprisonment cannot be laid at the door of radical changes in the volume and character of women's crime.

This becomes even more obvious if we look at the characteristics of women in U.S. prisons. The American Correctional Association (ACA) recently conducted a national survey of imprisoned women in the United States and found that overwhelmingly they were young, economically marginalized, women of color, and mothers of children with serious drug problems; the majority had experienced one or more types of abuse (Task Force on the Female Offender, 1990).

Most of these women were first imprisoned for larceny-theft or drug offenses. At the time of the survey, they were serving time for drug offenses, murder, larceny-theft, and robbery. While some of these offenses sound serious they, like all behavior, are heavily gendered. Research indicates, for example, that of women convicted of murder or manslaughter, many had killed husbands or boyfriends who repeatedly and violently abused them. In New York, for example, of the women committed to the state's prisons for homicide in 1986, 49% had been the victims of abuse at some point in their lives and 59% of the women who killed someone close to them were being abused at the time of the offense. For half of the women committed for homicide, it was their first and only offense (Huling, 1991).

Other recent figures suggest even more strongly that the "war on drugs" has translated into a war on women. In California, for example, a comparison of the institutional populations of women for the years 1984 and 1989 shows that the proportion of women incarcerated for violent offenses actually fell from 32.7 to 23.9% in that 5-year period. By contrast, the number of women incarcerated for drug offenses climbed from 17.9 to 37.9%. Looking more closely at these numbers reveals that over a third (37%) of these women in California prisons were incarcerated simply for possession of drugs or for marijuana offenses. If the offense category "possession for sale" is included, the figure jumps to 64.1% (California Prisoners and Parolees, 1990). Again, these figures do not indicate large numbers of women in prison for high-level drug trafficking.

The war on drugs, coupled with the development of new technologies for determining drug use (e.g., urinalysis), plays another less obvious role in increasing women's imprisonment. In California, of the over 6,000 women incarcerated in 1990, nearly half (48%) were imprisoned due to parole violations (Bachler, Bedrick, Brigham, Miller, Minnick, et. al., 1992). This figure clearly helped that state earn the dubious distinction of having over 100,000 people in prison, giving it one of the highest incarceration rates in the world (Garnett & Schiraldi, 1991). Many of these returns were the result of failed urinalysis (Garnett, 1991).

The profiles of women under lock and key suggest that women's crime has not gotten more serious. Instead, the whole system is now "tougher" on all offenses, including those that women have traditionally committed. Basically, we are now imprisoning women who, in past years, would have received nonincarceratory sentences.

Is this our only choice? Definitely not. Every dollar spent locking up women could be better spent on services that would prevent women from resorting to crime and violence. These are not simply hypothetical trade-offs. New York state, for example, has just spent $180,000 per bed to add 1,394 new prison spaces for women. Yet 12,433 women and children in that state were denied needed shelter in 1990 and nearly three-quarters of these denials were because of lack of space (Huling, 1991).

In our view, we must declare a moratorium on the construction of women's prisons immediately, and we must begin to decarcerate those women who are currently in prison. Such a moratorium is in the best interests of women and, since so many are mothers, their children too. Clearly, such a moratorium is also in the best interests of the taxpayers. In order for the decarceration of women to begin, however, states must begin to undertake new initiatives directed toward the needs of women in prison.

Assessments of the Characteristics and Needs of Women Offenders

States need to conduct quick investigations of the type of women they have in their prisons and the special needs of these groups. Studies in Connecticut, Delaware, Illinois, Maryland, Massachusetts, and New Jersey have reviewed the characteristics and treatment of female prisoners as they begin to identify and address the specific circumstances and needs of imprisoned women (Avallone & Talisano, 1989; Miller, 1990; Herr, 1988).

The Connecticut Correctional Institution at Niantic, for example, is the state's only women's prison, and it has been overcrowded throughout the 1980s. For this reason, it has also been the subject of a lawsuit by the Connecticut Civil Liberties Union for much of this period. Nonetheless, the Governor's Task Force on Jail and Prison Overcrowding, established in

1981 to define and implement programs and policies to reduce correctional crowding, has failed, in nine annual reports, to specifically address alternatives for female offenders.

Two noncorrectional groups have filled this void. In 1985 a task force formed as part of a legal settlement with the state's Department of Corrections identified the need to explore alternatives to confinement for women imprisoned for victimless and nonviolent crimes. In 1989 a report prepared by the state's Permanent Commission on the Status of Women found that less than 10% of imprisoned women were incarcerated for violent offenses (Avallone & Talisano, 1989). Most imprisoned women were confined for probation violations, failure to appear in court, prostitution, and operating a vehicle under suspended license or registration. The commission also found that communities had severely limited services designed for women offenders' special needs and circumstances and that neither the state's Bail Commission nor its Office of Adult Probation had specialized units for female offenders.

Studies like those done by women's groups in Connecticut have recommended that a comprehensive range of pretrial, sentencing, residential, and outpatient services could reduce the number of incarcerated women. These options include: a specialized bail unit; expanded nonincarcerative options for women; the reclassification of offenses such as prostitution and the possession of small amounts of marijuana; supervised home release for women who have a history of being physically or sexually abused and who were imprisoned for violent behavior; and increased drug and alcohol counseling and treatment services.

In Illinois, the Dwight Correctional Center, the state's only women's prison, has been overcrowded throughout the 1980s, despite the 1988 transfer of 72 women to a men's facility where women now comprise 9% of the total population. Women transferred to the men's facility report that they have lost good time for behavior that would have been considered a minor rule violation when they were incarcerated at Dwight. They have also had difficulty continuing vocational programs begun at Dwight, and have been frustrated by excess unscheduled and unstructured free time. One consequence of the inadequately planned mixing of male and female correctional populations, however, was that 12 pregnancies occurred within 10 months of the transfer.

The Citizens' Assembly, a bipartisan legislative agency, supported a study of the feasibility of sentencing program alternatives for women offenders. They found that over 80% of incarcerated women in the state are mothers and that 82.7% of them are single-parent heads-of-household. Most of the women at Dwight are from Chicago, 80 miles away, and transportation services between the two places is inadequate. Forty-three percent of the women housed at Dwight are classified as minimum security (Citizens' Council on Women, 1986, 1987).

In this context, the Citizens Assembly's Citizen Council on Women concluded the following: the forced separation of women prisoners from their children causes long-lasting and severe psychological harm; county jails and work release programs now being used to alleviate prison crowding merely complicate the parent–child reunification process; and community-based alternative sentencing programs are cost-effective and result in less recidivism than imprisonment.

A screening process can identify offenders facing a strong likelihood of being imprisoned. Courts and community programs can use standard prison risk instruments based on such variables as current charges, prior convictions, and length of time spent in jail awaiting trial to identify the women who are probably going to receive prison sentences. In New York, for example, one community service program combines the use of a research-based profile of jail-bound offenders with the in-court assessments of project staff to identify possible clients (McDonald, 1986). In North Carolina, alternative programs use a prison risk score sheet, based on a cross-sectional study of sentenced felons in the state, to identify offenders who have a strong probability of being convicted and sentenced to an active prison term (Wallace & Clarke 1984).

Advocates—probation officers, community case planners, and others—can then prepare alternative sentencing plans that make use of community service, individual or group counseling, day care provisions, educational opportunities, employment, restitution, and/or third-party supervision. Central to the success of these plans is an assessment of these women's needs, monitoring of their progress, and aftercare support services.

Most importantly, states need to reduce the number of imprisoned women as a matter of public policy. Delaware, for instance, is currently providing a good example of what a state might do to reduce its use of imprisonment for women offenders. The Women's Correctional Institution in Claymont, Delaware, has been overcrowded with both pretrial and sentenced women. The prison's capacity was 66 prisoners when it opened in 1975. This number was expanded to 90 several years later. Nonetheless, the prison housed an average of 145 women during 1988. The women's prison population increased by 39% between 1986 and 1988.

In 1988 the National Center on Institutions and Alternatives (NCIA) developed a profile of women incarcerated in the state and made specific recommendations to reduce the number imprisoned, including the use of empty work-release beds, creation of additional work-release beds, immediate classification of all women prisoners serving sentences of less than 1 year, increased pretrial staff to supervise women in the community, and more residential drug treatment space (Hayes, 1989; Roche, 1989).

NCIA also recommended establishing a unit within the state's probation and parole agencies that would be assigned smaller caseloads and be trained in the areas of most immediate concern to most female offenders, for example, obtaining child support and AFDC benefits, identifying women's shelters and family violence counseling, and accessing the appropriate vocational, educational, and other special services. This unit could prepare release plans that address the specific problems of female offenders.

Corrections policymakers in Delaware reviewed these recommendations and asked NCIA to prepare release plans for women currently held at the Women's Correctional Institution. NCIA interviewed approximately six women prisoners one day and prepared release plans for them the following day. This brief, labor-intensive process was coordinated with and approved by classification and release review committees located at the women's prison. The expeditious release of a significant number of female prisoners initiated a process designed to reduce the state female prisoner population according to NCIA's recommendation that no more than 80 women required incarceration.

Later, the governor's office in Delaware organized a one-day meeting of employment, mental health, substance abuse, and social service providers in the state to encourage the development of proposals to provide alternatives to incarceration for women in conflict with the law. Finally, women prisoners were again surveyed to identify what they felt were their most compelling needs. Issues facing women returning to the community include the need for work, a lack of adequate housing, the temptation of returning to substance abuse, and adjusting to a changed community.

Delaware currently contracts with Corrections Alternatives and Concepts, Inc., a private nonprofit agency, to purchase services as an alternative to confinement for women who have violated community supervision requirements. The program uses a simple referral process. A project coordinator consults with probation and parole agents who have clients facing incarceration. Together, they establish elements of a plan that is appropriate for the particular offender. Aspects of this plan depend on level of risk, areas of need, and the cost and availability of services. The coordinator then contacts the community service provider about what type of services are needed and how they will be funded. This valuable program relies on already existing services, although new interventions can be developed where necessary.

In essence, these state initiatives emphasize the role that can be played by the construction of a quick profile of women offenders and their needs in most state prison systems; this work, though, needs to be complemented by the creation of a political and social climate receptive to the decarceration of women. A key component of this task is to publicize the relatively low risk associated with the release of women offenders and the clear value to their children of such a release. Women's imprisonment stands in stark contrast to most widely accepted reasons for incarcerating anyone, since female offenders overwhelmingly commit crimes that, while unacceptable, pose little threat to the physical safety of the community at large (see American Correctional Association, 1986; Milgram, 1981).

Moreover, if released, women offenders are less likely than their male counterparts to recidivate. A Wisconsin study, for example, observed women for 2 years after their release from the women's prison at Tay-cheedah (Wagner, 1986). Few of these women had those personal or criminal history characteristics associated with a high risk of criminal behavior. They were found 44% less likely than male releasees to commit further criminal offenses, and they were also found to be one-third less likely to commit a serious, person-related offense if they did recidivate. In New York, another study found that women prisoners had a substantially lower rate of being returned to prison (16.9%) than male prisoners (37.3%) (McDermott, 1985).

Most imprisoned women are mired in serious economic, medical, mental health, and social difficulties that are often overlooked and frequently intensified when women are incarcerated (Pollock-Byrne, 1990; Rafter, 1990). Generally, prisons have failed to address women's specific needs, and they have failed to provide women with the same level of programs and services they make available to male prisoners.

Community-based programs are better suited to meet women offenders' diverse needs, and these services are more effective than incapacitation in enabling women to lead law-abiding lives in the community (DeJesus & Gibney, 1988; McDonald, 1986). In Pennsylvania, for example, the Program for Women Offenders found that its services reduce the recidivism of women who complete its program. In 1981 a random sampling of more than 1,000 clients found an extraordinarily low 3.2% rate of recidivism. In 1988 another random sample study found a rate of recidivism—17.7%— that was higher but nonetheless far below recidivism rates found in studies of other interventions with male offenders.

Creation of Community-Based Resources

For decarceration to really succeed, states must begin now to support existing community-based resources for women and to create new ones where none now exist. Fortunately, there are a few models of how this process should occur. The Georgia Department of Corrections established a planning division for female offenders in the late 1970s. Soon, a continuum of programs stressing economic independence was designed to take a balanced approach toward multidimensional problems faced by women offenders. Several years later, the Minnesota Department of Corrections also set up a planning division responsible for developing programs based on the special needs of women offenders.

Unfortunately, such systemic planning is rare. More typical is the lack of attention given women offenders by most policy and planning groups. In the 1980s, for instance, task forces in more than 20 states forged recommendations to reduce prison overcrowding. Only four of these states made recommendations specifically for incarcerated females. Three states focused on expanding prison space for women or the use of cocorrectional institutions. Only one state suggested the use of more halfway houses for women. Finally, even where planning has been done, incarcerative policies may still dominate. Georgia's continuum of programs has not been fully implemented, and in Minnesota a second facility for women prisoners has been opened at Moose Lake State Hospital to eliminate the overcrowding at the state's Correctional Facility at Shakopee.

Recent public opinion polls show that Americans support rehabilitative and nonincarcerative sanctions for nonviolent offenders (see Immarigeon & Chesney-Lind, 1986; Dable, 1987). Against this backdrop, the deincarceration of large numbers of women prisoners should be an attainable goal. But is this fair? Is focusing so exclusively the need to deincarcerate women unfair to male inmates, many of whom could also benefit from community-based programs? There are two ways in which to respond to this question. First, as we have seen, women are especially appropriate for community-based programs because they are disproportionately incarcerated for nonviolent offenses. Second, despite the fact that women prisoners are clearly the best candidates for alternatives to incarceration, few states faced with overcrowding in their facilities has focused directly on their women inmates. Hence, a specific focus on this neglected population is long overdue and may provide a model for deincarceration that could ultimately benefit male prisoners too. This approach also addresses the needs of the greatest number of children of prisoners who have been separated from their primary caregiving parent.

Having said this, halting the rush to build new women's prisons will not be easy. Many women's prisons are makeshift and overcrowded, and some are under court order to improve conditions. Those who favor alternatives to women's imprisonment must recognize that careful planning is now an essential ingredient in any systematic effort to reduce the female prison population. Women prisoners are no longer few in number, and, as a consequence, existing community-based resources (e.g., drug treatment programs) will need to be expanded to accommodate larger numbers of women. In addition, states and local communities must develop new nonincarcerative pretrial and sentencing options for women who are otherwise likely to receive a jail or prison term.

The growth in women's prison populations has been dramatic. To date, most correctional leaders have responded to this crisis by attempting to build their way out of it. This chapter argues that there is another option, and that the money currently being allocated to build cells could instead be diverted to support alternatives to women's incarceration. Overcrowding and overuse of women's prisons can be avoided by planning creatively for reduced reliance on imprisonment for women offenders. Practitioners working with women offenders have advanced several recommendations that should guide such an approach, including:

- Criminal justice officials need to learn more about the characteristics of women who are on probation or parole as well as those who are imprisoned. Are probation and parole agencies doing all they can to divert women from incarceration? Are the services of these agencies specific enough for the different types of interventions women need to lead law-abiding lives?
- Jurisdictions need to identify women who will likely be imprisoned so community resources can be marshaled to address their needs. Few jurisdictions use formal methods to target this population.
- Criminal sanctions for women should be based on the least restrictive alternative consistent with public safety. Women offenders recidivate at a much lower rate than men offenders. Studies indicate that women are more likely to recidivate when support services are lacking in the community. Women can be safely diverted or released from confinement when these services are made available.
- Criminal sanctions should directly address social and economic problems faced by women offenders. Intermediate sanctions such as home confinement and intensive supervision can be useful if they provide direct services to women in need. They are less likely to be successful, however, if they are used primarily as a means of discipline or surveillance. Boot camps and electronic monitoring, for instance, may not be as constructive for women as other forms of intervention.
- Community resources should be better coordinated and used more routinely in fashioning sanctions for women offenders. While programs that can successfully divert women from dysfunctional behavior often can be established more easily within the community, women frequently must go from agency to agency to have their needs addressed. This can be counterproductive for women trying to rebuild their lives. Recognizing how disruptive this can be, several years ago the New Jersey Association on Corrections initiated a regular series of meetings for local service providers so that they could coordinate their efforts to help women being released from jail or prison. In many cases, too, programs that can successfully divert women from dysfunctional behavior can be more easily established within the community.

The dramatic increases in women's imprisonment seen in the last decade are likely to continue unless meaningful alternative programs are used more widely in place of confinement. Although they have grown significantly in recent years, the populations of women's prisons are still sufficiently small that a well-planned and coordinated effort is likely to show meaningful results. In the process, we may also learn more about how to develop cost-effective and humane methods of reducing our reliance on imprisoning men.

References

American Correctional Association. (1986). *Public policy for corrections: A handbook for decision-makers.* College Park, MD: Author.

Arnold, R. (1991). Processes of victimization and criminalization of black women. In M. Baca Zinn & B. Thornton Dill (Eds.), *Women of color in American society.* Philadelphia: Temple University Press.

Avallone, A. V., & Talisano, R. D. (1989). *Task Force on Women, Children, and the Criminal Justice System: Executive summary/final report and recommendations.* Hartford, CT: Permanent Commission on the Status of Women.

Bachler, K., Bedrick, B., Brigham, T., Miller, J., Minnick, L., et. al. (1992). *Come into the sun: Findings and recommendations on the needs of girls and women in the justice system.* San Francisco: Delinquency Prevention Commission and Commission on the Status of Women.

Citizens' Council on Women. (1987). *Annual report, 1986.* Springfield, IL.: Citizens' Assembly.

Citizens' Council on Women. (1988). *Annual report, 1987.* Springfield, IL.: Citizens' Assembly.

Dable, J. (1987). *Crime and punishment: The public's view.* New York: Public Agenda Foundation.

DeJesus, A., & Gibney, W. D. (1988). *The case for expanding work release for women.* New York: Prisoners Legal Services of New York.

Federal Bureau of Investigation. (1991). *Uniform crime reports 1990.* Washington DC: U.S. Department of Justice.

Garnett, R., & Schiraldi, V. (1991). *Concrete and crowds: 100,000 prisoners of the state.* San Francisco: Center on Juvenile and Criminal Justice.

Hayes, L. M., et al. (1989). *The female offender in Delaware: Population analysis and assessment.* Alexandria, VA: National Center on Institutions and Alternatives.

Herr, K., et al. (1988). *Services for women offenders in Massachusetts: A report of the Advisory Group on Female Offenders.* Boston: Executive Office of Human Services.

Huling, T. (1991). *Breaking the silence.* New York: Correctional Association of New York.

Immarigeon, R. (1986, Fall). Surveys reveal broad support for alternative sentencing. *National Prison Project Journal,* pp. 1–4.

Immarigeon, R., & Chesney-Lind, M. (1992). *Women's prisons: Overcrowded and overused.* San Francisco: National Council on Crime and Delinquency.

McDermott, M. J. (1985). *Female offenders in New York State.* Albany: New York State Division of Criminal Justice Services.

McDonald, D. C. (1986). *Punishment without walls.* New Brunswick, NJ: Rutgers University Press.

Milgram, R. B. (1981). *Women, families and prison.* Raleigh, NC: Governor's Advocacy Council on Children and Youth.

Miller, M. L. (1990). *Perceptions of available and needed programs by female Offenders in Delaware.* Delaware Council on Crime and Justice.

Pollock-Byrne, J. (1990). *Women, prison, and crime.* Pacific Grove, CA: Brooks/ Cole. Prison and Jail Crowding Commission. (1989). *Prison and jail overcrowding: A report to the governor and legislature.* Hartford, CT: Office of Policy and Management.

Rafter, N. H. (1990). *Partial justice: Women, prisons and social control.* New Brunswick, NJ: Transaction Books.

Roche, T. J. (1989). *Addendum to NCIA's Report on the Female Offender in Delaware.* Alexandria, VA: National Center on Institutions and Alternatives.

Task Force on the Female Offender. (1990). *The female offender: What does the future hold?* Washington, DC: American Correctional Association.

U.S. Department of Justice. (1991a). *Jail inmates in 1990* (Report No. NCJ-129756). Washington, DC: Bureau of Justice Statistics.

U.S. Department of Justice. (1991b). *Prisoners in 1990* (Report No. NCJ-129198). Washington, DC: Bureau of Justice Statistics.

Wagner, D. (1986). *Women in prison: How much community risk?* Madison: Wisconsin Department of Health and Social Services.

Wallace, L. W., & Clarke, S. H. (1984). *The Institute of Government's Prison Risk Scoresheet: A user's manual.* Chapel Hill: University of North Carolina Press.

Conclusion

Denise Johnston

Children of prisoners and other offenders have historically received very little attention from professionals or the public. The dramatic increase in arrest, conviction, and incarceration rates over the past three decades has led to corresponding increases in what we know about these children and in our awareness of what we do not know.

Numbers of Children of Offenders

We know from consistent findings in national studies that about three quarters of all female prisoners and three fifths of all male prisoners are parents, and that they have, respectively, an average of 2.4 and 2.0 children each. Therefore, there are at least 1.5 million children of prisoners and at least 3.5 million children of offenders on probation or parole in the United States on any given day this year. The number of children who have been exposed to parental crime, arrest, and incarceration during their lifetime may be many times greater.

BUT

This information is essentially unknown, even among legislators, policy makers and children's advocates.

Parental Characteristics of Offenders

We know a great deal about children and their incarcerated mothers. Children of women offenders most often come from single-parent, low-income households headed by young women with little education, few job skills, and extensive histories of childhood victimization, domestic violence, and substance dependency. These mothers nevertheless have appropriate parental attitudes, characteristics, and concerns. There is no evidence that they are abusive or neglectful at greater rates than the general population. However, children of women offenders are at extremely high risk of permanent separation from their mothers due to termination of maternal rights; this occurs because women prisoners with children in foster care have difficulty working with child welfare systems.

BUT

We have limited information about the parental attributes of male offenders. We know very little about children's experiences with their incarcerated fathers; preliminary studies suggest that these relationships have unique characteristics. Most incarcerated fathers, for example, did not live with their children prior to arrest and do not have ongoing relationships with their children's mothers, yet most also want contact with their children and a role in the children's lives.

Parental Recidivism

Evidence suggests that parental (and particularly maternal) recidivism is the most damaging aspect of parental incarceration. And, we have some promising information about intensive family interventions such as therapeutic visitation that appear to dramatically decrease recidivism.

BUT

We have been unable to integrate what we know into criminal justice and correctional policy and practice; as a result, recidivism rates among parents (and other prisoners) are increasing.

Effects of Parental Incarceration

We know that the available demographic data on children of prisoners is remarkably consistent throughout the United States. These studies tell us that they are poor and disproportionately children of color; they most often live in homes characterized by high levels of stress and a lack of material resources; the majority are in the care of single and/or elderly women. They are members of families characterized by a lack of social support and high levels of intergenerational behaviors, including incarceration. We know something about the emotional and behavioral characteristics of children of offenders, and something about the developmental effects of parental arrest and incarceration. Much of this information overlaps with what is known about the effects of parent–child separation and parental susbtance-dependency.

We also know a great deal about the children of offenders who are most like their parents. We have good descriptive information about the characteristics of those children of offenders who are likely to become offenders themselves; we know that they respond to enduring trauma and parent–child separation with aggressive and other trauma-reactive behaviors which, when patterned in adolescence, lead to early entry into the criminal justice system. We also have some information about other contributors to and rates of intergenerational incarceration.

BUT

We don't know enough about all children of offenders. Existing research conducted directly on the children has identified and described only clinical samples or those who have distinguishing behavioral characteristics. Most studies on children of offenders have actually been no more than surveys of their parents. Advocates need to redirect their research efforts towards an examination of the lives of these children in the communities where they live and wait.

Parent–Child Visitation in Jails and Prisons

We recognize the problems with correctional visiting environments and we know how to create child-adapted contact visitation settings and programs. We know about the value of parent–child prison visitation and the emotional and behavioral reactions that children are likely to have to visiting.

We also know that what distinguishes and shapes children of offenders is not the relatively short periods in which their parents are incarcerated but rather their entire life experience, which is typically characterized by enduring trauma, multiple parent–child separations, and an inadequate quality of care due to poverty.

BUT

We don't know how to change the focus of the criminal justice and corrections systems from the isolated offender to families and communities. In fact, early advocacy efforts for children of incarcerated parents adopted that focus by developing interventions that were solely prison-based and served children only as adjuncts of their parents.

Other Interventions

We know from limited experience that some interventions, especially those comprehensive programs including therapeutic and family support services, can produce significant improvements in the lives of children of offenders.

Equally important are the effects of such services on reducing the behaviors that appear to be leading some children of offenders towards crime and incarceration.

BUT

There is little private or public funding available to support programs specifically for these children. Most intervention services received by children of offenders occur once they have entered the criminal justice system themselves.

The Effects of Poverty

We know that poverty is responsible for increased rates of every type of trauma (child abuse, domestic and community violence, parental substance-dependency, etc.) that children—including children of offenders—suffer. It is also responsible for the high levels of stress that prevent families from providing children of offenders with adequate care and support.

BUT

Our society is not working toward the major, systemic changes that must occur in order to improve the lives of large numbers of children of offenders. In addition, advocates for offenders and their children have not joined forces with their most natural allies: organizations that fight poverty and/or work towards a redistribution of income.

Implications for the Future

We have found that the post-traumatic behaviors that lead to crime and incarceration may be an *adaptive* response to life-threatening environments and experiences. The implications of this finding, which arose out of research and therapeutic projects at the Center for Children of Incarcerated Parents and the work of other advocates for these children, are profound. They challenge our society to examine the lives of these children more thoroughly and to disseminate research findings widely and more quickly. For if compulsive behaviors and criminal activity represent relatively resilient responses to life in poor, violent, chaotic families and neighborhoods, then our society is condemned to incarcerating an ever-increasing number of the people who live in these circumstances, unless we can help them to reduce the poverty, violence, and chaos in their lives.

Index

About the Contributors

Ellen Barry, J.D. is the founding director of Legal Services for Prisoners with Children. She has been lead counsel or co-counsel on a variety of major lawsuits on behalf of incarcerated women, pregnant prisoners, and women parolees. She is the Chair of the Board of Directors of the National Network for Women in Prison, recipient of the 1990 Annual Legal Services Achievement Award, Chair of the State Bar Committee on Legal Services for Prisoners, and Commissioner of the California Commission on Female Inmates and Parolees.

Barbara E. Bloom, M.S.W. is a doctoral candidate and consultant specializing in research on women under criminal justice system supervision and their families. Among her publications is *Why Punish the Children? A Reappraisal of the Children of Incarcerated Mothers in America*, the report of a national survey.

Peter Breen, M.A., L.C.S.W. is the Executive Director of Centerforce, a non-profit agency providing services to families of incarcerated persons in California. He was formerly President of the American Public Welfare Association in Washington, D.C. and Welfare Director of Marin County, California.

Meda Chesney-Lind, Ph.D. is Professor of Women's Studies at the University of Hawaii at Manoa. She is the author of over 50 monographs and papers on the subject of women and crime, and she has recently published *Girls, Delinquency & Juvenile Justice*, written with Randall G. Shelden, which was awarded the American Society of Criminology's Michael J. Hindelang Award for "outstanding contribution to criminology" in 1992.

Katherine Gabel, J.D., Ph.D., M.S.W. has served as superintendent of two juvenile correctional facilities for girls, Dean of the Smith College School of Social Work, and President of Pacific Oaks College and Children's Programs. While at Smith College, she directed the Women in Prison Project addressing legal issues and resources for female offenders. At Pacific Oaks, she co-founded the Center for Children of Incarcerated Parents with Denise Johnston.

Phillip Genty, J.D. is the Director of the Family Advocacy Clinic of the Columbia University School of Law. He has worked as an attorney for Prisoners' Legal Services of New York, for the New York City Department of Housing, Preservation and Development and for the Bedford-Stuyvesant Community Legal Services Corporation. He implemented the Rikers Island Parents' Legal Rights Clinic, for which he received the 1986 Mayor's Volunteer Service Award.

River Ginchild, J.D. staff attorney with Legal Services for Prisoners with Children, coordinates the Grandparent Caregiver Advocacy Project and the Law Student Internship Project of that agency. She is a member of the State Bar Standing Committee on Legal Services for the Poor, and a member of the Board of Directors for Women in Legal Services.

Kathryn Girard, Ed.D. specializes in educational program design and evaluation. She is also a mediator and the author of two books on conflict resolution. She was Director of the Research Center at Pacific Oaks College & Children's Programs from 1985–1993 and currently runs a private educational consulting practice.

Creasy Finney Hairston, Ph.D. is Dean of the Jane Addams College of Social Work, University of Illinois at Chicago, and a researcher and program consultant on family-oriented corrections policies and programs. Her major interest is social welfare policies that impact the lives of poor women and other oppressed groups. Her recent research and advocacy have focused on efforts to improve programs and services for incarcerated parents and their families.

Russ Immarigeon is a policy research consultant and writes regularly on criminal justice and child welfare issues. He is a contributing writer to the National Prison Project *Journal* and is co-author, with Meda Chesney-Lind, of *Women's Prisons: Overcrowded and Overused*. He is also co-editor, with Meda Chesney-Lind, of a new book series on women, crime and criminology, published by the State University of New York Press.

Denise Johnston, M.D. has been the principal investigator in 16 research projects on offenders and their children, including the landmark *Children of Offenders Study* (1992) and she has published 27 monographs or papers on this population. She serves on the Boards of Directors of Phase ReEntry Programs, the National Network for Women in Prison, and Friends Outside of Los Angeles County. In 1990, she co-founded the Center for Children of Incarcerated Parents with Katherine Gabel.

Christina Jose-Kampfner, Ph.D. is a psychologist with 15 years experience in working with battered women, sexually abused children, and women prisoners and their children. She has conducted research and published extensively on the effects of maternal incarceration. She is currently a member of the Board of Directors of the National Network for Women in Prison, an Assistant Professor of Psychology and Education at Eastern Michigan University and a Lecturer in Women's Studies at the University of Michigan.

Julie A. Norman, J.D., M.S. was employed by the Illinois Department of Children and Family Services for 15 years as a social worker, supervisor and child protection investigator. She has also worked as a counselor for private child protection agencies and the Juvenile Court division of the Cook County Public Defender's Office. Currently, she is Program Director for M. Lee & Associates, a private counseling and consulting agency in Chicago.

Leonora Poe, Ph.D. is a clinical psychologist and licensed marriage, family and child therapist at West Coast Children's Center in El Cerrito, California. She leads a Grandparents As Parents support group in Oakland, California and recently authored *Grandparents as Parents*, a book that focuses on breaking the cycle of intergenerational behaviors.

Gail T. Smith, J.D. is the founding director of Chicago Legal Aid to Incarcerated Mothers (CLAIM) in 1985. She is a former high school teacher. She authored the *Handbook for Incarcerated Parents in Illinois* and she co-authored the *Legal Manual for Children's Caregivers in Illinois*. She is currently a member of the Board of Directors of the National Network for Women in Prison.

Rose Weilerstein, P.H.N. is co-founder and President of the Board of Directors of the Prison MATCH program, an organization that has been working to create a support network for prison inmates and their children since 1977. She directed the Berkeley Hills Nursery School, a parent cooperative, for 25 years and presently directs the Children's Center within the San Francisco County Jail in San Bruno, California.

About the Editors

KATHERINE GABEL, J.D., Ph.D., M.S.W. grew up in Rochester, New York and completed her education in the northeast. She has her B.A. from Smith College, her M.S.W. from Simmons College, her Ph.D. from Syracuse University, and her J.D. from Albany Law School of Union University.

As an undergraduate at Smith College she volunteered to assist the warden of the Framingham Women's Prison by entering the prison as an inmate. It was a transforming experience leading to a life-long interest in issues related to women and the criminal justice system.

At the age of 24, Katherine Gabel was appointed Acting Superintendent of the Georgia Training School for Girls. She was the youngest superintendent ever appointed in the United States. Later, she oversaw the building of the Adobe Mountain School, a juvenile correctional facility in Arizona, and was its first warden when it served a primarily female population. After winning the Smith College Medal, she was appointed Dean of the Smith School of Social Work. She currently serves as President of Pacific Oaks College in Pasadena, California.

DENISE JOHNSTON, M.D. is the founding director of the Center for Children of Incarcerated Parents. Elected to Phi Beta Kappa, she graduated with highest honors from Mills College and received her doctorate from the Stanford University School of Medicine. She is a specialist in maternal/child health and a leading national authority on children of offenders.

Dr. Johnston was previously an instructor at the University of California, Santa Cruz, and medical director of the Los Angeles Feminist Women's Health and Childbirth Center. She co-founded Phase ReEntry Programs, a self-help collective for mothers who have been jailed or imprisoned. Dr. Johnston is also a founding member of the Board of Directors of the National Network for Women in Prison, and serves on the National Steering Committee of the Family & Corrections Network and the Board of Directors of Friends Outside in Los Angeles County. She is also a member of the Steering Committee on Women Offenders of the National Association of Women Judges.

Under Dr. Johnston's direction, the Pacific Oaks Center for Children of Incarcerated Parents conducts seventeen research, educational, family reunification, and therapeutic projects. She has conducted seven major research projects for the center, including the landmark "Children of Offenders" study in 1992.